The

Public Record Research Tips Book

Insider Information for Effective Public Record Research

By Michael Sankey

PO Box 27869
Tempe, AZ 85285
800.929.3811
www.brbpub.com

The Public Record Research Tips Book

Insider Information for Effective Public Record Research

©2008 By Michael Sankey and BRB Publications, Inc.

First Edition

Written by: Michael Sankey
Edited by: Kim Ensenberger and Peter Weber
Cover Design by: Robin Fox & Associates

Publisher's Cataloging-in-Publication
(Provided by Quality Books, Inc.)
Sankey, Michael L., 1949-
      Public record research tips book : insider
information for effective public record research / by
Michael Sankey. -- 1st ed.
      p. cm.
      Includes index.
      ISBN-13: 978-1-889150-50-5
      ISBN-10: 1-889150-50-9

      1. Public records--Research--United States.
      2. Public records--United States--Information resources.
      I. Title.

    JK2445.P82S26 2008   352.3'87
                      QBI08-600048

The material in this book is presented for educational and informational purposes only and is not offered or intended as legal advice in any manner whatsoever. The materials should not be treated as a substitute for independent advice of counsel. All policies and actions with legal consequences should be reviewed by your legal counsel. Specific factual situations should also be discussed with your legal counsel. Where sample language is offered, it is only intended to illustrate a potential issue. A sample policy cannot address all specific concerns of a particular company and should not be relied on as legal advice.

Table of Contents

We Have You Covered; Key Elements to Evaluating Public Record Sources; The Difference Between a Record Search and a Document Request; The Importance of Identifiers; The Redaction Trend; The Access Methods for Public Records; About Record Fees and Charges; Online Access to Public Records - From the Government; Using the Web for Public Record Research; Using Internet Sites to Locate Public Record Links; An Example of How to Use Specialized Web Resources; Keeping Track of Your Research; Summary

How Criminal Proceedings Create Criminal Records; Record Searching and Identifiers; Searching State Repositories; Searching State Court Administrator Records; State Criminal Database Comparison Table; Criminal Records and Pre-Employment Screening; The National Criminal Record Search; Take Caution When Using Private Databases; Other Criminal Record and Criminal Record-Related Databases

The Four Court Levels; State Court Structure; Types of Court Records; Differences Between Criminal and Civil Court Files; Probate and Eviction Files; How Courts Maintain Records; Court Record Searching Tips; Tips from a Professional; Summaries of State Court Systems

Federal Court Structure; How Federal Trial Court Cases are Organized; Searching Records by Mail and In Person; Electronic Access to Federal Court Records; Search the U.S. Party/Case Index; PACER; Case Management/ Electronic Case Files (CM/ECF); Voice Case Information System (VCIS); More Federal Courts Searching Hints; What If the Record Search Results Do Not Include Identifiers?; Federal Records Centers and the National Archives; Identifiers and Case Files for U.S. District and U.S. Bankruptcy Court Records; Other Federal Courts; U.S. Court of Federal Claims; U.S. Tax Court; U.S. Court of International Trade

The Difference Between Personal Property and Real Property; Types of Liens and Security Interests; Types of Real Estate Recorded Documents; The Search

Introduction

There is a lot of misinformation around about public record searching. How many of the following six statements about public record searching do you believe to be true?

- It's all free online. Why should I have to pay for it?
- I can find all the information I need using Google.
- To find criminal records, all I need to do is use a national database.
- I do background checks for employers, but I am not a consumer reporting agency because I don't provide credit reports.
- I can do all my public record searching with my membership web account that gives me access to 35,000+ databases of public records.
- Certain records may be open to the public in one state, but in another state they are not open.

The reality is that only the *last statement* is *true*.

There is No Free Lunch

The first five statements above represent common myths thought to be true by individuals who are looking for the easy way to find public records. If you are someone who practices due diligence when using public records for decision-making, you are already a step ahead. Regardless of what camp you fall into – the legal professional or casual requester – to some degree this book will change the way you search for public records. It may even knock your socks off.

Before You Start

This book will assist you in **how to search for public records**. Besides the many searching tips herein, this resource is especially helpful for finding where **certain types** of government records can be accessed, accurately and inexpensively.

The *Public Record Research Tips Book* is presented in a rather unique format. Chapter 1 is an introduction to the key techniques used in public record searching. This basic concepts chapter sets a foundation to understand and implement the searching tips and procedures found throughout this book.

Chapters 2 though 7 examine the most widely used records searching categories. Chapter 8 is an in-depth analysis of public record vendors and how to find the best vendor for your public record needs.

Chapter 9, as Paul Harvey would say, is the "rest of the story." Called *Searching A thru Z*, Chapter 9 presents key record topics in alphabetical order, from *Archives* to *Worker's Compensation*. Each record topic is packed with searching tips and unique resources.

The Appendix with its Glossary of record searching terms and the Index are quite helpful to find specific information on a particular topic or term.

The text printed below is significant. As your public record searching takes you from county-to-county and state-to-state, this is the one important truth to keep in mind—

> **"Just because records are maintained in a certain way in your state or county, do not assume that any other county or state does things the same way."**

———

There are a number of public record searching experts who contributed their time and written words to this manuscript. To Cynthia, Lynn, and Michele, as well as Bill, Carl, Larry, Les, and Mike for their help and encouragement I sincerely thank you for your valuable time and assistance!

To the users of this manual I sincerely hope that you find this publication a useful resource. Best of luck to you and *your* public record searching!

Michael Sankey
February, 2008

Chapter 1

The Fundamentals of Public Record Searching

The depth and scope of information that exists on people, businesses, and places is staggering. What used to be mostly paper and microfiche trails of data have turned into cyber trails of bytes managed by the government and by private companies. These trails, be they cyber or paper, reflect major events in people's lives – from birth to the first car and house, to death, wills, and probate. And today's society treats this information as a commodity.

According to www.freedictionary.com, a **public record** is *any information, minutes, files, accounts or other records which a governmental body is required to maintain, and which must be accessible to scrutiny by the public. This includes the files of most legal actions.*

And it's all on the Internet, right? No, not at all.

We Have You Covered

"Yes," says the clerk at the County Recorder's Office. "All our recorded documents are online."

She neglected to mention that only the index is online – not document images. She failed to mention the index only goes back to 2001, except for the records lost in the flood in the spring of 2003. She failed to say only real estate related records are in the index, only the debtors' names are searchable, and there are no identifiers to distinguish the subject. Oh yes, the system is managed by a private company that requires a user name and password. The clerk doesn't know the phone number, but it doesn't matter anyway because the company doesn't return calls.

This story may sound far-fetched, but it is closer to the truth than you might think. Actually many of the searching idiosyncrasies mentioned really do exist on searchable websites for many counties and towns.

There is no easy way to generalize about government-held records because of the diverse nature and variations of public policies associated with them. In reality some records are closed or restricted.

The purpose of this chapter is to set the foundation on how to perform public record searching. As you read about how to search for many types of government-held records, you will find that not all records are completely "public." For example, in some states or jurisdictions a specific category of records (birth records) is severely restricted and therefore, those records are not "public." But that very same category of records may be 100% open in other states. Also, records may be fully accessible, but only with certain personal information removed. Examples include motor vehicle records and criminal records. And, records may have restrictions to access imposed by state statutes.

Knowing when records are public and or not public is an important tool for any public record researcher. Just as important is an understanding of the relationship between the records, the record holders, and the users.

Key Elements to Evaluating Public Record Sources

There are two places you can find public records—

1. At a government agency
2. Within the database of a private company

There are key components that determine the thoroughness and attributes of the record source, regardless if it's government or privately-held. Consider these questions—

- How are the records stored?
- How far back are records kept?
- How are records indexed?
- What are the access procedures?
- Are there restrictions involved?
- Are record images available?

Finding the answers to these questions about data fundamentals is important when deciding if the source will match your needs and the best access method to use.

Most of the text in this section addresses direct record searching at government agencies. But there are many important items to consider when working with public record search vendors. For more information about vendors, including *Tips on Searching Vendor Databases* by Lawrence Lopez, see the *Working With Public Record Vendors* chapter.

Record Storage

Record storage methods used by government agencies are quite diverse; they maintain records in a variety of ways. Typical formats include paper, microfiche, microfilm, electronic records, magnetic tapes, maps, disks, photographs, film and sound recordings. Of course, most federal agencies and state agencies are computerized. So are many highly populated county or local level agencies (including parishes, cities, town, villages, etc.). But it is surprising how many local level agencies are not so sophisticated. Many agencies still use microfiche, microfilm, index cards, and paper as the primary method to store images, files, and indexes. Everything is NOT online, and everything is NOT electronic.

To computerize the records themselves, government agencies at one time must have converted their document files to electronic images. The paper documents were then destroyed or placed in archival storage, per the law or per the whim of the administration. Depending on the type of agency, the State Archives will often warehouse these files and is a good place to search if you are looking for old records. Sometimes it is the only place.

A key point to remember is – agencies that have converted to computerized storage will not necessarily place complete file records on their system; they are more apt to include only an index or summary data from the files.

The storage procedures used by **private companies** (vendors) is dependent upon the media format when the records were purchased or gathered. Vendors usually develop their databases by buying records in bulk from specific government agencies or by sending personnel to a government office to make copies or key in information on a laptop computer. A third common method is to buy data from other vendors.

Data Retention and Currency

This brings us to the questions: *How far back are records kept? How current are they?* and *When are records purged?* The need for due diligence may require that a record searcher research a certain time period. This may be seven years or longer, and it obviously is beneficial to know the record retention period. Any answer except a clear, concise date is not going to be adequate.

Knowing how "fresh" the information is – when it was last updated – is also an important factor. An index of records may have been updated last week at a courthouse or at a web page, but this data may reflect a 60-day delay or backlog. This update gap is extremely common with the state criminal record agencies like the State Police or Department of Public Safety who receive and hold criminal case information from the courts. Per a U.S. Department of Justice Study,[1] 27 states report they have a significant backlog (from 160 man-hours to 30,400 man-hours needed) for entering court data into the criminal history database.

---

[1] U.S. Department of Justice, Bureau of Justice Statistic's Survey of State Criminal History Information Systems, 2003 (released in 2006) found at www.ojp.usdoj.gov/bjs/abstract/sschis03.htm.

Similarly, many web vendors offering public record content do not state how up-to-date they are.

Ideally, when you search for or purchase items of information you should be provided access to a statement of accuracy without having to ask.

Record Indexing

A record index serves as a pointer system to the location of file documents such as recordings, case files, deeds, and articles of incorporation. If you are searching an unfamiliar location, then the makeup of the index is one of first items you need to check. The index can be electronic, on card files, in books, on microfiche, etc. A record index can be organized in a variety of ways – by name, by year, by case or file number, or by name and year. Depending on the type of public record, an alpha index could be by plaintiff and/or defendant, by grantor and/or grantee, by address, etc. Perhaps you check a microfiche reader or card file for a record on an individual and find nothing. That does not mean no record exists. The case or document files could be listed in another media index for that time period or perhaps you are searching using the wrong criteria.

As covered in the *Searching State and Local Court Records* chapter, if you are searching an index of court records, you are searching **dockets**. A docket can be a list of cases on a court's calendar *or* a log containing the schedule and all the actions involved within a court case.

An important fact to take note of is that the primary search that government agencies provide is a search of the index. When someone tells you "I can find xxx county court records online," this person is most likely talking about an index summary of records and not about the records themselves.

The Difference Between a Record Search and a Document Request

There is a significant difference between searching an index to determine if a public record exists versus obtaining or viewing file copy documents. Many times the latter cannot be accomplished without first doing the former.

Asking government personnel to perform a search of public records usually incurs a fee. Asking government personnel to provide you a specific file or case usually does not incur a search fee if the document is readily available and you have provided the exact file or case number.

Name Searching

Let's say you wish to determine if an individual has a criminal record or, say, if an individual has collateralized certain assets such as a real estate holding or ownership of equipment used in a business. The best way to perform this research is to do a "name search" – also known as an "alpha search" – of an index at the government agency that holds the records. An index may or may not contain dates, the date of birth, or even a partial Social Security Number due to privacy concerns. Obviously, having this additional information – often referred to as "PI," which stands for "personal identifiers" – can be quite helpful, see below.

Using an Internet site to perform a name search often is merely a *supplemental search* since many agencies withhold personal identifiers from appearing on the web. Some government agencies allow a researcher to view a record index; others do not permit the public to research. Where the public is not allowed to do its own on-site search the agency almost always imposes a fee for a government employee to do the name search. Other agencies, such as many of the county-based Supreme Courts in New York, refuse to allow the public to view an index in person AND refuse to perform a name search. These NY courts direct searchers of criminal records to the New York State Office of Court Administration (OCA) for a statewide criminal history search (CHRS) for a $52 fee.

Requesting a Specific Document

When you know the "document number" or exact location of a record, it becomes much easier to view or obtain a copy. If you are requesting a specific document, the government personnel are much more apt to help you compared to asking them to do a name search.

Using a government web page to search for a specific document is often easier when you have the document number or an identifier like the docket number. Remember, images of all the pages in the file may not be available online. This is especially true when searching court records or real estate recordings.

The Importance of Identifiers

As mentioned, every record source will require certain identifiers to accurately process a search request. For example, an agency may ask for the full name, Social Security Number (SSN), date of birth (DOB), sex, hair color, and even the last known address of the person to be checked. These identifiers serve two different though related purposes.

First, the identifiers of the subject must be used to analyze a public record for the purpose of determining if the record is about the subject. Perhaps the records are indexed by the last name and also by either the DOB or part of a SSN. If so, the searcher needs a DOB or SSN to search accurately.

Second, the identifiers act as an important safeguard for both the requesting party and the subject of the search. There is always the chance that the "Harold Johnson" on whom a given repository has a record is not the same "Harold Johnson" on whom a check has been requested. The possibility of a misidentification can be decreased substantially if other identifiers can match the individual to the record. Providing an identifier as simple as a middle initial is likely to identify the correct Harold Johnson.

There will be times when personal identifiers are not readily available. This is especially true when searching the index or even the document files for state and county civil records, and for any federal court records. Per record searching expert Lynn Peterson: "This [lack of identifiers] is why it is so difficult to determine relevance when researching civil litigation. This is seldom the situation with criminal court records. With criminal case files you will almost always find identifiers that enable you to determine relevance."

Matching Logic

Matching logic means using the identifiers given with a search request in order to determine if the record found does, in fact, belong to the subject. For example, before reporting results to clients, pre-employment screening companies are responsible for determining the level of matching logic that will meet Fair Credit Reporting Act (FCRA) rules.

According to the search standards of the Public Record Retriever Network (PRRN)[2] there are three levels of matching logic—

- **Partial Name Match Logic**—Match Logic that requires only a partial match of the subject's name to a result.
- **Name Match Only**—Results of a search that uses the subject's full name as a match.
- **Strict Match Logic**—Match logic that requires a minimum of two and, when possible, three subject identifiers before reporting.

Of course, using three subject identifiers is best. Even then you can have problems. Consider when a Jr. and Sr. are living at the same house; there are many possibilities of identifiers getting crossed.

Strictest matching logic available should be applied if negative or derogatory information is found.

When government personnel are doing the look-up in the index, it is good practice to provide them with personal identification information beyond the minimum whenever possible. Every available piece of information *could* aid their search. For example, maiden name, alias, or other previous names should be included when possible. Although no repository can be expected to give a 100% positive identification (unless

---

[2] See www.brbpub.com/prrn

it is a match of fingerprints), the more pointers matched, the smaller the chance of a mistake.

What If the Index Doesn't Have Matching Identifiers?

You will often find that if an index does not contain a personal identifier, one may be found within in the record file or in associated paperwork.

Let's say you are searching for a record on Joe B. Cool with a DOB of 01/01/1985. And let's say the index gives you an index showing a possible record match of J Cool with no DOB, and another possible match with a Joseph Cool with a partial DOB match. The next step is to examine the two files. The content in the file may contain the matching personal identifiers you are looking for. If you are a professional and the highest form of accuracy is vital, then you may have times where a common name requires you to view dozens of files.

Again, the chapters to follow contain searching search techniques and procedures you can use if you need to search for records and you only have a name.

The Redaction Trend

Redaction is simply removing or hiding certain elements within a record itself or the record index. Almost daily news stories appear related to ongoing privacy debates and efforts to remove personal identifiers from public records.

One way that government agencies and legislatures are dealing with identity theft problems is by remove identifiers from public records. In some cases, the anticipated cost of redacting records is forcing government agencies to instead block public access to the records. Yet at the same time many government officials understand the importance and benefits attached to the openness of public records. The balance of privacy interests versus public jeopardy goes beyond the purposes of this book. However, the key point here is to be aware of change and know that redactions can and will alter public record searching procedures.

An excellent article by Lynn E. Sudbeck titled *Placing Court Records Online: Balancing the Public and Private Interests* appeared in Vol 27, Number 3 (2006) of the *Justice System Journal*. The summarized list below of Sudback's recommendations is a figurative roadmap to what has been occurring to court records since the article was written, with the exception of a limited adoption of #2—

1. Limit information in the case record
2. Vary levels of access for different users
3. Provide access to case records at public access terminals in the clerk's office

4. Provide electronic storage of case records

The Access Methods for Public Records

The following is a how-to look at the various methods available to access public records from government agencies. Keep in mind—

- There is a distinction between performing a name search versus asking for a specific document copy.
- Many government agencies will not do a name search for the public, but will retrieve a specific document file.

Visit in Person

Direct access is easy if you live close by. Many courthouses and recorders offices provide "free use" public access terminals but charge to make copies of file documents. This is also true for certain state-held records such as corporate or Uniform Commercial Code (UCC) records generally found at the Secretary of State office. The index or the documents in a record file can be viewed for free, but a fee is charged if copies are requested.

Not every agency will permit walk-in traffic. Agencies such as the State Police, Workers Compensation Bureau, and even certain Motor Vehicle agencies and Occupational Licensing Boards will not honor in person requests.

There is one key distinction to make about in person searches at courthouses and recording offices: who is permitted to do a name search of the index? At some agencies, only government personnel can do the searching. At others, the government personnel will not help and only the public can do a search of the index. Still other agencies offer a choice. If the only way to do a record search is to do it yourself, and if you do not live close by, you will need to hire a record retriever (see the *Working With Public Record Vendors* chapter) to visit the agency and perform the search for you.

The on-site method is certainly under the influence on the kind of day the clerical staff at an agency is having. If someone woke up on the wrong side of the bed or if personnel are extremely busy, then you might not have your request serviced. Ongoing search requesters always find ways to make friends with the staff, but sometimes it is necessary to remind staff about a particular law in their jurisdiction that dictates what is public record and open.

Mail

While most agencies will process a request for a specific document or file if allowed by law, there are a number of agencies that do not honor a name search request by mail. Do not assume all do.

Some agencies do not charge to "find" a record but charge a fee to make a document copy or print a computer screen image. Call first and ask about the fees.

When mailing the request, an insider tip is to use a large, priority mail envelope. A 9 x12 envelope stands out and demands to be dealt with.

Another worthy piece of advice is to always include a **SASE** (the acronym for a self-addressed stamped envelope) or a prepaid express delivery return envelope. Providing either one insures the agency is not going to reject your request because you did not include postage. You may go to the top of the request pile!

Fax

Generally, fax service – for requesting or returning documents, or both – is only available to pre-approved requesters, especially if fees are involved. If you prepay a request and ask for a return of results by fax, some agencies will oblige only if the call is local or to a toll-free telephone number. While most courts will not offer to fax results of search requests, many will fax specific documents if the case file or docket number is given, again, to a toll-free number.

Some agencies (state vital record agencies, for example) consider fax requesting to be an expedited service that triggers additional fees.

Telephone

A limited number of agencies that permit telephone requests merely answer "Yes" or "No" to questions such as "Does John Doe have a civil court case in his name?" Several state motor vehicle agencies offer some rather sophisticated read-back dial-up systems as a service to ongoing accounts.

Professional searchers know that name search requests and results by telephone are not adequate in a due diligence situation. The reasons include that there is no assurance the court personnel keyed in the correct spelling and there is nothing in writing to back up the assertion that no records were found.

If the agency provides telephone service to pre-approved accounts or a fee-based "900" phone service, then the searcher may feel the agency personnel would do a better job of searching. But calling a public record agency for a name search should be performed only as a "quick and dirty" search investigation.

Online

Online access to public records comes in several varieties and packages, the primary sources being government agencies and vendors. Online access can be an instant path to viewable or downloadable record data or the means to transmit record information along an information chain. The web is the primary conduit, but there are a few dial systems (non-

Internet) that still exist for access to some subscription services. There are many useful web pages maintained by the government and by private enterprise that provide valuable information about public records.

Since online access is such an important topic, we will come back to it later in this chapter to discuss in more detail.

Bulk or Database Purchases

Many agencies offer the ability to purchase all or parts of their database for statistical or commercial purposes. Purchasing records for statistical purposes is often easy. Purchasing for commercial purposes is not so easy. "Commercial purposes" means the data will be used for marketing products or by database vendors building their proprietary database products for record sales to interested parties. Whether or not a government agency will sell the records is determined by restrictions imposed by law or administrative rule OR if it has the personnel, means, and time to fulfill a request.

Typically, records are available to those who qualify in the following media types: FTP, cartridges, paper printouts, labels, disks or CD files, microfiche, and microfilm.

Monitoring and Notification Programs

Some government agencies offer the ability to notify clients if there is activity on records. This may be on a submitted-list basis (such as monitoring commercial drivers or insured drivers) or an alert of activity related to a certain record type. An example is the LENS Program with the New York DMV, which registers drivers of participating employers or organizations.

Hire Someone Else

As mentioned previously, one method to access public records is through a vendor. Vendors must comply with state and federal laws governing the release of records. Thus, if the government agency will not release a full record to the public, neither will the vendor (at least the reputable ones do not). See the *Working With Public Record Vendors* chapter.

Using the Freedom of Information Act (FOIA)

The Federal Freedom of Information Act (FOIA) is only applicable to records held by federal agencies. The Federal FOIA has no bearing on state, county, or local government agencies because these agencies are subject to only that state's individual act. A great resource for FOIA and also for finding state's open record laws is **The Open Government Guide** at www.rcfp.org/ogg. Also, see the Appendix for more information about FOIA and other laws affecting privacy to government records.

About Record Fees and Charges

Remember that public records are records of incidents or transactions. It costs money (time, salaries, supplies, etc.) to record, store, and track these events. Although public records may be free of charge to view, they are not necessarily free of charge when obtaining file copies. Certainly fees are to be expected if government personnel must perform searches.

Common charges found at the government level include **copy fees** (to make copies of documents), **search fees** (for clerical personnel to search for the record), **certification fees** (to certify a document as being accurate and coming from the particular agency), and **expedite fees** (to place you at the "front of the line").

Fees can and do vary widely from jurisdiction to jurisdiction for the same record type. Copy fees vary from $.10 to $10 per page. In the U.S., search fees range from under a dollar to $52 search fee for government personnel to perform a name search. Also, expect additional fees if records must be pulled from an archives or from off-site storage.

According to public record searching expert Lawrence Lopez, many states have a superintendent of public documents who can be a real advocate. Superintendents often intercede if you have problems with agencies charging higher fees than allowed, or claiming they don't have to give you a certain document.

Note: BRB's Public Record Research System (PRRS) and *Sourcebook To Public Record Information* both indicate all the specific fees involved with all record access methods at more than 20,000 government agencies.

Online Access to Public Records – From the Government

First and foremost, let's look at three important facts—

1. Less than 50% of the available public records from the government can be found online.

2. Most **free** government public record websites contain no personal identifiers beyond the name.

3. Usually the searchable and viewable information found online is limited to name indexes and summary data rather than document images. Most access sites – especially the free access sites – permit the former, not the latter.

Many government websites offering online record access include a warning or disclosure stating that the data can have errors and/or should be used for informational purposes only. Such sites should be considered as supplemental or secondary sources only. Using a criminal record search from such a source usually does not in and by itself comply with Fair Credit Reporting Act regulations involving pre-employment screening.

Government Agencies and Identifiers

The federal, state, and local agencies that maintain public record systems make substantial efforts to limit the disclosure of personal information such as Social Security Numbers, phone numbers, and addresses. The Social Security Number is no longer the key search tool identifier it was in the 1980s and early 1990s.

The lack of identifiers displayed when searching online is a real problem for employers or financial institutions who require a certain level of due diligence. The existence of any possible adverse information must be checked by a hands-on search to insure the proper identity of the subject. Even then the identifiers may be removed.

The government agencies that offer online access on a fee or subscription basis, usually to pre-approved requesters, are more apt to disclose personal identifiers such as the date of birth, than the free access sites. Very few give Social Security Numbers and those that do usually cloak or mask the first five digits. Some now even cloak the month and day of the birth and only release the year of birth. For example, most U.S. District Court and Bankruptcy Court search systems give little or no personal identifiers on search results, thus making a reliable "name search" nearly impossible.

Government Subscription Accounts

The use of subscription accounts is more prevalent than many people may be aware. Also, many agencies, such as state motor vehicle agencies, only provide access to pre-approved, high-volume, ongoing accounts. Typically, this contractual access involves fees and a specified, minimum amount of usage.

A growing trend is offering online access to information on a pay-as-you-go basis, usually with a credit card payment online. Some agencies will give you a glimpse of the index or docket, but will charge a fee for the record copy. Some allow the record to be printed on the spot, other times it is mailed.

Have you heard of the **National Information Consortium (NIC)**? You may be aware of its services but not realize how widespread this company's services are in the U.S. NIC is a provider of government web portals. NIC designs, manages, and markets eGovernment services on behalf of 21 states and a number of local governments. NIC does this without spending taxpayer dollars.

The state affiliates of the NIC offer services that range from managing the look-ups found at states' web pages to managing record access subscription accounts for MVRs, UCC filings, and court records. Examples of states with NIC affiliates include www.alabama.gov, www.kansas.gov, and www.idaho.gov. Of course, access to restricted records involves account approval from the managing state agency. Visit the NIC at www.nicus.com for a list of all affiliates and services.

Google is also getting involved in making public information more searchable on the web. Arizona, California, Utah, and Virginia have made their public databases more accessible to Google's crawler by using sitemaps to identify the structure of their sites. Visit http://blog.searchenginewatch.com/blog/070430-000946.

Sometimes the only way to obtain certain records online is from a vendor. A vendor may provide access to many records that otherwise may not be found online via the government online sources.

The topic of using and evaluating vendor databases is discussed in the *Working with Public Record Vendors* chapter. The remainder of Chapter 1 examines web link lists and specialized web search techniques useful for public record searching.

Using the Web for Public Record Research

Using the web for any extensive research involves knowledge of search engines, directories, and using effective search strategies. Web research is quite important, but not the subject matter of this book. To learn more about overall web research fundamentals, we recommend books such as *Extreme Searcher's Internet Handbook* by Randolph Hock or *Find It Online* by Alan Schlein. For an excellent overview of how to use the Internet for legal and law-related research along with many useful links and guides, check out *The Virtual Chase* at www.virtualchase.com.

The Internet is a good place to find general information about a government agency and many websites contain detailed descriptions of policies and regulations. Where records or indices are not searchable on an agency website, the site may enable one to download or print record request forms.

The primary federal government site for finding information about federal government agencies is www.usa.gov. A true wealth of information is accessible there.

The Internet is also filled with web pages offering free link lists to public records sites and low-cost record searching deals, some suspect.

Link Lists and People Searching

What happens when you type the words "public records" at Google? Your search result will be a huge list of web pages that are mostly *people finders* and *links lists*. These sites offer to do name searches for a fee or for free, or provide links to thousands of free government record databases. These sites are called *consumer sites* since they are targeting the casual requester of public records. A casual requester is typically someone looking for a lost relative or classmate, or perhaps looking to find information about a neighbor or a person dating a relative. Some searchers may be "wannabe" private investigators.

A number of consumer sites are cited throughout this book since they can be quite useful if their limitations are kept in mind. For example, some offer a quick one-search of multiple free sites at once, which can be advantageous. Others offer access to specific, special searches such as a "reverse-phone directory."

Watch for These "Red Flags" at Consumer Links List Sites

Some consumer sites are more helpful than others for someone who really is looking for a lost relative or classmate. But some of these sites are misleading. They often try to disguise themselves as sites used by professionals or they tout unrealistic features.

There are a few considerations to review before spending money on public record research at certain free links list sites. If I find a site using any of the marketing schemes listed below, a giant red flag pops up in my mind and I take a closer look—

- **Charging membership fees for the ability to view free links lists**

  The most common is charging a $29 to $35 fee for a one to five-year membership term. Some sites even offer an affiliate program to set up your own site in order to sell memberships to others. The "benefit" of membership leads the buyer to either a free link or to a series of free links pages belonging to others. This is nothing but a rip-off. Another money-making concept is to offer links access for free, but charge a monthly fee to avoid sitting through twenty seconds of pop-ups before the free link connects.

- **Show endorsement by a phony or suspect trade association**

  Several of the suspect public records membership sites tout an endorsement from a national association of private investigators. Do a Google search on that association's name and read the results.

- **Promote non-FCRA compliant employment screening**

  Any public record professional will agree that you cannot purchase a "background check" on a new hire for $15 and be truly protected from a negligent hiring lawsuit or be in compliance with the Federal Fair Credit Reporting Act (FCRA). You may be able to do quick record search from a couple web pages or court repository, or from a supplementary database vendor, but that does not equate to due diligence or to a full background check.

- **Over exaggerate the number of free public record sites with links**

    If a people-searching site or free links list claims to access more than 35,000 or more "databases," then something is misstated. There are not 35,000+ government web addresses in the U.S., each with a searchable database of free public records. The 35,000 number is calculated probably by duplicating the count of possible record types and jurisdictions within an existing database. For example, the docket index search for Iowa court records at www.judicial.state.ia.us includes criminal, civil, probate and traffic case data from all 99 Iowa counties. This is one database. But an over-exaggerator will count this one database as 396 databases (4 x 99) in the advertising text. Making the number count high won't fool a professional, but it can mislead the novice consumer.

Michele Stuart, a licensed private investigator from Arizona, is a nationally known speaker and public record searching expert. In the article below she offers her expertise on searching and using links list sites, and we sincerely thank her. She can be reached at www.jaginvestigations.com.

Using Internet Sites to Locate Public Record Links

By Michele Stuart

Remember the days before the Internet became such a powerful search utility tool? When I started in this business, 18 years ago, we really didn't have access to databases and the Internet as we do now. I remember having stacks of cases placed before me with the instructions to find any and all assets affiliated to the subjects and/or businesses. This was the beginning of my education into public records researching.

Today, public records such as corporate, UCCs, property, civil and criminal records, inmates, sex offenders, births, deaths and marriages are now easily accessible at many levels. However, with the constant barrage of privacy advocates and the threat of identity theft, the Federal government and independent states are trying to close or restrict our access to these records. Thus, our ability to ascertain these records is becoming more limited year after year. For now, learn how to find them and how to use them.

Most of public records are accessible free of charge or for a small fee. Of course, we also have the ability to sign up and search numerous pay as you go types of databases. However, with the use of the Internet with just a click away, I want to share with you some sites that will provide you with an enormous amount of links for every state (and many county levels).

One site - www.brbpub.com - provides links to thousands of public record sites and maintains a "public records blog" full of updated information concerning new sites, upcoming conferences, and legislative issues. Additionally, it maintains a link to "The Public Record Retriever Network," an interactive area where you can search for companies throughout the United States that can provide you information from state or local agencies.

The following links also provide an abundance of free informational sites:

- www.virtualgumshoe.com/resources/
- www.freeprf.com/state.html
- http://publicrecords.onlinesearches.com/
- www.publicrecordcenter.com
- www.freepublicrecords.us
- www.blackbookonline.info
- www.statelocalgov.net/index.cfm

One site that I personally like is www.searchsystems.net. Although there is a minimum fee associated with this website for the same information found for free on other sites, searchsystems.net offers some excellent links for record searching in Canada, Australia, and Europe.

Each one of these links will take you to many levels of public records. Remember when you are doing research to 'think outside the box.' Check to see if your state has access to dog permits, hunting and fishing licenses, even political contribution sites. There is a vast amount of information out there. Never stop clicking!

An Example of How to Use Specialized Web Resources

The public record searching guidelines and tips presented throughout this book will give you a solid knowledge foundation. But you must also keep in mind that the creative use of web resources is an art. Knowing where special topic web pages are is important, but knowing **how to use these pages** to your advantage is more important.

Cynthia Hetherington[3], author of *Business Background Investigations,* is a very sought-after public speaker on this subject. Her article below provides some insight on using the web to discover hard-to-find information about corporations and their people.

Tips from a Professional

The catchphrase "lateral thinking" is very appropriate when using the web to discover facts about corporations and corporate personnel. Here are ten creative ways to look at discovery from a different perspective.

1. Don't discount social networks as being for kids alone. Many adults are using myspace.com, linkedin.com and spoke.com to outline their lives and professions.

2. Use more than one search engine to conduct your search. Google.com is the market share leader today, but smaller engines like Exalead.com are gaining momentum, and offering alternative views to search results.

3. Search by phone number, especially with fax numbers. Often a fraudulent company will set up different phone numbers for different business fronts, but will share the fax number.

4. Use Zoominfo.com to locate resume like dossiers on individuals, where information was captured from websites.

5. Need to find disgruntled employees? Check out technorati.com or icerocket.com, and search these blog engines with the expression, "I hate my job" + <company name>.

6. Look through Guidestar.org for any non-profit activity that the subject company may be involved in.

7. Check out IPmenu.com to look for any registered patents or trademarks which may turn out to be valuable assets owned by your subject.

8. See if anyone has posted videos of the area your subject is located through youtube.com, or internal office photographs through flickr.com. Search by company name or location.

9. Searching in Canada? For generalized information check out Canada411.com for more than 12 million residential and business listings.

---

[3] Hetherington is a licensed private investigator and a managing director for a national risk management company. She can be reached at ch@data2know.com.

10. Bookmark brbpub.com to get direct link access to the federal, state, and local government public records.

Keeping Track of Your Research

If you are searching for a specific public record or records from a government agency, then keeping track of your search results should not be difficult. But it may be wise to record the different aspects of the search such as cost, the period of time searched, and the record searching logic used. This is especially important if you are also hired to do the record retrieval. Creating a search form or perhaps a simple file on a spreadsheet program such as Microsoft's Excel is a good way to maintain a written progress report.

If your record searching entails extensive research at different locations or web pages, and the research branches off into many avenues, then it is imperative to take notes and record *where* you have researched and *what* you found.

Below are some ideas that may be quite useful when tracking your record searching techniques and results.

- Define your needs. What record are you searching for?
- Know the keywords or acronyms – MVR is a driving record, UCC is a uniform commercial code filing, etc.
- Define your search logic – time frame of search, name match only.
- Evaluate the sources – primary source vs. secondary, if data throughput dates indicated.
- Record the information found – if cannot be printed, then write results on paper or in a card file.
- Keep a log or an electronic folder. Record information you might need in case you what to find the source again.

Summary

Searching public records is not easy. Becoming an expert at public record searching is even harder. There are no shortcuts. If you hurry through your searches, eventually you are going to miss imperative information!

Hopefully this chapter has given you some highpoints on how to search and the chapters to follow will place you on the right road to becoming an expert.

Searching Criminal Records

Criminal records are widely used in the U.S. Nearly everyone who has applied or been hired for a job, or has applied or been issued an accredited license related to an occupation, has probably been the subject of a criminal record search.

The information trail of a criminal record starts with a criminal case tried at one the 10,000+ county, town, and municipal courts, state trial courts, or federal courts. The county, local, and state courts usually forward record information to a centralized state repository controlled by a state law enforcement agency. The centralized state repositories and the federal courts forward records to the FBI.

Criminal records also exist in other repositories. A number of states have unified court systems that collect case record data, usually statewide. Other *criminal-related* record sources are prison systems, sexual predator lists, federal government sanction and watch lists, and vendor databases.

There are a lot of **misconceptions** about searching criminal records in the U.S. These misconceptions can be traced to a lack of understanding about two key factors that affect criminal record searching–

1. **Criminal Records Are Not All Created Equal.**
2. **Criminal Records Are Not Always Open to the Public.**

This chapter examines the reasons why criminal records are not created equal, when criminal records may be incomplete or "full of holes," the pros and cons of searching different repositories including the so-called national databases, and legal issues affecting how records are searched and reported.

Note: As a point of organization and to avoid text duplication, please refer to the next two chapters – *Searching State and Local Court Records* and *Searching Federal Court Records* – for in-depth discussions and searching tips for all types of courts records.

How Criminal Proceedings Create Criminal Records

Criminal records have three distinct classes – **felonies**, **misdemeanors**, and **infractions**. Felonies are the most serious offenses, usually punishable by a jail or prison sentence of one year or more and/or probation. Misdemeanors are less serious offenses; if a jail term is imposed, it is usually one year or less. Depending on the degree or severity of the offense, some offenses may be classified as a felony in one state and a misdemeanor in another state. Also, whether an offense is tried as a felony or misdemeanor could depend on how the prosecuting attorney chooses to file charges, or how a judge views the offense or the offender. Infractions are minor offenses such as traffic tickets, municipal code violations, or minor crimes such public drunkenness or disturbing the peace. None of these offenses are punishable by a jail term. Offenses that can be tried as either a felony or a misdemeanor are commonly referred to as "wobblers."

The term **disposition** is frequently used when discussing or searching criminal records. A disposition is the final outcome of a criminal court case. A disposition is an important piece of information on a criminal record or record index, along with the defendant's name, some type of personal identifier, the charge, and the case number.

Lynn Peterson, a very highly regarded professional public record searcher, has been gracious to provide this book with her **Criminal Case Flowchart**. This chart, shown on the following page, maps the events during a "criminal proceeding" at a court.

While the flowchart may be simplified, it does point out the four key situations when a **criminal record** is **created** or **modified**.

1. At a **Booking (arrest record)**. Notice that the record is reported to the state central repository of records and then in turn to the FBI. Because the defendant is not booked, misdemeanor citations frequently are not reported to the state repository. If the case is from a federal court, the information is not reported to a state agency.

2. At **Filing of Charges with Court**. Misdemeanor citation records may get picked up here. The court docket index begins.

3. At the **Disposition and Sentencing** connection. Notice that at the sentencing the case is again reported to the state and forwarded to the FBI. Also notice on the chart the dotted line from the Dismissed box to May Go to State and FBI box. **A dismissal is not always automatically reported to the state (and FBI).** Courts sometimes neglect to forward information regarding convictions to the state repository. More about this later.

4. At the **Incarceration and Jail/Prison** connection. The Jail and Prison boxes reflect secondary criminal records. The state prison records are readily available. While some sheriff departments provide online inmate locators, most do not.

CRIMINAL CASE FLOWCHART

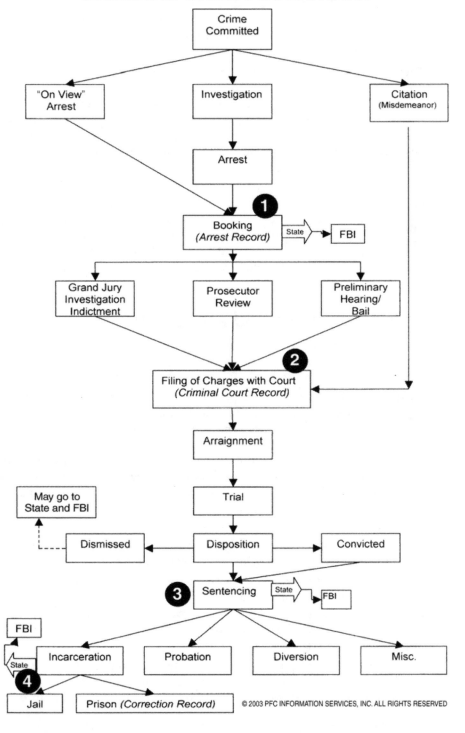

© 2003 PFC INFORMATION SERVICES, INC. ALL RIGHTS RESERVED

The Flowchart's Record Creation Points

Each one of the four record-creation points is very significant to searchers and to the end-users of criminal records. We will reference the significance of these record-creation points throughout this chapter and also in the two court record searching chapters to follow.

The chart distinctly illustrates the three different kinds of records that are often generically referred to as "criminal records" – **arrest records**, **criminal court records**, and **correction records**. They come into the flow at different points in the process and include different information. But to a record searcher, these criminal records will vary widely in substance, accuracy, and purpose, as you will learn throughout this chapter.

Fingerprints, usually taken at the time of a booking, also can become part of a criminal record. The flow chart also indicates when major misdemeanors and felony arrest records, and convictions are submitted to a central state repository. In turn, these state repositories submit criminal record activity to the FBI's National Crime Information Center. When these transfers take place, the fingerprints are normally submitted as well.

Record Searching and Identifiers

There are two primary approaches to searching *direct* criminal records – go to the courthouse or go to the state repository. There are pluses and minuses for each method.

Most criminal record searches performed by the public at the courts are "name searches." This means a name is submitted or researched against a record docket index to determine if a record exists on the subject. Usually the DOB and sometimes the SSN is also provided or used by the requester when searching open records. Many courts provide public access terminal to search the index if they do not provide their personnel to do a look-up. All courts will not honor search requests by mail and certainly not by phone.

Using an exact name and a DOB gives record requesters a higher likelihood that the record found is that of the subject, opposed to name search with a partial DOB or to search with name only.

A smart researcher will search the record file and look for clues to identifiers that will confirm the record does indeed belong to the subject of the search, especially if the name is common like Williams and Smith. This holds true regardless if you are searching records at courthouses or at state agencies.

The "other" criminal records – incarceration, sexual predator, and from database vendors – can usually be searched with a name and some personal identifiers. However, if case details are needed, then an on-site search must be made at the appropriate court. Note that industry professionals generally consider these records to be supplementary in nature. They are certainly worthwhile, but professional researchers know these records should not be used as the *only search source.*

Open or Closed

There is a huge difference on record access depending on the repository location. Consider the following—

- Records at the courts or at the jails and prison systems are generally open to the public.
- Records at the state repository may be open, open but with restrictions on access or use, or closed.
- Records at the FBI are closed to the public unless accessed by the subject or mandated by statute to be accessed by a regulatory licensing body.

If access restrictions are in place, this generally means that either fingerprints or a signed release, or both, are required to obtain a criminal record check.

The Fingerprint Factor

All states, except Massachusetts, maintain fingerprint files that can be used for criminal record searching. When government agencies such as the courts or law enforcement agencies need criminal record checks, they generally provide fingerprints for the search. These agencies are often called *criminal justice agencies.* When state repository agencies check their databases of names and fingerprints for a criminal justice agency, they generally do a fingerprint check with the FBI as well. The same holds true when state statutes require an FBI check to be performed before licenses are issued for certain occupations involved with jobs or industries such as nursing, child care, securities, liquor sales, gaming, etc.

But if a search is requested by a non-criminal justice agency (the private sector, such as an employer), usually only a name search is requested and performed, even if a check of the state's fingerprint database may be available. One reason is the time factor since it may take weeks or months to obtain results, and the employer needs to hire right away. Another reason is the cost factor with fingerprints. Also, access to the FBI fingerprint database is not available to employers unless an FBI check is required per statute as described above.

The next section covers how to search records at the state repositories.

Searching State Repositories

As mentioned, all states have a central repository of criminal records of those individuals who have been subject to that state's criminal justice system. The database is managed by a law enforcement agency, usually known as the State Police or Department of Public Safety. The information at the state repository is submitted by state, county, parish, and municipal courts as well as from local law enforcement. Information forwarded to the state includes notations of arrests and charges, sometimes the disposition, and a set of fingerprints.

There are two factors that must be taken into account when searching criminal records at the state law enforcement repositories:

1. **Access Restrictions**
2. **Accuracy of Record Content**

Record searchers and record vendors need to be aware of these factors. Often this means educating the end-users of the records.

Restrictions to Access Factor

You do not waltz into a state police headquarters and demand to view the record index like you would at a courthouse. A key point for a criminal record searcher is once a record from the court reaches the law enforcement agency in more than half the states the record is no longer public. Most law enforcement agencies impose a set of requirements for access and do not offer on-site searching. Often a set of fingerprints must be submitted to do a record search.

Consider the following statistics from BRB Publications[4] about restrictions on criminal record requests from the public —

- 23 states release criminal records (name search) to the general public without consent of the subject.
- 18 states require a signed release from the subject.
- 9 state require submission of fingerprints
- 6 states have closed their records.

Several states, Minnesota for example, offer access to limited and to full records, depending if the requester presents a signed release.

The table presented on page 35 specifies the states in each of the categories mentioned above.

Note that all states will process record requests from requesters who have legislative authority to obtain records. These requesters include criminal justice-related agencies (courts), occupational licensing boards, and often industries dealing with the healthcare, or with the care of the young or aged.

The Accuracy of the Records

As noted, many employers and state licensing boards depend on state criminal record repositories as their primary resource when performing

---

[4] Taken from the *Public Record Research System*, BRB Publications, Inc. www.brbpub.com

a criminal record background check. But in some states this can be a questionable practice if this is the only resource used, even if fingerprints are submitted.

There are four reasons why the completeness, consistency, and accuracy of state criminal record repositories are open to accuracy concerns—

- Level of Automation
- Level of Quality Control
- Timeliness of Receiving Arrest and Disposition Data
- Timeliness of Entering Arrest and Disposition Data into the Repository

The Disposition Reporting Factor

Remember the Criminal Case Flowchart? One of the key record creation points is when a case receives a disposition. The problem is that in many states, there is no automated system that insures the disposition is reported by the courts to the state. This includes a guilty or a not-guilty verdict. Thus a record search may indicate an open case when in fact the case was dismissed or the subject may have already served time or probation.

The lack of dispositions can complicate things. State and federal laws are very strict about what records employers can and cannot use when making hiring decisions. There can be strict compliance rules in place. Many states have enacted laws that prohibit the disclosure of criminal information if a disposition is missing. The following is a case example from Lynn Peterson:

> For example, in Pennsylvania, if you conduct a criminal check using the State Police Index (EPATCH) and the subject has a criminal record but the disposition is missing, you will receive a message that the request is pending. If the State Police do not come up with the disposition, they will eventually mail you a report that indicates "no record." This means that the State Police may very well report someone as being clear, when, in fact, the person has a record.

So how widespread is the disposition problem? Consider these examples—

- Only 30 states generate lists of arrests with no dispositions in order to give notice to criminal justice agencies and courts about obtaining missing dispositions.
- 12 states report they each have from 7,000 to 148,500 final court dispositions that cannot be linked to an arrest record.
- Only 21 states report they receive final felony trial court dispositions for 70% or more arrests within last five5 years.

The Data Entry Factor

Recording dispositions is not the only problem state repositories are facing. Many states have funding concerns and non-automated systems that may lead to delays in data input—

- 27 states report they have a significant backlog (from 160 man-hours to 30,400 man-hours needed) for entering court data into the criminal history database.

- Only 25 states have fully automated criminal history files with a master name index. The remaining 25 states are partially automated.

The statistics shown above and the statistics in the table below come from the U.S. Department of Justice, Bureau of Justice Statistic's *Survey of State Criminal History Information Systems, 2003* (released in 2006)[5] with updated content researched by BRB Publications.

Table of State Repository Record- Keeping

State	% Arrests with Final Dispositions	Average # of Days to Receive and Process Submitted Arrest Data	Average # of Days to Receive and Process Submitted Dispositions
AL	45%	37	30+
AK	87%	30	n/a
AR	81%	37-44	60
AZ	58%	1	70
CA	75%	1	60
CO	17%	2-4	2
CT	100%	213	2-4
DE	94%	2	2
DC	46%	2	2
FL	70%	12	63
GA	70%	3	197
HI	90%	1-7	57
IA	95%	2	80
ID	66%	42	17
IL	52%	10	150
IN	45%	17	1
KS	50%	11	21
KY	69%	1-90	30
LA	40%	3-15	n/a

---

[5] The DOJ survey is available at www.ojp.usdoj.gov/bjs/abstract/sschis03.htm.

State	% Arrests with Final Dispositions	Average # of Days to Receive and Process Submitted Arrest Data	Average # of Days to Receive and Process Submitted Dispositions
MA	100%	1-30	2
MD	90%	1	61-63
ME	90%	1-14	1
MI	80%	15-30	1-180
MN	41%	20	4
MO	76%	114	n/a
MS	40%	105	1000
MT	85%	28	3
NC	89%	1-18	1
ND	86%	n/a	n/a
NE	62%	25-50	180
NH	80%	35-56	7-14
NJ	84%	2-12	2
NM	32%	75	3
NV	37%	2	60
NY*	85%	1	1
OH	65%	15	22
OK	32%	95-97	n/a
OR	50%	1-22	30
PA	60%	1	n/a
RI	86%	1-67	5
SC	70%	13	2-4
SD	98%	1-10	28
TN	23%	1-12	35
TX	66%	1-9	30
UT	64%	48-52	31
VA	84%	2-8	3-16
VT	96%	17	24
WA	79%	4	32
WI	77%	9	6
WV	40%	10	n/a
WY	73%	9	n/a

* NY statistics refer to the record repository maintained by the Office of Court Administration.

The Common Sense Approach

Please don't misunderstand the message here – there are certainly good reasons for performing a search of a state repository record database. A statewide search covers a wider geographic range than a county search. And a state search is certainly less expensive than a separate search of each county. Many states do have strong database systems. But for proper due diligence for performing a criminal record search, using a state search AND a county search of criminal records AND even a search from a database vendor should be considered. This is extremely critical for employers making hiring decisions in states with legislative limitations on using criminal records without dispositions or using misdemeanor records. (See *Criminal Records and Pre-Employment Screening* later in this chapter.)

However, a few states do make this approach somewhat difficult. Some court clerks are instructed not to honor mail requests to perform criminal record name searches. The state administration instructs the clerk to send the requester to the state police repository. Unless the requester can do an on-site search of the index or hire a researcher on-site, there is always a question of *how accurate is the state search?*

Searching the State Court Administrator's Records

In some states there is an alternative to searching the central state repository. Every state has a court administration that oversees the state's trial and appellate court system. In a surprising number of states – 23 – some or all of the state trial courts at the county (or parish) forward court records to the administrative office of the courts, often referred to as the AOC. The AOC then offers a searchable database to the public.

A Valuable Resource

A search from one of these court systems can be a particularly useful tool in those states that do not permit a state repository search – such as New York, North Carolina, or Utah.

Another value to using these record systems is there may be a higher likelihood that the disposition records are forwarded in a timely manner. Thus, the database may be very current.

State-by-State Variations

But there are many nuances to these searches. The value of an AOC court search varies by state. All counties may not be included. There may be no uniformity with respect to the length of time criminal activity is archived. For example, one county may have cases dating back for seven years, while another county may have only two years of history.

The use or lack of identifiers as part of the search varies widely from state-to-state, but searches do not involve fingerprints.

When an AOC system is available, you need to know (1) the court structure in that state, (2) which particular courts are included in their online system, and (3) what types of cases are included.

The *State Criminal Database Comparison Table* gives a quick guide to the states with an AOC access. The Table also shows the restrictions imposed by the main state repositories.

For in-depth details about each state's court system including the AOC databases, see the *State Court Summary Section* in the *Searching State and Local Court Records* chapter.

State Criminal Database Comparison Table

SR = Sign Release Needed

FP = Fingerprints

State	Central State Repository	State AOC Database
AL	Restrictions-SR; FP-Optional	
AK	Open; FP-Optional	Partial Coverage
AZ	Restrictions-Purpose; FP-Required	Partial Coverage
AR	Restrictions-SR; FP-Optional	
CA	Closed to Public	
CO	Open with Disclaimer; FP-Optional	Outsourced via designated 3rd party, fees
CT	Open; No FP	No name searches, but will pull case files, fees
DE	Restrictions-SR; FP-Required	
DC	Restrictions-SR; No FP	Direct for Superior Court
FL	Open; FP-Optional	
GA	Open (SR if requested at any local law enforcement); FP-Optional	
HI	Open; FP-Optional	Yes, but with disclaimer
ID	Open; FP-Optional	
IL	Open; FP-Optional	
IN	Restrictions-SR; FP-Optional	
IA	Open; FP-Optional	Yes, fee and free systems
KS	Open; FP-Optional	Only for 8 counties, fees
KY	Restrictions-SR; No FP	Yes, but with disclaimer
LA	Closed to Public	
MA	Open; No FP	Yes, but only for attorneys
MD	Restrictions-Purpose; FP-Required	Yes, except for 2 counties
ME	Open; FP-Optional	
MI	Open; FP-Optional	
MN	Limited is Open; Full-SR; No FP	
MO	Open; FP-Optional	Yes, partial

State	Central State Repository	State AOC Database
MS	Closed to Public	Yes, but will service fax requests only, fees
MT	Open; FP-Optional	
NC	Closed to Public	Yes, fees
ND	Open, (but subject notified if no SR); FP-Optional	
NE	Open; No FP	Yes, except Douglas County, fees
NH	Restrictions-SR; No FP	
NJ	Restrictions-Purpose; FP-Optional	Civil only, fees
NM	Restrictions-SR; No FP	Yes, except Bernalillo Metro
NV	Restrictions-SR; FP-Required	
NY	Closed to Public	Yes, fees
OH	Restrictions-SR; FP-Required	
OK	Open; FP-Optional	2 partial, outsourced systems
OR	Open; No FP (unless request submitted by subject)	Yes, but one county per search, fees
PA	Open; No FP	Yes, but with disclaimer
RI	Restrictions-SR; FP-Optional	Yes, but with disclaimer
SC	Open; No FP	
SD	Restrictions-SR; FP-Required	Yes, for mail or fax requesters, fees
TN	Open; FP-Optional	
TX	Limited Record Open; Full Record SR and FP Required	
UT	Closed to Public	Yes, fee based
VA	Restrictions-SR; No FP	Yes, but one county per search, fees
VT	Restrictions-Purpose, SR; No FP	Civil only, partial, fees
WA	Open; FP-Optional	Yes, free and fee systems
WI	Open; FP-Optional	Yes, except probate from one county
WV	Restrictions-SR; FP-Required	
WY	Restrictions-SR; FP-Required	

Criminal Records and Pre-Employment Screening

By far, the vast majority of criminal records requested, outside of law enforcement and criminal justice agencies, are used for employment purposes. These records are part of what is generally referred to as pre-employment screening or background checks. (See the *Employment Screening* section in the *Searching A thru Z* chapter.)

A background screen is not meant to stop an individual who has a criminal record in the past from being hired. The purpose of a background screen is to enable the employer to verify the information presented by the applicant and determine if the applicant is truthful about the past and is not using a false ID. Employers encourage and expect applicants to be truthful about past activity and employment.

Employers must also follow state and federal laws about what employers can and cannot ask or data to use when making hiring decisions.

State Issues

The following statements pertain to state restrictions on criminal record use by employers[6]—

- 19 states prohibit, under certain conditions, the use of arrest records (i.e., non-conviction records)
- 5 states prohibit, under certain conditions, the use of misdemeanor convictions
- 13 states explicitly prohibit the use of expunged or sealed records, with certain exceptions
- 4 states restrict the use of records based on time periods
- 2 states limit the use of first offense records

A discussion of these rules and the specific legalities involved goes well beyond the intent of this chapter and book. For those of you strongly concerned about these issues, it is recommended to obtain a copy of the Hinton and Henry book.

Federal Issues

The federal regulations concerning the use of criminal records by employers come from the Fair Credit Reporting Act (FCRA). If you are an employer ordering criminal records on potential employees, or a pre-employment screening company, it is imperative to become familiar with this law.

Per the authors of *The Criminal Records Manual*, "...there are three main areas in which the FCRA can affect an employer ordering criminal records—

- **Releases**—What notifications must be made and permissions granted from the subject of the search?
- **Arrest vs. convictions**—What information can appear on the report, and what must be suppressed?
- **Aged public record for employment purposes**—When vendor database records are used, what additional notifications to the subject must be performed?"

For detailed specifics regarding FCRA and criminal records, we recommend *The Criminal Records Manual* and *The Safe Hiring Manual* by Lester R. Rosen (see below).

---

[6] Taken from *The Criminal Records Manual* by Derek Hinton and Larry Henry, Facts on Demand Press, 2008.

The National Criminal Record Search

"Ha ha," you may say. "There is no need to search the state and county agencies. I can find a national criminal record search on the Internet for as little as $15."

The reality is that there is no such truly national database available to the public. Remember the discussion in the last chapter about people finders and links list sites? These web pages can lead to examples of entities offering the so-called national database searches of criminal records. They are marketing this search to consumers, unsuspecting employers, and others who may not be very knowledgeable about criminal records and the FCRA.

It is important to note that there are also perhaps a dozen companies with proprietary databases of criminal record data who are very knowledgeable about the compliance issues employers and vendors face with the FCRA. Most of these database vendors do NOT sell to consumers or to entities without an associated FCRA purpose. And these companies readily admit the benefits and the limitations of using these databases.

The following article is copyrighted text appearing in Chapter 12 of *The Safe Hiring Manual*, written by Lester R. Rosen and published by Facts On Demand Press. Rosen has done an excellent job explaining how these databases are created and how they can be used. We sincerely thank him for giving his permission to reprint his text in this book.

Take Caution When Using Private Databases

By Lester R. Rosen

A new tool being touted to employers is a "national database search" of criminal records. A number of vendors advertise they have, or have access to, a "national database of criminal record information." These services typically talk about having over 160 million records from 38 or more states. When sexual offender data is added, these services claim even more states and records are covered. Unfortunately, this form of advertising can create an impression in an employer's mind that they are getting the real thing — access to the nation's criminal records. Nothing could be further from the truth.

These databases are compiled from a number of various state repositories, correctional, and county sources. There are a number of reasons why this database information may not be accurate or complete. It is critical to understand that these multi-state database searches represent a **research**

tool only, and under no circumstances are they a substitute for a hands-on search at the county level.

There are values to using these databases, but there are also limitations.

Database Values

These database searches are of value because they cover a much larger geographical area than traditional county-level searches. By casting a much wider net, a researcher may pick up information that might be missed. The firms that sell database information can show test names of subjects that were "cleared" by a traditional county search, but criminal records were found in other counties through their searchable databases. In fact, it could be argued that failure to utilize such a database demonstrates a failure to exercise due diligence given the widespread coverage and low price.

Overall, the best use of these databases is as a secondary or supplemental research tool, or "lead generator" which tells a researcher where else to look.

Database Limitations

The compiled data typically comes from a mix of state repositories, correctional institutions, courts and any number of other counties agencies. The limitations of searching a private database are the inherent issues about completeness, name variations, timeliness, and legal compliance.

Completeness Issues

The various databases that vendors collect may not be the equivalent of a true all-encompassing multi-state database. First, the databases may not contain complete records from all jurisdictions — not all state court record systems contain updated records from all counties. Second, for reporting purposes, the records that are actually reported may be incomplete or lack sufficient detail about the offense or the subject. Third, some databases contain only felonies or contain only offenses where a state corrections unit is involved. Fourth, the database may not carry subsequent information or other matter that could render the results not reportable, or result in a state law violation concerning criminal records use.

The result is a crazy quilt patchwork of data from various sources, and lack of reliability. These databases can be more accurately described as "multi-jurisdictional databases."

Name and Date of Birth Issues

An electronic search of a vendor's database may not be able to recognize variations in a subject name, which a person may potentially notice if manually looking at the index. The applicant may have been arrested under a different first name or some variation of first and middle name. A female applicant may have a record under a previous name. Some database vendors have attempted to resolve this problem with a wild card first name search (i.e. instead of Robert, use Rob* so that any variations of ROB will come up). However, there are still too many different first and middle name variations. There is also the chance of name confusion for names where a combination of mother and father's name is used. In addition, some vendors require the use of date of birth in order to prevent too many records from being returned. Also, if an applicant uses a different date of birth it can cause errors.

Also, there are some states where a date of birth is not in the court records. Since databases match records by date of birth, search when no DOB exists is of little value since no "hits" will be reported. In those situations, it is necessary to run a search in just the state in question and then individually review each name match. That can be tedious, especially if a common name is being searched.[7]

Timeliness Issues

Records in a vendor's database may be stale to some extent. These records are normally updated monthly, at best. Even after a vendor receives new data, there can be lag time before the new data is downloaded into the vendor database. Generally the most current offenses are the ones less likely to come up in a database search.

Legal Compliance Issues

When there is a "hit" an employer must be concerned about legal compliance. If an employer uses a commercial database via the Internet,

---

[7] Technically, the issue comes down to how broad or how narrow the database provider sets the search parameters. If a database sets the search parameters on a narrow basis, so it only locates records based upon exact date of birth and last name, then the number of records located not related to the applicant would be reduced. In other words, there will be less "false positives." However, it can also lead to record being missed, either because of name variations or because some states do not provide date of birth in the records. That can lead to "false negatives." Conversely, if the parameters are set broadly to avoid missing relevant records, then there is a greater likelihood of finding criminal records relating to the applicant, but at the same time, there are likely to be a number of records that do not belong to the applicant. That can happen for example in a state where no date of birth is provide, and the database is run on a "name match only basis. The bottom-line: with use of databases, employers need to understand there is the possibility of both "false negatives" and "false positives," depending upon how the particular background firm runs the databases.

the employer must have an understanding of the proper use of criminal records in that state. If the employer acts on face value results without any additional due diligence research, potentially the applicant could sue the employer if the record was not about them.

If a screening firm locates a criminal hit, then the screening firm has an obligation under the FCRA Section 613 (a)(2) to send researchers to the court to pull the actual court records. This section requires that a background-screening firm must—

…maintain strict procedures designed to insure that whenever public record information, which is likely to have an adverse effect on a consumer's ability to obtain employment, is reported, it is complete and up-to-date. For purposes of this paragraph, items of public record relating to arrests, indictments, convictions, suits, tax liens, and outstanding judgments shall be considered up-to-date if the current public record status of the item at the time of the report is reported.

As discussed in Chapter 6, FCRA section 613(a)(1) provides an alternative procedure. Instead of going to the courthouse, a CRA can notify the consumer that public record information is being reported by the consumer reporting, and give name and address of the requester. However, some states arguably do not permit this alternative procedure. This is a potential compliance issue for employers who operate in states that do not allow the "notification" procedure to be used instead of the "strict procedure" method of double-checking at the courthouse.

The best approach for an employer is to insist that a CRA always confirm the details of a database search by going to the courthouse to review the actual records.[8] Additional information about the FCRA and databases is covered in Chapters 6 and 10 in *The Safe Hiring Manual*, not this book.

Conclusion About Private Databases—

Just because a person's name appears in one of these databases it does not mean the subject is a criminal. On the other hand, if a person's name does not appear, this likewise should not be taken as conclusive the person is not a criminal. In other words, these databases can result in "false negatives" or "false positives;" and an over-reliance can cause one to develop a false sense of security.

---

[8] For a detailed discussion about the legal uses of a database, see an article co-written by Lester R. Rosen and national FCRA expert Carl Ernst titled *"National" Criminal History Databases* at www.brbpub.com/articles/CriminalHistoryDB.pdf

Criminal record vendors and background firms should make clear, and employers need to understand, the exact nature and limitations of any database they access. These private database searches are ancillary and can be very useful, but proceed with caution. In other words, it cannot be assumed that a search of a proprietary criminal database by itself will show if a person is or is not a criminal, but these databases are outstanding secondary or supplemental tools with which to do a much wider search.

Other Criminal Record and Criminal Record-Related Databases

For detailed information on the following topics, see the *Searching A thru Z* chapter:

- Incarceration Records
- Sexual Predator Records
- Federal Sanctions and Watch Lists Databases
- Securities and Securities Dealers – SEC – Enforcement Actions

Searching State and Local Court Records

Court records are perhaps the most widely sought public record in the U.S., and researching court records can be very complicated because of the extensive diversity of the courts and their record keeping systems.

Before searching an online index of court records or trudging into a courthouse and demanding to view a document, you should first familiarize yourself with basic court structures and procedures.

The Four Court Levels

Courts exist at four levels: federal, state, county, and local municipalities. All four levels can be within the same county.

Each state has its own court system, created by statutes or constitution to enforce state civil and criminal laws. Sometimes the terms "state court" and "county court" can be a source of confusion because state trial courts are located at county courthouses. In this book we will refer to state courts as the courts belonging to the state court systems, and county courts as those administered by county authority. Local municipal courts can be managed by the local city, town or village government whose laws they enforce. Some lower level courts are called justice courts.

In Louisiana the word *Parish* is equivalent to what is a county in another state. Alaska is organized by *Boroughs*, and a few states have cities that are equivalent to counties. Rather than to continually restate these facts, we will assume the reader knows that if the text is speaking of state courts, these other courts are included.

Courts may have divisions – such as criminal and civil – that only hear specific case types. For instance there are courts that only hear appeals. Whether the case is filed in a state, municipal, or federal court, each case follows a similar process.

The federal court system is covered in the next chapter.

State Court Structure

An important first step in determining where a particular state court case is located is to know how the court system is structured in that particular state. The general structure of all state court systems has four tiers:

- **Appellate courts**
- **Intermediate appellate courts**
- **General jurisdiction trial courts**
- **Limited jurisdiction trial courts**

The two highest levels, appellate and intermediate appellate courts, only hear cases on appeal from the trial courts. "Opinions" of these appellate courts are of particular interest to attorneys seeking legal precedents for newer cases. However, opinions can be useful to record searchers because they summarize facts about the case that will not show on an index or docket.

General jurisdiction trial courts oversee a full range of civil and criminal litigation, usually handling felonies and higher dollar civil cases. The general jurisdiction court will often serve as the appellate court for cases appealed from limited jurisdiction courts and even from the local courts. Many court researchers refer to general jurisdiction courts as **upper courts**.

There are some courts — sometimes called **special jurisdiction** courts — that have general jurisdiction but are limited to one type of litigation. An example is the Court of Claims in New York which only processes liability cases against the state.

Limited jurisdiction trial courts come in several varieties. Many limited jurisdiction courts handle smaller civil claims (usually $10,000 or less), misdemeanors, and pretrial hearings for felonies. Localized municipal courts are also referred to as courts of limited jurisdiction. Many court researchers refer to limited jurisdiction courts as **lower courts**.

A number of states, Iowa for instance, have consolidated their general and limited court structure into **one combined court system**.

About Municipal, Town, and Village Courts

These localized courts preside over misdemeanors, infractions, and city ordinance violations at the city, town or township level. Sometimes these courts may be known as *justice courts*. Notable is the state of New York where nearly 1,400 Town and Village Justice Courts handle misdemeanors, local ordinance violations, and traffic violations including DWIs.

In most states there is a distinction between state-supported courts and the local courts in terms of management and funding.

Watch for Divisions and Name Variations

Do not assume that the structure of the court system and the names used for courts in another state are anything like your own. Civil and criminal records may be handled by different divisions within a court or sometimes by completely different courts with different names. For example, in Tennessee the Chancery Court oversees civil cases but criminal cases are tried in Circuit Courts, except in districts with separate Criminal Courts as established by the state legislature. Also, in one state, the Circuit Court may be the highest trial court whereas in another it is a limited jurisdiction court. In New York, the Supreme Court is not very "supreme" and the downstate court structure varies from counties upstate.

Types of Court Records

Below is a summary of the types of court cases and records found at the state or local level. Note that bankruptcies are not found on this list because bankruptcy cases are filed at the federal level.

- **Civil Actions** - For money damages usually greater than $5,000. Also, some states have designated dollar amount thresholds for upper or lower (limited) civil courts. Most civil litigation involves torts or contract.
- **Small Claims** - Actions for minor money damages, generally under $5,000, no juries involved.
- **Criminal Felonies** - Generally defined as crimes punishable by one year or more of jail time. There can be multiple levels or classes.
- **Criminal Misdemeanors** - Generally defined as minor infractions with a fine and less than one year of jail time. Misdemeanors also have multiple levels or classes.
- **Probate** - Estate matters, settling the estate of a deceased person, resolving claims and distributing the decedent's property.
- **Eviction Actions** - Landlord/tenant actions, can also known as a unlawful detainer, forcible detainer, summary possession, or repossession.
- **Domestic Relations** – Sometimes known as *Family Law*, with authority over family disputes, divorces, dissolutions, child support or custody cases.
- **Juvenile** – Authority over cases involving individuals under a specified age, usually 18 years but sometimes 21.
- **Traffic** – May also have authority over municipal ordinances.
- **Specialty Courts** – Water, equity in fiduciary questions, tort, contracts, tax, etc.

The next two pages show how court systems are structured in West Virginia and Michigan, including which courts oversee which cases.

West Virginia Court System

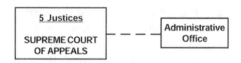

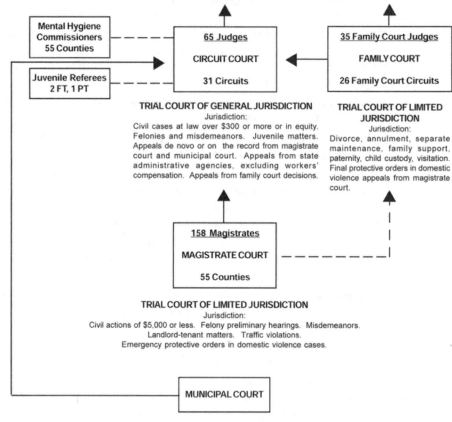

```
        ┌─────────────────┐              ┌──────────────────┐
        │   5 Justices    │ - - - - - -  │  Administrative  │
        │                 │              │     Office       │
        │ SUPREME COURT   │              └──────────────────┘
        │  OF APPEALS     │
        └─────────────────┘
```

COURT OF LAST RESORT
Jurisdiction:
Original jurisdiction in proceedings of habeas corpus, mandamus, prohibition, and certiorari. Appellate jurisdiction in civil cases at law over $300 or in equity, in cases involving constitutionality of a law, in felony and misdemeanor matters appealed from circuit court. Appeals of divorce and other domestic relations decisions in family court if both parties agree not to first appeal to circuit court. The Supreme Court also receives workers' compensation appeals directly from the state administrative agency and receives other state administrative appeals from the circuit court.

```
┌──────────────────┐     ┌─────────────────┐      ┌────────────────────────┐
│  Mental Hygiene  │     │   65 Judges     │      │ 35 Family Court Judges │
│  Commissioners   │- - -│                 │      │                        │
│   55 Counties    │     │  CIRCUIT COURT  │ ◄──  │     FAMILY COURT       │
└──────────────────┘     │                 │      │                        │
┌──────────────────┐     │   31 Circuits   │      │ 26 Family Court Circuits│
│ Juvenile Referees│- - -│                 │      └────────────────────────┘
│   2 FT, 1 PT     │     └─────────────────┘
└──────────────────┘
```

TRIAL COURT OF GENERAL JURISDICTION
Jurisdiction:
Civil cases at law over $300 or more or in equity. Felonies and misdemeanors. Juvenile matters. Appeals de novo or on the record from magistrate court and municipal court. Appeals from state administrative agencies, excluding workers' compensation. Appeals from family court decisions.

TRIAL COURT OF LIMITED JURISDICTION
Jurisdiction:
Divorce, annulment, separate maintenance, family support, paternity, child custody, visitation. Final protective orders in domestic violence appeals from magistrate court.

```
            ┌─────────────────┐
            │ 158 Magistrates │
            │                 │
            │ MAGISTRATE COURT│ - - - - - -
            │                 │
            │   55 Counties   │
            └─────────────────┘
```

TRIAL COURT OF LIMITED JURISDICTION
Jurisdiction:
Civil actions of $5,000 or less. Felony preliminary hearings. Misdemeanors. Landlord-tenant matters. Traffic violations. Emergency protective orders in domestic violence cases.

```
            ┌─────────────────┐
            │ MUNICIPAL COURT │
            └─────────────────┘
```

TRIAL COURT OF LIMITED JURISDICTION
Jurisdiction:
Ordinance and traffic violations.
Municipal courts are organized and operated at the local level.

Source: www.state.wv.us/wvsca

MICHIGAN JUDICIAL BRANCH

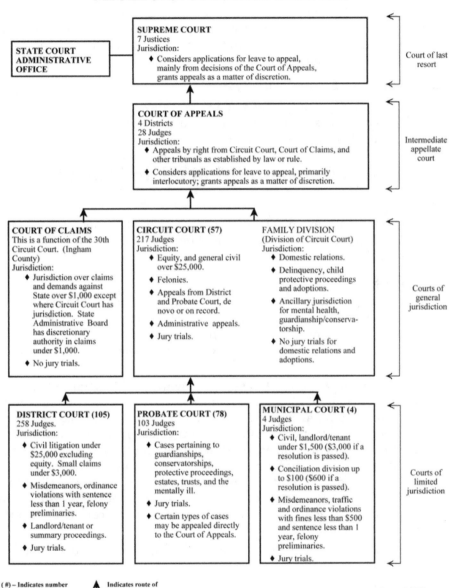

STATE COURT ADMINISTRATIVE OFFICE

SUPREME COURT
7 Justices
Jurisdiction:
♦ Considers applications for leave to appeal, mainly from decisions of the Court of Appeals, grants appeals as a matter of discretion.

Court of last resort

COURT OF APPEALS
4 Districts
28 Judges
Jurisdiction:
♦ Appeals by right from Circuit Court, Court of Claims, and other tribunals as established by law or rule.
♦ Considers applications for leave to appeal, primarily interlocutory; grants appeals as a matter of discretion.

Intermediate appellate court

COURT OF CLAIMS
This is a function of the 30th Circuit Court. (Ingham County)
Jurisdiction:
♦ Jurisdiction over claims and demands against State over $1,000 except where Circuit Court has jurisdiction. State Administrative Board has discretionary authority in claims under $1,000.
♦ No jury trials.

CIRCUIT COURT (57)
217 Judges
Jurisdiction:
♦ Equity, and general civil over $25,000.
♦ Felonies.
♦ Appeals from District and Probate Court, de novo or on record.
♦ Administrative appeals.
♦ Jury trials.

FAMILY DIVISION
(Division of Circuit Court)
Jurisdiction:
♦ Domestic relations.
♦ Delinquency, child protective proceedings and adoptions.
♦ Ancillary jurisdiction for mental health, guardianship/conservatorship.
♦ No jury trials for domestic relations and adoptions.

Courts of general jurisdiction

DISTRICT COURT (105)
258 Judges
Jurisdiction:
♦ Civil litigation under $25,000 excluding equity. Small claims under $3,000.
♦ Misdemeanors, ordinance violations with sentence less than 1 year, felony preliminaries.
♦ Landlord/tenant or summary proceedings.
♦ Jury trials.

PROBATE COURT (78)
103 Judges
Jurisdiction:
♦ Cases pertaining to guardianships, conservatorships, protective proceedings, estates, trusts, and the mentally ill.
♦ Jury trials.
♦ Certain types of cases may be appealed directly to the Court of Appeals.

MUNICIPAL COURT (4)
4 Judges
Jurisdiction:
♦ Civil, landlord/tenant under $1,500 ($3,000 if a resolution is passed).
♦ Conciliation division up to $100 ($600 if a resolution is passed).
♦ Misdemeanors, traffic and ordinance violations with fines less than $500 and sentence less than 1 year, felony preliminaries.
♦ Jury trials.

Courts of limited jurisdiction

(#) – Indicates number of courts.

↑ Indicates route of appeal

January 1, 2005

Source: http://courts.michigan.gov/scao/

Be Careful About Making Generalizations

As you can see per the charts, generalizations should not be made about where specific types of cases are handled in the various states. Misdemeanors, Probate, landlord/tenant (evictions), domestic relations, and juvenile cases may be handled in either or both the general and limited jurisdiction courts.

Summaries of State Court Systems

An in-depth summary of each state's court systems is provided later in this chapter. These summaries also indicate searching tips and online search capabilities for each state.

Differences Between Criminal and Civil Court Files

There are significant differences between civil and criminal court cases filings which affect how records should be searched and the relevance of the records

Who Files

In a **criminal case**, the government files the case. The government brings the action against the defendant for violation of one or more of its statutes. The Criminal Case Flowchart in the last chapter shows how a criminal case progresses and the key points when criminal records are created.

In most instances, a **civil case** is brought to trial by an individual or company, usually through their attorney. The defendant responds to the complaint with an answer. After this initial round, there may be literally hundreds of activities before the court issues a judgment. These activities can include amended complaints and their answers, motions of various kinds, discovery proceedings (including depositions) to establish the documentation and facts involved in the case. All of these activities are listed on **dockets**, (see below). Once the court issues a civil judgment if money is involved the winning side can usually file a judgment lien with the county recorder.

Appellate divisions usually deal only with legal issues and not the facts of the respective cases.

Burden of Proof

In criminal cases guilt must be proved "beyond a reasonable doubt." However, the standard is lower in civil cases and proof only has to be determined by a "preponderance of the evidence."

Penalties

In criminal cases the penalties may involve incarceration in jail or prison, probation, fines, diversions, delayed adjudication, or community service. In civil cases the judgments usually involve money.

A defendant may not be convicted in a criminal case, but may still lose in a civil case. O.J. Simpson and Michael Jackson are good examples. While they were not criminally convicted, they lost or settled the civil suits against them.

Probate and Eviction Files

Probate is process of court actions to prove a will. Individual cases may involve wills, decedents' estates, trusts, guardianships, and conservatorships. The probate record file may contain the will or letters of administration, renunciations, inventories, lists of sales, estate vouchers or releases, administration bonds, executor accounts, distributive settlements, guardian bonds and accounts, and any stated exceptions.

Two significant terms may appear on records: a guardian is a court-appointed person responsible for the care, custody, and control of the respondent; a conservator is a person appointed by the court to manage the estate of the respondent.

The organization of probate courts in the U.S. is state dependant, there is no true consistency. About half the states have a formal probate court established by state statute; the other states assign probate to a division in a general or limited jurisdiction court. Some counties have more than one probate court. Some states assign other case types, such as the jurisdiction of involuntary civil commitment and adoption cases to a probate court. Probate records are important to genealogists, in fact there are many archival sites available for record dating back several centuries.

Evictions, frequently called forcible detainers, are civil actions where a judgment has been rendered against a renter or leaser entity for non-payment. The court record will indicate plaintiff, defendant, disposition and amount of judgment. These court records are generally held in assigned division at either a general or limited jurisdiction court, depending on the state. Eviction records are important for tenant screening purposes.

Probate and eviction records are accessed in a similar manner as other court records, using an index and a case file. Many jurisdictions offer online access to the index. See the State Court Summaries section to follow for details on each state's probate court system and location of eviction records.

How Courts Maintain Records

Case Numbering

When a case is filed, a case number is assigned. Use of a case number is the primary indexing method in every court. Therefore, to search specific case records, you will need to know – or find – the applicable case number.

Be aware that case numbering procedures are not necessarily consistent throughout a state court system. One district may assign numbers by district while another may assign numbers by location (division) within the district, or by judge. Remember: case numbers appearing in legal text citations may not be adequate for searching unless they appear in the proper form for the particular court in which you are searching.

The Docket Sheet

Information from cover sheets and from documents filed as a case goes forward is recorded on the docket sheet. Thus the docket sheet is a running summary of a case history from initial filing to its current status. While docket sheets differ somewhat in format from court to court, the basic information contained on a docket sheet is consistent. All docket sheets contain:

- Name of court, including location (division) and the judge assigned;
- Case number and case name;
- Names of all plaintiffs and defendants/debtors;
- Names and addresses of attorneys for the plaintiff or debtor;
- Nature and cause (e.g., statute) of action.

File Storage and Computerization

Most courts enter the docket data into a computer system. Within a state or judicial district, the courts *may* be linked together via a single computer system.

But docket sheets from cases closed before the advent of computerization may not be in the computer system. And in some locations all docket information is non-computerized. Media formats include microfilm, microfiche, index cards, and paper that may even be hand-written.

As mentioned, case document images are not generally available online because courts are still experimenting and developing electronic filing and imaging. Generally, copies of case documents are only on-site.

Dispositions, Expungments, and Sealed Records

When a case is decided, a decision or *disposition* is rendered. **(See the previous chapter for information about the importance of the**

disposition in a criminal case.) The disposition is entered onto the docket or index.

There are some cases where decisions were rendered, but the results are not recorded or the case file number is removed from the index. In certain situations, a judge can order the case file sealed or removed – expunged – from the public repository. Examples include if a defendant enters a diversion program (drug or family counseling), or a defendant makes restitution as part of a plea bargain; these cases may not be searchable. The only way to gain direct access to these types of case filings is through a subpoena. However, savvy researchers and investigators will sometimes search news media sources if need be.

Court Record Searching Tips

1. Learn the Index & Record Systems

Most civil courts index records by both plaintiffs and defendants, but some only index by the defendant name. A plaintiff search is useful, for example, to determine if someone is especially litigious.

Determine if there is a computerized indexing system and/or if the court used index books or cards. The throughput dates are important to know.

2. Understand the Search Requirements

There is a strong tendency for courts to overstate their search requirements. For civil cases, the usual reasonable requirement is a defendant (or plaintiff) name – full name if it is a common name – and the time frame to search – e.g., 1993-2002. For criminal cases, the court may require more identification, such as date of birth (DOB), to ascertain the correct individual. Other information "required" by courts – such as Social Security Number (SSN) – is often just "helpful" to narrow the search on a common name.

3. Be Aware of Restricted Records

Courts have types of case records, such as juvenile and adoptions, which are not released without a court order. The presiding judge often makes a determination of whether a particular record type is available to the public. Some criminal court records include the arresting officer's report. In some locations this information is regarded as public record, while in other locations the police report may be sealed.

4. Know the Fees and Other Requirements

As previously mentioned, most courts charge fees for their searching, copying, and certification services.

Sometimes there is a difference in the copy fee depending if the court makes the copy or if a self-serve machine is used. Ask first when you hire someone to pull copies for you.

Some courts do not accept personal checks, some do not even take business checks. If in doubt, send a money order or certified funds.

Assume or at least ask if the court requires a self-addressed stamped envelope (**SASE)** to accompany a written search request. Even where it is not indicated, we recommend including a SASE with a mail request.

5. Watch for Multiple Courts as Same Location

When the general jurisdiction and limited jurisdiction courts are in the same building and use the same support staff, chances are the record databases are combined as well. But that does not necessarily mean you will receive a search of both databases and pay for one search unless you **ask for it**. Do not assume.

Look for the situation when a county wide database exists for outlying limited jurisdictional courts. Make sure you ask if you are receiving a search of all limited jurisdiction courts in the county or just the court you are speaking to.

The same holds true when using public access computer terminals. Ask what courts the index covers. In some states you can only view the case at the court, but other courts provide access to a statewide system!

6. Be Aware Not All Courts Conduct Name Searches

The reality of court record searching is many courts will not perform name searches. You must search the index yourself or hire someone to do an on-site search. In some states, such as Kentucky, the courts refer the searcher to a central state repository, and the agency that maintains a database combining individual court records, which may not be current. In other states, Nebraska for instance, the court has public access terminals or microfilm/fiche readers available for public use.

If you need copies of a specific case record and you know the case number, court personnel generally will honor mail, fax, and sometimes phone requests to make copies for you. Also, court personnel may certify the document for you for a fee.

If you cannot come to the courthouse yourself, and the court personnel will not perform the search for you, then you must hire a local retrieval firm or other individual to conduct the search. An excellent source of local court record searchers is the Public Record Retriever Network found at www.brbpub.com/prrn.

7. Online Searching is Generally Limited to Docket Sheets

Most courts that offer online access limit the search to the docketsheet data. But checking a courthouse's computer online docket index is the quickest way to find if case records exist online. Just be sure to check all name variations and spelling variations. (See the *Tips From a Professional Searcher* in the *Searching Liens and Recorded Documents* chapter)

8. Watch for Overlapping Jurisdictions

In some states, the general jurisdiction court and the limited jurisdiction court have overlapping dollar amounts for civil cases. That means a case could be filed in either court. Check both courts; never assume.

9. Using the State Court Administrator's Office

The state court administrator oversees the state court system and the web page is a good place to find opinions from supreme courts and appeals courts.

In some states, the state court administration office oversees a statewide online access system to court records. Some of these systems are commercial fee-based. Other systems offer free access, but are usually very limited by comparison. The *Searching Criminal Records* in the previous chapter provides a table summary. The *Summaries of State Court Systems* to follow gives detailed information about how to access to these centralized (sometimes) index of trial court records.

10. Additional Searching Tips from a Pro

The following tips mention other search considerations to keep in mind. The information was provided by Lynn Peterson[9], a public records expert and President of PFC Information Services, Inc. We sincerely thank her for allowing us to share her comments and ideas.

Tips from a Professional

By Lynn Peterson

Geographic and Time Considerations

Geographic considerations play a significant role when determining which courts you will need to research. If searching for civil or criminal cases and the subject is an individual, you probably will want to search the courts in all of the locations identified where the individual has worked or lived. And you will also have to determine how many years back to search. If the research is being conducted for employment purposes, state laws and FCRA may limit the period of time involved. However, if the situation

---

[9] Also, Ms. Peterson is an adjunct instructor at the University of North Carolina, School of Journalism and Mass Communication, where she co-teaches a course in public records and investigative research. See www.pfcinformation.com.

calls for some serious due diligence, you might need to go back many years.

The situation becomes more complicated when you are searching for civil litigation involving a company. A suit could be filed just about anywhere, particularly if the company has several locations. For example, let's say you are looking for a suit involving a contract case. In addition to searching the company's physical locations, it would be wise to also search locations where the contract was signed or where it was breached.

Name Relevance

Often criminal dockets are simply an alpha index of defendant names. When the defendant's name is John Smith, you may have to review each file involving defendants named John Smith to determine relevance. Criminal case files normally include information regarding the identity of the defendant. Name, AKA's, and date of birth are usually listed in the file. Sometimes Social Security Number, driver's license number, and address are also listed. Therefore, it normally isn't difficult to determine the relevance of a particular criminal case.

Determine the relevance of names in civil court cases can be much more difficult. Again, the civil docket might provide nothing more than the names of the parties involved. If you found a case involving a John Smith and the co-defendant was Eloise Smith. This could provide you with a clue concerning relevance—if you happened to know that your subject's wife's name was Eloise. In the absence of clues provided by the names of co-defendants or co-plaintiffs, the case files would have to be examined for relevance. This is where the process can get difficult, as it is not uncommon for the file itself to contain absolutely no identifying information. In this case, all you can do is to guess at relevance.

Note: Look in the *Searching Liens and Recorded Documents* chapter for additional searching tips about name variants and using indexes and card files. These suggestions are very applicable to court record searching.

Summaries of State Court Systems

The following profiles each state's court system, include structure, jurisdiction, online capabilities, and specific searching tips.[10]

Alaska

Administration - Office of the Administrative Director, 907-264-8232; Records: 907-264-0491. www.state.ak.us/courts

Structure & Jurisdictions - Alaska has a unified, centrally administered, and totally state-funded judicial system with 4 Judicial Districts. Municipal governments do not maintain separate court systems. Alaska has 15 boroughs, not counties. 3 are unified home rule municipalities that are combination borough and city, and 12 boroughs. There are also 12 home rule cities which do not directly coincide with the 4 Judicial Districts. In other words, judicial boundaries cross borough boundaries.

The four levels of courts are the Supreme Court, the Court of Appeals, the Superior Court, and the District Court. There are also Magistrate Courts that preside over certain District Court matters. The magistrate is a judicial officer of the District Court.

The Superior Court hears felony cases and civil cases generally involving $100,000 or more. The court also hears cases involving children, property of deceased or incompetent persons, involuntary commitment of persons to institutions for the mentally ill, probate, and domestic relations matters. It serves as an appellate court for appeals from civil and criminal cases which have been tried in the district court and for appeals from some administrative agencies.

The District Court cases involve hear state misdemeanors and violations of city and borough ordinances, first appearances and preliminary hearings in felony cases, record vital statistics (in some areas of the state), civil cases valued up to $100,000, small claims cases ($10,000 maximum), cases involving children on an emergency basis, and domestic violence cases.

Online Access – A name search of a partial statewide Alaska Trial Courts database index is at www.courtrecords.alaska.gov. Since the Alaska Court System is migrating to a new electronic case information system called CourtView, there is an old and a new system. Search results give case number, file date, disposition date, charge, and sentence. Be aware that the intial index gives the only the name used on the first pleading.

---

[10] To find detailed searching procedures, fees, and access methods on over 7,000 courts, please see BRB Publication's *The Sourcebook to Public Record Information* or the PRRS online subscription (www.brbpub.com).

The home web page gives access to Appellate opinions. The site at http://government.westlaw.com/akcases/ provides access to opinions of the Alaska Supreme Court and Alaska Court of Appeals.

Searching Tips - Magistrate Courts vary in how records are maintained and hours of operation; some are open only a few hours per week.

Alabama

Administration – Director of Courts, 334-954-5000. www.alacourt.gov

Structure & Jurisdictions - Alabama courts include Supreme Court, Court of Civil Appeals, Court of Criminal Appeals, Circuit Courts, District Courts, Probate Courts and Municipal Courts. Circuit Courts are the courts of general jurisdiction, handling felonies and civil cases of $3,000 or more. District Courts have limited jurisdiction in civil matters, up to $10,000 and handle small claims (up to $3,000). The Circuit and District Courts are combined in all but eight larger counties. Also, Barbour, Coffee, Jefferson, St. Clair, Talladega, and Tallapoosa Counties have **two court locations** within the county. Jefferson County (Birmingham), Madison (Huntsville), Marshall, and Tuscaloosa Counties have **separate criminal divisions** for Circuit Courts and/or District Courts. All counties have separate probate courts.

Misdemeanors committed with felonies are tried with the felony. The Circuit Courts are appeals courts for misdemeanors. District Courts can receive guilty pleas in felony cases. 250+ Municipal Courts handle misdemeaner, DWI/DUI, and as ordinance violations.

Online Access – A commercial online subscription service at www.alacourt.com draws its data from the State Judicial Information System (SJIS). This system is comprehensive and user friendly, includes civil, criminal, DR, traffic, warrants, and trial court dockets statewide. It also features multiple monthly payment plans. State Supreme Court and Appellate decisions are available at www.alalinc.net and at http://www.judicial.state.al.us/

Searching Tips - Although in most counties Circuit Courts and District Courts are combined, each index may be separate. Therefore, when you request a search of both courts, be sure to state that the search is to cover "both the Circuit and District Court records." A number of courts do not perform searches, you must hire a retriever. Many courts offer public access computer terminals.

Arizona

Administration - Administrative Office of the Courts, 602-452-3300. www.supreme.state.az.us

Structure & Jurisdictions - Superior Court is the court of general jurisdiction. Justice of the Peace Courts and Municipal Courts generally have separate jurisdiction over case types. Probate and estate cases are handled by Superior Court. Civil cases between $5,000 and $10,000 may be filed at either Justice Courts or Superior Courts.

Online Access - The Public Access to Court Case Information at (Click on *Public Access – Case Lookup* from home page) provides a resource for information about court cases from 142 out of 180 courts in Arizona. Courts not covered include certain parts of Pima, Yavapai, Mohave, and Maricopa counties. Information includes docket information, the parties in the case (not including victims and witnesses), and the court mailing address and location. Opinions from the Supreme Court and Court of Appeals are available from www.supreme.state.az.us.

Searching Tips - Many offices do not perform searches due to personnel or budget constraints but many provide public access computer terminals. Public access to all Maricopa County court case indexes is available at a central location - 1 W. Madison Ave in downtown Phoenix. However, file copies must be obtained from the court where the case is heard.

Arkansas

Administration - Administrative Office of Courts, 501-682-9400, 501-682-6849. www.courts.state.ar.us

Structure & Jurisdictions - Circuit Courts are the courts of general jurisdiction and are arranged in 28 circuits with five subject matter divisions: criminal, civil, probate, domestic relations, and juvenile. A Circuit Clerk handles the records and recordings, however some counties have a County Clerk that handles probate. District Courts, formerly known as Municipal Courts, exercise countywide jurisdiction over misdemeanor cases, preliminary felony cases, and in civil cases for matters of less than $5,000, including small claims. City Courts operate in smaller communities and exercise citywide jurisdiction where District Courts do not exist.

Online Access - Access to Supreme Court Opinions and Appellate Court dockets is at http://courts.state.ar.us/online/or.html where you will also find Court of Appeals dockets, corrected opinions, and parallel citations. An attorney search, court rules and administrative orders are also available. Online access to individual courts at the county level remains almost non-existent.

Searching Tips - Many courts that allow written search requests require an SASE. Fees vary widely across jurisdictions as do prepayment requirements.

California

Administration - Administrative Office of Courts, 415-865-3688. www.courtinfo.ca.gov

Structure & Jurisdictions - The Superior Court is the trial court in this state and handles all cases. However, in higher population counties, there are Limited Superior Courts. Civil cases under $25,000 is in a Limited Civil Court, over $25,000 is in Unlimited Civil Court, and if both covered in one court, then the court is a Combined Civil Court. It is important to note that Limited Courts may try minor felonies.

Online Access - The website at www.courtinfo.ca.gov offers access to all opinions from the Supreme Court and Appeals Courts from 1850 to present. Opinions not certified for publications are available for the last 60 days. There is no statewide online computer access available. However, a number of counties have developed their own online access sytems and provide internet access at no fee. Los Angeles County has an extensive free and fee-based online system at www.lasuperiorcourt.org.

Searching Tips - If muliple courts of the same level are in a county, where the case is tried and where the record is held depends on how a citation is written, where the infraction occurred, or where the filer chose to file the case. Case file information may need to be obtained from the exact court of record.

Some courts require a signed release from the subject for criminal searches and no longer allow the public to conduct such searches.

Colorado

Administration - State Court Administrator, 303-861-1111. www.courts.state.co.us

Structure & Jurisdictions - The District Court is the trial court of general jurisdiction and handles felony matters, probate and domestic relations. The County court handles misdemeanor cases. The District and County Courts have overlapping jurisdiction over civil cases involving less than $15,000 ($10,000 prior to 9/1/2001). Fortunately, District and County Courts are combined in most counties. Co-located with seven district courts are divisions known as Water Courts located in Weld, Pueblo, Alamosa, Montrose, Garfield, Routt, and La Platta counties. There are over 200 municipal courts in the state.

The Denver Court System differs from the rest of the state, in part because Denver is both a city and a county. The Denver County Court functions as a municipal and a county court and is paid for entirely by Denver taxes, rather than by state taxes and is not part of the state court system; the District Court is.

On November 15, 2001, Broomfield City & County came into existence, derived from parts of counties of Adams, Boulder, Jefferson, and Weld. A District and County Court (in 17th Judicial District) was established.

Municipal courts only have jurisdiction over traffic, parking, and ordinance violations. Denver is the only county where the Probate Court and Juvenile Court is separate from the District Court.

Online Access - LexisNexis CourtLink was appointed to act as agent for the Colorado Judicial Department to provide access to ICON (Integrated

Colorado Online Network) to the general public and serve as the gateway for other vendors. For a fee, these vendors permit users to look at a name index - the Register of Actions - to court filings and appearance dates. Images or copies of documents are not available from any of the commercial sites and may only be obtained by contacting the individual court where the documents were filed.

Opinions from the Court of Appeals are available from the state website.

Searching Tips - Nearly every court requires a self-addressed, stamped envelope (SASE) for return of information. Many combined courts search both civil or criminal indexes for a single fee, but be sure to ask. To retrieve a Water Court record, one must furnish the case number or the legal description (section, township, and range) or the full name of the respondent (case number or legal description are preferred).

Connecticut

Administration - Chief Court Administrator, 860-757-2100. www.jud.ct.gov

Structure & Jurisdictions - The Superior Court is the sole court of original jurisdiction for all causes of action, except for matters the Probate Courts have jurisdiction as provided by statute. There are 15 Judicial Districts, 20 Geographic Area Courts, and 14 Juvenile Districts. The Superior Court - comprised primarily of the Judicial District Courts and the Geographical Area Courts - has five divisions: Criminal, Civil, Family, Juvenile, and Administrative Appeals. When not combined, the Judicial District Courts handle felony and civil cases while the Geographic Area Courts handle misdemeanors and most handle small claims. Divorce records are maintained by the Chief Clerk of the Judicial District Courts. Probate is handled by city Probate Courts and are not part of the state court system.

Online Access - The judicial branch provides access to civil and family court records, small claims, and housing (landlord issues) at http://civilinquiry.jud.ct.gov. Name search and docket searchers are offered. The Housing/Eviction case information offered is for only 6 locations- Bridgeport, Hartford, New Haven, New Britain, Norwalk, and Waterbury. After selecting from among the four search sites, click on "Party Names." Warning - some, not all, online civil case information goes back a maximum of 10 years after disposition date, and many are only available for as little as one year per Connecticut Practice Book Sections 7-10 and 7-11. Of limited value is the daily criminal and traffic daily docket search for apparently all 33 courts.

Opinions from the Supreme Court and Appellate Courts are available from the general website, www.jud.ct.gov/. Click on Opinions. You may also search for 'Upcoming Cases' for these 2 court branches from this main website after clicking on 'Courts.'

Searching Tips - Probate information request requirements are consistent across the state – requesters must provide full name of decedent, year and place of death, and SASE. Personal checks must have name and address printed on the check. If requesting in person, the check must have same address as on the drivers' license.

The Superior Court Record Center in Enfield, CT is the repository for criminal and some civil records. Case records are sent to the Enfield Record Center from 3 months to 5 years after disposition by the courts. Records are maintained 10 years for misdemeanors and 20+ years for felonies. Only written requests are accepted. **Enfield does not do name searches.** Connecticut Record Center, 111 Phoenix Avenue, Enfield, CT 06082, telephone 860-741-3714.

Delaware

Administration - Administrative Office of the Courts, 302-255-0090 http://courts.delaware.gov

Structure & Jurisdictions - The Superior Court has original jurisdiction over criminal and civil cases except equity cases with exclusive jurisdiction over felonies and almost all drug offenses. The Court of Common Pleas has jurisdiction in civil cases where the amount in controversy, exclusive of interest, does not exceed $50,000. The Court of Common Pleas handles all misdemeanors except certain drug-related offenses and traffic offenses. The Court of Chancery has jurisdiction to hear all matters relating to equity – litigation in this tribunal deals largely with corporate issues, trusts, estates, other fiduciary matters, disputes involving the purchase of land, and questions of title to real estate as well as commercial and contractual matters. The Justice of the Peace Court has jurisdiction over civil cases in which the disputed amount is less than $15,000 and for certain misdemeanors. Justices of the Peace may act as committing magistrates for all crimes. Alderman's Courts handle traffic matters.

Online Access - Chancery, Superior, Common Pleas, and Supreme Courts opinions and orders are available free online at http://courts.state.de.us/opinions. Supreme, Superior, and Common Pleas Courts calendars are available free at http://courts.delaware.gov/calendars.

There is no statewide online access to trial court data. However, Chancery Courts and Supreme Courts filings are available from a vendor at www.virtualdocket.com. Registration and fees required.

Searching Tips - Search fees and copy fees vary widely. The fee schedule on the web appears to provide limits on copy and certification fees rather than specific fees.

District of Columbia

Administration - Executive Office, 202-879-1700.
www.dccourts.gov/dccourts/index.jsp

Structure & Jurisdictions - The Superior Court handles all local trial matters, including civil, criminal, family court, probate, tax, landlord-tenant, small claims, and traffic. Divisions include Civil, Criminal, Family, Domestic, and Probate. Eviction records are found at the Landlord & Tenant Branch, telephone 202-879-4879.

Online Access - The Superior Court and Court of Appeals offer access to opinions at the web page above.

Searching Tips - Public access terminals are available. This court recommends that you contact the Metro DC Police to perform a "police clearance" record check. ID and signed release is required. Metro Police is at 202-727-4245.

Florida

Administration - Office of State Courts Administrator, 850-922-5081.
www.flcourts.org

Structure & Jurisdictions - The Circuit Court, the court of general jurisdiction, has general trial jurisdiction over matters not assigned by statute to the County Courts and also hear appeals from county court cases. Thus, Circuit Courts are simultaneously the highest trial courts and the lowest appellate courts in Florida's judicial system.

The trial jurisdiction of Circuit Courts includes original jurisdiction over civil disputes involving more than $15,000; estates of decedents, minors, and persons adjudicated as incapacitated; juveniles; criminal prosecutions for all felonies; tax disputes; actions to determine the title and boundaries of real property; suits for declaratory judgments; and requests for injunctions. The trial jurisdiction of County Courts is established by statute and extends to civil disputes involving $15,000 or less. Many counties have combined Circuit and County Courts.

Online Access - Search Supreme Court dockets online at http://jweb.flcourts.org/pls/docket/ds_docket_search.

Many courts offer online access to the public, usually through the Clerk of the Circuit Court.

Searching Tips - All courts have one address and switchboard, however the divisions within a court are completely separate. Requesters should specify which court and which division – e.g., Circuit Civil, County Civil, etc. – to direct the request, even though some counties will automatically check both with one request. Most courts have very lengthy phone recording systems.

Georgia

Administration - Court Administrator; 404-656-5171.
www.georgiacourts.org

Structure & Jurisdictions - The Georgia court system has five classes of trial-level courts: Magistrate, Probate, Juvenile, State, and Superior. In addition, approximately 350 municipal courts operate locally. The Superior Court, arranged in 49 circuits, is the court of general jurisdiction and assumes the role of a State Court if the county does not have one. State Courts exercise limited jurisdiction for misdemeanors including traffic violations, issue search and arrest warrants, hold preliminary hearings in criminal cases and try civil matters not reserved exclusively for the Superior Courts.

Magistrate Courts also issue arrest warrants and set bond on all felonies. Magistrate Courts also have jurisdiction for bad checks, arrest warrants, preliminary hearings, and county ordinance violations. The Magistrate Court has jurisdiction over civil actions under $15,000, also one type of misdemeanor related to passing bad checks. Two counties (Bibb, Richmond) have Civil/Magistrate courts with varied civil limits.

Probate Courts can, in certain cases, issue search and arrest warrants, and hear miscellaneous misdemeanors.

Online Access - Search the dockets of the Court of Appeals at www.gaappeals.us/. Search dockets of the Supreme Court at www.gasupreme.us/computer_docket.php. Make online purchases of certificates of admission and good standing and certified copies of Supreme Court opinions at www.gasupreme.us/purchase_online.php.

A limited number of county courts offer online access to court records, but there is no statewide online access available statewide.

Searching Tips - Many Georgia courts will not perform criminal or civil record searches. Using an in person search or hiring a record retriever is advised. Many Georgia counties are small and no retriever may be available; if so, it is best to engage a retriever in a neighboring county or take the advice of most court clerks by asking a local law firm to search.

Hawaii

Administration - Administrative Director of Courts, Judicial Branch, 808-539-4900. www.courts.state.hi.us/index.jsp

Structure & Jurisdictions - Hawaii's trial level is comprised of Circuit Courts (includes Family Courts) and District Courts. These trial courts function in four judicial circuits: First (Oahu), Second (Maui-Molokai-Lanai), Third (Hawaii County), and Fifth (Kauai-Niihau). The Fourth Circuit was merged with the Third in 1943.

Circuit Courts are general jurisdiction and handle all jury trials, felony cases, civil cases over $20,000, probate, and guardianship. There is concurrent jurisdiction with District Courts in civil non-jury cases that specify amounts between $10,000-$20,000. The District Court handles criminal cases punishable by a fine and/or less than one year imprisonment, some civil cases up to $20,000, landlord/tenant, and DUI cases. The Family Court Division rules in all legal matters involving children, such as delinquency, waiver, status offenses, abuse and neglect, termination of parental rights, adoption, guardianships and detention. Also hears traditional domestic-relations cases, including divorce, nonsupport, paternity, uniform child custody jurisdiction cases and miscellaneous custody matters.

Online Access - Free online access to all Circuit Court and Family Court records, civil records from the District Courts, and the traffic case index is available at the web, click on "Search Court Records" under Legal References. These records are not considered "official." Search by name or case number. Most courts have access back to mid 1980s. Opinions from the Appellate Court are available at the home page. Click on "Opinions."

Searching Tips - Most Hawaii state courts offer a public access terminal to search records at the courthouse.

Idaho

Administration - Administrative Director of Courts; 208-334-2246. www.isc.idaho.gov

Structure & Jurisdictions - Idaho has two levels of trial courts: District and Magistrate. District judges hear felony criminal cases and civil actions for amounts over $10,000, and appeals of decisions of the Magistrate Division. The Magistrate Division hears probate, divorce, juvenile, preliminary felony proceedings, misdemeanors, infractions, and civil cases when the amount in dispute does not exceed $10,000. Magistrates hear Small Claims cases, established for disputes of $4,000 or less. 44 of 46 counties have combined courts.

Online Access - Although appellate and supreme court opinions are available from the website, but there is no statewide computer system offering external access to trial court records. ISTARS is a statewide intra-court/intra-agency system run and managed by the State Supreme Court. All counties are on ISTARS, and all courts provide public access terminals on-site.

Searching Tips - A statewide court administrative rule states that record custodians do not have a duty to "compile or summarize information contained in a record, nor ... to create new records for the requesting party." Under this rule, some courts will not perform searches. A detailed description of the court rules regarding access to records may be found in Idaho Court Administrative Rule 32. Many courts require a signed release for employment record searches, when done.

Illinois

Administration - Administrative Office of Courts; 217-558-4490. www.state.il.us/court/

Structure & Jurisdictions - The Circuit Court is the only trial court in Illinois. Cases are decided by Circuit Judges and Associate Judges. Circuit judges can hear any kind of case. Associate Judges may not preside over criminal cases in which the defendant is charged with a felony, unless approval is received from the Supreme Court. Illinois is divided into 22 judicial circuits; 3 are single county: Cook, Du Page (18th Circuit) and Will (12th Circuit). The other 19 circuits consist of 2 or more contiguous counties.

The Circuit Court of Cook County is the largest unified court system in the world. Its 2,300-person staff handles approximately 2.4 million cases each year. The civil part of the various Circuit Courts in Cook County is divided as follows – under $30,000 are "civil cases" and over $30,000 are "civil law division cases."

Probate is handled by the Circuit Court in all counties.

Online Access - While there is no statewide public online system available, other than Appellate Court and Supreme Court opinions from the website. A number of Circuit Courts offer online access, many through a vendor at www.judici.com.

Searching Tips - The search fee, set by the Clerk of Courts Act (705 ILCS 105), has different pricing court filings and services based on county population tiers (under 500,000, between 500,000 and 3,000,000, and over 3,000,000) . The higher the population, the higher the fee. The statute gives a minimum and maximim that that can be charged with rules how to reach the maximim. Searching is supposed to be calculated at a per year searched basis. Not all courts follow the pricing mansdates; you will find pricing all over the board.

At least 90% of the courts offer public access terminals to look-up docket data.

Indiana

Administration - State Court Administrator; 317-232-2542. www.in.gov/judiciary

Structure & Jurisdictions - Trial courts include Circuit Courts, Superior Courts, County Courts, and local City or Town Courts. Indiana has 92 counties, and 88 of these counties comprise their own circuit, with their own Circuit Court. The remaining four small counties (Ohio, Dearborn, Jefferson, and Switzerland Counties) have been combined to form two circuits with two counties in each circuit. In counties without Superior or County Courts, the Circuit Courts in addition to all other cases, also handle small claims cases for civil disputes involving less than $6,000 and minor offenses, such as misdemeanors, ordinance violations, and Class D felonies. County Courts are gradually being restructured into divisions of the Superior Courts. Small Claims cases in Marion County are heard at the township and records are maintained at that level.

Online Access - There is no statewide trial court records service available, but the home page gives free access to an index of docket information for Supreme, Appeals, and Tax Court cases.

A vendor is working closely with many counties to provide electroinc access. An expanding limited free search of open case index is available at www.doxpop.com/prod/welcome.jsp. Full access to case records requires registration and subscription fees.

Searching Tips - The Circuit Court Clerk/County Clerk in a county is the same individual and is responsible for keeping all county judicial records. We a record request indicate which court heard the case (Circuit, Superior, or County). Many courts do not perform searches, especially criminal searches, based on a 7/8/1996 statement by the State Board of Accounts.

Iowa

Administration – Iowa State Court Administrator; 515-281-5911. www.judicial.state.ia.us

Structure & Jurisdictions - The District Court has general jurisdiction of all civil, criminal, juvenile, and probate matters in the state. In each of Iowa's 99 counties, a Clerk of District Court Office manages and maintains all trial court records filed in the county.

Online Access - From the home page www.judicial.state.ia.us one may access Supreme Court and Appellate Court opinions. District criminal, civil, probate, and traffic information is available from all 99 Iowa counties at www.iowacourts.state.ia.us/ESAWebApp/SelectFrame. Name searches are available on either a statewide or specific county basis. Names of juveniles who are 10 to 17 will appear only for completed cases with a guilty verdict. There is no fee for basic information. A pay system is offered for more detailed requests. While this is an excellent site with much information note that dates of historical records offered vary on a county-by-county basis.

Searching Tips - Most courts do not do searches and recommend either in person searches or use of a record retriever. Most courts have a public access terminal for access to the record index.

Kansas

Administration - Judicial Administrator, Kansas Judicial Center; 785-296-3229. www.kscourts.org

Structure & Jurisdictions - District courts are the trial courts of general original jurisdiction over all civil and criminal cases, including divorce and domestic relations, damage suits, probate and administration of estates, guardianships, conservatorships, care of the mentally ill, juvenile matters, and small claims. There are 110 courts in 31 districts in 105 counties. There are 350 Municipal Courts that deal with violations of city ordinances. If an individual in Municipal Court wants a jury trial, the request must be filed de novo in a District Court.

Online Access - Commercial online access for civil and criminal records is available for District Court Records in eight counties – Anderson, Coffey, Franklin, Johnson, Osage, Sedgwick, Shawnee, and Wyandotte. Access is web-based at www.accesskansas.org. The system also provides state criminal records and motor vehicle records as well. For additional information, call 800-452-6727 or visit the web page.

The Kansas Appellate Courts offer free online access to case information at www.kscourts.org. Published opinions from the Appellate Courts and Supreme Court are also available.

Searching Tips - Five counties - Cowley, Crawford, Labette, Montgomery, and Neosho - have two hearing locations but only one record center. Many Kansas courts do not perform criminal record searches and refer all criminal name searches to the Kansas Bureau of Investigation.

Kentucky

Administration - Administrative Office of Courts, Pre-Trial Services Records Unit, 502-573-1682. http://courts.ky.gov/

Structure & Jurisdictions - The Circuit Court is the court of general jurisdiction and the District Court is the limited jurisdiction court. Circuit Courts have jurisdiction for capital offenses and felonies, divorces, adoptions, terminations of parental rights, land dispute title problems, and contested probates of will. Juvenile matters, city and county ordinances, misdemeanors, traffic offenses, uncontested probate of wills, felony preliminary hearings, and civil cases involving $4,000 or less are heard in District Court.

Online Access – A free but limited access system is at http://apps.kycourts.net/CourtRecords/. Search daily court calendars by county free at http://apps.kycourts.net/dockets. KY Bar attorneys may use the comercial system KCOJ for court records data at http://apps.kycourts.net/courtrecordsKBA. One may search online opinons and case informaion for the Supreme Court and Court of Appeals at http://courts.ky.gov/research/.

Searching Tips - Most of Kentucky's counties combined the courts into one location and records are co-mingled. Until 1978, county judges handled all cases. Therefore, most District Court and Circuit Court records go back only to 1978. Records prior to that time are archived.

Contact the Administrative Office of the Courts about its commercial service of statewide criminal background checks provided via fax, standard mail, walk-in, or drive-thru service.

Louisiana

Administration - Judicial Administrator, Judicial Council of the Supreme Court; 504-310-2550. www.lasc.org

Structure & Jurisdictions - The Louisiana court structure includes 5 Courts of Appeal, 42 District Courts, 5 Family or Juvenile courts, 50 City Courts and 3 Parish Courts. The trial court of general jurisdiction in Louisiana is the District Court. A District Court Clerk in each Parish holds all the records for that Parish. Each Parish has its own clerk and courthouse. City Courts are trial courts of record and generally exercise concurrent jurisdiction with the District Court in civil cases where the amount in controversy does not exceed $15,000. City Courts generally have jurisdiction over ordinance violations and misdemeanor violations of state law. City judges also handle many traffic cases. Parish Courts exercise jurisdiction in civil cases worth up to $10,000 and criminal cases punishable by fines of $1,000 or less, or imprisonment of six months or less. Cases are appealable from the Parish Courts directly to the courts of appeal. A municipality may have a Mayor's Court; the mayor may hold trials over minor matters, there are no records.

Online Access - Search opinions from the state Supreme Court at www.lasc.org/opinion_search.asp. Online records go back to 1995. There is no statewide system open to the public for trial court dockets, but a number of parishes offer online access.

Searching Tips - The courts vary widely in terms of fees. 80% of the courts offer a public access terminal.

Maine

Administration - State Court Administrator; 207-822-0792. www.state.me.us/courts

Structure & Jurisdictions - A Superior Court – the court of general jurisdiction – is located in each of Maine's sixteen counties, except for Aroostook County which has two Superior Courts. Both Superior and District Courts handle misdemeanor and felony cases, with jury trials being held in Superior Court only. The District Court hears both civil and criminal and always sits without a jury.

Within the District Court is the Family Division, which hears all divorce and family matters, including child support and paternity cases. The District Court also hears child protection cases, and serves as Maine's juvenile court. Actions for protection from abuse or harassment, mental health, small claims cases, and money judgments are filed in the District Court. Traffic violations are processed primarily through a centralized Violations Bureau, part of the District Court system. Prior to year 2001, District Courts accepted civil cases involving claims less than $30,000. Now, District Courts have jurisdiction concurrent with that of the Superior Court for all civil actions, except cases vested in the Superior Court by statute.

Probate Courts are part of the county court system, not the state system. Although the Probate Court may be housed with other state courts, it is on a different phone system; calls may not be transferred.

Online Access - The website offers access to Maine Supreme Court opinions and administrative orders, but not all documents are available online. The website offers access to trial court schedules by region and case type. Some county level courts are online through a private vendor.

Searching Tips - Most mail requests of a name search for full criminal history record information are returned to the sender, referring them to the State Bureau of Investigation. Mail requests that make a specific inquiry related to an identified case are responded to in writing. You must also include all appropriate copy and attestation fees. Some courts search both civil and criminal indices for the same search fee.

Maryland

Administration - Court Administrator, Administrative Office of the Courts; 410-260-1400, 410-260-1488. www.courts.state.md.us

Structure & Jurisdictions - The Circuit Court, in each county of Maryland and in Baltimore City, is the upper court. The jurisdiction of the District Court, the lower court, includes all landlord/tenant cases, replevin actions, motor vehicle violations, misdemeanors and certain felonies. In civil cases the District Court has exclusive jurisdiction in claims for amounts up to $5,000, and concurrent jurisdiction with the circuit courts in claims for amounts above $5,000 but less than $25,000. The jurisdiction in criminal cases is concurrent for offenses in which the penalty may be confinement for three years or more or a fine of $2,500 or more; or offenses which are felonies. The Circuit Court handles probate in only Montgomery and Harford counties. In other counties, probate is handled by the Register of Wills and is a county, not a court, function.

Online Access - Appellate opinions are available from www.courts.state.md.us/opinions.html. There are two systems offering trial court record indices. The free search at http://casesearch.courts.state.md.us/inquiry/inquiry-index.jsp includes all district courts and most circuirt courts except case information from Montgomery and Prince George's Counties Circuit courts. This free system includes basic summary information and much of the details found on the old dial-up system. All case information may be searched by party name or case number. The older dial-up (non-Internet) system is being phased out.

Bulk subscription of civil record data can be requested for a fee using a form found at www.courts.state.md.us/district/forms/acct/dca107.pdf. Plans are underway for subscribing parties to access statewide Case Search bulk data and data extracts through a standards-based interface in XML format. Also, there is an attorney's Calendar Service that displays information related to a trial and hearing schedule.

Searching Tips - In most Circuit Courts and District Courts, copies are $.50 per page and certification is $5.00.

Massachusetts

Administration - Chief Justice for Administration and Management; 617-742-8575. www.mass.gov/courts/admin/index.html

Structure & Jurisdictions - There are seven Trial Court Departments: the Boston Municipal Court, the District Court, the Housing Court, the Juvenile Court, the Probate and Family Court, the Superior Court, and the Land Court. The Superior Court handles felony cases. While Superior Courts and District Courts have concurrent jurisdiction in civil cases, the practice is to assign cases less than $25,000 to the District Court and those over $25,000 to Superior Court. In addition to misdemeanors, District Courts and Boston Municipal Courts have jurisdiction over certain minor felonies. Eviction cases may be filed at a county District Court or at the regional "Housing Court." A case may be moved from a District Court to a Housing Court, but never the reverse. Housing Courts also hear misdemeanor "Code Violation" cases and prelims for these. There are five Housing Court Regions - Boston (Suffolk County), Worcester (County), Southeast (Plymouth and Bristol Counties), Northeast (Essex County), and Western (Berkshire, Franklin, Hampden and Hampshire Counties). The Southeast Housing Court has three branches - Brockton, Fall River, and New Bedford.

There are 15 Probate and Family Court locations in Massachusetts - one per county plus two in Bristol.

Online Access - Opinions from the Supreme Court and Appellate Courts can be found at http://massreports.com. Online access to records on the statewide Trial Courts Information Center website with both criminal and civil superior court cases is available to ONLY attorneys and law firms at www.ma-trialcourts.org/tcic/welcome.jsp. **Searching Tips** - In Massachusetts courts, "attestation" is the term for what is known as certification in other states. In Massachusetts, a "certificate" is a separate authentification page with a gold seal.

Michigan

Administration - State Court Administrator; 517-373-0130. http://courts.michigan.gov/scao/

Structure & Jurisdictions - The Circuit Court is the court of general jurisdiction. District Courts and Municipal Courts have jurisdiction over certain minor felonies and handle all preliminary hearings. The Family Division of the Circuit Court hears domestic relations actions and juvenile cases, including criminal and abuse/neglect. Mental health and estate cases are handled by Probate Courts. A Court of Claims in Lansing that is a function of the 30th Circuit Court with jurisdiction over claims against the state of Michigan.

Several counties (Barry, Berrien, Iron, Isabella, Lake, Washtenaw) and the 46th Circuit Court are participating in a "Demonstration" pilot project designed to streamline court services and consolidate case management. They may refer to themselves as County Trial Courts.

Online Access - There is a wide range of online computerization of the judicial system from "none" to "fairly complete," but there is no statewide court records network. A few offer remote online to the public. Subscribe to free email updates of appellate opinions at http://courtofappeals.mijud.net/resources/subscribe.htm.

Searching Tips - Court records are considered public except for specific categories: controlled substances, spousal abuse, Holmes youthful trainee, parental kidnapping, set aside convictions and probation, and sealed records. Courts will, however, affirm that cases exist and provide case numbers. Some courts will not perform criminal searches, rather they refer requests to the State Police. Search requirements, and procedures vary widely because each jurisdiction may create its own administrative orders. Some courts provide public access terminals in clerk's offices and some courts are developing off-site electronic filing and searching capability.

Minnesota

Administration - State Court Adminstrator; 651-296-2474. www.mncourts.gov/default.aspx

Structure & Jurisdictions - The District Court is the orginating court for civil actions, criminal actions, family, juvenile, probate, and violations of city ordinances.

There are 97 District Courts (some counties have divisional courts) comprising 10 judicial districts. The limit for small claims is $7500 unless the case involves a consumer credit transaction then the limit is $4000. The Conciliation Division handles civil disputes up to $7,500.

Online Access - Minnesota offers the Trial Court Public Access (MPA) at http://pa.courts.state.mn.us/default.aspx. Search statewide or by county. Records available include criminal, civil, family, and probate. Searches can be performed using a case number or by name.

But there are a number of caveats. Name searches for criminal case records will not return pre-conviction criminal records. A statewide case inquiry may exclude district courts that have not yet converted to the system. Interestingly, the public access terminals found at the courthouses do not use this system. For example, party street address and name searches on criminal pre-conviction case records are publicly accessible and available at the courthouse, but not online. Electronic copies of public documents filed by parties also cannot be viewed online, but are on the public terminals. The federal Violence Against Women Act (VAWA) also prevents the state from displaying harassment and domestic abuse case records online, but these are available at the courthouse. Comment fields for all case types are not available online but are available at the courthouse. Online users are not notified when such public data is restricted from online viewing.

The bottom line is the online system is not very accurate and is supplemental at best; public access terminals found at courthouses are still the most accurate searching locations. In Judicial Districts (arranged by number and often covering several counties) many court's public access terminals contain court records for that entire district.

The state provides free access to Appellate and Supreme Court opinions at www.mncourts.gov/default.aspx?page=1650. An approved bail bond agent list search is also free.

Searching Tips - Most Judicial Districts no longer perform criminal record name searches for the public but may do civil name searches. An exact name is required to search, e.g., a request for "Robert Smith" will not result in finding "Bob Smith." The requester must request both names and pay two search fees. When a search is permitted by "plaintiff or defendant," most jurisdictions state that a case is indexed by only the first plaintiff or defendant. Second or third party names would not be sufficient information for a search.

Mississippi

Administration - Court Administrator; 601-354-7406.
www.mssc.state.ms.us

Structure & Jurisdictions - The court of general jurisdiction is the Circuit Court with 70 courts in 22 districts. Justice Courts were first created in 1984, replacing Justice of the Peace Courts. Prior to 1984, records were kept separately by each Justice of the Peace, so the location of older records is often unknown. Probate is handled by the Chancery Courts, as are property matters.

Online Access - The website offers searching of the MS Supreme Court and Court of Appeals Decisions and dockets. There is no online access to trial court records or to an index.

Searching Tips - A number of Mississippi counties have two Circuit Court Districts. A search of either court in such a county will include the index from the other court. Full name is a search requirement for all courts. DOB and SSN are very helpful for differentiating between like-named individuals.

The Court Administration Office provides a statewide search via fax requesting with a 24 hour turnaround time. Felony and civil case information are provided. Misdemeanor records are not. Fees are involved. Call 601-354-7449 for details.

Missouri

Administration - State Court Administrator; 573-751-4377. www.courts.mo.gov

Structure & Jurisdictions - Circuit Courts are courts of original civil and criminal jurisdiction. Within the Circuit Court, are Divisions, including associate circuit, small claims, municipal, family, probate, criminal, and juvenile. There are 45 circuits comprised of 115 county Circuit Courts and one independent City Court. The Associate Circuit Courts have limited jurisdiction. A growing trend is to form Combined Courts (23 consolidated in 2005/2006). Municipal Courts only have jurisdiction over traffic and ordinance violations.

Online Access – Missouri CaseNet is available free at www.courts.mo.gov/casenet/cases/searchCases.do. CaseNet is a growing online system for access to docket data. The system includes at least 110 counties as well as the Eastern, Western, and Southern Appellate Courts, the Supreme Court, and Fine Collection Center. Some counties only offer probate case data. Cases can be searched case number, filing date, or litigant name from 6AM-1AM M-F. Also, search Supreme Court and Appellate Court opinions at the home page.

Searching Tips - Many Circuit Courts and Associate Courts no longer accept mail or fax requests to perform criminal record searches. Instead, the courts instruct requesters to mail criminal search requests to the State Highway Patrol Criminal Records Division or use CaseNet.

While the Missouri State Statutes set the Civil Case limit at $25,000 for the Associate Courts, and over $25,000 for the Circuit Courts, a great many county courts have adopted their own Local Court Rules regarding civil cases and the monetary limits. A suggestion is to call the County's Court Clerk to determine the court location of the case.

Montana

Administration - Court Administrator; 406-444-2621. www.montanacourts.org

Structure & Jurisdictions - The District Courts have no maximum amount for civil judgment cases. Most District Courts handle civil cases over $7,000 but there are exceptions that handle a civil minimum as low as $5,000. Limited Jurisdiction Courts, which are also known as Justice Courts or City Courts or Municipal Courts handle real property rights cases up to $7,000. The Small Claims limit is $3,000. Some Justice Courts and City Courts have consolidated.

Online Access - Supreme Court opinions, orders, and recently filed briefs may be found http://searchcourts.mt.gov. There is no statewide access to docket information from the trial courts.

Searching Tips - Most District Courts charge $2.00 per name per year, first 7 years, then $1.00 per year for searching. Many Montana Justices of the Peace maintain case record indexes on their personal computers, which does speed the retrieval process.

Nebraska

Administration - Court Administrator 402-471-3730. http://court.nol.org/

Structure & Jurisdictions - District courts have original jurisdiction in all felony, equity, domestic relations, and civil cases where the amount in controversy involves more than $51,000. District Courts also have appellate jurisdiction in certain matters arising out of County Courts. Prior to the current level, on Sept. 1, 2001 the state raised the County Court limit on civil matters from $15,000 to $45,000. County Courts have original jurisdiction in probate, violations of city or village ordinances, juvenile court matters without a separate juvenile court, adoptions, preliminary hearings in felony cases, and eminent domain proceedings. The County Courts have concurrent jurisdiction in civil matters when the amount is $51,000 or less, misdemeanors, infractions, some domestic relations matters, and paternity actions. Nearly all misdemeanor cases are tried in the County Courts.

County Courts have juvenile jurisdiction in all but 3 counties. Douglas, Lancaster, and Sarpy counties have separate Juvenile Courts.

Online Access - An online access subscription service is available for Nebraska District Courts and County courts, except Douglas County District Court. Case details, all party listings, payments, and actions taken for criminal, civil, probate, juvenile, and traffic is available. Users must be registered with Nebraska.gov; there is a start-up fee and various acess fees. Also, for a fee access the JUSTICE Court Case System statewide at https://www.nebraska.gov/justicecc/ccname.cgi. Call 402-471-7810 or go to www.nebraska.gov/faqs/justice or for more info and details on how far back records go per county. Supreme Court opinions are available from http://court.nol.org/opinions.

Searching Tips - Most Nebraska courts require the public to do their own in person searches and will not respond to written search requests. The State Attorney General has recommended that courts not perform searches because of the time involved and concerns about legal liability.

Nevada

Administration - Supreme Court of Nevada, Administrative Office of the Courts; 775-684-1700. www.nvsupremecourt.us/index.php

Structure & Jurisdictions - 17 District Courts are the courts of general jurisdiction and are within 9 judicial districts. Their minimum civil limit raised from $7,500 to $10,000 on Jan 1, 2005. The Justice Courts, named for the township of jurisdiction, handle misdemeanor crime and traffic matters, small claims disputes, evictions, and other civil matters less than $10,000. The Justices of the Peace also preside over felony and gross misdemeanor arraignments and conduct preliminary hearings to determine if sufficient evidence exists to hold criminals for trial at District Court. Due to their small populations, some townships no longer have Justice Courts. Probate is handled by the District Courts.

Online Access - Only Clark and Washoe counties offer online access to the public. A statewide court automation system is being implemented. The Supreme Court website gives access to opinions.

Searching Tips - Many Nevada Justice Courts are small and have very few records. Their hours of operation vary widely and contact is difficult. It is recommended that requesters call ahead for information prior to submitting a written request or attempting an in person retrieval.

New Hampshire

Administration - Administrative Office of the Courts, 603-271-2521. www.courts.state.nh.us

Structure & Jurisdictions - The Superior Court, the court of general jurisdiction, has jurisdiction over a wide variety of cases, including criminal, domestic relations, and civil cases, and provides the only forum in this state for trial by jury. Felony cases include Class A misdemeanors. The District Court oversees family, juvenile, small claims ($5,000), landlord tenant matters, minor crimes and violations and civil cases in which the disputed amount does not exceed $25,000. The Superior Court and the District Court share jurisdiction over domestic violence cases. In Grafton and Rockingham Counties, the Family Division Pilot Project has jurisdiction over divorce, custody/support and domestic violence cases

Filing a civil case in the monetary "overlap area" between the Superior Court minimum and the District Court maximum is at the discretion of the filer. Older Municipal Courts have all been closed, the caseload and records were absorbed by the nearest District Court.

Online Access - While there is no statewide access available for trial court records, the home page has useful information including opinions and directives from the Supreme Court, Superior Courts, and District Courts; search at www.courts.state.nh.us/search/index.htm.

Searching Tips - Fees for searching, copies, and certification are set by the New Hampshire Supreme Court. The fee structure has a flate rates based if number of names on list it up to 10 names or if 10 or more names in one request. Most courts follow this fee schedule.

New Jersey

Administration - Administrative Office of the Courts; 609-984-0275. www.judiciary.state.nj.us

Structure & Jurisdictions - The Superior Court is the court of general jurisdiction. Each Superior Court has 2 divisions; one for Civil and another for Criminal. Search requests should be addressed separately to each division. There are over 530 Municpal Courts that handle city ordiances and many misdemeanor cases.

Civil cases in which the amount in controversy exceeds $15,000 are heard in the Civil Division of Superior Court. Cases between $3,000 and $15,000 are heard in the Special Civil Part of the Civil Division. Cases involving amounts less than $3,000 also are heard in the Special Civil Part and are known as Small Claims cases. Probate is handled by Surrogates.

Online Access - The Judiciary's civil motion calendar and schedule is searchable at www.judiciary.state.nj.us/calendars.htm. The database includes all Superior Court Motion calendars for the Civil Division (Law-Civil Part, Special CivilPart and Chancery-General Equity), and proceeding information for a six-week period (two weeks prior to the current date and four weeks following the current date). Another useful website giving decisions is maintained by the Rutgers Law School at http://lawlibrary.rutgers.edu/search.shtml. Supreme and Appellate case data is found at www.judiciary.state.nj.us/opinions/index.htm.

Restricted online access to all civil records is available through the ACMS, AMIS, and FACTS systems. The fee is $1.00 per minute of use. For more information, contact the Superior Court Clerk's Office, Electronic Access Program at 609-292-4987. Ask for the Inquiry System Guidebook containing hardware and software requirements and an enrollment form.

Searching Tips - The Judgment Unit at 609-292-4804 will confirm if a case is still open or closed; requester must submit docket number. Criminal searches may be done in person at the courts on their public access terminals, but the Superior Court usually directs mail inquiries to the New Jersey State Police Records and ID Section at 609-882-2000, x2991 or x2918. State Police records are fingerprint-based searches. For purchase information of the statewide public access criminal records databases, call 609-882-2000.

Originally developed for county prosecutors, the Promis/Gavel is an automated criminal case tracking system that provides the function of docketing, indexing, noticing, calendaring, statistical reporting, and case management reporting, etc. Promis/Gavel is interactive with the courts as well as with the NJSP. But rules do not allow the public to access the complete Promis/Gavel system—only a filtered Promis/Gavel Public Access (PGPA) system is available on the public access terminals in the courts. Also, the PGPA does not include offenses or petty offenses recorded in 530+ municipal courts, unless filed with indictables. The more serious of these petty offenses include drug offenses, violence, theft, sexual assault, and pedophilia. An AOC press release about the PGPA states: "The court records obtained from Promis/Gavel do not constitute a criminal history records check, which must be obtained through law enforcement." So, be careful when using this system.

Note that Cape May County offices are located in City of Cape May Court House, and not in City of Cape May.

New Mexico

Administration - Administrative Office of the Courts, Judicial Information Division; 505-476-6900. www.nmcourts.com

Structure & Jurisdictions - The 30 District Courts in 13 districts are the courts of general jurisdiction and hear tort, contract, real property rights, estate. District Courts also hear exclusive domestic relations, mental health, appeals for administrative agencies and lower courts, miscellaneous civil jurisdiction; misdemeanor; exclusive criminal appeals jurisdiction; and exclusive juvenile jurisdiction.

The 54 Magistrate Courts are courts of limited jurisdiction that hear tort, contract, landlord/tenant rights ($0-10,000); felony preliminary hearings; misdemeanor, DWI/DUI and other traffic violations. The Magistrate Courts handle civil cases up to $10,000, and cases are referred to as Small Claims. The Bernalillo Metropolitan Court has jurisdiction in cases up to $10,000.

Municipal Courts handle petty misdemeanors, DWI/DUI, traffic violations, and other municipal ordinance violations.

County Clerks handle "informal" (uncontested) probate cases, and the District Courts handle "formal" (contested) probate cases.

Online Access - Supreme Court opinions may be researched at www.supremecourt.nm.org. The home page above offers free access to District Courts and Magistrate Courts case information (except Bernalillo Metropolitan Court, see below). In general, records are available from June, 1997 forward. The site also offers a DWI Offender History name search tool for researching an individual's DWI history.

A commercial online service is available for the Metropolitan Court of Bernalillo County. There is a set up fee and usage fee. The system is available 24 hours daily. Call 505-345-6555 for more information.

Searching Tips – Be aware there are some "shared courts" in low-populated counties in New Mexico, with one county handling cases arising in another.

New York

Administration - New York State Unified Court System, Office of Court Administration (OCA), 212-428-2700. www.courts.state.ny.us

Structure & Jurisdictions - "Supreme and County Courts" are the highest trial courts in the state, equivalent to Circuit or District Courts in other states. New York's Supreme and County Courts may be administered together or separately. When separate, there is a clerk for each. Supreme and/or County Courts are not appeals courts. Supreme Courts handle civil cases – usually civil cases over $25,000 – but there are many exceptions. County Courts handle felony cases and, in many counties, these County Courts also handle misdemeanors.

City Courts handle misdemeanors and lower-value civil cases, small claims, and eviction cases. Since not all counties have City Courts, these cases go to the Supreme and County Courts respectively, or, in a many counties, to the small Town and Village Courts, which can number in the dozens within a county.

Probate is handled by Surrogate Courts. Surrogate Courts may also hear Domestic Relations cases in some counties.

Online Access - OCA offers a subscription service to its database of criminal case records from all boroughs and all counties including Supreme Courts, County Courts, and most City Courts. In at least 20 New York Counties, misdemeanor records are only available at city, town, or village courts. This is also true of small claims and eviction records. An accurate search for all misdemeanor records is nearly impossible since over 1400 Town and Village Courts in NY may or may not be accurately reporting all open and closed case records to the OCA. The Criminal History Record Search Unit can be reached at 212-428-2943 or www.nycourts.gov/apps/chrs.

Visit https://iapps.courts.state.ny.us/caseTrac/jsp/ecourt.htm for access to a number of records, including WebCrims for criminal case dockets with future appearance dates in 13 counties, open landlord tenant cases from NYC, and open family court cases from all 62 counties. Also from here access or monitor Supreme Court and Family Court case information on open cases for all 62 New York counties. Appellate decisions available at www.nycourts.gov/ctapps/latdec.htm.

Searching Tips – The OCA offers mail, fax, and in-person searching of its criminal record database. Requesters receive information back via email. Call OCA for how to set up an account.

In all but a few NY counties, the Supreme and County Court records are maintained in the County Clerk's office, which (with the exception of New York City and its boroughs) may index civil cases by defendant, whereas the courts themselves maintain only a plaintiff index. And, while most criminal courts in the state are indexed by defendant and plaintiff, many New York City courts are indexed by plaintiff only.

Almost all County Courts (felony records) will provide a Certificate of Disposition that indicates the disposition of a case.

Some County Clerks (and a limited number of Supreme and County Court Clerks) provide countywide criminal record searches. Some County Clerks or Chief Clerks instruct criminal record searchers to contact OCA. This information is subject to change, and does.

Most City Courts no longer do criminal record searches and send misdemeanor record requesters to the OCA.

North Carolina

Administration - Administrative Office of the Courts; 919- 890-1000. www.nccourts.org

Structure & Jurisdictions - The Superior Court is the court of general jurisdiction; the District Court is limited jurisdiction. Counties have combined the courts, thus searching is done through one court, not two, within the county. Small Claims Court is part of the District Court Division and handles civil cases where a plaintiff requests assignment to a magistrate and the amount in controversy is $5,000 or less (raised up from $4,000 in Summer, 2005). Small Claims Court also handles summary ejectment (eviction). Probate is handled by County Clerks.

Online Access - The state AOC has public access for approved requesters on its Virtual Private Network. Charges are based on screens viewed rather than a specific fee per name. A lesser valued product known as the Criminal Extract is available, but does not have the depth and quality of data as the Virtual Private Network. Call 919-716-5088 for details on these programs. Also, search the District and Superior Court Query system free for current criminal defendants at http://www1.aoc.state.nc.us/www/calendars/CriminalQuery.html.
There are also queries for Impaired Driving, Citations, and Current Civil and Criminal Calendars. Appellate and Supreme Court opinions are at www.aoc.state.nc.us/www/public/html/opinions.htm.

Searching Tips - Many courts recommend that civil searches be done in person or by a retriever and that only criminal searches be requested in writing. Companies offering NC online criminal records are found at www.nccourts.org/Citizens/GoToCourt/Documents/WebsiteListing.pdf.

Many courts have archived their records prior to 1968 in the Raleigh State Archives, 919-807-7280.

North Dakota

Administration - State Court Administrator, North Dakota Judiciary; 701-328-4216. www.ndcourts.com

Structure & Jurisdictions - The District Courts are general jurisdiction over criminal, civil, and juvenile matters. Municipal courts in North Dakota have jurisdiction of all violations of municipal ordinances, with some exceptions. At one time there were County Courts, but these courts merged with the District Courts statewide in 1995. The older County Court records are held by the District Court Clerks.

Online Access - Access district court criminal index on the state system at www.ndcourts.gov/publicsearch/contactsearch.aspx. This includes 9 municipal courts as well. Each counties index only goes back to their month of computerization. Search North Dakota Supreme Court dockets and opinions at www.ndcourts.com by docket number, party name, or anything else that may appear in the text. Records are from 1982 forward. Email notification of new opinions is also available.

Searching Tips - For search requests fo records back to 1995 or further, state "include all County Court cases" in your request.

Ohio

Administration - Administrative Director, Supreme Court of Ohio; 614-387-9000. www.sconet.state.oh.us

Structure & Jurisdictions - The Court of Common Pleas is the court of general jurisdiction for matters involving criminal, civil, probate, domestic relations, and juvenile. County Courts and Municipal Courts have limited jurisdiction over misdemeanor, civil cases up to $15,000, and traffic. Actually, Ohio Common Pleas Courts may name their own civil action limits, although most courts elect to use $15,000 as a standard minimum, but some use $3,000 and some $10,000. So these Common Pleas courts may take any civil cases. However, civil maximum limits for Ohio's County Courts and Municipal Courts remains the same – $15,000.

Online Access - There is no statewide computer system for trial court dockets but a number of counties and many municipal courts offer online access. Appellate and Supreme Court opinions may be researched from the website above.

Searching Tips - There is no standardization followed for fees. The most common copy fee is $.25. Over 80% of the courts offer a public access terminal to view a docket index.

Oklahoma

Administration - Administrative Director of Courts; 405-521-2450. www.oscn.net

Structure & Jurisdictions - The District Court is the court of general jurisdiction with 82 courts in 26 judicial districts. Two cities with populations in excess of 200,000 (Oklahoma City and Tulsa) have criminal Municipal Courts of Record. Cities with less than 200,000 have a Municipal Court Not of Record.

The Supreme Court determines all issues of a civil nature, and the Oklahoma Court of Criminal Appeals decides all criminal matters, there is also a Court of Civil Appeals.

Online Access - Free Internet access to docket information is available for District Courts in 13 counties and all Appellate courts at www.oscn.net. Both civil and criminal docket information is available for the counties involved. Also, search the Oklahoma Supreme Court Network from the website.

Also, the Oklahoma District Court Records free website at www.odcr.com offers searching for over 60 District Courts. More counties are being added as they are readied and hope to eventually feature all Oklahoma District Courts.

Searching Tips - Case information is available in bulk form, call the Administrative Director of Courts. Over 80% of the courts offer a public access terminal.

Oregon

Administration - Court Administrator, Supreme Court Bldg; 503-986-5500. www.ojd.state.or.us

Structure & Jurisdictions - Oregon has two types of state trial courts, the Circuit Courts, which are general jurisdiction courts, and the Oregon Tax Court, whose jurisdiction is limited to cases involving taxes. Until January 1998, Oregon had a third state trial court called the District Court, which had limited jurisdiction over smaller civil cases and lesser crimes. On January 15, 1998, the District Courts merged into the Circuit Courts.

Probate is handled by the Circuit Court, except in six counties (Gilliam, Grant, Harney, Malheur, Sherman, and Wheeler) probate in handled by County Courts. There are over 100 Municipal Courts and 35 Justice Courts that oversee minor misdemeanor, traffic, and ordinance cases.

Online Access - Online access is available to state court case data through the Oregon Judicial Information Network (OJIN). There is a one-time setup fee plus usage fees. The database contains criminal, civil, small claims, tax, domestic, usually probate when not at the county court, and some but not all juvenile records. However, it does not contain any records from municipal or county courts. For further information visit www.ojd.state.or.us/ojin, or call 800-858-9658 or 503-986-5588.

Appellate opinions are found at www.publications.ojd.state.or.us.

Searching Tips - Many Oregon courts indicated that using in person searchers would markedly improve request turnaround time as court offices are understaffed or spread very thin to handle mail requests. Most Circuit Courts with computerized records have public access terminals. Most records offices close from noon to 1PM for lunch. No staff is available during that period.

Pennsylvania

Administration - Administrative Office of PA Courts; 717-795-2097. www.courts.state.pa.us

Structure & Jurisdictions - The Courts of Common Pleas are the general trial courts, with jurisdiction over both civil and criminal matters and appellate jurisdiction over matters disposed of by the special courts. The civil records clerk of the Court of Common Pleas is called the Prothonotary. The Superior Court is a Court of Appeals. Probate is handled by the Register of Wills. There are over 550 lower level Magisterial District Courts.

Small claims cases are usually handled by the District Justice Courts. These courts, designated as "special courts," also handle civil cases up to $8,000. However, all small claims and civil actions are recorded through the Prothonotary Section of the Court of Common Pleas, which then holds the records. Other courts of note include the Philadelphia Municipal Court, the Philadelphia Traffic Court, the Pittsburgh Magistrate Court.

Online Access - The web page offers access to a variety of the Judiciary's Electronic Services (E-Services) such as Web Docket Sheets, DA Link, Superior Court's Web Docketing Statements, etc. Web Docket provides public access to view and print case docket sheets from the criminal cases of the Courts of Common Pleas and from the Appellate Courts and Criminal Cases. Search by docket number, name or organization. Go to http://ujsportal.pacourts.us.

The Infocon County Access System provides a commercial direct dial-up access to court record information for at least 25 counties. Fees are involved. For information, call Infocon at 814-472-6066 or visit www.infoconcountyaccess.com.

Searching Tips - Fees vary widely among jurisdictions. Many courts will not conduct searches due to a lack of personnel or, if they do search, turnaround time may be excessively lengthy. Many courts offer public access terminals for in-person searchers.

Rhode Island

Administration - Court Administrator, Supreme Court; 401-222-3266. www.courts.state.ri.us

Structure & Jurisdictions - The Superior Court has general jurisdiction on all felony matters and on civil matters over $5,000. The District Court oversees misdemeanor and civil matters under $10,000. Civil claims between $5000 and $10,000 may be filed in either Superior Court or District Court at the discretion of the filer.

Rhode Island has five counties but only four Superior/District Court Locations— 2nd-Newport, 3rd-Kent, 4th-Washington, and 6th-Providence/Bristol Districts. Bristol and Providence counties are completely merged at the Providence location. For questions regarding the Superior Courts, telephone 401-222-2622. For questions regarding the District Courts, telephone 401-458-5201. Probate is handled by the Town Clerk at the 39 cities and towns across Rhode Island

Online Access - The Rhode Island Judiciary offers free access to an index of county criminal cases statewide at http://courtconnect.courts.state.ri.us. A word of caution, this website is provided as an informational service only and should not be relied upon as an official record of the court. Supreme Court and Appellate opinions are available from the home page.

Searching Tips - Limited in-person searching of Supreme, District, Superior, and Family court cases are available. Most records available are from the mid 1980's to the present.

South Carolina

Administration - Court Administration, 803-734-1800 www.sccourts.org

Structure & Jurisdictions - The 46 SC counties are divided among 16 judicial circuits. Circuit Courts are the courts of general jurisdiction and consist of a Court of General Sessions (criminal) and a Court of Common Pleas (civil). A Family Court (juveniale cases) and Probate Court are found in each county. There are combined 300+ different Magistrate and Municipal Courts (often referred to as "Summary Courts") that handle misdemeanor cases involving a $500.00 fine and/or thirty days or less jail time.

Online Access - Appellate and Supreme Court opinions are available from the web. Although there is no statewide access to trial court records, a number of counties offer online access. From the home page, one may view a map of the state and those counties with online access are hot-linked.

Searching Tips - Most South Carolina courts will not conduct name searches. For those that do, search fees vary widely and are set by each county individually. If requesting a record in writing, it is recommended that the phrase "Request that General Session, Common Pleas, and Family Court records be searched" be included in the request.

South Dakota

Administration - State Court Administrator; 605-773-3474 www.sdjudicial.com

Structure & Jurisdictions - The state re-aligned their circuits from 8 to 7 effective June, 2000. The Circuit Courts are the general trial courts of the Unified Judicial System and have original jurisdiction in all and criminal cases and civil cases involving more than $10,000 in damages. Circuit Courts also have jurisdiction over appeals from Magistrate Court decisions. Generally, Magistrate Courts assist the Circuit Courts in processing minor criminal cases and less serious civil actions.

There are 66 counties, but 64 courts. Cases for Buffalo County are handled at the Brule County Circuit Court. Cases for Shannon County are handled by the Fall River County Circuit Court.

Online Access - Supreme Court calendar, opinions, rules and archived oral arguments may be searched from the website.

Records of all active money judgments and inactive civil money judgments from 04/19/2004 forward are available from a web subscription service offered by the State Court Administration Office. Fees are monthly, annual, or pay as you go basis from a credit card. Visit https://apps.sd.gov/applications/judgmentquery/login.aspx. The money judgment system permits bulk downloading of information. However, the agreement with the agency disallows any resell of the data. Note this subscription system does not include probate or criminal information. For more details contact Ms. Jill Gusso at 605-773-8437.

Searching Tips - Most South Dakota courts do not allow the public to perform an on-site name search, searches must be performed by the clerk for a fee. All clerks offices require written requests. A special Record Search Request Form must be used and can be found at www.sdjudicial.com/downloads/prcdr/rsrf.pdf. An inaccurate date of birth, SSN, driver's license number or other incomplete demographic information may result in inaccurate search results. Clerks are not required to respond to telephone or fax requests, but many courts return records via fax to ongoing commercial accounts.

For fastest service, the state asks that all mail requests be directed to one of three processing centers; the Miner County Clerk of Court, PO Box 265, Howard SD 57349 or to Aurora County Clerk of Court, PO Box 366, Plankinton, SD 57368-0366. Also, the State Court Administration provides a statewide criminal request system. Fax 605-773-8437 or email jill.gusso@ujs.state.sd.us for details.

Tennessee

Administration - Administrative Office of the Courts; 615-741-2687 www.tncourts.gov

Structure & Jurisdictions - The trial courts are the Chancery, Criminal, Circuit and Probate Courts. Lower courts are the General Sessions, Juvenile and Municipal Courts. Circuit Courts hear civil and criminal cases and appeals of decisions from City, Juvenile, Municipal and General Sessions courts. Criminal cases are tried in Circuit Court except in districts with separate Criminal Courts established by the General Assembly. Criminal Courts relieve Circuit Courts in areas where they are justified by heavy caseloads. Criminal Courts exist in 13 of the 31 judicial districts. The Chancery Courts, in addition to handling probate, also hear certain types of equitable civil cases. The jurisdiction of Circuit Courts often overlaps that of the Chancery Courts. Combining of Circuit Court and General Sessions Courts varies by county.

Online Access - Appellate Court opinions are found at www.tsc.state.tn.us/geninfo/Courts/AppellateCourts.htm. There is no statewide access system but several counties offer online access.

Searching Tips - Fees vary widely. Over 67% of the general jurisdiction courts offer public access terminals to view docket indices.

Texas

Administration - Office of Court Administration; 512-463-1625. www.courts.state.tx.us

Structure & Jurisdictions - The legal court structure for Texas is explained extensively in the "Texas Judicial Annual Report." Generally, Texas District Courts have general civil jurisdiction and exclusive felony jurisdiction, along with typical variations such as contested probate and divorce. There can be several districts in one courthouse.

The County Court structure consists of two forms of courts - "Constitutional" and "At Law." The Constitional upper claim limit is $100,000 while the At Law upper limit is $10,000. County Courts handle misdemeanors and general civil cases. In some counties the District Court or County Court handles evictions. District Court and County Court are combined in 69 counties.

Probate is handled in Probate Court in the ten largest counties and in District Courts or County Courts At Law elsewhere. The County Clerk is responsible for the records in every county.

Online Access - A number of local county courts offer online access to their records but there is no statewide system of local level court records. Case records of the Supreme Court can be searched at www.supreme.courts.state.tx.us. Appellate Court case information is searchable free at the website of each Appellate Court, reached online from www.courts.state.tx.us/courts/coa.asp. Court of Criminal Appeals opinions are found at www.cca.courts.state.tx.us.

Searching Tips - Often, a record search is automatically combined for two courts, for example a District Court with a County Court, or both County Courts. Less than half the courts have public access terminals to view docket indices. For civil matters up to $10,000, we recommend searchers start at the Constitutional County Court as they, generally, offer a shorter waiting time for cases in urban areas.

Utah

Administration - Court Administrator; 801-578-3800. www.utcourts.gov

Structure & Jurisdictions - The District Court has original jurisdiction to try all civil cases, all criminal felonies and misdemeanors in certain circumstances, domestic relations cases, and probate. 41 District Courts are arranged in 8 judicial districts. Branch courts in larger counties, such as Salt Lake, which were formerly Circuit Courts and now elevated to District Courts have full jurisdiction over felony as well as misdemeanor cases. Justice Courts are established by counties and municipalities and have the authority to deal with class B and C misdemeanors, violations of ordinances, small claims, and infractions committed within their territorial jurisdiction. The Justice Court shares jurisdiction with the Juvenile Court over minors 16 or 17 years old who are charged with certain higher level traffic offenses

Online Access - Case information from all Utah District Court locations is available online through Xchange; however, misdemeanor B's, C's, infractions and small claims cases are often filed in limited jurisdiction courts and not available through this site. Fees are involved. Information about XChange and the subscription agreement is found at http://www.utcourts.gov/records. One may search for Supreme Court or Appellate Courts opinions at the main website.

Searching Tips - Most District Courts charge hourly to do a name search, some give the first 15-20 minutes free. The Salt Lake District Court has an automated information phone line that provides court appearance look-ups, outstanding fine balance look-ups, and judgment/divorce decree lookups. Call 801-238-7830.

Vermont

Administration - Administrative Office of Courts, Court Administrator; 802-828-3278. www.vermontjudiciary.org

Structure & Jurisdictions - The Superior Court hears predominantly civil, tort, real estate, and small claims cases. On rare occasion it hears criminal cases, but the District Court hears predominantly criminal cases. Specialty courts include Probate Courts Family Courts. In Vermont, the Judicial Bureau has jurisdiction over traffic, municipal ordinances, and Fish & Game violations, minors in possession, hazing.

Online Access - Vermont Courts Online provides access to civil and small claim cases and court calendar information from 12 of the county Superior Courts at https://secure.vermont.gov/vtcdas/user. Access is not offered for Chittenden and Franklin. Records are in real-time mode, fees are involved.

Supreme Court opinions are available from the main website and are also maintained by the Vermont Department of Libraries at http://dol.state.vt.us.

Searching Tips – Most court follow a similar fee schedule for search, certification, and copy.

Virginia

Administration - Executive Secretary, Administrative Office of Courts; 804-786-6455. www.courts.state.va.us

Structure & Jurisdictions - The Circuit Courts in 31 districts are the courts of general jurisdiction. There are 132 District Courts of limited jurisdiction. A district can be either a county or a city (see below). The General District Court decides all criminal offenses involving ordinances laws, and by-laws of the county or city where it is located and all misdemeanors under state law. A misdemeanor is any charge that carries a penalty of no more than one year in jail or a fine of up to $2,500, or both.

Records of civil action from $4,500 to $15,000 can be at either the Circuit Court or District Court as either can have jurisdiction. **Check both record locations** as there is no concurrent database or index.

Online Access - There are 3 available systems. None are statewide; each county must be searched separately. Cases from 132 General District Courts may be searched free at www.courts.state.va.us/courts/gd.html. You can search records from over 120 Circuit courts at www.courts.state.va.us/courts/circuit.html. These 2 online systems do not include DOBs, SSNs or addresses. An older dial-up access system known as LOPAS (Law Office & Public Access System) is available free for District and Circuit records. Results include full name & address. Call Marguerite Steele, 804-786-6455 for LOPAS details. The web page www.courts.state.va.us provides Supreme Court and Appellate opinions.

Searching Tips - Fifteen independent cities share the Clerk of Circuit Court with the county - Bedford, Covington (Alleghany County), Emporia (Greenville County), Fairfax, Falls Church (Arlington or Fairfax County), Franklin (Southhampton County), Galax (Carroll County), Harrisonburg (Rockingham County), Lexington (Rockbridge County), Manassas and Manassas Park (Prince William County), Norton (Wise County), Poquoson (York County), South Boston (Halifax County), and Williamsburg (James City County).

Charles City and James City are counties, not cities. The City of Franklin is not in Franklin County, but is its own separate jurisdiction. The City of Richmond is not in Richmond County, but is its own separate jurisdiction. The City of Roanoke is not in Roanoke County, but is its own separate jurisdiction.

Washington

Administration - Court Administrator; 360-753-3365.
www.courts.wa.gov

Structure & Jurisdictions - The Superior Court is the court of general jurisdiction, but District Courts have criminal jurisdiction over misdemeanors, gross misdemeanors, and criminal traffic cases. Many Municipal Courts combine their record keeping with a District Court housed in the same building.

Washington has a mandatory arbitration requirement for civil disputes for $35,000 or less. However, either party may request a trial in Superior Court if dissatisfied with the arbitrator's decision.

Online Access - The web offers free look-up of docket information at http://dw.courts.wa.gov/. Search by name or case number. This is an unofficial search. For more detailed case data, the AOC provides facilities that allow one to access information in the Judicial Information System's (JIS) program called JIS-Link. JIS-Link provides access to all counties and court levels. Case records include criminal, civil, domestic, probate, and judgments. Fees are involved. Call 360-357-3365 or visit www.courts.wa.gov/jislink.

Supreme and Appellate opinions and a notification service are found at www.courts.wa.gov/appellate%5Ftrial%5Fcourts.

Searching Tips - District Courts retain civil records for ten years from date of final disposition, then the records are destroyed. District Courts retain criminal records forever. An SASE is required in most courts that respond to written search requests.

West Virginia

Administration - Administrative Office, Supreme Court of Appeals; 304-558-0145. www.state.wv.us/wvsca

Structure & Jurisdictions - Records are held at the County Commissioner's Office. The trial courts of general jurisdiction are the Circuit Courts which handle civil cases at law over $300 or more or in equity, felonies, misdemeanors, and probate. The Magistrate Courts, which are akin to small claims courts, issue arrest and search warrants, hear misdemeanor cases, conduct preliminary examinations in felony cases, and hear civil cases with $5,000 or less in dispute. Magistrates also issue emergency protective orders in cases involving domestic violence.

The Circuit Courts hear appeals of Magistrate Court cases. The highest court is the Supreme Court of Appeals of West Virginia.

Family Courts, created by constitutional amendment of January 1, 2002, hear cases involving divorce, annulment, separate maintenance, family support, paternity, child custody, and visitation. Family Court judges also conduct final hearings in domestic violence cases.

Online Access - Supreme Court of Appeals Opinions and Calendar are available at the web page. 18 circuit courts have accessible records at www.swcg-inc.com/circuit-express.php. Fees are involved, records go back to 02/1997.

Searching Tips - There is a statewide requirement that search turnaround times not exceed five business days. However, most courts do far better than that limit. Release of public information is governed by WV Code Sec.29B-1-1 et seq.

Wisconsin

Administration - Director of State Courts, Supreme Court; 608-266-6828. http://wicourts.gov

Structure & Jurisdictions - The Circuit Court is the court of general jurisdiction for civil and criminal matters. The majority of Municipal Court cases involve traffic and ordinance matters.

Probate filing is a function of the Circuit Court, however each county has a Register in Probate who maintains and manages the probate records, guardianship, and mental health records. Most Registers in Probate are putting pre-1950 records on microfilm and destroying the hard copies. This is done as "time and workloads permit," so microfilm archiving is not uniform across the state.

Online Access - Wisconsin Circuit Court Access (WCCA) allows users to view Circuit Court case information at http://wcca.wicourts.gov. Data is available from all counties (except only probate records are available from Portage). Searches can be conducted statewide or county-by-county. WCCA provides detailed information about circuit cases and for civil cases, the program displays judgment and judgment party information and offers the ability to generate reports. Appellate Courts and Supreme Court opinions are available from the main web page.

Searching Tips - Public access terminals are available at each court. In about half the Circuit Courts, a search fee is charged even if the case number is provided.

Wyoming

Administration - Court Administrator; 307-777-7583. www.courts.state.wy.us

Structure & Jurisdictions – The District Court is higher jurisdiction and the Circuit Court is limited jurisdiction. Circuit Courts handle civil claims up to $7,000 and small claims to $5,000. The District Courts take cases over the applicable limit in each county. Municipal courts operate in all incorporated cities and towns and cover all ordinance violations but no civil jurisdiction. Probate is handled by the District Court. Effective January 1, 2003 all Justice Courts became Circuit Courts and follow Circuit Court rules.

Online Access - Wyoming's statewide case management system is for internal use only. Planning is underway for a new case management system that will ultimately allow public access. Supreme Court opinions are listed by date at the home page.

Searching Tips - Three counties have two Circuit Courts each: Fremont, Park, and Sweetwater. Cases may be filed in either of the two court offices in those counties, and records requests are referred between the two courts.

Searching Federal Court Records

Searching records at the federal court system can be one of the easiest or one of the most frustrating experiences that public record searchers may encounter. Although the federal court system offers advanced electronic search capabilities, at times it is practically impossible to properly identify a subject when searching civil or criminal records.

Before reviewing searching procedures, a brief overview is in order.

Federal Court Structure

At the federal level, all cases involve federal or U.S. constitutional law or interstate commerce. The federal court system includes three levels of courts, plus several specialty courts.

United States District Courts

The United States District Courts are the courts of general jurisdiction, or trial courts. There are 89 districts in the 50 states, which are listed with their divisions in Title 28 of the U.S. Code, Sections 81-144. District courts also exist in Puerto Rico, the U.S. Virgin Islands, the District of Columbia, Guam, and the Northern Mariana Islands. In total there are 94 U.S. district courts in 500 court locations. Some states, such as Colorado, are composed of a single judicial district. Others, such as California, are composed of multiple judicial districts – Central, Eastern, Northern, and Southern.

The task of locating the right court is seemingly simplified by the nature of the federal system—

- All court locations are based upon the plaintiff's county of domicile.
- All civil and criminal cases go to the U.S. District Courts.
- All bankruptcy cases go to the U.S. Bankruptcy Courts.

Bankruptcy Courts are separate units of the district courts and have exclusive jurisdiction over bankruptcy cases. States with more than one court are divided further into judicial districts — e.g., the State of New York consists of four judicial districts: the Northern, Southern, Eastern, and Western. Further, many judicial districts contain more than one court location, usually called a division.

The bankruptcy courts generally use the same hearing locations as the district courts. If court locations differ, the usual variance is to have fewer bankruptcy court locations.

A plaintiff or defendant may have cases in any of the 500 court locations, so it is really not all that simple to find them.

United States Court of Appeals

The United States Court of Appeals consists of thirteen appellate courts that hear appeals of verdicts from the district and bankruptcy courts. Courts of Appeals are designated as follows:

- **The Federal Circuit Court of Appeals** hears appeals from the U.S. Claims Court and the U.S. Court of International Trade. It is located in Washington, DC.

- **The District of Columbia Circuit Court of Appeals** hears appeals from the district courts in Washington, DC as well as from the Tax Court.

- Eleven geographic **Courts of Appeals** — each of these appeal courts covers a designated number of states and territories.[11]

Supreme Court of the United States

The Supreme Court of the United States is the court of last resort in the United States. The Supreme Court is located in Washington, DC, where it hears appeals from the United States Courts of Appeals and from the highest courts of each state.

Other Federal Courts of Note

There are three significant special/separate courts created to hear cases or appeals for certain areas of litigation that demand special expertise. These courts are the U.S. Tax Court, the Court of International Trade, and the U.S. Court of Federal Claims. A profile of each of these courts is located at the end of this chapter.

How Federal Trial Court Cases are Organized

Indexing and Case Numbering

When a case is filed with a federal court, a case number is assigned. District courts index by defendant and plaintiff as well as by case number. Bankruptcy courts usually index by debtor and case number. Therefore, when you search by name you will first receive a listing of all cases where the name appears, both as plaintiff and defendant.

To view case records you will need to know or find the applicable case number.

---

[11] The profiles at the end of the chapter list the circuit numbers (1 through 11) and location of the Court of Appeals for each state.

Case numbering procedures are not consistent throughout the federal court system. One judicial district may assign numbers by district while another may assign numbers by location (division) within that judicial district or by judge within the division. Remember that case numbers appearing in legal text citations may not be adequate for searching unless they appear in the proper form for the particular court.

Docket Sheet

As in state court systems, information from cover sheets and from documents filed as a case goes forward is recorded on the **docket sheet**, which then contains the case history from initial filing to its current status. While docket sheets differ somewhat in format, the basic information contained on a docket sheet is consistent from court to court. As noted previously in the state court chapter, all docket sheets contain—

- Name of court, including location (division) and the judge assigned;
- Case number and case name;
- Names of all plaintiffs and defendants/debtors;
- Names and addresses of attorneys for the plaintiff or debtor;
- Nature and cause (e.g., U.S. civil statute) of action;
- Listing of documents filed in the case, including the date, docket entry number, and a short description (e.g., 12-2-92, #1, Complaint).

All basic civil case information entered onto docket sheets and into computerized systems like the Case Management/Electronic Case Filings (CM/ECF) starts with standard form JS-44, the Civil Cover Sheet, or the equivalent.

Assignment of Cases and Computerization

At one time, cases were assigned within a district based on the county of origination. Although this is still true in most states, computerized tracking of dockets has led to a more flexible approach to case assignment. For example in Minnesota and Connecticut, rather than blindly assigning all cases from a county to one judge, their districts use random numbers and other methods to logically balance caseloads among their judges.

This trend may appear to confuse the case search process. Actually, finding cases has become significantly easier with the wide availability of the U.S. Party/Case Index and PACER.[12] Also helpful is when on-site terminals in each court location contain the same database of district-wide information.

---

[12] PACER - Public Access to Court Electronic Records - is explained on pages to follow.

Searching Records by Mail and In Person

There are certain pre-set standards for federal courts that most all courts follow.

The search fee is $26 per item. 'A search' is one party name or case number. The court copy fee is $.50 per page. Certification fee is $9 per document, double for exemplification, if available. If you request documents by mail, it is best to always enclose a stamped self-addressed envelope unless a court indicates otherwise. Most courts accept fax requests or will suggest a copying/search vendor. Before releasing records, assume that the court will require prepayment, as most do.

Nearly all courts offer Internet access via CM-ECF or PACER as described in the next section.

Electronic Access to Federal Court Records

Numerous programs have been developed for electronic access to federal court records. Over the years, the Administrative Office of the United States Courts in Washington, DC has developed a number of innovative public access programs—

- The U.S. Party/Case Index
- PACER
- Case Management/Electronic Case Files (CM/ECF)
- VCIS (via the telephone)

Search the U.S. Party/Case Index

The U.S. Party/Case Index, actually part of PACER, is a national locator index for U.S. District, Bankruptcy, and Appellate courts. By using the U.S. Party/Case Index searchers may conduct nearly nationwide search to determine whether or not a party is involved in federal litigation.

If you find there is a case in existence involving a particular subject, then you need to visit the PACER or CM/ECF site for the particular jurisdiction where the case is located. The *Case Number* field in the output will be a direct link to the full case information on the court's computers, whether the court is running the Internet version of PACER or the newer PACER on the CM/ECF system.

You may access the U.S. Party/Case Index via the Internet at http://pacer.uspci.uscourts.gov. Subscribers to PACER automatically have access to the U.S. Party/Case Index. Subscribers may use their existing PACER login and password.

The U.S. Party/Case Index allows searches 1) by party name or Social Security Number in the bankruptcy index, 2) party name or nature of suit in the civil index, 3) defendant name in the criminal index, and 4) party name in the appellate index. The information provided by the search result will include the party name, the court where the case is filed, the case number and the filing date.

To find the date ranges for the cases in a particular court, choose the option "Date Ranges" at the main menu. This option provides how far back the search will go and the date the U.S. Party/Case Index was last updated for each court.

To retrieve more information on a particular case found while searching the U.S. Party/Case Index, access the PACER system for the jurisdiction where the case resides as indicated by the court abbreviation. Usually the Case Number will be a link to the case summary information at that court's PACER site.

At press time, there were a number of courts not participating in the U.S. Party Case Index. Non-participating Appellate Courts include the Second, Fifth, Seventh, and Eleventh Circuits. Non-participating District Courts include the Indiana Southern District, New Mexico District, and the U.S. Virgin Islands District.

PACER

PACER, the acronym for **P**ublic **A**ccess to **E**lectronic **C**ourt **R**ecords, provides docket information online for open and some closed case information at **all U.S. Bankruptcy Courts** and **most U.S. District Courts**. Cases for the U.S. Court of Federal Claims are also available.

A key point to consider is that each court maintains its own database with case information and decides what to make available on PACER. Also, several courts provide case information on Internet sites without support of the PACER Service Center.

PACER sign-up and technical support is handled at the PACER Service Center in San Antonio, Texas; phone 800-676-6856. A single sign-up is good for all courts; however, some individual courts may require further registration procedures. Many judicial districts offer to send a PACER Primer that has been customized for that district. The primer contains a summary of how to access PACER, how to select cases, how to read case numbers and docket sheets, some searching tips, who to call for problem resolution, and district specific program variations.

You may search by case number, party name, SSN, or tax identification number in the U.S. Bankruptcy Courts. You may search by case number, party name, or filing date range in the U.S. District Courts. You may search by case number or party name in the U.S. Courts of Appeals.

PACER provides the following information

- A listing of all parties and participants including judges, attorneys, trustees
- A compilation of case related information such as cause of action, nature of suit, dollar demand
- A chronology of dates of case events entered in the case record
- A claims registry
- A listing of new cases each day in the bankruptcy courts
- Appellate court opinions
- Judgments or case status
- Types of case documents filed for certain districts.

PACER Problems

There are two inherent problems when searching PACER records—

1. How far back records are kept
2. Lack of identifiers

Since each court determines how records will be indexed and when records will be purged, this can leave a searcher guessing how a name is spelled or abbreviated, and how much information about closed cases a search will uncover. The bottom line is that a PACER search may not come close to matching a full seven-year search of the federal court records available by written request from the court itself or through a local document retrieval company.

Another problem is the lack of identifiers. Most federal courts do not show the full DOB on records available to the public. Some courts show no DOB at all. Thus, if the name searched for is common and the search results show two or more hits, each individual case file may need to be reviewed to determine if the case belongs to the subject in mind.

An excellent FAQ on PACER is at http://pacer.psc.uscourts.gov/faq.html.

Miscellaneous Online Systems

RACER is a comparable system to PACER. A few courts still maintain and offer access through RACER. Over the years some courts have developed their own legacy online systems. In addition to RACER, Idaho's Bankruptcy and District Courts have other searching options available on their websites. Likewise, the Southern District Court of New York offers CourtWeb, which provides information to the public on selected recent rulings of those judges who have elected to make information available in electronic form.

Case Management/Electronic Case Files (CM/ECF)

CM/ECF is the relatively new case management system for the Federal Judiciary for all bankruptcy, district, and appellate courts, replacing the aging electronic docketing and case management systems. CM/ECF allows courts to accept filings and provide access to filed documents over the Internet. Attorneys may use CM/ECF to file documents and manage official documents related to a case. Case Management/Electronic Case Files case information is available to the public. Searchers access CM/ECF via PACER.

For details, visit http://pacer.psc.uscourts.gov/cmecf/index.html.

It is important to note that when you search ECF, you may be searching ONLY cases that have been filed electronically. Since a case may not have been filed electronically through CM/ECF, you must still conduct a search using PACER to determine if a case exists.

Most individual courts offer tutorials on how to use CM/ECF for their district. Functioning as a search mechanism, CM/ECF attaches to the relevant docket entries and to PDF versions of related documents filed with or issued by the court. A user may access PDF attachments through a hyperlink that appears with the docket entry.

Because PACER and CM/ECF database systems are maintained within each court, each jurisdiction will have a different URL or modem number. Accessing and querying information from PACER and CM/ECF is comparable; however the format and content of information provided may differ slightly.

Voice Case Information System (VCIS)

Another access system is **VCIS** – Voice Case Information System. At one time, nearly all of the U.S. Bankruptcy Court judicial districts provided **VCIS**, a means of accessing information regarding OPEN bankruptcy cases by merely using a touch-tone telephone. The advantage? There is no charge. Individual names are entered last name first with as much of the first name as you wish to include. For example, Joe B. Cool could be entered as COOLJ or COOLJOE. Do not enter the middle initial. Business names are entered as they are written, without blanks.

VCIS, like the RACER System, is being replaced by newer technology. Each bankruptcy court that still offers VCIS access is shown in the court profiles section at the end of this chapter.

VCIS should only be used to locate information about open cases. Do not attempt to use VCIS as a substitute for a PACER search.

More Federal Courts Searching Hints

- Check the assigned counties of jurisdiction for each court within a state. Usually accessible from the web, this is a good starting point for determining where case records may be found.

- Searchers need to be sure that the court's case index includes all cases open or closed for that particular period, especially important if using CM/ECF. Be aware that some courts purge older, closed paper case files after a period of time, making a search there incomplete after the purge date. Purge times vary from court to court and state to state. **Some courts purge within a few months of a case closing.**

- Often, court personnel are very knowledgeable open cases, but are sometimes fuzzy in answering questions about how far back case records go on PACER, and whether closed cases have been purged. If you are looking for cases older than a year or two, there is no substitute for paying for a real, on-site search performed by court personnel or by a local document retriever. An accurate on-site search can be performed if the court allows full access to its indexes, and most do through public access terminals in their offices.

- Most federal courts no longer provide the date of birth or the Social Security Number on search results. However, a handful will provide the last four digits of the SSN, or they may provide the birth month and year of birth, but not the day. **The court summary pages at the end of this chapter show which districts provide personnel identifiers for record searchers.**

- Some courts may be more willing than others to give out information by telephone. This is because most courts now have fully computerized indexes that clerks can access while on the phone.

What If the Record Search Results Do Not Include Identifiers?

Approximately 5 percent of the criminal records in the U.S. are records of federal offenses. A well-known concern of the employment screening industry is the fact it is next to impossible for employers to verify that a new hire does not have a federal criminal record.

This is a struggle and a tough problem to solve, especially if a searcher is dealing with a common name. Here are several ideas for trying to ferret out a false-positive:

View Case Files

If possible, review the documents found in the case files for any hints of identification. At some district courts, clerks will look at paper case file records, if any, to determine if other identification exists that can match the requester's identifiers.

Incarceration Records

Searching prison records is sometimes an excellent alternative means for identity verification. See *Incarceration Records – Bureau of Federal Prisons* in the *Searching A thru Z* chapter. The agency's web page offers a free inmate locator for all inmates housed starting in 1982. A search will show release dates. Age is given, but not the DOB.

News Media

Some record searchers have been successful in confirming an identity by using news media**Error! Bookmark not defined.** sources such as newspapers and web news media. Even blogs may help.

Some Background to This Problem

Why the lack of identifiers? The court administrators and judges at the federal level and the attorneys who routinely file and try cases at the federal level formed a panel and decided to protect the identities of witnesses and victims by redacting (or not including) certain information from the case record. However, this methodology also redacted the identifiers of the convicted criminals. The decision makers apparently did not take into account that the biggest users of criminal records (employers) in the U.S. already had written authorization to search, had full identifiers to match, and were complying with federal law, mainly the Fair Credit Reporting Act. Today, most of the public hiring that takes place is done so without checking the court record repositories or databases. In hindsight, perhaps the record "creators" should have asked the record "users" to be part of the decision making process (as opposed to giving public testimony). What if the U.S. Department of State went along with a notion that 5 percent of the foreigners visiting this country do not need to have passport to enter? Sounds crazy doesn't it?

Federal Records Centers and the National Archives

After a federal case is closed, the documents are held by the federal courts location for a predetermined number of years. This can be as little as six months, or, rarely, until the court reaches its capacity to store files. The closed cases are then sent to and stored at a designated Federal Records Center (FRC). After 20 to 30 years, the records are then transferred from the FRC to the regional archives offices. All of these offices are administered by the National Archives and Records Administration (NARA).

Each court has its own transfer cycle and determines access procedures to its case records even after they have been sent to the FRC.

When case records are sent to an FRC, the boxes of records are assigned accession, location, and box numbers. These numbers, which are called *case locator information*, must be obtained from the originating court and are necessary to retrieve documents from the FRC. Some courts will provide case locator information over the telephone, but other courts may require a written request. In certain judicial districts this information is now available on PACER.

The Federal Records Center location for each state is shown below. For the address and contact information for each of these centers, along with details about other information found at the Archives offices, see *Archives (National)* in the *Searching A thru Z* chapter.

Federal Record Center Locater Table

State	Circuit	Appeals Court	Federal Records Center
AK	9	San Francisco, CA	Anchorage (Some records are in temporary storage in Seattle)
AL	11	Atlanta, GA	Atlanta
AR	8	St. Louis, MO	Fort Worth
AZ	9	San Francisco, CA	Los Angeles
CA	9	San Francisco, CA	Los Angeles (Central & Southern CA) San Francisco (Eastern & Northern CA)
CO	10	Denver, CO	Denver
CT	2	New York, NY	Boston
DC		Washington, DC	Washington, DC
DE	3	Philadelphia, PA	Philadelphia
FL	11	Atlanta, GA	Atlanta
GA	11	Atlanta, GA	Atlanta
GU	9	San Francisco, CA	San Francisco
HI	9	San Francisco, CA	San Francisco
IA	8	St. Louis, MO	Kansas City, MO
ID	9	San Francisco, CA	Seattle
IL	7	Chicago, IL	Chicago
IN	7	Chicago, IL	Chicago
KS	10	Denver, CO	Kansas City, MO
KY	6	Cincinnati, OH	Atlanta
LA	5	New Orleans, LA	Fort Worth
MA	1	Boston, MA	Boston
MD	4	Richmond, VA	Philadelphia
ME	1	Boston, MA	Boston
MI	6	Cincinnati, OH	Chicago
MN	8	St. Louis, MO	Chicago
MO	8	St. Louis, MO	Kansas City, MO

State	Circuit	Appeals Court	Federal Records Center
MS	5	New Orleans, LA	Atlanta
MT	9	San Francisco, CA	Denver
NC	4	Richmond, VA	Atlanta
ND	8	St. Louis, MO	Denver
NE	8	St. Louis, MO	Kansas City, MO
NH	1	Boston, MA	Boston
NJ	3	Philadelphia, PA	New York
NM	10	Denver, CO	Denver
NV	9	San Francisco, CA	Los Angeles (Clark County, NV) San Francisco (Other NV counties)
NY	2	New York, NY	New York
OH	6	Cincinnati, OH	Chicago (Dayton has some bankruptcy)
OK	10	Denver, CO	Fort Worth
OR	9	San Francisco, CA	Seattle
PA	3	Philadelphia, PA	Philadelphia
PR	1	Boston, MA	New York
RI	1	Boston, MA	Boston
SC	4	Richmond, VA	Atlanta
SD	8	St. Louis, MO	Denver
TN	6	Cincinnati, OH	Atlanta
TX	5	New Orleans, LA	Fort Worth
UT	10	Denver, CO	Denver
VA	4	Richmond, VA	Philadelphia
VI	3	Philadelphia, PA	New York
VT	2	New York, NY	Boston
WA	9	San Francisco, CA	Seattle
WI	7	Chicago, IL	Chicago
WV	4	Richmond, VA	Philadelphia
WY	10	Denver, CO	Denver

Identifiers and Case Files for U.S. District and U.S. Bankruptcy Court Records

Listed in order by state are brief summaries for U.S. District Courts, and U.S. Bankruptcy Courts. Summaries include the district's website URL, the district's VCIS phone numbers if available, what personal identifiers appear on search results if any, and duration before closed case files are shipped to the Federal Records Center for archiving. Also shown are the division locations within the district. In most cases, a court's website reveals if specific counties are under its jurisdiction.

Alabama Middle District- US District Court www.almd.uscourts.gov
Search results do not include DOB or SSN. **Divisions-** Dothan, Montgomery, Opelika.

Alabama Middle District- US Bankruptcy Court www.almb.uscourts.gov
VCIS: 334-954-3868. Search results include SSN. Case files sent to archives 3 years after closed. **Location-** Montgomery.

Alabama Northern District- US District Court www.alnd.uscourts.gov
Search results do not include SSN or DOB. Case files sent to archives 18 months after closed. **Divisions-** Birmingham, Gadsden, Huntsville, Jasper.

Alabama Northern District- US Bankruptcy Court www.alnb.uscourts.gov
VCIS: 877-466-0795, 205-254-7337. Search results include last 4 SSN digits. Paper case files sent to archives 1 years after closed; cases kept electronically indefinitely. **Divisions-** Anniston, Birmingham, Decatur, Tuscaloosa.

Alabama Southern District- US District Court www.als.uscourts.gov
Search results do not include SSN, DOB. **Divisions-** Mobile (South), Selma (North).

North Southern District- US Bankruptcy Court www.alsb.uscourts.gov
VCIS: 251-441-5637. Search results include SSN. **Location-** Mobile.

Alaska- US District Court www.akd.uscourts.gov
VCIS: 907-222-6940. Search results do not include SSN or DOB. Tried case files sent to Anchorage Records Center. If the case did not go to trial, file sent to Seattle Records Center. **Divisions-** Anchorage, Fairbanks, Juneau, Ketchikan, Nome.

Alaska- US Bankruptcy Court www.akb.uscourts.gov
VCIS: 888-878-3110, 907-271-2658. Search results do not include DOB; SSN only before 12/04. If a case was tried, file sent to Anchorage Records Center. If the case did not go to trial, file sent to Seattle Records Center. Case records sent to a Center 3 months after case closed. **Location-** Anchorage.

Arizona- US District Court www.azd.uscourts.gov
Search results do not include SSN or DOB. Case files sent to archives 5 years after closed. **Divisions-** Phoenix, Prescott, Tucson.

Arizona- US Bankruptcy Court www.azb.uscourts.gov
VCIS: 602-682-4001. Search results include last 4 SSN digits. Closed case files kept 6 months; electronic files kept indefinitely. **Divisions-** Phoenix, Tucson, Yuma.

Arkansas Eastern District- US District Court www.are.uscourts.gov
Search results do not include SSN or DOB. Case files sent to archives 4 years after closed. **Divisions-** Batesville, Helena, Jonesboro, Little Rock, Pine Bluff.

Arkansas Eastern District- US Bankruptcy Court www.areb.uscourts.gov
VCIS: 800-891-6741, 501-918-5555. Search: Index includes last 4 SSN digits and any other identifiers remaining on document. Case files sent to archives 6 month to a year after closed. **Location-** Little Rock.

Arkansas Western District- US District Court www.arwd.uscourts.gov
Search results do not include SSN or DOB. Closed cases sent to archives after 5 years. **Divisions-** El Dorado, Fayetteville, Fort Smith, Hot Springs, Texarkana.

Arkansas Western District- US Bankruptcy Court www.arb.uscourts.gov
VCIS: 800-891-6741, 501-918-5555. Search results include last 4 SSN digits. All paper files have been sent to archives. **Location -** Fayetteville.

California Central District- US District Court www.cacd.uscourts.gov
Search results do not include SSN or DOB. Case files sent to archives 2-3 years after closed. **Divisions-** Los Angeles (Western), Riverside (Eastern), Santa Ana (Southern).

California Central District- US Bankruptcy Court www.cacb.uscourts.gov
VCIS: 866-522-6053, 213-894-4111. Search results include last 4 SSN digits. Case files sent to archives 1 year after closed. **Divisions-** Los Angeles, Riverside (East), San Fernando Valley, Santa Ana, Santa Barbara (Northern).

California Eastern District- US District Court www.caed.uscourts.gov
Search results do not include SSN or DOB. Case files sent to archives at varying intervals, usually as time permits. **Divisions-** Fresno, Sacramento.

California Eastern District- US Bankruptcy Court www.caeb.uscourts.gov
Search results include last 4 SSN digits. All cases before 3/99 sent to archives. **Divisions-** Fresno, Modesto, Sacramento.

California Northern District- US District Court www.cand.uscourts.gov
Search results do not include SSN or DOB, but office can confirm or deny. Case files sent to archives 6 months after closed. **Divisions-** Oakland, San Francisco, San Jose.

California Northern District- US Bankruptcy Court www.canb.uscourts.gov
VCIS: 888-457-0604, 415-705-3160. Search results include last 4 SSN digits. Case files sent to archives up to 1 year after closed. **Divisions-** Oakland, San Francisco, San Jose, Santa Rosa.

California Southern District- US District Court www.casd.uscourts.gov
Search results do not include SSN or DOB. When local space becomes unavailable, closed cases are transferred to archives. **Location -** San Diego.

California Southern District- US Bankruptcy Court www.casb.uscourts.gov
VCIS: 619-557-6521. Search results include last 4 SSN digits. Case files sent to archives 6 months after closed. **Location-** San Diego.

Colorado- US District Court www.co.uscourts.gov
Search results do not include SSN or DOB. Closed records sent to archives at irregular intervals. **Location-** Denver.

Colorado- US Bankruptcy Court www.cob.uscourts.gov
VCIS: 720-904-7419. Search results do not include SSN or DOB. Docket sheet includes last 4 digits of SSN. Closed electronic cases not purged. **Location-** Denver.

Connecticut- US District Court www.ctd.uscourts.gov
Search results do not include SSN or DOB. **Divisions-** Bridgeport, Hartford, New Haven.

Connecticut- US Bankruptcy Court www.ctb.uscourts.gov
VCIS: 800-800-5113. Search results include last 4 SSN digits, also address. Case files sent to archives 1 year after closed. **Divisions-** Bridgeport, Hartford, New Haven.

Delaware- US District Court www.ded.uscourts.gov
Search results do not include SSN or DOB. Closed cases are not sent to the archives for a minimum of 6 months. **Location-** Wilmington.

Delaware- US Bankruptcy Court www.deb.uscourts.gov
VCIS: 302-252-2560. Search results include last 4 SSN digits. Case files sent to archives when court has collected 150 records boxes. **Location-** Wilmington.

District of Columbia- US District Court www.dcd.uscourts.gov
Search: Criminal search results include DOB; civil returns name only. Case files sent to archives 5 years after closed.

District of Columbia- US Bankruptcy Court www.dcb.uscourts.gov
VCIS: 202-208-1365. Search results include last 4 SSN digits. Case files sent to archives 1 year after closed.

Florida Middle District- US District Court www.flmd.uscourts.gov
Search results do not include SSN or DOB. Case files sent to archives 3 years after closed. **Divisions-** Fort Myers, Jacksonville, Ocala, Orlando, Tampa.

Florida Middle District- US Bankruptcy Court www.flmb.uscourts.gov
VCIS: 866-879-1286, 904-301-6490. Search results include last 4 SSN digits. No specific time when closed records sent to Atlanta Records Center. **Divisions-** Jacksonville, Orlando, Tampa.

Florida Northern District- US District Court www.flnd.uscourts.gov
Search results do not include SSN or DOB. Closed cases sent to archives depending on case type. **Divisions-** Gainesville, Panama City, Pensacola, Tallahassee.

Florida Northern District- US Bankruptcy Court www.flnb.uscourts.gov
VCIS: 850-435-8477. Search results include last 4 SSN digits. All case files are electronicly stored. **Divisions-** Pensacola, Tallahassee.

Florida Southern District- US District Court www.flsd.uscourts.gov
Search: Recent cases do not include SSN or DOB. Case files sent to archives 5 years after closed, then sent to Atlanta Records Center. **Divisions-** Fort Lauderdale, Fort Pierce, Key West, Miami, West Palm Beach.

Florida Southern District- US Bankruptcy Court www.flsb.uscourts.gov
VCIS: 800-473-0226, 305-536-5979. Search results do not include SSN or DOB. Case files sent to archives 6 months after closed. **Divisions-** Fort Lauderdale, Miami, West Palm Beach.

Georgia Middle District- US District Court www.gamd.uscourts.gov
Search results do not include SSN or DOB. Case files sent to archives 2 years after closed. **Divisions-** Albany/Americus, Athens, Columbus, Macon, Thomasville, Valdosta.

Georgia Middle District- US Bankruptcy Court www.gamb.uscourts.gov
VCIS: 800-211-3015, 912-752-8183. Search results do not include SSN or DOB. **Divisions-** Columbus (West), Macon (East).

Georgia Northern District- US District Court www.gand.uscourts.gov
Search results include last 4 SSN digits. **Divisions-** Atlanta, Gainesville, Newnan, Rome.

Georgia Northern District- US Bankruptcy Court www.ganb.uscourts.gov
VCIS: 800-510-8284, 404-730-2866. Search results include last 4 SSN digits. Paper case files archived 6 months after closing; electronic files maintained indefinitely. **Divisions-** Atlanta, Gainesville, Newnan, Rome.

Georgia Southern District- US District Court www.gasd.uscourts.gov
Search results do not include SSN or DOB. **Divisions-** Augusta, Brunswick, Savannah.

Georgia Southern District- US Bankruptcy Court www.gas.uscourts.gov
Search results include last 4 SSN digits. **Divisions-** Augusta, Savannah.

Guam- US District and Bankruptcy Court www.gud.uscourts.gov
Search results include last 4 SSN digits only. All closed case records maintained here.

Hawaii- US District Court www.hid.uscourts.gov
Search results do not include SSN or DOB. Case files sent to archives 1 year after closed.

Hawaii- US Bankruptcy Court www.hib.uscourts.gov
VCIS: 808-522-8122. Search results include last 4 SSN digits.

Idaho- US District Court www.id.uscourts.gov
Search results do not include SSN or DOB. **Divisions-** Boise, Coeur d' Alene, Moscow, Pocatello.

Idaho- US Bankruptcy Court www.id.uscourts.gov
VCIS: 208-334-9386. Search results include last 4 SSN digits and address. **Divisions-** Boise, Coeur d' Alene, Moscow - Northern, Pocatello.

Illinois Central District- US District Court www.ilcd.uscourts.gov
Search results do not include SSN or DOB; court will confirm if identifiers provided in request. Case files sent to archives 5-7 years after closed. **Divisions-** Peoria, Rock Island, Springfield, Urbana.

Illinois Central District- US Bankruptcy Court www.ilcb.uscourts.gov
VCIS: 800-827-9005, 217-431-4820. Search results do not include SSN or DOB. No paper files available. **Divisions-** Danville, Peoria, Springfield.

Illinois Northern District- US District Court www.ilnd.uscourts.gov
Search results do not include SSN or DOB. Case files sent to archives 1-5 years after closed. **Divisions-** Chicago (Eastern), Rockford (Western).

Illinois Northern District- US Bankruptcy Court www.ilnb.uscourts.gov
VCIS: 888-232-6814, 312-408-5089. Search results include last 4 SSN digits. **Divisions-** Chicago (Eastern), Rockford.

Illinois Southern District- US District Court www.ilsd.uscourts.gov
Search results do not include SSN or DOB. Case files sent to archives as deemed necessary. **Divisions-** Benton, East St Louis.

Illinois Southern District- US Bankruptcy Court www.ilsb.uscourts.gov
VCIS: 800-726-5622, 618-482-9365. Search results do not include SSN or DOB. **Divisions-** Benton, East St Louis.

Indiana Northern District- US District Court
www.innd.uscourts.gov/fortwayne.shtml
Search results do not include SSN or DOB. **Divisions-** Fort Wayne, Hammond, Lafayette, South Bend.

Indiana Northern District- US Bankruptcy Court www.innb.uscourts.gov
VCIS: 800-755-8393, 574-968-2275. Search results do not include full SSN. Paper files sent to archives 2 years after closed. **Divisions-** Fort Wayne, Hammond, Hammond at Lafayette, South Bend.

Indiana Southern District- US District Court www.insd.uscourts.gov
Search results include SSN or DOB year for criminal cases; civil includes only last 4 SSN digits. **Divisions-** Evansville, Indianapolis, New Albany, Terre Haute.

Indiana Southern District- US Bankruptcy Court www.insb.uscourts.gov
VCIS: 800-335-8003, 317-229-3888. Search results include last 4 SSN digits. Paper case files sent to archives as cases are closed. Electronic cases maintained indefinitely. **Divisions-** Evansville, Indianapolis, New Albany, Terre Haute.

Iowa Northern District- US District Court www.iand.uscourts.gov
Search results do not include SSN or DOB or any personal identifiers. **Divisions-** Cedar Rapids (Eastern), Sioux City (Western).

Iowa Northern District- US Bankruptcy Court www.ianb.uscourts.gov
VCIS: 800-249-9859, 319-286-2282. Search results include name and address only. **Divisions-** Cedar Rapids (Eastern), Sioux City (Western).

Iowa Southern District- US District Court www.iasd.uscourts.gov
Search results do not include SSN or DOB. Case files are all electronic; never purged. **Divisions-** Council Bluffs (Western), Davenport (Eastern), Des Moines (Central).

Iowa Southern District- US Bankruptcy Court www.iasb.uscourts.gov
VCIS: 888-219-5534, 515-284-6427. Search results include dba, fka (alias) **Location-** Des Moines.

Kansas- US District Court www.ksd.uscourts.gov
Search results do not include SSN or DOB. Case files sent to archives 12 months after closed. **Divisions-** Kansas City, Topeka, Wichita.

Kansas- US Bankruptcy Court www.ksb.uscourts.gov
VCIS: 800-827-9028, 316-269-6668. Search results include last 4 SSN digits. Case files sent to archives every 6 months. **Divisions-** Kansas City, Topeka, Wichita.

Kentucky Eastern District- US District Court www.kyed.uscourts.gov
Search results do not include SSN or DOB. Case files sent to archives 5 years after closed. **Divisions-** Ashland, Covington, Frankfort, Lexington, London, Pikeville.

Kentucky Eastern District- US Bankruptcy Court www.kyeb.uscourts.gov
VCIS: 800-998-2650, 859-233-2650. Search results include last 4 SSN digits only. **Location-** Lexington.

Kentucky Western District- US District Court www.kywd.uscourts.gov
Search results do not include SSN or DOB. **Divisions-** Bowling Green, Louisville, Owensboro, Paducah.

Kentucky Western District- US Bankruptcy Court www.kywb.uscourts.gov
VCIS: 800-263-9385, 502-627-5660. Search results include last 4 SSN digits only. **Location-** Louisville.

Louisiana Eastern District- US District Court www.laed.uscourts.gov
Search results do not include SSN or DOB. Case files sent to archives 6 months after closed. **Location-** New Orleans.

Louisiana Eastern District- US Bankruptcy Court www.laeb.uscourts.gov
VCIS: 504-589-7879. Search results do not include SSN or DOB. **Location-** New Orleans.

Louisiana Middle District- US District Court www.lamd.uscourts.gov
Search results do not include SSN or DOB but pre-2003 crim recs may have DOBs. Case files sent to archives 1 year after closed. **Location-** Baton Rouge.

Louisiana Middle District- US Bankruptcy Court www.lamb.uscourts.gov
VCIS: 225-382-2175. Search results include last 4 SSN digits and address. Almost all closed paper files have been sent to archives. **Location-** Baton Rouge.

Louisiana Western District- US District Court www.lawd.uscourts.gov
Search results do not include SSN or DOB. Cases files now all electronic; never purged. **Divisions-** Alexandria, Lafayette, Lake Charles, Monroe, Shreveport.

Louisiana Western District- US Bankruptcy Court www.lawb.uscourts.gov
VCIS: 800-326-4026, 318-676-4234. Search results include last 4 SSN digits only. Case files sent to archives 5 years after closed. **Divisions-** Alexandria, Lafayette-Opelousas, Lake Charles, Monroe, Shreveport.

Maine- US District Court www.med.uscourts.gov
Search results include partial DOB; no SSN. There is no set date when closed case files sent to archives. **Divisions-** Bangor, Portland.

Maine- US Bankruptcy Court www.meb.uscourts.gov
VCIS: 800-650-7253, 207-780-3755. Search results include last 4 SSN digits only. Case files sent to archives 2 years after closed. **Divisions-** Bangor, Portland.

Maryland Northern District- US District Court www.mdd.uscourts.gov
Search results do not include SSN or DOB. Case files sent to archives 3 years after closed. **Location-** Baltimore.

Maryland Northern District- US Bankruptcy Court www.mdb.uscourts.gov
VCIS: 800-829-0145, 410-962-0733. Search results include name and address only. Case files sent to archives 6 months after closed. **Location-** Baltimore.

Maryland Southern District- US District Court www.mdd.uscourts.gov
Search results do not include SSN or DOB. Case files sent to archives 3 years after closed. **Location-** Greenbelt.

Maryland Southern District- US Bankruptcy Court www.mdb.uscourts.gov
VCIS: 800-829-0145, 410-962-0733. Search results include SSN. Case files sent to archives 6 months after closed. **Location-** Greenbelt.

Massachusetts- US District Court www.mad.uscourts.gov
Search results do not include SSN or DOB. Criminal case files sent to archives 4 years after closed; 3 years for civil. **Divisions-** Boston, Springfield, Worcester.

Massachusetts- US Bankruptcy Court www.mab.uscourts.gov
VCIS: 888-201-3572, 617-565-6025. Search results include SSN last 4 digits only, partial address. Case files sent to archives 6 months after closed. **Divisions-** Boston, Worcester.

Michigan Eastern District- US District Court www.mied.uscourts.gov
Search results do not include SSN or DOB. Closed cases are kept electronically; paper files sent to archives. **Divisions-** Ann Arbor, Bay City, Detroit, Flint.

Michigan Eastern District- US Bankruptcy Court www.mieb.uscourts.gov
VCIS: 877-422-3066. Search results include last 4 SSN digits. Case files sent to archives 2 years after closed. **Divisions-** Bay City, Detroit, Flint.

Michigan Western District- US District Court www.miwd.uscourts.gov
Search results do not include SSN or DOB. Closed electronic cases not purged. **Divisions-** Grand Rapids, Kalamazoo, Lansing, Marquette-Northern.

Michigan Western District- US Bankruptcy Court www.miwb.uscourts.gov
VCIS: 866-729-9098, 616-456-2075. Search results include last 4 SSN digits. Case files sent to archives 1 year after closed. **Divisions-** Grand Rapids, Marquette-Northern.

Minnesota- US District Court www.mnd.uscourts.gov
Search results do not include SSN or DOB. **Divisions-** Duluth, Minneapolis, St Paul.

Minnesota- US Bankruptcy Court www.mnb.uscourts.gov
VCIS: 800-959-9002. Search results include last 4 SSN digits. **Divisions-** Duluth, Fergus Falls, Minneapolis, St Paul.

Mississippi Northern District- US District Court www.msnd.uscourts.gov
Search results do not include SSN or DOB. Civil cases sent to archives 5 years after disposition; 10 years for criminal. **Divisions-** Aberdeen-Eastern, Delta, Greenville, Oxford-Northern.

Mississippi Northern District- US Bankruptcy Court www.msnb.uscourts.gov
VCIS: 800-392-8653, 662-369-8147. Search results include last 4 SSN digits. **Location-** Aberdeen.

Mississippi Southern District- US District Court www.mssd.uscourts.gov
Search results do not include SSN or DOB. **Divisions-** Eastern, Hattiesburg, Jackson, Southern, Western.

Mississippi Southern District- US Bankruptcy Court www.mssb.uscourts.gov
VCIS: 800-601-8859, 601-965-6106. Search results include last 4 SSN digits only; court can also verify using address. **Divisions-** Biloxi, Jackson.

Missouri Eastern District- US District Court www.moed.uscourts.gov
Search results do not include SSN or DOB, but they may verify over phone. Case files sent to archives 4 years after closed. **Divisions-** Cape Girardeau, St Louis.

Missouri Eastern District- US Bankruptcy Court www.moeb.uscourts.gov
VCIS: 888-223-6431, 314-244-4999. Search results include last 4 SSN digits, address. Case files sent to archives 4-5 years after closed. **Location-** St Louis.

Missouri Western District- US District Court www.mow.uscourts.gov
Search results do not include SSN or DOB. Case files sent to archives as deemed necessary. **Divisions-** Jefferson City - Central, Joplin - Southwestern, Kansas City - Western, Springfield-Southern, St Joseph.

Missouri Western District- US Bankruptcy Court www.mow.uscourts.gov
VCIS: 888-205-2527, 816-512-5110. Search results include last 4 SSN digits. **Location-** Kansas City - Western.

Montana- US District Court www.mtd.uscourts.gov
Search results do not include SSN or DOB. Case files sent to archives 4-5 years after closed. **Divisions-** Billings, Butte, Great Falls, Helena, Missoula.

Montana- US Bankruptcy Court www.mtb.uscourts.gov
VCIS: 888-879-0071, 406-782-1060. Search results include last 4 SSN digits. **Location-** Butte.

Nebraska- US District Court www.ned.uscourts.gov
Search results do not include SSN or DOB or gender; Pre-2004 cases may provide some identifiers. Case files sent to archives approx. 1 year after closed. **Divisions-** Lincoln, North Platte, Omaha.

Nebraska- US Bankruptcy Court www.neb.uscourts.gov
VCIS: 800-829-0112, 402-221-3757. Search results include last 4 SSN digits, address. Case files sent to archives 6 months after closed. **Divisions-** Lincoln, North Platte, Omaha.

Nevada- US District Court www.nvd.uscourts.gov
Search results do not include SSN or DOB. **Divisions-** Las Vegas, Reno.

Nevada- US Bankruptcy Court www.nvb.uscourts.gov
VCIS: 800-294-6920, 702-388-6708. Search results include last 4 SSN digits. All cases stored electronically and kept indefinitely. **Divisions-** Las Vegas, Reno.

New Hampshire- US District Court www.nhd.uscourts.gov
Search results do not include SSN or DOB. Paper case files sent to archives 1 years after closed; electronic maintained indefinitely **Location-** Concord.

New Hampshire- US Bankruptcy Court www.nhb.uscourts.gov
VCIS: 800-851-8954, 603-222-2626. Search results include last 4 SSN digits. Case files sent to archives 1 year after closed. **Location-** Manchester.

New Jersey- US District Court www.njd.uscourts.gov
Search: Court will examine identifiers for possible match. Closed case files sent to archives irregularly. **Divisions-** Camden, Newark, Trenton.

New Jersey- US Bankruptcy Court www.njb.uscourts.gov
VCIS: 877-239-2547, 973-645-6044. Search results include last 4 SSN digits. **Divisions-** Camden, Newark, Trenton.

New Mexico- US District Court www.nmcourt.fed.us/web/DCDOCS/dcindex.html
Search results do not include SSN or DOB on civil; older criminal cases may include last 4 SSN digits. Case files sent to archives 6 months after closed. **Location-** Albuquerque.

New Mexico- US Bankruptcy Court
www.nmcourt.fed.us/web/BCDOCS/bcindex.html
VCIS: 888-435-7822, 505-348-2444. Search results include last 4 SSN digits. Case files sent to archives 5 years after closed. **Location-** Albuquerque.

New York Eastern District- US District Court www.nyed.uscourts.gov
Search results do not include SSN or DOB after 2003 **Divisions-** Brooklyn, Central Islip.

New York Eastern District- US Bankruptcy Court www.nyeb.uscourts.gov
VCIS: 800-252-2537, 718-852-5726. Search results do not include SSN or DOB; pre-2003 closed cases may include SSN. Paper closed case files sent to archives 1 year after closed; computer records never purged. **Divisions-** Brooklyn, Central Islip.

New York Northern District- US District Court www.nynd.uscourts.gov
Search results include last 4 SSN digits, also birth year. Results do not include SSN or DOB if case after 2003. Case files sent to archives 1 year after closed. **Divisions-** Albany, Binghamton, Syracuse, Utica.

New York Northern District- US Bankruptcy Court www.nynb.uscourts.gov
VCIS: 800-206-1952. Search results may include SSN. **Divisions-** Albany, Syracuse, Utica.

New York Southern District- US District Court www.nysd.uscourts.gov
Search results do not include SSN or DOB, though DOB may appear on records prior to 2004. Case files sent to archives 5 years after closed (due to construction, closed cases were recently purged.) **Divisions-** New York City, White Plains.

New York Southern District- US Bankruptcy Court www.nysb.uscourts.gov
VCIS: 212-668-2772. Search results include last 4 SSN digits. Case files sent to archives approx. 2 years after closed. **Divisions-** New York, Poughkeepsie, White Plains.

New York Western District- US District Court www.nywd.uscourts.gov
Search results do not include SSN or DOB. Closed electronic cases are not purged. **Divisions-** Buffalo, Rochester.

New York Western District- US Bankruptcy Court www.nywb.uscourts.gov
VCIS: 800-776-9578, 716-551-5311. Search results include last 4 SSN digits. Closed electronic cases not purged. **Divisions-** Buffalo, Rochester.

North Carolina Eastern District- US District Court www.nced.uscourts.gov
Search results do not include SSN or DOB. Civil records retained 2 years. All criminal records after 1979 forwarded to Raleigh. **Divisions-** Eastern, Northern, Southern, Western.

North Carolina Eastern District- US Bankruptcy Court www.nceb.uscourts.gov
VCIS: 888-847-9138, 919-856-4618. Search results include last 4 SSN digits. **Divisions-** Raleigh, Wilson.

North Carolina Middle District- US District Court www.ncmd.uscourts.gov
Search results do not include SSN or DOB, only case numbers and cases found. Closed electronic cases not purged. **Divisions-** Greensboro.

North Carolina Middle District- US Bankruptcy Court www.ncmb.uscourts.gov
VCIS: 888-319-0455, 336-338-4057. Search results include full name and attorney. **Divisions-** Greensboro, Winston-Salem.

North Carolina Western District- US District Court www.ncwd.uscourts.gov
Search results do not include SSN or DOB. Closed cases sent to archives after 5 years. **Divisions-** Asheville, Bryson City, Charlotte, Statesville.

North Carolina Western District- US Bankruptcy Court www.ncwb.uscourts.gov
VCIS: 800-324-5614, 704-350-7509. Search results do not include SSN or DOB. Case files sent to archives upon closing. Cases after 1/1997 are scanned and not retired. **Location-** Charlotte.

North Dakota- US District Court www.ndd.uscourts.gov
Search results do not include SSN or DOB. Records posted after 11/2005 are retained indefinitely. **Divisions-** Bismarck-Southwestern, Fargo-Southeastern, Grand Forks-Northeastern, Minot-Northwestern.

North Dakota- US Bankruptcy Court www.ndb.uscourts.gov
VCIS: 701-297-7166. Search results include last 4 SSN digits. **Location-** Fargo.

Ohio Northern District- US District Court www.ohnd.uscourts.gov
Search results include full name and case number only. Case files sent to archives 5 years after closed. **Divisions-** Akron, Cleveland, Toledo, Youngstown.

Ohio Northern District- US Bankruptcy Court www.ohnb.uscourts.gov
VCIS: 800-898-6899. Search results include SSN. Prior to 1995, closed cases sent to Chicago Records Center; case records now sent to Dayton Records Center every few years. **Divisions-** Akron, Canton, Cleveland, Toledo, Youngstown.

Ohio Southern District- US District Court www.ohsd.uscourts.gov
Search results do not include SSN or DOB. Closed cases sent to archives after 5 years. **Divisions-** Cincinnati, Columbus, Dayton.

Ohio Southern District- US Bankruptcy Court www.ohsb.uscourts.gov
VCIS: 800-726-1004, 937-225-2544. Search results include last 4 SSN digits. Case files sent to archives 6 months after closed. **Divisions-** Cincinnati, Columbus, Dayton.

Oklahoma Eastern District- US District Court www.oked.uscourts.gov
Search results do not include SSN or DOB. Case files sent to archives 3-5 years after closed. **Location-** Muskogee.

Oklahoma Eastern District- US Bankruptcy Court www.okeb.uscourts.gov
VCIS: 877-377-1221, 918-756-8617. Search results include last 4 SSN digits. Closed cases prior to 1998 sent to archives; electronic case held indefinitely. **Divisions-** Okmulgee.

Oklahoma Northern District- US District Court www.oknd.uscourts.gov
Search results do not include SSN or DOB. Case files sent to archives 1 year after closed. **Location-** Tulsa.

Oklahoma Northern District- US Bankruptcy Court www.oknb.uscourts.gov
VCIS: 888-501-6977, 918-699-4001. Search results include last 4 SSN digits only. Closed electronic cases not purged. **Location-** Tulsa.

Oklahoma Western District- US District Court www.okwd.uscourts.gov
Search results do not include SSN or DOB. Closed civil case files sent to archives 5 years after closed, 7 for criminal. **Location-** Oklahoma City.

Oklahoma Western District- US Bankruptcy Court www.okwb.uscourts.gov
VCIS: 800-872-1348, 405-231-4768. Search results include all or partial SSN. Closed cases prior to 1996 have been sent to the archives; newer files available electronically. **Location-** Oklahoma City.

Oregon- US District Court www.ord.uscourts.gov
Search results do not include SSN or DOB. The Documentation index may have DOBs on judgments. Case files sent to archives 3-5 years after closed. **Divisions-** Eugene, Medford, Portland.

Oregon- US Bankruptcy Court www.orb.uscourts.gov
VCIS: 800-726-2227, 503-326-2249. Search results include last 4 SSN digits or DOB; debtor may have chosen to release full SSN. Case files sent to archives irregularly after at least 6 months. **Location-** Eugene, Portland.

Pennsylvania Eastern District- US District Court www.paed.uscourts.gov
Search results do not include SSN or DOB. Closed electronic cases not purged. **Divisions-** Allentown/Reading, Philadelphia.

Pennsylvania Eastern District- US Bankruptcy Court www.paeb.uscourts.gov
VCIS: 215-597-2244. Search results do not include SSN or DOB. Cases sent to archives as early as 6 months after closed. **Divisions-** Philadelphia, Reading.

Pennsylvania Middle District- US District Court www.pamd.uscourts.gov
Search results do not include SSN or DOB. Closed electronic cases not purged. **Divisions-** Harrisburg, Scranton, Williamsport.

Pennsylvania Middle District- US Bankruptcy Court www.pamb.uscourts.gov
VCIS: 877-440-2699. Search results include last 4 SSN digits. Case files sent to archives 6 months after closed. **Divisions-** Harrisburg, Wilkes-Barre.

Pennsylvania Western District- US District Court www.pawd.uscourts.gov
Search results do not include SSN or DOB. Closed electronic cases not purged. **Divisions-** Erie, Johnstown, Pittsburgh.

Pennsylvania Western District- US Bankruptcy Court www.pawb.uscourts.gov
VCIS: 412-355-3210, 866-299-8515. Search results include last 4 SSN digits. Closed cases are sent to archives as storage space fills. **Divisions-** Erie, Pittsburgh.

Puerto Rico- US District Court www.prd.uscourts.gov
Search results do not include SSN or DOB, but judgments may have SSN. Case files sent to archives 1 year after closed.

Puerto Rico- US Bankruptcy Court www.prb.uscourts.gov
Search results include SSN. Cases shipped to Missouri Records Center 3 months after closed.

Rhode Island- US District Court www.rid.uscourts.gov
Search results do not include SSN or DOB. Case files maintained at court 25 years after closed.

Rhode Island- US Bankruptcy Court www.rib.uscourts.gov
VCIS: 800-843-2841, 401-626-3076. Search results include last 4 SSN digits. All closed files on paper have been sent to the archives.

South Carolina- US District Court www.scd.uscourts.gov
Search results do not include SSN or DOB. **Divisions-** Anderson, Beaufort, Charleston, Columbia, Florence, Greenville, Greenwood, Spartanburg.

South Carolina- US Bankruptcy Court www.scb.uscourts.gov
VCIS: 800-669-8767, 803-765-5211. Search results include last 4 SSN digits. Closed case files sent to archives irregularly. **Location-** Columbia.

South Dakota- US District Court www.sdd.uscourts.gov
Search results do not include SSN or DOB. Case files sent to archives 6 months after closed. **Divisions-** Aberdeen, Pierre, Sioux Falls, Western Div - Rapid City.

South Dakota- US Bankruptcy Court www.sdb.uscourts.gov
VCIS: 800-768-6218, 605-357-2422. Search results include partial SSN. Case files are all electronic; never purged. **Divisions-** Pierre, Sioux Falls.

Tennessee Eastern District- US District Court www.tned.uscourts.gov
Search results do not include SSN or DOB. Closed electronic cases not purged. **Divisions-** Chattanooga, Greeneville, Knoxville, Winchester.

Tennessee Eastern District- US Bankruptcy Court www.tneb.uscourts.gov
VCIS: 800-767-1512. Search results include last 4 SSN digits only. Closed records sent to archives 2-3 years after closing. **Divisions-** Northeastern, Northern, Southern.

Tennessee Middle District- US District Court www.tnmd.uscourts.gov
Search results do not include SSN or DOB. Case files sent to archives 1 year after closed. **Divisions-** Columbia, Cookeville, Nashville.

Tennessee Middle District- US Bankruptcy Court   http://www2.tnmb.uscourts.gov
VCIS: 615-736-5584 x4. Search results include last 4 SSN digits. Closed case files sent to archives at variable intervals. **Location-** Nashville.

Tennessee Western District- US District Court   www.tnwd.uscourts.gov
Search results do not include SSN or DOB. **Location-** Jackson, Memphis.

Tennessee Western District- US Bankruptcy Court   www.tnwb.uscourts.gov
VCIS: 888-381-4961, 901-328-3509. Search results include last 4 SSN digits only. Case files sent to archives 3-6 months after closed. **Divisions-** Jackson/Eastern, Memphis/Western.

Texas Eastern District- US District Court   www.txed.uscourts.gov
Search results do not include SSN or DOB. Case files sent to archives 1 year after closed. **Divisions-** Beaumont, Lufkin, Marshall, Sherman, Texarkana, Tyler.

Texas Eastern District- US Bankruptcy Court   www.txeb.uscourts.gov
VCIS: 800-466-1694, 903-590-3251. Search results do not include SSN or DOB; you may call and they may verify. Case files sent to archives 1 year after closed. **Divisions-** Beaumont, Marshall, Plano, Texarkana, Tyler.

Texas Northern District- US District Court   www.txnd.uscourts.gov
Search results do not include SSN or DOB. Closed case files sent to archives yearly. **Divisions-** Abilene, Amarillo, Dallas, Fort Worth, Lubbock, San Angelo, Wichita Falls.

Texas Northern District- US Bankruptcy Court   www.txnb.uscourts.gov
VCIS: 800-886-9008, 214-753-2128. Search results include last 4 SSN digits, address and name. Case files sent to archives 6 months after closed. **Divisions-** Amarillo, Dallas, Fort Worth, Lubbock, Wichita Falls.

Texas Southern District- US District Court   www.txs.uscourts.gov
Search results do not include SSN or DOB. Case files sent to archives 6 months after closed. **Divisions-** Brownsville, Corpus Christi, Galveston, Houston, Laredo, McAllen, Victoria.

Texas Southern District- US Bankruptcy Court   www.txsd.uscourts.gov
VCIS: 800-745-4459, 713-250-5049. Search results include last 4 SSN digits only. Case files sent to archives 6 months after closed. **Divisions-** Corpus Christi, Houston.

Texas Western District- US District Court   www.txwd.uscourts.gov
Search results do not include SSN or DOB. Case files kept a minimum 2 years before sending to archives. **Divisions-** Austin, Del Rio, El Paso, Midland, Pecos, San Antonio, Waco.

Texas Western District- US Bankruptcy Court   www.txwb.uscourts.gov
VCIS: 888-436-7477, 210-472-4023. Search results do not include SSN or DOB; clerk will verify if your SSN is correct. Case files sent to archives 6-8 months after closed. **Divisions-** Austin, El Paso, Midland/Odessa, San Antonio, Waco.

Utah- US District Court   www.utd.uscourts.gov
Search results do not include SSN or DOB; will include case number and date of sentencing. Case files sent to archives 3-4 years after closed.

Utah- US Bankruptcy Court   www.utb.uscourts.gov
VCIS: 800-733-6740, 801-524-3107. Search results include last 4 SSN digits only.

Vermont- US District Court   www.vtd.uscourts.gov
Search results do not include SSN or DOB. Closed electronic cases not purged. **Divisions-** Burlington, Rutland.

Vermont- US Bankruptcy Court   www.vtb.uscourts.gov
VCIS: 800-260-9956, 802-776-2007. Search results include last 4 SSN digits and possibly address. Closed electronic cases not purged. **Location-** Rutland.

Virginia Eastern District- US District Court www.vaed.uscourts.gov
Search results do not include SSN or DOB. Closed electronic cases not purged.
Divisions- Alexandria, Newport News, Norfolk, Richmond.

Virginia Eastern District- US Bankruptcy Court www.vaeb.uscourts.gov
VCIS: 800-326-5879. Search results include last 4 SSN digits. Closed electronic cases not purged. **Divisions-** Alexandria, Newport News, Norfolk, Richmond.

Virginia Western District- US District Court www.vawd.uscourts.gov
Search results may include last 4 SSN digits. Case files sent to archives 1 year after closed.   **Divisions-** Abingdon, Big Stone Gap, Charlottesville, Danville, Harrisonburg, Lynchburg, Roanoke.

Virginia Western District- US Bankruptcy Court www.vawb.uscourts.gov
Search results include last 4 SSN digits. Paper case files sent to archives 2 years after closed. Electronic cases maintained indefinitely.   **Divisions-** Harrisonburg, Lynchburg, Roanoke.

Washington Eastern District- US District Court www.waed.uscourts.gov
Search results do not include SSN or DOB. Case files sent to archives 6 months after closed. **Divisions-** Spokane, Yakima.

Washington Eastern District- US Bankruptcy Court www.waeb.uscourts.gov
VCIS: 509-353-2404. Search results do not include SSN or DOB. **Location-** Spokane.

Washington Western District- US District Court www.wawd.uscourts.gov
Search: Most results do not include SSN or DOB. Case files sent to archives 2-3 years after closed. **Divisions-** Seattle, Tacoma.

Washington Western District- US Bankruptcy Court www.wawb.uscourts.gov
VCIS: 888-409-4662, 206-370-5285. Search results include last 4 SSN digits. Closed paper files sent to archives; electronic cases maintained indefinitely. **Divisions-** Seattle, Tacoma.

West Virginia Northern District- US District Court www.wvnd.uscourts.gov
Search results do not include SSN or DOB. Civil cases sent to archives every 5 years; every 10 years for criminal. **Divisions-** Clarksburg, Elkins, Martinsburg, Wheeling.

West Virginia Northern District- US Bankruptcy Court www.wvnb.uscourts.gov
VCIS: 800-809-3028, 304-233-7318. Search results include last 4 SSN digits. Case files sent to archives 2 years after closed. **Location-** Wheeling.

West Virginia Southern District- US District Court www.wvsd.uscourts.gov
Search results do not include SSN or DOB. Paper case files sent to archives as deemed necessary.   **Divisions-** Beckley, Bluefield, Charleston, Huntington, Parkersburg.

West Virginia Southern District- US Bankruptcy Court www.wvsd.uscourts.gov
VCIS: 304-347-5680. Search results include last 4 SSN digits. Closed electronic cases not purged. **Location-** Charleston.

Wisconsin Eastern District- US District Court www.wied.uscourts.gov
Search results include last 4 SSN digits, also birth year. Case files sent to archives 3 years after closed. **Location-** Milwaukee.

Wisconsin Eastern District- US Bankruptcy Court www.wieb.uscourts.gov
VCIS: 877-781-7277, 414-297-3582. Search results include full SSN. Case files sent to archives once 100-150 boxes are filled. **Location-** Milwaukee.

Wisconsin Western District- US District Court www.wiwd.uscourts.gov
Search results do not include SSN or DOB. Closed electronic cases not purged.
Location- Madison.

Wisconsin Western District- US Bankruptcy Court
www.wiw.uscourts.gov/bankruptcy
> VCIS: 800-743-8247, 608-264-5035. Search results include last 4 SSN digits. **Divisions-** Eau Claire, Madison.

Wyoming- US District Court www.wyd.uscourts.gov
> Search results do not include SSN or DOB. Case files sent to archives when the right number of boxes filled. **Location-** Cheyenne.

Wyoming- US Bankruptcy Court www.wyb.uscourts.gov
> VCIS: 888-804-5537, 307-433-2238. Search results include last 4 SSN digits only. Case files sent to archives 1 year after closed. **Location-** Cheyenne.

Other Federal Courts

U.S. Court of Federal Claims

The Court of Federal Claims is authorized to hear primarily money claims in regard to federal statutes, executive regulations, the Constitution, or contracts, expressed- or implied-in-fact, with the United States. Approximately a quarter of the cases involve complex factual and statutory construction issues in tax law. About a third of the cases involve government contracts. Cases involving environmental and natural resource issues make up about 10 percent of the caseload. Another significant category of cases involve civilian and military pay questions. In addition, the Court hears intellectual property, Indian Tribe, and various statutory claims against the United States by individuals, domestic and foreign corporations, states and localities, Indian Tribes and Nations, and foreign nationals and governments.

Direct questions to the U.S. Court of Federal Claims, Attention: Clerks Office, 717 Madison Place, NW, Washington, DC 20005, or call 202-357-6400.

www.uscfc.uscourts.gov and www.uscfc.uscourts.gov/opinions.htm

U.S. Tax Court

The jurisdiction of the U.S. Tax Court includes the authority to hear tax disputes concerning notices of deficiency, notices of transferee liability, certain types of declaratory judgment, readjustment and adjustment of partnership items, review of the failure to abate interest, administrative costs, worker classification, relief from joint and several liability on a joint return, and review of certain collection actions. For a less formal and speedier disposition in certain tax disputes involving $50,000 or less, taxpayers may choose to have the case conducted under the Court's simplified small tax case procedure. However, these decisions may not be appealed.

Docket information is available for cases filed on or after May 1, 1986. Call Docket Information at 202-521-4650. For case records, call Records and Reproduction at 202-521-4688.

Direct questions to United States Tax Court, 400 Second Street, NW, Washington, DC 20217. The main number is 202-521-0700. Dockets and opinions also may be searched on the web at www.ustaxcourt.gov.

U.S. Court of International Trade

The U.S. Court of International Trade oversees disputes within the international trade community including individuals, foreign and domestic manufacturers, consumer groups, trade associations, labor unions, concerned citizens, and other nations.

The geographical jurisdiction of the United States Court of International Trade extends throughout the U.S. The court does hear cases anywhere in the nation and is also authorized to hold hearings in foreign countries.

Appeals from final decisions of the court may be taken to the United States Court of Appeals for the Federal Circuit and, ultimately, to the Supreme Court of the United States.

The Court provides online access to opinions and judgments. From 1999-2006, the Court published only the slip opinions online. Starting January 1, 2007, the online postings contain both the slip opinion and judgment in each case. Registered users of the CM/ECF system have the ability to open a case as of October 11, 2006.

The Court's Administrative Office is located at One Federal Plaza, New York, New York 10278-0001, or call 212-264-2800.

www.cit.uscourts.gov

Searching Liens and Recorded Documents

Recorded documents and liens notices are two of the most widely found categories of public records. Documents are recorded for a number of reasons. Once properly recorded, they can show proof of ownership (deed to your house) or show when an asset is used as collateral for a loan (mortgage on your house). The benefits of having public recorded documents are many. Real estate records are public so that everyone can know who owns what property. Liens on real estate must be public so potential lenders and buyers know all the facts about the chain of title. Finding recorded documents and lien notices is a necessity to making informed business-related decisions and these documents lead to a virtual treasure trove of data. Private investigators and attorneys research liens and recorded documents when doing an **Asset Lien** search. Since liens are part of an information trail in the public record, finding liens will lead to finding assets or to other liens which could lead to other assets.

The function of searching the many types of liens and recorded documents found in the U.S. public record is truly an art because—

- There are over 4,000 locations in the U.S. where one may file a lien notice or record a document.
- There are no standard rules or practices among these locations.

The 4,000+ locations where liens and recorded documents are found can be at any of three levels: local municipality, county or parish, or state agency. The level at which to file a form of notice, like a tax lien, varies from one state to another. The jurisdictions maintain indexes to these recorded documents. Some government agencies maintain an overall index of all recorded documents and liens notices, while others maintain a series of separate indices within the same office. In other words, a researcher must know the particular index to search for a particular record. A good searcher knows to search ALL the indices.

There are many types of records covered in the chapter, but the publicly recorded documents most often accessed are generally related to:

- Real Estate Transactions
- Uniform Commercial Code Filings
- Tax Liens
- Tax Assessor Records

That does not imply that other records such as vital records, voter registration rolls, and fictitious names are inconsequential – far from it. But this chapter is organized by the four key records mentioned above.

The Difference Between Personal Property and Real Property

An important first distinction to know when searching recorded public records is the difference between personal property and real property. This is because each of these categories requires different documents or forms that need to be recorded or filed when loans are made or other liens are incurred. Generally, documents related to real property are recorded in different locations from personal property records.

Personal property includes items such as bank accounts, vehicles, jewelry, computers, etc. It can be business collateral or 'consumer goods.' Often when personal property is given as collateral, the lender will secure the loan by filing a Uniform Commercial Code (UCC) financing statement on the asset.

Real property involves real estate related assets such as homes, apartment building, land, etc. A mortgage is an example of a recorded document that secures the associated loan to finance real property.

Types of Liens and Security Interests

Liens - With or Without Consent

A lien is a lawful claim or right against property or funds for payment of a debt or for services rendered. There are **two types of liens** that are recorded: those **with consent (voluntary) or without consent (involuntary).**

Examples of liens placed with the consent of an asset holder include mortgages, loans on car and vessels, and Uniform Commercial Code filings on business assets such as equipment or accounts receivable.

Examples of liens placed without the consent of an asset holder include federal and state tax liens, mechanic's liens, and liens filed on assets as the result of judgments issued by courts.

About Judgments

When a judgment is rendered in court, the winning party usually files and records a lien notice (called an abstract of judgment in many states) against real estate owned by the defendant or party against whom the judgment is given. Sometimes judgments can be used to garnish wages or can be placed on bank accounts.

Judgments can be searched at the local or county level usually in the same index as real estate records. Many times judgments are bought and sold as commodities. An Assignment of Judgment is the transfer of the title and interest in a judgment from one person to another person.

Types of Real Estate Recorded Documents

There many types of lien notices and recorded documents related to real estate files. Below are common names for documents that a public record researcher may find when searching real estate records. This list is certainly not all inclusive; there are many, many more. Also keep in mind that name variations will occur from state to state.

Deed of Trust or Mortgage of Deed of Trust Generally a mortgage that secures a debt, and names three parties - the borrower (trustor), the beneficiary (lender), and the trustee who holds title to real property under the terms of a deed of trust.

Bill of Sale A Bill of Sale will be recorded to show the transfer of most any kind of personal property.

Assignment of Deed of Trust A transfer or sale of a Deed of Trust from the current lender (beneficiary) to a new beneficiary.

Abstract of Judgment A court issued money judgment to secure payment to the creditor, usually creates a general lien on real property of the judgment debtor.

Declaration of Homestead A document recorded by either a homeowner or head of household on their primary residence to protect his home from forced sale in satisfaction of certain types of creditors' claims.

Mechanic's Lien A document recorded to create a lien in favor of persons contributing labor, material, supplies, etc., to a work of improvement upon real property.

Notice of Default A notice to show that the borrower under a mortgage or deed of trust is behind in payments.

Notice of Lis Pendens A notice that litigation is pending in court which may affect the title of the real estate involved.

Notice of Trustee's Sale This document is recorded to notify the public of pending the foreclosure sale by the trust for non-payment or non-performance of the conditions of the deed of trust.

Power of Attorney This document delegates the authority of an entity to an agent (attorney-in-fact) to allow this agent to act behalf of the entity in a designated capacity.

Quitclaim Deed A form of deed that conveys or releases any interest that the grantor may have acquired in real property. Many times this type of deed is issued without title insurance.

Reconveyance   The instrument releases the loan that was a lien against real property. Can also be called a satisfaction of the loan or a release of lien or a release of mortgage.

Satisfaction of Mortgage   Release of the loan that was a lien against real property. This document may also be called a release of mortgage.

Subordination Agreement   This document is recorded when a current lender agrees to makes their encumbrance deed of trust beneath or junior to another loan. These loans are sometimes called seconds.

Trustee Deed in Lieu of Foreclosure   Document indicates the transfer of real property from the defaulting borrower to the beneficiary (lender) in lieu of foreclosure.

Trustee's Deed   Deed given by the trustee when the real property is sold under the power of sale in a deed of trust in a foreclosure proceeding.

Writ or Notice of Levy   A document to notify a party served with writ of execution that specific property is being taken to satisfy a debt.

The Search Location Problem

Keeping variations in state laws and filing locations straight is a major challenge to the professional public record searching specialist. Where to search for recorded documents and property liens can be a perplexing puzzle. Just because a mailing address is Schenectady NY doesn't mean the property is located in Schenectady County. The property could be physically located in neighboring Albany County. The fact is over 8,000 of the 45,000 or so ZIP Codes cross county lines. Having access to an enhanced ZIP Code/place name/county locator product is a must. Finding involuntary liens—such as federal and state tax liens—and UCC filings can be even harder.

So, unless you know exactly where the real or personal property is located, and you are certain that everyone else who has filed or recorded liens also knows where to go, you may have a problem. You may have to search more than one county, town, city (or even state) to find the property or liens you need to know about. But knowing about the *County Rule* helps.

The County Rule

In most states, transactions are recorded at one designated recording office in the county where the property is located. But the key word in the last sentence is *most*. One of the most important searching tips to have in hand when searching for liens and recorded documents is the **County Rule**.

Below is an article written by Mr. Carl Ernst of Ernst Publishing.[13] We sincerely thank Mr. Ernst for allowing us to reproduce the article.

The County Rule

By Ernst Publishing

Where to search for recorded documents usually isn't a difficult problem to overcome in everyday practice. In most states, these transactions are recorded at one designated recording office in the county where the property is located.

We call this the "County Rule." It applies to types of public records such as real estate recordings, tax liens, Uniform Commercial Code (UCC) filings, vital records, and voter registration records. However, as with most government rules, there are a variety of exceptions which are summarized here.

The Exceptions

The five categories of exceptions to the County Rule (or Parish Rule, if searching in Louisiana) are listed below [**Editor's Note: details for each state are listed in the State Profiles Section which follows.**]—

1. Special Recording Districts (AK, HI)

2. Multiple Recording Offices (AL, AR, IA, KY, ME, MA, MS, TN)

3. Independent Cities (MD, MO, NV, VA)

4. Recording at the Municipal Level (CT, RI, VT)

5. Identical Names—Different Place
   (CT, IL, MA, NE, NH, PA, RI, VT, VA)

The Personal Property Problem and the Fifth Exception

The real estate recording system in the US is self-auditing to the extent that you generally cannot record a document in the wrong recording office. However, many documents are rejected for recording because they are submitted to the wrong recording office. There are a number of reasons why this occurs, one of which is the overlap of filing locations for real estate and UCC.

---

[13] Ernst Publishing publishes two extensive industry manuals - *The UCC Filing Guide* and *The Real Estate Recording Guide*. Visit www.ernstpublishing.com for more information.

Finding the right location of a related UCC filing is a different and much more difficult problem from finding a real estate recording. In the majority of states, the usual place to file a UCC financing statement is at the Secretary of States office—these are called central filing states. In the dual and local filing states, the place to file, in addition to the central filing office, is usually at the same office where your real estate documents are recorded. However, where there are identical place names referring to two different places, it becomes quite confusing, so hence, the fifth exemption.

Searching Real Estate Records

Every local entity (i.e. county, parish or town recorder of Deeds) records documents that transfer or encumber title. Examples of these documents include deeds, deeds of trust, liens, mortgages, and releases of liens. A list of typical documents is shown later in this chapter. As with court records, the recording office maintains an index and file copies. Documents are recorded by date and include a recording file number. Although many of the searching tips found in the *Searching State and Local Court Records* chapter are also applicable here, there are specific searching tips that will enhance any record search for real estate records.

Learn How to Use the Local Index & Record Systems

To perform a name search or a property search, the first step is to understand how the index works. About half of the recording offices in the U.S. use one index for all recorded documents, the rest use multiple indices. Each index may be organized on a yearly basis or a certain number of years, perhaps based on the media type. Indices may be kept in books (mostly older records), card files, microfiche, microfilm, or be computerized. Generally the index is alphabetized using the last names of Grantors (the party transferring title) AND Grantees (the recipients of title). Thus, one may search for debtors or lenders. The index listing generally includes the date of transfer, and cross-references to the book and page or document number where a copy of the document was recorded and can be examined. This is a key instrument in tracking a chain of title.

More than 50% of the recording offices will *not* perform a name search for you. Therefore you must come in and perform the search yourself or hire someone to search for you. Most recording offices offer public access terminals that permit a search of the index. But nearly 25% of the recording offices do not have a computerized index, so a hand search of the available index(es) must be performed.

The Grantor-Grantee Index

Perhaps the most commonly used term to describe an index of recorded documents at a county/parish/city/town recorder's office is the **Grantor-Granter Index**.

The **Grantor** is the party that is a **transferring** title or some type of interest that involves a recording. The **Grantee** is the party that is the **recipient** of the title, interest or document. For example, if you purchase or re-finance real estate and borrow money from a bank, an instrument called a mortgage or deed of trust is generally involved. You, the borrower, are the Grantor since you giving a lien on the property to the bank. The bank is recorded as the Grantee since it is the recipient of the interest in the property as collateral for the loan. Sometimes the Grantor-Grantee Index is known as the **Forward-Reverse** or **Direct-Indirect** Index.

Below is a useful table that shows who is the grantor and the grantee based on the type of document that is recorded. The table was provided by Dallas Record and Abstract Service, courtesy of Perry McDaniel ... Thank you!

Instrument	Who's Who: Grantor/Grantee
Deed	Grantor/Direct – Seller Grantee/Indirect - Buyer
Deed of Trust	Grantor/Direct – Borrower Grantee/Indirect – Lender
Mechanics Lien	Grantor/Direct – Borrower Grantee/Indirect – Lender or Contractor
Abstract of Judgment	Grantor/Direct – Plaintiff Grantee/Indirect – Defendant
State Tax Lien	Grantor/Direct – State of XX Grantee/Indirect – Tax Payer
Federal Tax Lien	Grantor/Direct – Tax Payer Grantee/Indirect – IRS
Release of State Tax Lien	Grantor/Direct – State of XX Grantee/Indirect – Tax Payer
Release of Federal Tax Lien	Grantor/Direct – IRS Grantee/Indirect – Tax Payer
Release of Judgment	Grantor/Direct – Plaintiff Grantee/Indirect - Defendant
Release of Deed of Trust or Mechanics Lien	Grantor/Direct – Lender Grantee/Indirect – Borrower
Affidavit of Heirship	Grantor/Direct – Affiant Grantee/Indirect – Deceased Person

Understand the Search Requirements

As you can imagine, it is important to know the fields that you can search by, and the variances or wild card terms the office provides. Ask the clerk how to differentiate between a William or Bill, Debra or

Deborah, etc. Does each name require a separate search? Can you use Initials? What personal identifiers can you search by, i.e.: DOB, year in DOB, middle initial, sex?

The article below presents useful hands-on tips to keep in mind when doing name searches from an index. The article was written by William C. Asher, a licensed Texas private investigator and agency owner.[14] Many thanks to Mr. Asher for allowing us to reprint his words of wisdom.

Tips from a Professional Searcher

By William C. Asher

- The search algorithms to use will vary quite a bit depending on the system. Start with a broad search, then narrow the search. Be careful not to be overly restrictive. Sometimes you must assume the system is weak or shot full of holes and you will have to look for work-arounds.

- Searching with variant names is important. For example, if the subject's name is Kermit T. Frog, also search using Kermit Frog, Kermie Frog, K.T. Frog, T.K. Frog, T. Frog, etc. In other words, search using all the variants. Other classic variant names include John vs. Jack, William vs. Bill vs. Wm, and Robert vs. Bob, among others.

- A number of government databases have weird proprietary search software that can do some strange things. So, often it is wise to start the search on Kermit T. Frog use "J." Frog to start. Starting with the letter "J" will at some point give you a full listing of all items starting with "K" Frog to appear on the screen or index. Then you can view all the variant names that might be applicable.

- Always double check your search. Believe it or not, some computers can give different results at different times for the same search parameters. This is often caused by a minor power dip or surge which can sometimes throw off a different set of results, which can happen for a variety of reasons. Examples include when new equipment is brought into an older building or offices are consolidated and the electrical systems are insufficient.

- If you are searching index cards a tip is to search several cards on either side of the name you are searching. This is because cards get put

---

[14] Mr. Asher is a writer and editor for multiple investigative journals, and is also active in federal legislative matters for the industry. He can be reached at washer@ticnet.com.

back incorrectly and sometimes are misfiled just a few cards on either side of where they should be. You will find that searcher paid by the hour, rather than paid by the name tends to do more of a thorough job by searching "around" the location.

The bottom line is the fact that computers and hand searches can miss "stuff," and there are techniques to help catch these misses.

Know the Fees

As with the courts, most recording offices charge fees for performing a search, providing copies, or certifying document copies.

Sometimes there is a difference in the copy fee depending if the office makes the copy or if a self-serve machine is used. Be sure to find out the fee structure if you must hire someone to search and/or pull copies for you. For example, the self-serve copy fee may be $.25 per page, but should government personnel make the copy, the fee may $1.00 or more per page.

Look at the Tax Assessor and Tax Collector Records

There is a county, parish, or local municipality official, usually called the Assessor, who is required by law to determine the value of all taxable property in a jurisdiction for property taxing purposes. This official publishes assessment reports and provides it to property owners with valuation notices. The official may also be known as the Auditor or Property Valuator.

Usually tax assessment records are searchable by name or by legal description (plat number), and not necessarily by the address. These records are very public, very valuable, and often available online.

Records of unpaid property taxes can be found in the office of the treasurer or tax collector.

There are several good web pages that offer links lists to Tax Assessor offices. The site at www.pulawski.net is very easy to use, and indicates when pages are last updated. Another excellent site specializing in listing tax assessors and recorder offices with web pages offering record searching capabilities is http://publicrecords.netronline.com.

Searching Online For Real Estate Records

Many county, city, and parish government jurisdictions provide online access to indices of real estate records and recorded documents. Most sites are free if viewing an index, but an increasing number of government agencies will charge a fee to view or print an image or copy of a page within the file.

As with other types of public records, many investigators and researchers use these online resources as a pre-search or preliminary search, especially if dealing with an uncommon name.

Keep in mind there are a number of private companies who compile and maintain these records. Some offer free searching on the web as a way to drive users to their web pages. Some vendors offer bulk data for resale. Vendors are a very comprehensive resource to obtain electronic records.

In the state summaries pages at the end of this chapter you will see a number of online resources who provide wide geographic coverage. To find the individual county, parish, or municipal coverage sites with free access, visit www.brbpub.com or http://publicrecords.netronline.com.

There are a number of web pages that information on the property of specific homes (addresses). Check www.zillow.com and www.trulia.com. A site highly recommended by Michele Stuart is RealPedia found at www.billdoll.com/dir/r/biz/re/re.html. For interactive map information, check out http://nationalmap.gov.

Real Estate Records and the County Rule

Remember the earlier article on the County Rule? The second, third and fourth County Rules are very important to observe when searching real estate records in the states listed below.

- **Multiple Recording Offices (AL, AR, IA, KY, LA, ME, MA, MS, TN)**
  In these states, some counties have more than one recording office.

- **Independent cities (MD, MO, NV, VA)**
  Independent cities should be treated just as if they are counties. For example, St Louis City and St. Louis County are separate jurisdictions with separate sets of data.

- **Recording at municipal level of government (CT, RI, VT)**
  In these states, the recording jurisdiction is the town, not the county. The county clerk's office does not record documents.

Uniform Commercial Code and Tax Lien Records

Uniform Commercial Code

As mentioned above, Uniform Commercial Code (UCC) filings are to personal property what mortgages are to real estate property. UCCs indicate where personal property, usually business related, is placed as collateral. A UCC recording allows potential lenders to be notified that certain assets of a debtor are already pledged to secure a loan or lease. Therefore, examining UCC filings is an excellent way to find many types of assets, security interests, and financiers.

Tax Liens

Tax liens are non-consensual liens placed by a government agency for non-payment of taxes. The federal government and every state have some sort of taxes, such as sales, income, withholding, unemployment, and/or personal property. When these taxes go unpaid, the appropriate state agency can file a lien on the real or personal property of the subject.

Tax liens filed against individuals are frequently maintained at separate locations from those liens filed against businesses. For example, a large number of states require liens filed against businesses to be filed at a central state location (i.e., Secretary of State's office) and liens against individuals to be filed at the county level (i.e., Recorder, Registrar of Deeds, Clerk of Court, etc.).

UCC and Tax Lien Searching Tips

Tax liens and UCC recordings are filed, according to state law, either at the state or local (county, town, parish) level. Normally, the state agency that maintains UCCs records also maintains the tax liens filed at the state level but this is not true in all states.

The same tips discussed for searching real estate records are applicable here. However, there are some important points to keep in mind about UCC and tax liens. Most state agencies will not perform name searches by phone but offer search services online, by mail, and on-site. Most agencies prefer that searchers use online access when available. All state jurisdictions (except Delaware) offer extensive online search capabilities to their indices and sometimes even to images. A state table of online access sites is presented at the end of this chapter.

Where to Search for Tax Liens

Liens on a company may not all be filed in the same location. A federal tax lien will not necessarily be filed (recorded) at the same location/jurisdiction as a state tax lien. Plus there can be different filing locations when these liens are filed against individuals versus filed against businesses. These variances are shown in the *Recording Offices Summaries* section later in this chapter. In general, state tax liens on personal property will be found where UCCs are filed and tax liens on real property will be found where real property deeds are recorded, with few exceptions.

Unsatisfied state and federal tax liens may be renewed if prescribed by individual state statutes. However, once satisfied, the time the record will remain in the repository before removal varies by jurisdiction. Many states will show a release of lien filing rather than deleting the original recording of the lien.

Where to Search for UCC

The place to file against individuals is the state where the person resides. Most UCC filings against businesses are found at the state where a business is organized, not where the collateral or chief executive offices are located. Therefore, you will need to know where a company is organized in order to know where to find recent UCC filings against it. However federal tax liens are still generally filed where the chief executive office is located.

The location to search UCC records changed dramatically in many states with the enactment of Revised Article 9 (see below).

Online Searching of UCC Records

Delaware is the only state that does not offer online access to an index of UCC records, except through certain contracted firms. South Carolina offers access, but only to records filed prior to 10/27/2003. Most state UCC websites provide a free search of the index. A few will permit free access to images, but most states charge a fee to access the full records, which usually involves a subscription service and registration, login, and password.

A number of private companies compile their own proprietary database of UCC and tax lien records or offer real time gateway services. Vendors are a very comprehensive resource to obtain electronic records over multiple jurisdictions.

The table at the end of the chapter gives the web address for each state's central repository. Also, for specific links and updated information, visit the free public record searching sites found at www.brbpub.com.

Affect of Revised Article 9

A significant change in UCC filing that took effect in most states in July 2001 made significant changes about where to find UCC filings. Prior to that date UCC documents were recorded either at a centralized state agency or at a local recording office. At the time, there were over 4,200 locations in the U.S. that recorded UCCs. Revised Article 9 of the Code mandated effective July 2001 that all UCC documents were to be filed and recorded at a state level agency with the exception of certain real estate filings such as farm-related real estate (see Searching Real Estate Related UCC Collateral to follow).

Until June 30, 2001, liens on certain types of companies required dual filing (must file at BOTH locations) in some states, and records could be searched at BOTH locations. As of July 1, 2001, UCC filings other than those that go into real estate records were no longer filed at the local filing offices. According to the UCC Filing Guide (see www.ernstpublishing.com) now less than 3% of filings are done at the local level.

Although there are significant variations among state statutes, the state level is now the best starting place to uncover liens filed against an individual or business, but it is not the only place to search. Strict due diligence may require a local search also, depending on the state, how many years back you wish to search, and the type of collateral. The best technique is to check both locales of records.

General UCC Search Rules

As a result of Revised Article 9, the general rules for searching of UCC records are as follows:

- Except in former local filing states, a search at the state level is adequate to locate all legally valid UCC records on a subject.
- Credit due diligence searching requires use of flexible search logic provided either by the state agency or private database vendors.
- Mortgage record searches will include any real estate related UCC filings.

Searching Real Estate Related UCC Collateral

A specific purpose of lien statutes under both the UCC and real estate laws is to put a buyer or potential secured creditor on notice that someone has a prior security interest in real or personal property.

One problem is that certain types of property have the characteristics of both real and personal property. In those instances, it is necessary to have a way to provide lien notice to two different categories of interested parties: those who deal with the real estate aspect of the property and those who deal with the "personal" aspect of the property. The solution is addressed by UCC filings on real estate.

In general, the definition of real estate related UCC collateral is any property that in one form is attached to land, but that in another form is not attached. For the sake of simplicity, we can define the characteristics of two broad types of property that meet this definition:

1. **Property that is initially attached to real property, but then is separated.**
Three specific types of collateral have this characteristic: *minerals* (including oil and gas), *timber*, and *crops*. These things are grown on or extracted from land. While they are on or in the ground they are thought of as real property, but once they are harvested or extracted they become personal property. Some states have a separate central filing system for crops.

2. **Property that is initially personal property, but then is attached to land, is generally called fixtures.**
Equipment such as telephone systems or heavy industrial equipment permanently affixed to a building are examples of

fixtures. It is important to realize that what is a fixture, like beauty, is in the eye of the beholder, since it is a somewhat vague definition.

UCC financing statements applicable to real estate related collateral must be filed where real estate and mortgage records are kept, which is generally at the county level — except in Connecticut, Rhode Island, and Vermont where the Town/City Clerk maintains these records.

The titles of the local officials who maintain these records for each state are indicated in the Recording Office Summaries by State section.

Search tip: Watch For the Odd Location

Do not be surprised if a search for liens and UCCs turns up an odd lien in a state where your subject is not located. A big company, say, based in Phoenix might show a tax lien in Utah. This should be followed up on because it could mean there is a second location for that company.

Regardless of the state, a search of county records may still be revealing even if you would normally search only at the state level based on the state's filing characteristics.

Other Types of Recorded Documents

There are numerous types of documents that can be recorded and are not related to real estate or personal property. Many of these documents are found at the same recording office that records real estate liens, and often times they appear in the same index. Mentioned below are several significant types.

Fictitious Names or Assumed Names

If a person operates a business not organized as a corporation, partnership, LLC, etc., under a name other his own, then it has a fictitious name. For example if Joe Cool is doing business as Costabunch General Store, that business name must be registered. Depending on the state, this registration can take place at municipal, county or state. A fictitious name is also known as a DBA – meaning **D**oing **B**usiness **A**s.

Forcible Detainer

A *Forcible Detainer* is a landlord's lien against a tenant's property for unpaid rent or damages. Sometimes the document is filed to essentially 'give notice.' If the tenant does not comply within a designated time period, the landlord can forcibly move the tenant's belongings off the property, usually with the assistance of local law enforcement.

Searching for evidence of a Forcible Detainer is part of the tenant screening process (see the *Tenant Screening* section in the *Searching A thru Z* chapter).

Vital Records

Births, deaths, marriages, and divorces may be recorded at the local level or state level, with copies of the documents found at both the state and local agencies. See *Vital Records* in the *Searching A thru Z* chapter for more.

Wills

Many people record their Last Will and Testament at the local recorder's office. Some people confuse a probate court with this function. A probate court is not a recording office, but has records concerning decedents which include their will (if any) and a listing of assets.

Recording Office Summaries – By State

(Includes Information on Assessor Data)

Alabama

How Organized and Location Anomalies—67 counties, 71 recording offices. The recording officer is the Judge of the Probate Court. Property tax records are located at the Assessor's Office. **Four counties have two recording offices** - Barbour, Coffee, Jefferson, and St. Clair. **Record Searching Tips**—Most counties do not perform real estate searches. Pre-Article 9 UCCs were filed with the Secretary of State. Only one-third of counties will perform UCC searches on real estate related records. Federal and state tax liens on personal property of businesses are filed with the Secretary of State. Other federal and state tax liens are filed with the County Judge of the Probate Court.

There is no statewide system for recorded documents and tax assessor data but a limited number of counties offer free online access. The Secretary of State's Lands and Trademarks Division offers free access to county-by-county tract books that reflect the original ownership of Alabama lands, see www.sos.state.al.us/GovtRecords/Land.aspx

Alaska

How Organized and Location Anomalies—The 23 Alaskan counties are called boroughs. However, real estate recording is per a system established at the time of the Gold Rush (1893-1916) with 34 Recording Districts. Some of the Districts are identical in geography to boroughs such as the Aleutian Islands, but other boroughs and districts overlap. Therefore, you need to know which recording district any given town or city is located in. A helpful Alaska government website www.dnr.state.ak.us/recorders/findYourDistrict.htm

Only twelve boroughs and thirteen cites levy a property tax, handled by the Assessor.

Record Searching Tips—Most Districts do not perform real estate names searches. UCC financing statements are filed at the Department of Natural Resources, except for real estate related collateral filed with the District Recorder. All state and federal tax liens are filed with the District Recorder, but they will perform separate tax lien name searches.

Online access to the state recorder's office (www.recorder.alaska.gov) database from the Dept. of Natural Resources is free at www.dnr.state.ak.us/ssd/recoff/search.cfm. This includes property data, liens, deeds, and more. Images go back to June, 2001; index to 2000. Also, a DNR "land records" database is searchable at http://plats.landrecords.info/. About ½ of Alaska's boroughs and cites have local assessor records online.

Arizona

How Organized and Location Anomalies—15 counties, 16 recording offices. The Navajo Nation Recorder is the 16th office and covers northern areas of Apache County and Navajo County. The recording officer is the County Recorder. Recordings are usually placed in a Grantor/Grantee index. Property tax records are located at the Assessor's Office. Arizona observes Mountain Time and does not change to Daylight Savings Time.

Record Searching Tips—Counties do not perform real estate searches. UCC financing statements are filed at the Secretary of State except for real estate related collateral filed with the County Recorder. Most counties will perform these UCC searches. Federal and state tax liens on personal property of businesses are filed with the Secretary of State. Federal and state tax liens on individuals are filed with the County Recorder. Several counties will do a separate tax lien search.

Nearly every county assessor offers online access.

Arkansas

How Organized and Location Anomalies—75 counties, 85 recording offices. The recording officer is the Clerk of Circuit Court who is Ex Officio Recorder.

Ten counties have two recording offices - Arkansas, Carroll, Clay, Craighead, Franklin, Logan, Mississippi, Prairie, Sebastian, and Yell.

Record Searching Tips—Most counties do not perform real estate searches. UCC financing statements are filed at the Secretary of State since 07/2001. Prior records and all real estate related collateral were filed with the County Circuit Clerk. However, few counties will perform these UCC searches. Federal tax liens on personal property of businesses are filed with the Secretary of State. Other federal and all state tax liens are filed with the Circuit Clerk. Many counties will perform separate tax lien searches.

There is no statewide access to assessor information; however, all counties cooperate with at least one commercial vendor. Check out www.arcountydata.com and www.actdatascout.com.

California

How Organized and Location Anomalies—58 counties, 58 recording offices. The recording officer is the County Recorder. Recordings are usually located in a Grantor/Grantee or General Index.

Record Searching Tips—Most California counties do not perform real estate name searches. UCC financing statements are filed at the Secretary of State except for real estate related collateral filed with the County Recorder. Few counties will perform these UCC searches. Federal and state tax liens on personal property of businesses are filed with the Secretary of State. Other federal and state tax liens are filed with the County Recorder, and state tax liens on individuals can be found at both the Secretary of State and county. Some counties will perform separate tax lien searches; fees vary.

A number of counties offer online access to assessor and real estate information. The Assessor system in Los Angeles County has an online commercial subscription system.

Colorado

How Organized and Location Anomalies—63 counties, 63 recording offices. The recording officer is the County Clerk and Recorder. Tax records are located in the Assessor's Office.

November 15, 2001, 'Broomfield City and County' came into existence, derived from portions of Adams, Boulder, Jefferson and Weld counties. To determine if an address is in Broomfield County, you may parcel search by address at the Broomfield County Assessor search site at www.co.broomfield.co.us/centralrecords/assessor.shtml or you may search www.broomfield.org/maps/IMS.shtml

Record Searching Tips—Counties do not perform real estate searches. UCC financing statements are filed at the state level except for real estate related collateral filed with the County Clerk and Recorder. Prior to July, 1996, personal property UCCs could be filed at the County Recorder OR at the state level. Nearly all counties perform UCC searches. Federal and some state tax liens on personal property are filed with the Secretary of State. However, some federal and state tax liens are filed with the County Clerk and Recorder. Many counties will perform a tax lien search, usually for the same fee as a UCC search.

At least 17 Colorado counties offer free access to property assessor basic tax roll records and sometimes sales via www.qpublic.net. For more data, there is a 3-level subscription service purchase plan.

Connecticut

How Organized and Location Anomalies—8 counties and 169 towns/cities. **There is no county recording in Connecticut; all recordings are done at the town/city level**. The recording officer is the Town/City Clerk.

Be careful not to confuse searching in the following towns/cities as equivalent to a countywide search (**since they have the same names**): Fairfield, Hartford, Litchfield, New Haven, New London, Tolland, and Windham.

Record Searching Tips—Many towns do not perform real estate searches. UCC financing statements are filed at the Secretary of State except for real estate related collateral filed only with the Town/City Clerk. All federal and state tax liens on personal property are filed with the Secretary of State. Federal and state tax liens on real property are filed with the Town/City Clerk, but many towns will not perform tax lien searches.

A number of towns offer free web access to assessor information. The State's Municipal Public Access Initiative has produced a website of Town and Municipality general information at www.munic.state.ct.us. Also, a private vendor has placed assessor records from a number of towns on the Internet. Visit http://data.visionappraisal.com

Delaware

How Organized and Location Anomalies—Delaware has 3 counties, 3 recording offices. Recording officer is the County Recorder.

Record Searching Tips—Counties do not perform real estate searches but will provide copies. There is no statewide online system for county recorded documents. UCC financing statements are filed at the Secretary of State except for real estate related collateral that is filed with the County Recorder. All counties perform these real estate related UCC searches. Federal tax liens on personal property of businesses are filed with the Secretary of State. Other federal and all state tax liens on personal property are filed with the County Recorder.

All non-"Search to Reflect" UCC Searches are outsourced to a Delaware Authorized Searcher, who performs the search for you. The website www.corp.delaware.gov/uccsearch.shtml maintains a list of these private vendors. All UCC searches performed by these agents are Certified UCC Searches.

District of Columbia

How Organized and Location Anomalies—Recording officer is the Recorder of Deeds.

Note: a taxpayer who resides outside the U.S. is deemed to be a resident of D.C.

Record Searching Tips—The District does not perform real estate searches. UCC financing statements are filed with the Recorder, including real estate related collateral. Federal tax liens on personal property of businesses are filed with the Secretary of State. Other federal and all state tax liens on personal property are filed with the Recorder.

Search the Recorder's database at www.washington.dc.us.landata.com. Registration is required; images are available for free, temporarily. Search the real property database and real estate sales database at http://otr.cfo.dc.gov/otr/cwp/view,a,1330,q,594345.asp

Recorded documents and UCC financing statements are at www.washington.dc.us.landata.com/. Registration required. Two commercial plans to purchase images are available.

Florida

How Organized and Location Anomalies—67 counties, 67 recording offices. The recording officer is the Clerk of the Circuit Court. Tax records are located at the Property Appraiser Office. 57 Florida counties observe Eastern Time and the 10 westernmost "panhandle counties" observe Central Time.

Record Searching Tips—All local transactions are recorded in the "Official Record," a grantor/grantee index. Some counties will search by type of transaction while others will return everything on the index. Any name searched in the "Official Records" will usually include all types of liens and property transfers for that name.

UCC financing statements are filed at the Secretary of State except for real estate related collateral filed at the Clerk of the Circuit Court. Few counties will perform these UCC searches. Federal tax liens on personal property of businesses are filed with the Secretary of State. All other federal and state tax liens on personal property are filed with the county Clerk of Circuit Court. Usually tax liens on personal property are filed in the same index with UCC financing statements and real estate transactions. Most counties will perform a tax lien as part of a UCC search.

There are numerous county agencies that provide online access to records, but the statewide system MyFlorida.com predominates and offers both a free and fee service.

Any person has the right to request the Clerk to redact/remove his or her Social Security Number from an image or copy of an Official Record that has been placed on a Clerk's publicly available website.

Georgia

How Organized and Location Anomalies—159 counties, 159 recording offices. The recording officer is the Clerk of Superior Court. All transactions are recorded in a "General Execution Docket."

Record Searching Tips—Most counties will not perform real estate searches. See below about the online indices.

UCCs are filed in a central index with the Georgia Superior Court Clerk's Cooperative Authority (GSCCCA). Only a few counties will perform local UCC searches. Prior to July, 2001, UCC records were only filed at the Clerk of Superior Court; older records should be searched there. All tax liens on personal property are filed with the Clerk of Superior Court in a "General Execution Docket" (grantor/grantee) or "Lien Index." Most counties will not perform tax lien searches.

The GSCCCA page at www.gsccca.org/search offers free access to a number of state indices including real state, liens, and UCC. The entire UCC Central Index System can be purchased on a daily, weekly, or biweekly basis. Visit the GSCCCA website for details.

Hawaii

How Organized and Location Anomalies—This is a central filing state. All UCC financing statements, tax liens, and real estate documents are filed centrally with the Bureau of Conveyances located in Honolulu. Property tax records are found at the county assessor.

Record Searching Tips—Real estate recordings, UCC filings, and tax liens are filed at the central Bureau of Conveyances. Several counties offer free access to assessor records; Hawaii County at www.hawaiipropertytax.com; Maui County at www.mauipropertytax.com and Honolulu property records at www.honolulupropertytax.com.

Idaho

How Organized and Location Anomalies—44 counties, 44 recording offices. The recording officer is the County Recorder. Many counties utilize a grantor/grantee index containing all transactions recorded with them. The uppermost 10 counties observe Pacific Time; the 34 others observe Mountain Time.

Record Searching Tips—Most counties will not perform real estate name searches. UCCs are at the Secretary of State except for real estate related filings at the County Recorder. All counties will perform these UCC searches. Until July 1, 1998, state tax liens were filed at the local county recorder. Now they are filed with the Secretary of State who has all active case files. Federal tax liens on personal property of businesses are filed with the Secretary of State. Other federal tax liens are filed with the county recorder. Some counties will perform a combined state and federal tax lien search while others will not perform tax lien searches.

Few counties offer direct web access but property data for a number of counties is found at www.etitlesearch.com. Fees and registration required.

Illinois

How Organized and Location Anomalies—102 counties, 102 recording offices. The recording officer is the County Recorder, but some counties prefer the name Recorder of Deeds. Tax records are usually located at the Treasurer's Office.

Record Searching Tips—Most counties will not perform real estate searches. A number of counties offer online access to real estate and assessor data. Many counties utilize a grantor/grantee index containing all transactions. Cook County had separate offices for real estate recording and UCC filing until they combined offices June 30, 2001. UCC financing statements are filed at the Secretary of State except for real estate related filings filed with the County Recorder. Federal tax liens on personal property of businesses are filed with the Secretary of State. Other federal and all state tax liens on personal property are filed with the County Recorder. Most counties will perform UCC searches. Some counties will perform tax lien searches; state and federal are separate searches in many of these counties.

Indiana

How Organized and Location Anomalies—92 counties, 92 recording offices. The recording officer is the County Recorder but see the office of the Circuit Clerk for state tax liens on personal property. Many counties utilize a "Miscellaneous Index" for tax and other liens. Indiana observes Eastern Time except Gibson, Jasper, Lake, LaPorte, Newton, Porter, Posey, Spencer, Vanderburgh, Warrick counties in CST.

Record Searching Tips—Most counties will not perform real estate name searches. UCC financing statements are filed at the Secretary of State, but real estate related collateral is filed with the County Recorder. Most counties perform UCC searches and copies are usually included in the search fee. All federal tax liens on personal property are filed with the County Recorder. State tax liens on personal property are filed with the Circuit Clerk. Most counties will not perform tax lien searches.

A growing number of agencies offer online access to official records. Perhaps the most notable is the subscription service offered by Marion County at www.civicnet.net

Iowa

How Organized and Location Anomalies—99 counties, 100 recording offices. The recording officer is the County Recorder. Lee County has two recording offices. Many counties utilize a grantor/grantee index containing all transactions recorded with them.

Record Searching Tips—Most counties are hesitant to perform real estate searches, but some will provide a listing from the grantor/grantee index with the understanding that it is not a certified list. UCC financing statements are filed at the Secretary of State since 7/2001, except for real estate related collateral that have always been filed with the County Recorder. Most Iowa counties will do UCC searches. Federal tax liens on personal property of businesses are filed with the Secretary of State. Other federal and all state tax liens on personal property are filed with the County Recorder. County search practices vary widely, but most provide some sort of tax lien search.

Land records are available for registered users on the "officially sponsored" state system at http://iowalandrecords.org. The County Land Record Information System offers free searching and pdf images of deeds, liens, even UCCs and judgments, though this service may begin charging at any time. Features for monitoring for new documents and saving documents are available.

A links list for assessor records for 66 counties plus cities of Ames, Cedar Rapids, Davenport, Dubuque, Iowa City, and Souix City is at www.iowaassessors.com, but note that many of the links are routed to http://beacon.schneidercorp.com. A statewide Property Tax lookup and payment page is at www.iowatreasurers.org/iscta/access/home.do. First, select the county then follow prompts to the search page where you can first look-up the name, then parcel information.

Kansas

How Organized and Location Anomalies—105 counties, 105 recording offices. The recording officer is the Register of Deeds. Tax records are located at the Appraiser's Office. Greeley, Hamilton, Sherman, Wallace counties use Mountain Time; all other counties observe Central Time. **Record Searching Tips**—Most counties will not perform real estate searches although some will do as an accommodation with the understanding that their results are not "certified searches." Some counties will also do a search to determine the owner based upon legal description. Many counties utilize a "Miscellaneous Index" for tax and other liens, separate from real estate records.

UCC financing statements are filed at the Secretary of State except for real estate related collateral filed with the Register of Deeds. Most counties will perform UCC searches. Federal tax liens on personal property of businesses are filed with the Secretary of State. Other federal tax liens and all state tax liens on personal property are filed with the county Register of Deeds. Most counties automatically include tax liens on personal property with a UCC search. Tax liens on personal property may usually be searched separately.

A number of counties have online access to recorder records; there is no statewide system.

Kentucky

How Organized and Location Anomalies—120 counties, 122 recording offices. The recording officer is the County Clerk. Kenton County has two recording offices. Jefferson County had a separate office for tax liens but filings are now at the County Clerk main office. Tax records are maintained by the Property Valuation Administrator. 80 counties use Eastern Time and 40 observe Central Time. Many offices are open until noon on Saturdays.

Record Searching Tips—Most counties will not perform real estate searches. A number of counties offer free access to assessor or real estate records. Several other counties offer commercial systems.

Under revised Article 9, Kentucky changed from a "local filing state" to a "central filing state" with filing now at the Secretary of State UCC Branch. Collateral on non-resident debtors were always filed at the Secretary of State. Real-estate related UCC records are still filed at the County Clerk. All federal and state tax liens on personal property are filed with the County Clerk, often in an "Encumbrance Book." Many clerks will not perform UCC searches or tax lien searches.

Louisiana

How Organized and Location Anomalies—64 parishes, 64 recording offices. One parish – St. Martin – has two non-contiguous segments. In Orleans Parish, deeds are recorded in a different office from mortgages. The recording officer is the Clerk of Court.

Record Searching Tips—Most parishes will perform a mortgage search Some will provide a record owner search. Many parishes include tax and other non-UCC liens in their mortgage records. UCC financing statements are filed with the Parish Clerk of Court and are entered onto a statewide database of UCC financing statements available for searching at any parish office. Most parishes perform UCC searches. All federal and state tax liens are filed with the Clerk of Court. Parishes usually file tax liens on personal property in the same index. However, tax liens are not kept on the same statewide database as UCCs. Most parishes will perform tax lien searches. Some parishes automatically include tax liens on personal property in a mortgage certificate search.

A number of parishes offer online access to recorded documents. Most are commercial fee systems but newer systems are allowing for free index searching, then a fee for images. A statewide system (excluding Jefferson Davis, Orleans, Sabine, St. Tammany, Terrebonne, and Winn Parishes) at www.latax.state.la.us/TaxRoll_ParishSelect.asp offers free access to assessor parish tax roll data.

Maine

How Organized and Location Anomalies—16 counties, 18 recording offices. The recording officer is the County Register of Deeds. Counties maintain a general index of all transactions recorded. **Aroostock and Oxford Counties each have two recording offices.** There are no county assessors; each town and city has its own.

Record Searching Tips—Counties do not usually perform real estate name searches but some will look up a name informally. Assessor and tax records are located at the town/city level. There is no statewide online system, however a number of counties offer access. Some counties outsource via vendors.

UCC financing statements are filed at the Secretary of State except for real estate related filings at the county Register of Deeds. Counties do not perform UCC searches. Supposedly tax liens on personal property are filed with the Secretary of State, but counties tend to have some of these. All tax liens on real property are filed with the Register of Deeds.

Maryland

How Organized and Location Anomalies—23 counties and one independent city; 24 recording offices. The recording officer is the Clerk of the Circuit Court. **Baltimore City has a recording office separate from the County of Baltimore.** Watch for ZIP Codes that include both the city and the county.

Record Searching Tips—Counties will not perform real estate searches. Until July, 1995 this was a dual filing state for UCCs. Now UCC filings are at the Department of Assessments & Taxation except farm products and real estate related filings are submitted to the Clerk of Circuit Court. All tax liens are filed with the county Clerk of Circuit Court. Counties will not perform name searches; hire a retriever to search.

Search statewide property records data free at http://sdatcert3.resiusa.org/rp_rewrite/. There is no name searching. Also, the Maryland State Dept. of Planning offers MDPropertyview with property maps/parcels and assessments on CD-rom or the web. Registration required; visit www.mdp.state.md.us/tax_mos.htm or call 410-767-4614. There is no name searching. Also, the state launched an experimental Digital Image Retrieval System for Land Record Indices at www.mdlandrec.net/msa/stagser/s1700/s1741/cfm/index.cfm. This service is currently being provided free to all those interested in testing the system. Users are encouraged to provide feedback and report any problems encountered.

Also, several notable vendors provide online access to county tax records and to land survey, condominium, and survey plats. Visit www.taxrecords.com or www.plats.net (use username "Plato" and password "plato#". No name searching.)

Massachusetts

How Organized and Location Anomalies—14 counties, 21 recording offices.

Berkshire and Bristol counties each have three recording offices. Essex, Middlesex, and Worcester counties each have two recording offices. Each town also has Assessor/Tax Collector/Treasurer offices from which limited real estate ownership and tax information is available. Cities/towns bearing the same name as a county are Barnstable, Essex, Franklin, Hampden, Nantucket, Norfolk, Plymouth, and Worcester. Real estate related recording is handled by the County Register of Deeds.

Record Searching Tips— Counties will not perform searches. Massachusetts was a dual filing state until July 1, 2001. Until then, financing statements could be filed with both the Town/City Clerk and at the state level except for real estate related collateral recorded at the county Register of Deeds. Now, all filings are at the state except for the real estate related collateral. Most town/city recording offices no longer perform UCC searches.

Federal tax liens on personal property are filed with the U.S. District Court in Boston as well as with the towns/cities. State tax liens on personal property are filed with the Town/City Clerk or the Tax Collector. All tax liens against real estate are filed with the county Register of Deeds. Some towns file state tax liens on personal property. Others perform a separate state tax lien search.

Many towns and several counties offer free web access to assessor records. Also, at www.visionappraisal.com/databases/mass/index.htm a private vendor offers assessor records from a number of towns.

Michigan

How Organized and Location Anomalies—83 counties, 83 recording offices. The recording officer is the County Register of Deeds. Ownership records are located at the Equalization Office. Tax records are located at the Treasurer's Office. 4 counties that border Wisconsin – Gogebic, Iron, Dickinson, Menominee – observe Central Time; all other counties observe Eastern Time.

Record Searching Tips—Some counties will perform real estate searches. UCC financing statements are filed at the Secretary of State except for real estate related collateral filed with the County Register. However, prior to July, 2001, UCCs on consumer goods were also filed at the County Register and these older records can be searched there. All counties will perform UCC searches. Federal and state tax liens on personal property of businesses are filed with the Secretary of State. Other federal and state tax liens are filed with the Register of Deeds. Most counties search each tax lien index separately. Some charge one fee to search both while others charge a separate fee for each one.

There is no statewide online access to assess or real estate records but a number of counties, including Wayne, offer online access.

Minnesota

How Organized and Location Anomalies—87 counties, 87 recording offices. The recording officer is the County Recorder.

Record Searching Tips—Many Minnesota counties perform real estate searches, including over the phone if you offer only short questions.

UCC financing statements are filed at the Secretary of Stat except real estate related collateral is recorded at the County Recorder. Federal and state tax liens on personal property of businesses are filed with the Secretary of State. Other federal and state tax liens are filed with the County Recorder. Most counties will still perform UCC searches; a UCC search can include tax liens. Some counties search each tax lien index separately using form UCC-12.

There is no statewide system to assessment or recorded deeds, but a number of counties offer web access to these.

Mississippi

How Organized and Location Anomalies—82 counties, 92 recording offices. The recording officers are Chancery Clerk, and Clerk of Circuit Court for state tax liens. Ten counties have two separate recording offices - Bolivar, Carroll, Chickasaw, Harrison, Hinds, Jasper, Jones, Panola, Tallahatchie, and Yalobusha.

Record Searching Tips—Very few counties will perform real estate searches. Until July, 2001, UCCs were filed either at the Secretary of State or with the Chancery Clerk, except for consumer goods, farm related and real estate related filings that were filed only with the Chancery Clerk. Now, only real estate related filings are filed at the county level.

Most counties will perform UCC searches. Federal tax liens on personal property of businesses are filed with the Secretary of State. Federal tax liens on personal property of individuals are filed with the county Chancery Clerk. State tax liens on personal property are filed with the County Clerk of Circuit Court. State tax liens on real property are filed with the Chancery Clerk. Chancery Clerk offices may perform a federal tax lien search.

A limited number of counties offer online access to records

Missouri

How Organized and Location Anomalies—114 counties and one independent city; 115 recording offices. **The city of St. Louis has its own recording office.** Watch for ZIP Codes that may be City of St. Louis or County of St. Louis. The recording officer is the Recorder of Deeds.

Record Searching Tips—A few counties will perform real estate searches. A number of counties offer online access.

Until July, 2001, UCC financing statements were filed either at the Secretary of State or with the County Recorder of Deeds. Now only farm related and real estate related filings are filed with the County Recorder. Most counties will perform UCC searches of their pre-7/2001 records. All federal and state tax liens are filed with the county Recorder of

Deeds. Tax liens are usually indexed together. Some counties will perform tax lien searches.

For an electronic copy of the image of the UCC filing, send email request to UCCMail@sos.mo.gov. The email must contain file number, name, and address of the filing.

Montana

How Organized and Location Anomalies—57 counties, 56 recording offices. Yellowstone National Park is considered a county but is not included as a filing location. The recording officer is the County Clerk and Recorder; the Clerk of District Court manages state tax liens.

Record Searching Tips—Many Montana counties will perform real estate searches. Search for a Montana property owner by name and county on the Montana Cadastral Mapping Project GIS mapping database at http://gis.mt.gov.

UCC financing statements are filed at the Secretary of State except for real estate related collateral filed with the Clerk and Recorder. All counties will perform these UCC searches. Federal tax liens on personal property of businesses are filed with the Secretary of State. Other federal tax liens are filed with the county Clerk and Recorder. State tax liens are filed with the Clerk of District Court. Usually tax liens on personal property filed with the Clerk and Recorder are in the same index with UCC financing statements. Most counties will perform tax lien searches, some as part of a UCC search.

Nebraska

How Organized and Location Anomalies—93 counties, 109 recording offices. The recording officers are County Clerk (UCCs and some state tax liens) and Register of Deeds (real estate and most tax liens). Most counties have a combined Clerk/Register office. Still, in combined offices, the Register of Deeds is frequently a different person from the County Clerk. **16 counties have separate offices for real estate recording and UCC filing** - Adams, Cass, Dakota, Dawson, Dodge, Douglas, Gage, Hall, Lancaster, Lincoln, Madison, Otoe, Platte, Sarpy, Saunders, Scotts Bluff. 19 western-most counties observe MST.

Record Searching Tips—Some Nebraska counties will perform real estate searches (including owner of record) when provided with the property's legal description. Address search requests and make checks payable to the Register of Deeds, not the County Clerk. Access real estate or personal property data for free for at least 40 counties at www.nebraskataxesonline.us.

UCC financing statements are filed at the Secretary of State; real estate related collateral are filed with the County Clerk. Prior to July, 2001, financing statements could be filed at any county. All but a few counties will perform UCC searches; the UCC statute allows for phone searches.

Most federal and state tax liens are filed with the County Register of Deeds. Some state tax liens on personal property are filed with the County Clerk. Some federal tax liens on individuals are filed at the Secretary of State's office. Most counties will perform tax lien searches, some as part of a UCC search.

Nevada

How Organized and Location Anomalies—16 counties and one independent city; 17 recording offices. The recording officer is the County Recorder. **Carson City has a separate filing office.**

Record Searching Tips—Most counties will not provide real estate searches. A number of counties have searchable databases online. A private company, GoverNet at www.governet.net/SurfNV/, offers online access to Assessor, Treasurer, Recorder and other county databases for Churchill, Clark, Esmeralda, and Pershing. Registration is required; sliding monthly and per-hit fees apply.

UCCs are filed at the Secretary of State except for real estate related collateral filed with the County Recorder. Federal tax liens on personal property of businesses are filed with the Secretary of State. Federal tax liens on personal property of individuals are filed with the County Recorder. Although not called state tax liens, employment withholding judgments have the same effect and are filed with the County Recorder. If available, some counties provide tax lien searches.

New Hampshire

How Organized and Location Anomalies—New Hampshire has 10 recording offices. There are 233 cities/town which previously handled the filing of UCCs. The recording officer is the Register of Deeds. Real estate transactions are recorded at the county level, and property taxes are handled at the town/city level. Local town real estate ownership and assessment records are usually located at the Selectman's Office.

Be careful to distinguish the **following names that are identical for both a town/city and a county** - Grafton, Hillsborough, Merrimack, Strafford, Sullivan. The following unincorporated towns do not have a Town Clerk, so all liens are located at the corresponding county: Cambridge (Coos), Dicksville (Coos), Green's Grant (Coos), Hale's Location (Carroll), Millsfield (Coos), and Wentworth's Location (Coos).

Record Searching Tips—Most New Hampshire counties will not perform real estate searches. Until July, 2001, financing statements were filed Secretary of State and with the Town/City Clerk, except for UCCs on consumer goods filed only with the Town/City Clerk, and for real estate related collateral which was and still is filed with the county Register of Deeds. Most recording offices will perform UCC searches.

Federal and state tax liens on personal property of businesses are filed with the Secretary of State. Other federal and state tax liens on personal property are filed at the Town/City Clerk. Federal and state tax liens on real property are filed with the county Register of Deeds. There is a wide variation in indexing and searching practices among recording offices.

The NH Counties Registry of Deeds website at www.nhdeeds.com allows free searching of real estate related records for Belknap, Cheshire, Coos, Hillsborough, Rockingham, Strafford, and Sullivan counties. Several vendors are worthy of mention; see www.visionappraisal.com/databases for free assessor records from a number of towns. For Property Card data for 75+ NH towns, see www.avitarofneinc.com. Fees apply.

New Jersey

How Organized and Location Anomalies—21 counties, 21 recording offices. The recording officer title varies depending upon the county, either the Register of Deeds or the County Clerk. The Clerk of Circuit Court records the equivalent of some state's tax liens.

Record Searching Tips—No counties will provide real estate searches. Assessment and tax offices are at the municipal level.

A vendor's statewide database of property tax records can be accessed at http://taxrecords.com. Search property data for New Jersey counties free at http://tax1.co.monmouth.nj.us. Use username "monm" and password "data" then select county.

UCC financing statements are filed at the Secretary of State, except for real estate related collateral filed with the County Clerk. About half of the recording offices will perform UCC searches.

All federal tax liens are filed with the County Clerk/Register of Deeds and are indexed separately from all other liens. State tax liens comprise two categories - certificates of debt are filed with the Clerk of Superior Court (some, called docketed judgments are filed specifically with the Trenton court), and warrants of execution are filed with the County Clerk/Register of Deeds. Few counties will provide tax lien searches.

New Mexico

How Organized and Location Anomalies—33 counties, 33 recording offices. The recording officer is the County Clerk.

Record Searching Tips—Most New Mexico counties maintain both a grantor/grantee index and a miscellaneous index. Most counties will not perform real estate searches.

A handful of counties offer online access but there is no statewide system of real estate record data.

UCC financing statements are filed at the Secretary of State except for real estate related collateral filed with the County Clerk. Only a few recording offices will perform UCC searches. All federal and state tax liens are filed with the County Clerk but most counties will not provide tax lien searches.

New York

How Organized and Location Anomalies—62 counties, 62 recording offices. Recording officer is the County Clerk except in the counties of Bronx, Kings, New York, and Queens where the recording officer is the New York City Register. Note that Staten Island/Richmond County has a County Clerk. Tax records located at Treasurer's Office.

Record Searching Tips—Some counties will perform real estate searches.

Since July, 2001, UCC financing statements are filed at the Secretary of State except for cooperatives, farm and real estate related collateral filed with the County Clerk (or the City Clerk in NYC). Previously all UCCs could be filed locally. Most counties will perform UCC searches.

Federal tax liens on personal property of businesses are filed with the Secretary of State. Other federal tax liens are filed with the County Clerk. State tax liens are filed with the County Clerk and placed on a master list - called state tax warrants - available at the Secretary of State's office. Federal tax liens are usually indexed with UCC records. State tax liens are usually indexed with other miscellaneous liens and judgments. Some counties include federal tax liens in their UCC search while others will search tax liens for a separate fee or not search at all.

Many counties and towns offer free internet access to assessor records and the number is growing. The New York City Register offers free access to all borough's real estate records (also including Staten Island) at http://nyc.gov/html/dof/html/home/home.shtml. Search by address or legal description. A private company offers property assessment data for most New York counties online at www.uspdr.com/consumer/ownersearch.asp.

North Carolina

How Organized and Location Anomalies—100 counties, 100 recording offices. The recording officer is the Register of Deeds, except for tax liens that are recorded with the Clerk of Superior Court.

Record Searching Tips—Counties will not perform real estate searches. Many counties offer free web access to assessor and real estate records.

Until July, 2001, UCC financing statements were both at the Secretary of State and with the County Register of Deeds, except for real estate related collateral that were only filed locally. Now only real estate related collateral is filed at the county level.

Most counties will perform UCC searches. Federal tax liens on personal property of businesses are filed with the Secretary of State. Other federal and all state tax liens are filed with the County Clerk of Superior Court. Even tax liens on real property are also filed with the Clerk of Superior Court, not with the Register of Deeds.

North Dakota

How Organized and Location Anomalies—53 counties, 53 recording offices. The recording officer is the County Recorder, changed from Register of Deeds as of August, 2001.

Record Searching Tips—Some counties will perform real estate searches by name or by legal description.

The North Dakota Recorders Information Network (NDRIN) is a electronic central repository representing a number of North Dakota counties - 37 currently, with more being added - and offering Internet access to records, indices and images. Register or request information via the website at www.ndrin.com

All UCCs are filed at the Secretary of State except for real estate related collateral filed only with the County Recorder or the County Register (which county official performs this duty varies by county). All counties access a statewide computer database of UCC filings and will perform UCC searches.

Federal tax liens on personal property of businesses are filed with the Secretary of State. Other federal and all state tax liens are filed with the County Recorder. All counties will perform tax lien searches. Be aware that federal tax liens on individuals may only be in the county lien books and not on the statewide system. Separate tax lien searches are usually available. Tax lien copies may be faxed back.

Ohio

How Organized and Location Anomalies—88 counties, 88 recording offices. The recording officer is the County Recorder. State tax liens are managed by the Clerk of Common Pleas Court.

Record Searching Tips—Counties will not perform real estate searches. Tax records are located at the Auditor's Office. Many, many counties offer web access to assessor and real estate data, usually free.

Ohio was a dual filing state until July 1, 2001. UCC financing statements were filed both at the Secretary of State and with the County Recorder except for farm and real estate related collateral filed only with the County Recorder. Now only real estate related collateral is filed at the county level. All counties will perform UCC name searches.

Federal tax liens are filed in the "Official Records" with the County Recorder where the property is located. All state tax liens are filed with the Clerk of Common Pleas Court. Most counties will not perform a separate federal tax lien search.

Oklahoma

How Organized and Location Anomalies—77 counties, 77 recording offices. The recording officer is the County Clerk.

Record Searching Tips—Many Oklahoma counties will perform real estate searches by legal description. UCC financing statements and Federal tax liens on personal property of businesses are filed centrally with the County Clerk of Oklahoma County. UCCs on farm and real estate related collateral are filed at the local County Clerk. Federal tax liens and all state tax liens are filed with the County Clerk. Usually state and federal tax liens on personal property are filed in separate indexes, state liens on businesses or individuals usually in the real estate index. All counties perform UCC searches; some perform tax lien searches.

Very little is available online directly from the counties. However, several vendors sites are worth mentioning: subscription access to assessor indices and property images for all but one Oklahoma county available at http://oklahoma.usassessor.com/. Almost all Oklahoma counties assessment data on CD-rom, also plats and land maps, are all at https://secure.vlsmaps.com/ecom_vls/store.php; and fees vary by county. Also, a limited free search is offered for all counties except Texas and Roger Mills at www.pvplus.com/freeaccess/free_login.aspx.

Oregon

How Organized and Location Anomalies—36 counties, 36 recording offices. The recording officer is the County Clerk. 35 Oregon counties observe Pacific Time; Malheur County observes Mountain Time.

Record Searching Tips—Some counties will not perform real estate searches. Where they do, counties will search all lien types together. The Assessor keeps tax and ownership records. A number of counties offer internet access to assessor records.

From a statewide perspective, the ORMAP Tax Viewing System at www.ormap.com/disclaimer.cfm provides maps for free, and searching by county, then by address. Though there is no name searching and maps are pdfs arranged in folders (and you may zoom in to a map location), this is a step toward owner identification.

UCC financing statements are filed at the Secretary of State except for real estate related collateral filed locally at the County Clerk. Many county clerks will perform UCC searches; calling first is suggested. All federal and state tax liens on personal property are filed with the Secretary of State. Other federal and state tax liens are filed with the County Clerk. Government agencies file 'warrants' that represent liens for unpaid taxes and other state fees. Certain warrants are filed with the Secretary of State such as those related to income tax and hazardous waste and are included in a UCC search. Other warrants are filed at the county level, such as those relating to employment taxes. Most counties will perform tax lien searches and include them with a UCC search.

Pennsylvania

How Organized and Location Anomalies—67 counties, 67 recording offices and 134 UCC filing offices. Each county has two different recording offices. The Prothonotary - Pennsylvania's term for "clerk" - accepted UCC and tax lien filings until July 1, 2001. The other office is the Recorder of Deeds who maintains real estate records.

Record Searching Tips—County Recorders of Deeds will not perform real estate searches. A number of counties provide web access to assessor data. Also, the Infocon County Access System provides internet and direct dial-up access to recorded record information for over twenty Pennsylvania counties; for information call Infocon at 814-472-6066 or visit www.infoconcountyaccess.com

Pennsylvania was a dual filing state. Until July 1, 2001, UCC financing statements on personal property were filed both at the Department of State and with the County Prothonotary, except for real estate related collateral which was and still is filed with the Recorder of Deeds. Now the Prothontary has only the pre-July, 2001 UCCs on personal property. Many county offices will not perform UCC searches.

All federal and state tax liens on personal property and on real property are filed with the Prothonotary. Usually, tax liens on personal property are filed in the Prothonotary's judgment index. Some Prothonotaries will perform tax lien searches.

Rhode Island

How Organized and Location Anomalies—5 counties and 39 towns, 39 recording offices. The recording officers are the Town/City Clerks who also usually serve as Recorder of Deeds. There is **no county recording** in RI. All recording is done at the city/town level.

Be aware that three cities bear the same name as their respective counties. Therefore, the recordings within the counties of **Bristol**, **Newport**, and **Providence** can relate to property located in cities/towns other than the individual cities of Bristol, Newport, and Providence.

Record Searching Tips—Towns/Cities will not perform real estate searches. UCC financing statements are filed at the Secretary of State except for farm and real estate related collateral filed with the Town/City Clerk and Recorder. Most local recording offices will not perform UCC searches. All federal and state tax liens on personal property and on real property are filed with the Recorder of Deeds. Towns/Cities will not perform tax lien searches.

A private vendor has placed assessor records from a number of towns on the web; visit www.visionappraisal.com/databases/ri/index.htm.

South Carolina

How Organized and Location Anomalies—46 counties, 46 recording offices. The recording officer is either the Register of Mesne Conveyances or the Clerk of Court; this varies by county. The Assessor maintains property tax records.

Record Searching Tips—Most counties will not perform real estate searches. There is no statewide system, but a number of counties offer free record data through their websites.

UCC financing statements are filed at the Secretary of State except for real estate related collateral filed with the County Register/Clerk. In general, recording offices will perform UCC searches.

All federal and state tax liens on personal property and on real property are filed with the Register of Mesne Conveyances or Clerk of Court. A few counties will perform tax lien searches.

South Dakota

How Organized and Location Anomalies—66 counties, 66 recording offices. Recording officer is the Register of Deeds. 18 western-most counties use Mountain Time; eastern counties use Central Time.

Record Searching Tips—Most counties will not perform real estate searches, though some will assist. Very little is found online.

UCC financing statements are filed at the Secretary of State except for real estate related collateral filed with the County Register of Deeds. All recording offices should perform UCC searches; all counties have access to a statewide database of UCC filings. Federal tax liens on personal property of businesses are filed with the Secretary of State. Other federal and state tax liens are filed with the County Register of Deeds. Most counties will perform tax lien searches.

Tennessee

How Organized and Location Anomalies—95 counties, 96 recording offices. The recording officer is the Register of Deeds. Sullivan County has two recording offices. Tax records are kept at the Assessor's Office. 66 counties including the state capital observe Central Time. The 29 eastern-most counties observe Eastern Time.

Record Searching Tips—Counties will not perform real estate searches. The State Comptroller of the Treasury Real Estate Assessment Database can be searched free at www.assessment.state.tn.us/. Select a county then search by name for real property information. Counties not on this system are Davidson, Hamilton, Knox, Shelby, and Unicoi.

Three noteworthy competing vendors offer access to a number of county's property and deeds indexes and images:

www.titlesearcher.com
www1.ustitlesearch.net

www.tnrealestate.com

UCC financing statements are filed at the Secretary of State except for real estate related collateral filed with the county Register of Deeds. All federal tax liens are filed with the County Register of Deeds. State tax liens are filed with the Secretary of State or the Register of Deeds. Counties will not perform tax lien searches.

Texas

How Organized and Location Anomalies—254 counties, 254 recording offices. The recording officer is the County Clerk. Each county has an "Appraisal District" that is responsible for collecting taxes. 2 counties by El Paso observe Mountain Time; all others use Central Time.

Record Searching Tips—Some counties will perform real estate searches. Financing statements are filed at the state level except for real estate related collateral which are filed with the County Clerk. Most Texas recording offices will perform UCC searches. Federal tax liens on personal property of businesses are filed with the Secretary of State. Other federal and all state tax liens are filed with the County Clerk. All counties will perform tax lien searches. Tax lien records are usually provided as part of a UCC search.

There are a number of competing vendors who provide free searching for tax appraisal assessor records. Some also have links to county grantor/grantee indices. Check each of the following for their respective county coverage:

www.txcountydata.com
www.taxnetusa.com
www.titlex.com
www.texaslandrecords.com

A good resource to many county appraisal districts web pages, and to some links to free searching, is found at http://appraisaldistrict.net.

Utah

How Organized and Location Anomalies—29 counties, 29 recording offices. The recording officers are the County Recorder for real estate and the Clerk of District Court for state tax liens.

Record Searching Tips—County Recorders will not perform real estate searches. A number of counties offer online access; some are fee-based.

UCC financing statements are filed at the Division of Corporations & Commercial Code except for real estate related collateral filed with the County Recorder (and at the state level in certain cases). Many county filing offices will not perform UCC searches. All federal tax liens are filed with the County Recorder, who do not perform searches. All state tax liens are filed with Clerk of District Court, many of which have online access and almost all will perform searches.

Vermont

How Organized and Location Anomalies—Vermont has 14 counties and 246 towns/cities which have 246 recording offices. There is **no county recording** in this state. All recording is done at the city/town level. Many towns are so small that their mailing addresses are in different towns. **4 towns have the same names as cities** - Barre, Newport, Rutland, St. Albans. 11 cities or towns bear the same name as a Vermont county - Addison, Bennington, Chittenden, Essex, Franklin, Grand Isle, Orange, Rutland, Washington, Windham, and Windsor.

Record Searching Tips—Most towns/cities will not perform real estate searches. There is limited online access to county recorded documents, and a growing number of towns have contracted out online services, usually offering property assessment records or property cards.

Vermont was a dual filing state until July 1, 1995 when UCC filings on personal property ceased to be filed at the Town/City Clerk, though real estate related collateral continues to be filed locally to this day. Many but not all recording offices will perform UCC searches.

All federal and state tax liens on personal property and on real property are filed with the Town/City Clerk in the lien/attachment book and indexed in real estate records. Most towns/cities will not perform tax lien searches.

Virginia

How Organized and Location Anomalies—95 counties and 41 independent cities; 123 recording offices statewide. The recording officer is the Clerk of Circuit Court.

There are many notable County Rule exceptions in Virginia.

Sixteen independent cities share the Clerk of Circuit Court with the county – Bedford (Bedford County); Covington and Clifton Forge (Alleghany County); Emporia (Greenville County); Fairfax (Fairfax County); Falls Church (Arlington or Fairfax County); Franklin (Southhampton County); Galax (Carroll County); Harrisonburg (Rockingham County); Lexington (Rockbridge County); Manassas and Manassas Park (Prince William County); Norton (Wise County); Poquoson (York County); South Boston (Halifax County); and Williamsburg (James City County).

Charles City and James City are counties, not cities. The City of Franklin is not in Franklin County. The City of Richmond is not in Richmond County. The City of Roanoke is not in Roanoke County.

Record Searching Tips—Only a few Clerks of Circuit Court perform real estate searches. The independent cities may have their own, separate Assessor offices. An increasing number of Virginia counties and cities provide free access to real estate related information via the Internet. A limited but growing private company network named

VamaNet provides free residential, commercial, and vacant property data and tax records; visit www.vamanet.com/info/home.jsp

Virginia was a dual filing state until July 1, 2001; UCC financing statements on personal property were filed at the Corporation Commission and with the Clerk of Circuit Court. Since July, 2001, only farm and real estate related collateral are filed with the Clerk of Circuit Court. Some of these local recording offices will perform UCC searches.

Federal tax liens on personal property of businesses are filed with the State Corporation Commission. Other federal and all state tax liens are filed with the county Clerk of Circuit Court, usually filed in a "Judgment Lien Book." Most Virginia counties will not perform tax lien searches.

Washington

How Organized and Location Anomalies—39 counties, 39 recording offices. The recording officer is the County Auditor. County records are usually combined in a Grantor/Grantee index.

Record Searching Tips—Many County Auditors will perform real estate searches, including record owner searches. If the Auditor does not provide searches, then contact the Assessor for record owner information. Contact the Treasurer (or, if it concerns King County, the Finance Department) for information about unpaid real estate taxes.

A number of counties offer web access to assessor or real estate records.

UCC financing statements are filed at the state Dept. of Licensing except for real estate related collateral filed with the County Auditor. Most of these county recording offices will perform UCC searches.

All federal tax liens are filed with the Department of Licensing. All state tax liens are filed with the County Auditor. Most counties will perform tax lien searches.

West Virginia

How Organized and Location Anomalies—55 counties, 55 recording offices. The recording officer is the County Clerk.

Record Searching Tips—Most County Clerks will not perform real estate searches. There is no statewide system open to public, but a growing number of counties offer online access. A private company offers subscription access to land book assessment information statewide at http://digitalcourthouse.com.

UCC financing statements are filed at the Secretary of State except for real estate related collateral filed only with the County Clerk. Many recording offices will perform UCC searches. All federal and state tax liens are filed with the County Clerk. Most counties will not perform tax lien searches.

Wisconsin

How Organized and Location Anomalies—72 counties, 72 recording offices. Recording officers are Register of Deeds for real estate and Clerk of Court for state tax liens. County Clerks hold marriage records and state tax liens. Treasurer maintains property tax records.

Record Searching Tips—Registers will not perform real estate searches. Counties do not have assessors, they are at the city level. A number of cities and a few counties offer online access to assessor and property records. The Wisconsin Register of Deeds Association website at www.wrdaonline.org/RealEstateRecords offers helpful guidance to which counties are online.

UCC financing statements and federal tax liens on personal property of businesses are filed at the state Dept. of Financial Institutions except for real estate related collateral filed with the Register of Deeds. Only federal tax liens on real estate are filed with the County Register of Deeds. State tax liens are filed with the Clerk of Court, and at the State Treasurer at the State Department of Revenue. Most but not all Registers will perform federal tax lien searches.

Wyoming

How Organized and Location Anomalies—23 counties, 23 recording offices. The recording officer is the County Clerk.

Record Searching Tips—County Clerks will not perform real estate searches. The county Assessor maintains property tax records. A growing number of counties offer online access to various property records and databases of recorded documents.

Since July 1, 2001, all UCC filings have been centralized at the Secretary of State. Prior, tax liens and UCC financing statements (except for out-of-state and A/Rs filed with the Sec. of State) were filed with the County Clerk. All recording offices will perform UCC searches of what records they have. Federal tax liens on personal property of businesses are filed with the Secretary of State. Other federal and all state tax liens are filed with the County Clerk. Most counties perform tax lien searches.

Web Access to the State UCC Filings Index or Images

This helpful table will lead you to the web page to find information on UCC filings maintained by the central state registry. A number of jurisdictions allow free searching of the index or of images. Many charge a fee or require a subscription service to obtain images. Usually the look-ups include all business entities types.

* No search capabilities offered in Delaware.

** In South Carolina, the index only has UCC records filed before 10/27/03. One may search by debtor name or number, there are no images. Information on filings after that date must be obtained by mail or email SCUCC@INFOAVE.NET.

State	Web Page
Alabama	www.sos.state.al.us/vb/inquiry/inquiry.aspx?area=UCC
Alaska	www.ucc.alaska.gov/search.cfm
Arizona	www.azsos.gov/scripts/ucc_search.dll
Arkansas	https://www.ark.org/sos/ucc/index.php (an alert system is also available for a fee)
California	https://uccconnect.ss.ca.gov/acct/acct-login.asp
Colorado	www.sos.state.co.us/pubs/business/search_records.htm
Connecticut	www.concord-sots.ct.gov/CONCORD/index.jsp
Delaware*	www.corp.delaware.gov/uccsearch.shtml (No searches offered)
District of Columbia	www.washington.dc.us.landata.com
Florida	www.floridaucc.com/pls/ucc/uccdba.searchoptions
Georgia	www.gsccca.org/search
Hawaii	http://bocweb.dlnrbc.hawaii.gov/boc/
Idaho	https://www.accessidaho.org/secure/sos/liens/search.html
Illinois	www.ilsos.gov/uccsearch
Indiana	www.in.gov/sos/services.html
Iowa	www.sos.state.ia.us/Search/UCC/search.aspx?ucc www.sos.state.ia.us/Search/UCCAlternative/search.aspx
Kansas	www.kssos.org/business/business_ucc.html
Kentucky	http://sos.ky.gov/business/ucc/online/.
Louisiana	http://www.sos.louisiana.gov/tabid/130/Default.aspx
Maine	h www.maine.gov/sos/cec/corp/debtor_index.shtml
Maryland	http://sdatcert3.resiusa.org/ucc-charter/
Massachusetts	http://corp.sec.state.ma.us/corp/psearch/default.asp
Michigan	www.michigan.gov/sosucc
Minnesota	www.sos.state.mn.us/home/index.asp?page=89
Mississippi	https://secure.sos.state.ms.us/busserv/ucc/soskb/SearchStandardRA9.asp
Missouri	www.sos.mo.gov/ucc/soskb/searchstandardRA9.asp.
Montana	http://app.mt.gov/uccs/.
Nebraska	www.sos.state.ne.us/business/ucc/
Nevada	https://esos.state.nv.us/NVUCC/user/login.asp
New Hampshire	https://www.sos.nh.gov/uccegov/
New Jersey	https://www.state.nj.us/treasury/revenue/dcr/filing/ucc_lead.htm https://accessnet.state.nj.us/home.asp
New Mexico	http://secure.sos.state.nm.us/ucc/default.asp
New York	http://appsext8.dos.state.ny.us/pls/ucc_public/web_search.main_frame
North Carolina	www.secretary.state.nc.us/ucc/
North Dakota	www.nd.gov/sos/businessserv/centralindex/index.html
Ohio	www.sos.state.oh.us/sos/ucc/ucc.aspx
Oklahoma	http://countyclerk.oklahomacounty.org/UCC-SearchSite.html

State	Web Page
Oregon	www.filinginoregon.com/ucc/index.htm
Pennsylvania	https://www.corporations.state.pa.us/ucc/soskb/SearchStandardRA9.asp
Rhode Island	http://ucc.state.ri.us/psearch
South Carolina**	www.scsos.com/uccsearch.htm
South Dakota	www.sdsos.gov/busineservices/ucc.shtm
Tennessee	www.ja.state.tn.us/sos/iets3/ieuc/PgUCCSearch.jsp
Texas	www.sos.state.tx.us/corp/sosda/index.shtml
Utah	https://secure.utah.gov/uccsearch/uccs
Vermont	www.sec.state.vt.us/seek/ucc_seek.htm
Virginia	www.scc.virginia.gov/division/clk/diracc.htm
Washington	https://fortress.wa.gov/dol/ucc
West Virginia	www.wvsos.com/UccSearch/index-noecomm.aspx
Wisconsin	www.wdfi.org/ucc/search/.
Wyoming	http://soswy.state.wy.us/uniform/uniform.htm

Searching Records of Business Entities

Business entities come in all sizes and flavors. Ownership of companies can be "public" or "private." They can be organized in any number of ways – as corporations, partnerships, non-profits, or sole proprietorships. They may be public companies – traded on a stock market – or private. Often they use fictitious names or trade names. Researching the public records connected to a business entity starts with having good basic knowledge about the type of entity.

This chapter first examines the types of U.S. business entities you will come across. The chapter provides record searching tips that include where public records about these entities can be found, how to access records, and how to analyze the sources.

An important tip to keep in mind when searching records on business entities – do not overlook the importance of searching public records on the officers or principals. Investigating – or backgrounding – an individual's filings or records may lead to other associated business entities or assets.

This chapter is not all all-encompassing; there are other types of public records that are very useful when researching business entities. See the *Searching A thru Z* chapter for coverage of:

- Copyrights
- Patents
- Federal Agency Sanctions and Watch Lists
- Trade Associations
- Securities and Securities Dealers

Business Entity Types

Knowing how a business is legally organized is extremely helpful when searching for public records. The type of entity a business is may dictate where to search and what information may be provided on public records.

In the U.S., if a business is a public company (selling shares of ownership to the public, via the stock market) it must be registered with the Securities and Exchange Commission (SEC) or with a state securities regulator, or both. A registration discloses information on the management and financial condition of the entity, and describes how the proceeds of the offering will be used. The statement also is filed with the appropriate securities exchanges and state securities regulators.

In general, businesses that are not public companies are registered at the state level, usually with its Secretary of State. This is required so the business name cannot be used by another entity. Its public location is registered in case service of process is required against the company, and the business is structured in accordance with the rules provided by the state. Fictitious names and trade names can be registered at either the local (county or city) or state level, depending on the state's specifications.

Below are quick but basic overviews of the types of business entities.

Corporations

A corporation is a legal entity or structure created under the authority of state law. A corporation is owned by shareholders, also known as stockholders. A corporation can enter into contracts, sue or be sued, and is liable for its own debts and obligations including income taxes. When ownership changes in a corporation, the corporation does not dissolve.

There are two common forms of corporation – a "C" and a "S" corporation. A "C" corporation is, as described above, a legal separate entity, but also with limited personal liability for business debts. In a "S" corporation (often referred to as a "Sub-S") the corporate earnings, profits, and the taxation are passed directly to the personal tax return of the shareholder on a prorated basis equal to his share of ownership. No taxes are paid on the corporate tax structure.

A foreign corporation is an existing corporation formed in one U.S. state or country that is registered to do business in another U.S. state. This allows a business entity to operate in multiple states or jurisdictions as one organization. The only alternative would be to form and register a separate corporation in each jurisdiction.

If corporations sell shares of ownership or securities they must be registered with the SEC, or file a D Exemption and then file at a state agency that oversees securities. See the section on Searching Publicly Owned (Traded) Companies later in this chapter.

Non-Profits

A non-profit corporation is formed to carry out a specific purpose that is charitable, educational, religious, literary, or scientific in nature. Often, a non-profit corporation is often referred to as a "501(c)3" or a "501(c)4" which come from Section 501(c) of the Internal Revenue Code. The IRS grants a tax exempt status, not non-profit status. Differences abound though in the different ways the non-profit is registered are used. For example, contributions to a 501(c)(3) organization can be claimed against income tax, but donations to a 501(c)(4) entity cannot. 501(c)3 types are more prevalent; those organized as 501(c)4 are usually organized for lobbying or political campaigning.

Organizational records for non-profits are filed with the same state agency that oversees the filing of corporation papers. Filing as a non-profit does not mean the entity is exempt from federal income taxes: in general it means that it cannot give out ownership shares or distribute share dividends.

Foundations and Charitable Trusts

Sometimes non-profits will fund their own non-profit foundations or charitable trusts for specific purposes or programs. Others of this type include community foundations and private foundations. Private foundations are usually funded by an individual or family. They can be single or limited purpose oriented or they may cover a wide range of purposes. Large foundations usually publish guidelines and have officers or staff.

Partnerships (Limited, Limited Liability, and General)

A partnership is a business that has more than one owner and has not filed papers with the state to become a corporation or LLC (limited liability company). There are two basic types of partnerships—general partnerships and limited partnerships. The general partnership is the simplest and least expensive, co-owned business structure to create and maintain. Many states allow the creation of special limited liability partnerships (LLPs).

A limited liability limited partnership (LLLP) is a relatively new modification of the limited partnership. An LLLP business entity is recognized under U.S. commercial law. Like a limited partnership, an LLLP is a limited partnership and, as such, consists of one or more general partners *and* one or more limited partners. Many LLLPs deal with real estate ownership and management.

Limited Liability Company

A limited liability company (LLC) combines the advantages of a corporation with the tax advantages and management flexibility of a partnership. Similar to a corporation, an LLC is created by a state filing, protects personal assets from business liabilities, and has few ownership restrictions. Perhaps the biggest difference between LLCs and corporations is that LLCs cannot issue stock. Like partnerships, LLCs are simply owned by members (usually managers) of the company.

Because of its simplicity and flexibility, an LLC is very popular for both start-up businesses and more-mature businesses. In many states now, the number of new LLCs forming is outpacing the number of new corporation filings.

Franchise

A franchise represent an agreement or contract between two or more persons by which a franchisee is granted the right offer, sell or distribute goods or services under a marketing plan or system dictated substantially by a franchisor. The business is substantially associated with the franchisor's trademark, service mark, trade name, advertising or other commercial symbol designating the franchisor or its affiliate. The franchisee is generally required to pay, directly or indirectly, a franchise fee.

Trade Names, Fictitious Names

"Trade names" is a relative term. Trade names may be referred to as "fictitious names," "assumed names," or "DBAs." Using a trade name or fictitious name allows a business owner or business entity to operate a company using a name other than its real name. (Marilou's Diner sounds more inviting than Eat at MLB Group, Inc.) Registering this additional name insures that another entity will not use the same or similar name.

Typically, the state agency that oversees corporation records usually maintains the files for trade names. Nearly all states provide a website to do a status check of names; most states also provide a verbal service.

Some states will administer "fictitious names" at the state level, while county agencies administer "trade names," or vice versa. Many California counties provide online fictitious business name lookups.

Employer Identification Number

For the purposes of accounting, for tax returns, for fraud prevention, and for claims verification, the U.S. Internal Revenue Service assigns individual Employer Identification Numbers (EINs) to business companies, estates, and trusts or non-profits operating in the U.S. or operated by U.S. citizens. This includes Indian Tribes, churches, farmers' cooperatives, plan administrators, and government agencies. Sometimes EINs are referred to as Federal Employer Identification Numbers or FEINs. An EIN is classified as a Taxpayer Identification Number (TIN), as is a Social Security Number (SSN).

All of the business entities mentioned in the above section must have an EIN. Within a large business conglomerate or corporate, different business entities may be assigned different EINs.

Sole proprietorships are not required to obtain EIN numbers; they may use the Social Security Numbers of the proprietor for identification if they wish.

A completed IRS W-9 Form – Request for Taxpayer Identification Number Certification – is often requested by companies from their suppliers to insure taxes are not withheld from monies paid to entities for supplies or services. The W-9 calls for the disclosure of the EIN if the entity is a business and an SSN if the entity is an individual or sole proprietor.

EINs as Location Tools

The EIN consists of nine digits, same as a Social Security Number. EINs are distinguishable by use of the two-digit code in front of the remaining seven numbers. In general, these two digits indicate the location or origin of the entity applying for the EIN.

Prior to 2001, the EIN's first two digits indicated the specific IRS office that issued the number, a great tool for determining where a business entity might be headquartered. Since 2001, numbers are only assigned by three major EIN offices (at Brookhaven [Holtsville] NY, Philadelphia, and Cincinnati), seven smaller IRS offices, and by EIN Internet and telephone assigning entities. While the state location cannot be determined under the new system, the Present Issuer may help. For example if issued by Cincinnati, the location state is likely to be Michigan, Illinois, Indiana, or Kentucky. So, the Present Issuer gives *somewhat* of a regional clue, but not a reliable one due to many exceptions.

The middle column of the chart shown below also indicates the *state of issue* for the first two digits on an EIN in the old, pre-2001 EIN system.

Table of EIN Issuing Offices Codes and Assigned States

EIN Prefix	Original Issuer (Pre-2001)	Present Issuer (2001 forward)
01	ME	Brookhaven
02	NH	Brookhaven
03	VT	Brookhaven
04	MA	Brookhaven
05	RI	Brookhaven
06	CT	Brookhaven
10		Andover
11	NY	Brookhaven
12		Andover
13	NY	Brookhaven
14	NY	Brookhaven
15		Fresno
16	NY	Brookhaven
20		Internet
22	NJ (2)	Brookhaven
23	PA	Brookhaven
24		Fresno
25	PA	Brookhaven

26		Internet; Philadelphia in pre-internet era
27	IL	Internet; Philadelphia in pre-internet era
30		Cincinnati
31	OH	Small Business Admin
32		Cincinnati
33	CA	Philadelphia
34	OH	Brookhaven
35	IN	Cincinnati
36	IL	Cincinnati
37		Cincinnati
38	MI	Cincinnati
39	WI	Philadelphia
40		Kansas City
41	MN	Philadelphia
42	IA	Philadelphia
43	MO	Philadelphia
44		Kansas City
45	ND	Philadelphia
46	SD	Philadelphia
47	NE	Philadelphia
48	KS	Philadelphia
50		Austin
51	DE	Brookhaven
52	DC	Brookhaven
53		Austin
54	VA	Brookhaven
54	WA	Brookhaven
55	WV	Brookhaven
56	NC	Brookhaven
57	SC	Brookhaven
58	GA	Brookhaven
59	FL	Brookhaven
60		Atlanta
61	KY	Cincinnati
62	TN	Philadelphia
63	AL	Philadelphia
64	MS	Philadelphia
65	FL	Brookhaven
66		Philadelphia
67		Atlanta
68	CA	Philadelphia
71	AR	Philadelphia
72	LA	Philadelphia

73	OK	Philadelphia
74	TX	Philadelphia
75	TX	Philadelphia
76	TX	Philadelphia
77	CA	Philadelphia
80		Ogden
81	MT	Philadelphia
82	ID	Philadelphia
83	WY	Philadelphia
84	CO	Philadelphia
85	NM	Philadelphia
86	AZ	Philadelphia
87	UT	Philadelphia
88	NV	Philadelphia
90		Ogden
91		Philadelphia
92	AK	Philadelphia
93	OR	Philadelphia
94	CA	Memphis
95	CA	Memphis
98		Philadelphia
99	HI	Philadelphia

The EIN Chart provides a great starting point to finding or researching a business entity, once you have secured an EIN. But the chart does not mean the entity is headquartered or even located in that state since businesses are not required to obtain a new EIN if they move or change names. But strict guidelines are in place when certain re-organizations occur. For example, a corporation requires a *new* EIN under any of these four conditions: it receives a new charter from a Secretary of State; it becomes a subsidiary of another corporation; it changes to a partnership or sole proprietorship; or, a new corporation is created as a result of a statutory merger. A new EIN is *not* required if you are simply a division of a corporation, the surviving corporation after a corporate merger, or the corporation declares bankruptcy. Nor is a new EIN needed if the corporation name or location changes, or if its status changes to an S corporation, or if a corporate reorganization changes only its identity or its home base.

To learn the requirements when other business entities need to change an EIN, see www.irs.gov/businesses/small/article/0,,id=98350,00.html.

Although the IRS does not make the identity of EINs public, EINs do find their way into the public record by circumstance. They can be found in bankruptcy cases, civil court actions, sometimes in local recorded documents, but mostly in state and federal filings.

A commercial vendor, freeERISA.com, LLC, provides three free searches of EINs and unlimited Internet access for its half a million subscribers at www.freeerisa.com. ERISA stands for Employee Retirement Income Security Act – monies held by retirement plans and monitored by the IRS. The EIN is used to identify the businesses involved. Some of the vendors in the section *Searching Non-Profits, Foundations and the Wealthy* later in this chapter also provide EIN data.

Searching Organization Records at State Agencies

As mentioned previously, businesses are organized and registered at the state level, usually with the Secretary of State. An initial search for a business entity's records usually starts there with a record index. An index "hit" will lead to a document file number or images of documents. Most states merge the indices of all their registered business entities (corporations, partnerships, LLCs, LLPs, etc.) and registered business names into one index. Usually this index is searchable at a public access terminal on-site and is also searchable online.

Note: Corporations that are publicly traded or offer shares of ownership and are exempt from filing with the SEC must register with a state securities regulator. This is another source of public records information. See *Searching Publicly Owned (Traded) Companies* later in this chapter.

Information Available

Information available from a registration file typically includes the date of registration, status, name and address of the registered agent and, sometimes, the names and addresses of officers, directors or principals. The **registered agent** is the person authorized to receive legal papers such as service of process. The registered agent can be a company attorney or a designated third party who specializes in representing business entities.

The registration file usually holds a myriad of other company documents. For example, a corporation registration file will typically include the articles of incorporation, annual reports, merger documents, name changes, and termination papers. Partnership and LLC filings may include similar documents with details such as how decisions are made, how profits are distributed, and names and addresses of all limited and general partners or owners. Finding this material is a good way to find the start of a paper trail and/or to find affiliates of the search subject.

All state agencies provide a business **name check** so that a new entity can make sure the name is not already used by an existing business entity. Doing a business name check is a good way to find where a business is located and leads to additional information about a business.

Checking to see if a company is currently incorporated is called a **status check.** If an entity's registration is current and there are no problems, a document known as a **Good Standing** may be purchased. If available, **articles of incorporation** or amendments to them as well as copies of **annual reports** also may provide useful information about an entity or business owner. Keep in mind corporate records may *not* be a good source for a business address because most states allow corporations to use a registered agent as their address for service of process.

State Nuances

Many large companies that do business in multiple states will incorporate in Delaware or Nevada.

Most states have one central agency that oversees business entity records and filings, but there are several exceptions of note.

- **Arizona** – The Corporation Commission oversees corporation and LLC records. The Secretary of State oversees all partnerships including LPs and LLPs; as well as trademarks, servicemarks, and trade names.

- **South Carolina** – The Corporation Division oversees corporation, LP, LLP, LLC, trademark and servicemark records. The Department of Revenue oversees annual reports and records of directors.

- **Kansas** – Kansas does not have statutes requiring or permitting the registration or filing of DBAs or fictitious names.

Searching Tips

Many of the searching tips previously described in the chapters on court records and recorded documents are very applicable to the search methodology for a business records index.

Regardless if the search is on-site or online, always familiarize yourself with the alphabetizing system in use. For example, knowing how to search properly for the following is crucial:

- **When a company name starts with the word *The.*** Should you search for *The ABC Company* or search by *ABC Company, The* ?

- **When a company name starts with a number.** Is the number alphabetized as a word? Are listings with numbers found at the front or the end of the index?

- **Watch for key words that may indicate name changes, former entities, or related companies.** For example, if a company is known as *YESS Embroidery and Screenprinting*, it would be worthwhile to search for *YESS Embroidery, YESS Screenprinting, YESS Screenprinting and Embroidery, The YESS*

Company, etc. Also, ascertain if the use of an "&" in place of the word "And" will modify the search.

- **Know the capacity for error and forgiving of typos**. If you can pull an alphabetical index list, make sure that screenprinting is not listed as screnprinting, or even screen printing, etc.

Often, an investigation of a business entity entails public record searching on associated officers or company principals. Finding the names of these people within business records is certainly a good way to start, and there are many other search avenues including occupational licensing databases, industry associations, and using the news media. These areas are covered in the *Searching A thru Z* chapter.

The last portion of this chapter discusses how to use online vendors to find business entity information, including a section devoted to searching non-profits.

Free Web Access to Corporation & Business Entity Records

Every state provides a business search tool on the web. This helpful table will lead you to the web page to find information on state-registered business entities. Usually the look-ups include all business entities types, including non-profits.

State	Web Page
Alabama	www.sos.state.al.us/vb/inquiry/inquiry.aspx?area=Corporations
Alaska	https://myalaska.state.ak.us/business/
Arizona – eFilings Search	http://edocket.azcc.gov/
Arizona – Registered Name Search	http://starpas.azcc.gov/scripts/cgiip.exe/WService=wsbroker1/main.p
Arkansas	www.sos.arkansas.gov/corps/
California	http://kepler.ss.ca.gov/list.html
Colorado	www.sos.state.co.us/pubs/business/main.htm
Connecticut	www.concord-sots.ct.gov/CONCORD/index.jsp
Delaware	https://sos-res.state.de.us/tin/GINameSearch.jsp
District of Columbia	http://mblr.dc.gov/corp/lookup/index.asp (No data searching, only checks name availability.)
Florida	www.sunbiz.org
Georgia – Site 1	https://corp.sos.state.ga.us/corp/soskb/login.asp
Georgia – Site 2	www.ganet.org/services/corp/individual.html
Hawaii	http://hawaii.gov/dcca/areas/breg/online/
Idaho	www.sos.idaho.gov/corp/corindex.htm
Illinois	www.ilsos.gov/corporatellc/
Indiana	www.in.gov/sos/business/corporations.html
Iowa	www.sos.state.ia.us/corp/corp_search.asp
Kansas	www.accesskansas.org/srv-corporations/index.do
Kentucky	http://sos.ky.gov/business/filings/online/
Louisiana	www400.sos.louisiana.gov/app1/paygate/crpinq.jsp

State	Web Page
Maine	https://icrs.informe.org/nei-sos-icrs/ICRS
Maryland	http://sdatcert3.resiusa.org/ucc-charter/CharterSearch_f.asp
Massachusetts	http://corp.sec.state.ma.us/corp/corpsearch/corpsearchinput.asp
Michigan	www.cis.state.mi.us/bcs_corp/sr_corp.asp
Minnesota	http://da.sos.state.mn.us/minnesota/corp_inquiry-find.asp?:Norder_item_type_id=10&sm=7
Mississippi	www.sos.state.ms.us/busserv/corp/soskb/csearch.asp
Missouri	https://www.sos.mo.gov/BusinessEntity/soskb/csearch.asp
Montana	http://app.mt.gov/bes/
Nebraska	https://www.nebraska.gov/sos/corp/corpsearch.cgi?nav=search
Nevada	https://esos.state.nv.us/SOSServices/AnonymousAccess/CorpSearch/CorpSearch.aspx
New Hampshire	https://www.sos.nh.gov/corporate/soskb/csearch.asp
New Jersey	https://accessnet.state.nj.us/home.asp
New Mexico	www.nmprc.state.nm.us/cii.htm
New York	http://appsext8.dos.state.ny.us/corp_public/CORPSEARCH.ENTITY_SEARCH_ENTRY
North Carolina	www.secretary.state.nc.us/Corporations/
North Dakota	https://secure.apps.state.nd.us/sc/busnsrch/busnSearch.htm
Ohio	www.sos.state.oh.us/sos/ucc/UCC.aspx?Section=101
Oklahoma	https://www.sooneraccess.state.ok.us/home/home-default.asp
Oregon	http://egov.sos.state.or.us/br/pkg_web_name_srch_inq.login
Pennsylvania	www.corporations.state.pa.us/corp/soskb/csearch.asp?corpsNav=|
Rhode Island	http://ucc.state.ri.us/CorpSearch/CorpSearchInput.asp
South Carolina	www.scsos.com/corp_search.htm
South Dakota	www.state.sd.us/applications/st02corplook/corpfile.asp
Tennessee	www.tennesseeanytime.org/soscorp/
Texas – Site 1	www.sos.state.tx.us/corp/sosda/index.shtml
Texas – Site 2	http://ecpa.cpa.state.tx.us/coa/Index.html
Vermont	www.sec.state.vt.us/seek/corpseek.htm
Virginia – Site 1	http://docket.scc.virginia.gov:8080/vaprod/main.asp
Virginia – Site 2	www.scc.virginia.gov/division/clk/diracc.htm
Washington	www.secstate.wa.gov/corps/search.aspx
West Virginia	www.wvsos.com/wvcorporations/
Wisconsin	www.wdfi.org/apps/CorpSearch/Search.aspx?
Wyoming	https://wyobiz.wy.gov/

Searching Publicly Owned (Traded) Companies

There are two important facts to know about finding information about publicly traded companies:

1. Publicly traded companies operating in the U.S. are required by federal law to register with the Securities and Exchange Commission (SEC).

2. If a publicly traded company does not meet certain "thresholds," it submits filings with a state regulatory securities agency instead of the SEC.

Either the SEC or these state agencies monitor the registered companies for any irregularities or potential fraudulent behavior.

EDGAR and the SEC

Publicly traded companies must inform the public the complete truth about their businesses' financial data. EDGAR – the **E**lectronic **D**ata **G**athering **A**nalysis and **R**etrieval system – was established by the SEC as the means for companies to make required filings to the SEC by direct transmission. As of May 6, 1996, all non-exempt companies (see below), foreign and domestic, are required to file registration statements, periodic reports, and other forms electronically through EDGAR. Thus, EDGAR is an extensive repository of U.S. corporation information available online. Anyone can access and download this information for free.

Companies must file the following reports with the SEC:

- 10-K – an annual financial report that includes audited year-end financial statements.

- 10-Q – a quarterly, unaudited report.

- 8K – a report detailing significant or unscheduled corporate changes or events.

- Securities offering, trading registrations, and final prospectus.

- DEF-14 – a definitive proxy statement offering director names, their compensation and position.

The list above is not all-inclusive. Other miscellaneous reports include items dealing with security holdings by institutions and insiders. Access to these documents provides a wealth of informative data about these companies.

EDGAR offers a guide on how to search publicly traded companies; go to www.sec.gov/investor/pubs/edgarguide.htm. The record searching site at EDGAR is www.sec.gov/edgar/searchedgar/webusers.htm.

A number of private vendors offer access to EDGAR records along with some added features and searching flexibilities. Recommended sites include www.edgar-online.com, www.secinfo.com, www.edgarlive.com, and www.lexisnexis.com.

For more information about other SEC databases including enforcement actions, see the *Securities and Securities Dealers* section in the *Searching A thru Z* chapter.

The Regulation D Rule

Under the Securities Act of 1933, any offer to sell securities must either be registered with the SEC or meet an exemption. Per the SEC Regulation D there are three exemptions – known as Rules 504, 505, and 506 – which allow many smaller companies to offer and sell their securities without having to register those securities with the SEC.

While companies using an exemption under Regulation D do not have to register their securities and usually do not have to file reports with the SEC, they must file what's known as a Form D after selling their securities. Form D includes the names and addresses of the company's owners and stock promoters, but not much else. These companies are regulated by state regulatory agencies per the state's **Blue Sky Laws** (see below).

Recently, the SEC adopted regulations to streamline Regulation D reporting and ease some of the disclosure requirements for smaller reporting companies.

To determine if a company has filed a Form D, call the SEC Office of Investor Education and Advocacy at 202-551-8090 or email publicinfo@sec.gov. If the company has filed a Form D, you can request a copy of the Form. For more information about the exemptions visit the SEC web page at www.sec.gov/answers/formd.htm.

State Regulatory Agencies and Blue Sky Laws

Every state has securities laws—often referred to as **"Blue Sky Laws"** — designed to protect investors against fraud. These laws, which do vary from state to state, typically require companies making small offerings to register their offerings before they can be sold in a particular state.

Records of the filings by companies registering under Blue Sky Laws, as well as any records of legal actions, are held by designated state regulatory securities agencies. These records are open to the public and can be a great source of data when searching for assets, ownership records, or doing background investigations. For example, a registration record that has valuable public data is the Small Corporate Offering Registration (SCOR) document used by small companies issuing stock directly to the public.

However, in many states the filing records are not generally available online and often will require in person visits to the agency. Records found more often on the web are reports of legal actions or sanctions, with extensive details on names and addresses. The state agency that oversees these filing and legal actions also usually licenses and holds records of brokerage firms, their brokers, and investment adviser representatives.

For links to all the state regulatory agencies visit the North American Securities Administrators Association web page at www.nasaa.org/QuickLinks/ContactYourRegulator.cfm. Another source is a vendor site at www.seclinks.com/id16.html.

Searching Franchise Records

Franchises are regulated by the Federal Trade Commission (FTC) and by state regulatory agencies. (See *Blue Sky Laws* above.) If the franchise involves a public offering, then records may also be in the SEC database.

A key public record document associated with a franchise is the Uniform Franchise Offering Circular (UFOC). Usually, this document may be obtained from a state agency or from a vendor, but not the FTC.

The International Franchise Association (IFA) is a great resource of basic information about member franchising and the members of this trade association. IFA can be reached in Washington, DC at 202-628-800 or www.franchise.org.

Other Resources

There are many resources available to find general information about a publicly traded company. Every major stockbrokerage firm offers some free information on the web. Search engines Yahoo! and Google provide in-depth data on publicly traded companies. Also, check out The Motley Fool at www.fool.com and the *Investors Business Daily* at www.investors.com.

Business registrations, changes, and annual reports are available via each state's Secretary of State web page. The web links are presented earlier in this chapter; see *Web Access to Corporation & Business Entity Records Table.* Also visit a site that offers free public record links such as - www.blackbookonline.info or www.brbpub.com.

Vendors provide company information. Several companies, including www.annualreports.com, tout access to annual reports. A Google search will uncover many more. A number of commercial vendors with extensive proprietary databases are mentioned later in the article *Recommended Online Database Services* by Cynthia Hetherington.

Several sites of note with free or pay information and other business related tools for searching public and private companies include–

www.hoovers.com/free

www.manta.com

www.spoke.com

Searching Private Companies

There are several distinctly different search avenues to explore to find information on private companies.

Search Company Records

Finding the ownership and records of private companies can be a difficult task. The entity may be registered at the state, but minimal public disclosure and required forms may be available. To the plus, there are a number of vendors who profile both public and private companies. Hoovers (www.hoovers.com) is perhaps the firm most widely known and used. Local Chambers of Commerce and Better Business Bureaus may be useful; to find their local offices go to www.worldchambers.com and www.bbb.org.

Other investigative resources are the business and credit report data that can be obtained from vendors such as Dun & Bradstreet (D&B), Experian, and SkyMinder.

Search by Ownership

Two websites are recommended in Cynthia Hetherington's *Business Background Investigations* book:

- https://solutions.dnb.com/wow/
- www.corporateaffiliations.com

Search by Industry

One of the most powerful resources for searching industrial information, products and services is ThomasNet (www.thomasnet.com). From the home page you can also link to the Thomas Global Register then search worldwide industrial Information from more than 700,000 suppliers in 28 countries.

At the end of this chapter are profiles of four unique global-in-nature business data resources.

Below is an excerpt taken from Cynthia Hetherington's book *Business Background Investigations*. We sincerely thank her for allowing us to reproduce this article and also her article at the end of this chapter.

Tips From a Professional Searcher

By Cynthia Hetherington

Do not underestimate news stories, press releases, and a company's website. The "About Us" section may accurately offer company history and ownership information. However, it is best to verify any company-produced literature. Given that investigators always verify their leads, take a look to see what is on the website that offers clues. Visiting the website will give you a sense of what the company has to say.

When the question comes down to "who owns whom?" I recommend two valuable resources for finding the ultimate parent of a company—

1. *The Directory of Corporate Affiliations* - www.corporateaffiliations.com, owned by LexisNexis.

Per their web page... "Our database provides current, accurate corporate linkage information and company profiles on nearly 200,000 of the most prominent global public and private parent companies and their affiliates, subsidiaries and divisions—down to the seventh level of corporate linkage.

"Not only does Corporate Affiliations publish corporate family trees, the database also contains over 700,000 corporate contacts, 110,000 board members, 150,000 brand names, and 140,000 competitors."

2. *Who Owns Whom* - https://solutions.dnb.com/wow, presented by Dun & Bradstreet.

This international database covers the following industries since January 2006— "...manufacturing, retail trade , wholesale trade, agriculture, mining, construction, financial services, educational institutions, business services, professional services, also public, private and government-run companies."

Searching Non-Profits and Foundations

Below are recommended organizations that are quite helpful for finding information on non-profits.

Capital Research Center (CRC) www.capitalresearch.org, established in 1984 to study non-profit organizations, provides a free database search of non-profits including associated activists and directors.

GuideStar is a non-profit entity that supplies detailed financial information about non-profits. Guidestar's fee-searching content includes searchable data from IRS Forms 990 and the IRS Business Master File, including comprehensive facts on employee compensation and grant activity. It also offers free access to basic information on 1.5 million non-profits. Registration is required. www.guidestar.org

The Foundation Center is a national organization that serves as an authoritative source of information on foundation and corporate giving. Publications include *The Foundation Directory*, various regional and reference books including *Securing Your Organization's Future, A Complete Guide to Fundraising Strategies* by Michael Seltzer. Many public libraries throughout the country participate in The Foundation Center's Cooperating Collections network. For further information on services, publications, and locations of cooperating collections, call 1-800-424-9836. http://foundationcenter.org

The Taft Group publishes the *Corporate Giving Directory* that provides comprehensive profiles on America's major corporate foundations and corporate charitable-giving programs. Search The Taft Group indices by company name, location, recipient type, or officers and directors names. The Taft Group also publishes *Guide to Private Fortunes* (profiles of wealthy philanthropic individuals and families) and *Who Knows Who: Networking Through Corporate Boards.* www.taftgroup.com

Enterprise Resources Database is another resource worth checking. The website provides fundraising tools with plenty of good information on how to find qualified prospects to donate money and help with fundraising. The site's search of qualifying potential donors is a quite useful as reference resource for finding personal and business assets and financial relationships. www.practitionerresources.org

The rest of this chapter is an excerpt from *Business Background Investigations* by Cynthia Hetherington.

===

Recommended Online Database Services

By Cynthia Hetherington

The key to learning more about any company is to find out who the administration is, what type of financials can be obtained, how many locations it has, and what type of industry it is involved in.

There are numerous online services to research both large and small corporations. The given for large companies is that the bigger they are, the easier it is to gather information on them. The tasking issues are discerning the volumes of data and deciding on what is valuable and current and what is not. Researching the target company by using online database vendors is a must.

Dun & Bradstreet

Dun & Bradstreet is the largest provider of business reports internationally, with more than 100 million companies in its database. Very small, one-man companies and very large, mega corporations are in its international collection. For investigators who conduct a lot of due diligence or who find themselves often looking into companies, D&B may be worth the starting subscription price of several thousand dollars.

The shortcoming of this service is its price. However, you can search for your company for free. At the page www.dnb.com/us, you will see the "Find a Company" search box. This "Find a Company" search box extends to international searches. Your company should be listed.

Special Tips for Searching D&B

Search by the person's last name or full name instead of the company name. This is especially handy for small companies. D&B will find the owner's name and cite it as "Also Trades As:."

Key things to know about searching D&B reports include:

- For information that contributes to an investigative reports report, use D&B reports as a lead, not the answer.
- The best part of the reports is not the financial information.

The best parts of a report for investigators are:

- Name of company and owner
- Phone and fax
- History of company and principals
- Public filings
- And the really best part of D&B is being able to search inside its database.

The following reasons illustrate the need to use D&B:

- Fraudulent companies often share fax numbers, even though they generate new phone numbers for business. ALWAYS SEARCH the FAX!
- Searching by the principal's name will often show current company interests and former company interests.
- Dun & Bradstreet automatically does Soundex searching. The name Bill will generate William hits.
- Address searches will show other companies listed at the same address, including mail drops and suspicious addresses.

If you can not afford D&B directly, you can access its reports through one of D&B's resellers such as Dialog, SkyMinder, LexisNexis or Bureau van Dijk. If you are a licensed investigator with an account at ChoicePoint or Accurint, both resell D&B reports. However, keep in mind that direct service subscribers get much better pricing.

Kompass.com

Kompass originated in Switzerland and is now present in 70 countries. It offers a very reasonably priced collection of information on more than two million companies globally. With a subscription you can locate the executives of companies and obtain addresses, corporate structures, names of key figures, company turnover information, company descriptions, product names and services, trade and brand names, and location of branches. Kompass offers free searches for the following topics:

- Region – Geographically locate all companies

- Products/Services – Type of product (i.e. clocks, telephones, hamburgers)
- Companies – Name of company
- Trade names – Name of product
- Executives – Search by 'person at the top'
- Codes – NAICS, SIC, and other government-related codes

This is a considerable amount of information when you are starting from nothing. The address and phone numbers are leads that can be explored at www.google.com or other databases, such as D&B. Having a ballpark number of employees also is helpful. The minimum amount of credit units you can buy is 50, which costs $150 (USD).

SkyMinder.com

SkyMinder, located in Tampa, Florida, is an affiliate of CRIBIS S.p.A., based in Bologna, Italy. SkyMinder is an incredible aggregator of corporate business and credit reports. Consider the following:

- Used by more than 330 Italian banking and financial institutions and more than 14,000 Italian, European, and U.S. companies.
- Supplies online credit and business information on more than 50 million companies in 230 countries.
- Only works with Internet Explorer version 5.0 and newer.
- One of the best places to buy inexpensive D&B header reports.
- Available data (per the web page) includes: marketing data, line of business, incorporation details, shareholders/owners, executives, employees, office and facilities, business structure (headquarters, parent, branches, subsidiaries), rating, credit limit, payment information, financials, banking relationships and accountants, litigations, etc.

For a complete source list visit, including how often updated, visit www.skyminder.com/basic/info_sources.asp.

Bureau van Dijk (BvDEP)

Because there is so much that Bureau van Dijk (www.bvdep.com) offers, it is difficult to catalog its many databases. With a unique name for each service, international databases such as ORBIS and Osiris are teamed up with country-specific services like Ruslana (Russia), Sabi (Spain), and Jade (Japan).

ORBIS is a global database that has information on more than 35 million companies. ORBIS covers:

- 48,000+ "publicly listed" companies worldwide
- 28,000+ banks and 7,700+ insurance companies
- 15 million+ European companies from 46 countries

- 14 million+ U.S. and Canadian companies
- 3 million+ South and Central American companies
- 1.3 million+ Japanese companies
- approximately 65,000 companies from countries in East and Central Asia
- approximately 39,000 African companies

Their information is sourced from more than 40 different information providers, all experts in their regions or disciplines. With descriptive information and company financials, ORBIS contains extensive detail on items such as news, market research, ratings and country reports, scanned reports, ownership, and mergers and acquisitions data.

ORBIS has several different reports for each company. View a summary report, a report that automatically compares a company to its peers, or view more detailed reports that are taken from BvDEP's specialist products.

Searching ORBIS can be done in basic or advanced modes. The advanced mode offers searches by company names, locations, board member and executive names, specific financials, mergers and acquisitions deals, etc.

Once a name is searched, a page with the number of results is offered. You can pay to look at all the results or choose a free preview in order to see if you are close to the results you want.

Unique database services of Bureau van Dijk include—

- **ZEPHYR** - A worldwide database of detailed information on rumored, announced or completed financial deals; it includes approximately 80,000 new deals a year.
- **CAMEO / TRACE** – Search for and verify any individual's name and address, anywhere in the United Kingdom, using the Electoral Roll.
- **FAME** - Company accounts, ratios, activities, ownership and management of the largest 2.4 million British and Irish companies, and summary information for an additional 950,000 smaller businesses.
- **JADE** - Company accounts, financial ratios, activities and management of more than 380,000 Japanese companies.
- **ODIN** - Standardized annual accounts, financial ratios, activities and ownership information for 700,000 companies in Scandinavia.
- **QIN** - Company accounts and financial ratios for 300,000 companies in mainland China in both standardized and local detailed formats.

Searching Motor Vehicle Records

Motor vehicle records, essential decision-making tools for hiring and rate determination. They are used by many industries and groups, particularly insurance companies, trucking firms, employers, lenders, and private investigators. In general, motor vehicle records can be made *public* only if personal information is not disclosed, depending on the type of record and the state involved. This chapter reviews the various types of motor vehicle records, when they are public or not, and how to search.

Overview

The types of records characterized as *motor vehicle records* for the purposes of this chapter include—

- Driving history (also known as an MVR)
- Driver license status
- Accident Report
- Traffic Ticket
- Vehicle registration, status
- Vehicle title (ownership), title history, liens
- Vessel registration
- Vessel title, title history, liens
- VIN – Vehicle Identification Number

In general, the databases for each of these record types are maintained by state agencies, but in some jurisdictions a local agency is empowered to process record requests.

Four Critical Rules

Before we proceed with a review of motor vehicle record searching procedures, keep in mind four important rules about state motor vehicle records—

1. Each state maintains its own separate database of licensed drivers, vehicle registrations, vehicle ownership, accident reports, and other associated records.

2. There is NO national database of driving records. [15]

3. The Federal Driver's Privacy Protection Act (DPPA)[16] sets specific standards when the personal information can be included on records – but not necessarily on whom can access records.

4. Many state jurisdictions impose restrictions on the access of motor vehicle records per DPPA. But many state agencies permit the public to obtain **sanitized records** (no personal information shown) without the consent of the subject.

The Similarities and Differences Among the States

Who is legally permitted to access driving or vehicle records? What degree of authority is needed to obtain a full record? What data is found on a record? What information is masked from the public's view? Will the records you request actually give you the information you seek?

Answers to these questions are all subject to individual state statutes, state administrative rules and regulations, and compliance with Federal laws. The manner in which states communicate internally or externally and their policies of reciprocity reflect the diversity that contributes to making each state unique.

The Affect of DPPA

As mentioned, the Driver's Privacy Protection Act (DPPA) has an important influence on motor vehicle records. This is because DPPA mandates that states differentiate between *permissible uses* (14 are designated in DPPA) and casual requesters. Thus the reason for the record requests determines who may receive a record with personal information. Records with personal information are only given to those with a listed permissible use or with the written consent of the driver.

All states are in compliance with the DPPA standards. Note that these standards are only minimal and states can be more restrictive. Nearly half of the states sell "sanitized records" (personal information redacted) to casual requesters. Some states refuse to disclose any certain personal information on their records to anyone. The state profile pages at the end of this chapter indicate which states sell sanitized records.

Driving Records

The acronym MVR comes from the phrase "Motor Vehicle Record" or "Moving Violation Record." The majority of the time when the term MVR is used it simply means a driving record.

---

[15] However, there are two national indices maintained by the National Driver Registry; one for commercial drivers (CDLIS) and one for problem drivers (PDPS).

[16] 18 USC Section 2721.

An MVR is a historical index of a driver's moving violation convictions, accidents, and license sanctions. Depending on the state's record reporting procedure, an MVR can show activity anywhere from 3 years to a lifetime. By far and away, the primary users of MVRS are the insurance and trucking industries. Together they account for easily over 90% of all record requests.

Note: If you talk to someone at a state motor vehicle department about records, be sure you are clear on what you want or mean. A state DMV official hearing the words motor vehicle record or MVR may think you are referring to a vehicle title or registration record, or perhaps a status record.

Typical Access Methods and Requirements

Few states will perform a (name search(without being provided with other key identifiers. Typically, a request for an individual's driving record must include the full name with middle initial, date of birth, and/or the driver license number. Similarly, vehicle record requests require the name and plate number and/or VIN (vehicle identification number).

Access methods fall into two overall categories – manual or electronic.

Manual access methods include in-person, fax, phone, and mail. Every state does not offer every access method. A limited number of states will provide fax or phone services for approved ongoing accounts – Missouri, Nevada, and Oregon for example. There are at least three states that do NOT provide businesses an in-person, counter service – California, Michigan, and Wisconsin.

Electronic access methods vary widely depending upon how orders are grouped or submitted, and by the media type. Most states provide **interactive processing**. This means the results of a record request is shown immediately. Usually single name requests are sent one at a time, perhaps in rapid succession. This method is popular if a quick decision needs to be made about hiring or about the issuance of a new insurance policy. Usually interactive processing is handled via the web or on a private access dial-up system.

Batch processing is when a group of record requests are submitted in bulk and results are obtained at a later time. Most states offer electronic batch processing online, usually by the web using File Transfer Protocol (FTP) technology, and a few states still offer access via cartridges and/or magnetic tapes.

Types of Driving Records

Depending on the state, driving records generally fall into one of several categories, often based on the reason for the request—

- Employment (Commercial Driver License holder - CDL)
- Non-Employment (without CDL data)

- Insurance
- Certified

Generally an employment record is limited to only reporting activity while driving a commercial motor vehicle (CMV). In most cases, certified records can only be obtained manually.

The License Status Report

A **status report** – the top or header portion of a driving record – can sometimes be obtained as a separate record. The license status report generally indicates three important pieces of information:

1. The type or class of license issued which in turn tells what types of vehicles (commercial, non-commercial, motorcycle) can be operated. Different commercial license classes regulate the size or weight of the vehicle licensed to be driven.

2. Any special conditions placed on the license holder. These permissions and limitations are known as endorsements and restrictions. A typical restriction is a requirement to have "corrective lenses" when driving. Another example is a CDL license may have an endorsement that regulates if hazardous material can be hauled.

3. If the license is valid or under suspension or revocation.

A handful of states offer online status checks. Some are free, some are for a fee. The state-by-state searching tips at the end of this chapter indicate states that offer free online status reports.

State Fees

The fees that states charge to access a motor vehicle record vary widely. For example, the fee for a driving record via electronic access ranges from $1.25 in Minnesota and Missouri to $19.25 in Rhode Island. Overall, the average fee for electronic access for all states is approximately $6.30. Access to MVRs represents a major source of revenue to the states. Over 700,000 driving record requests are processed daily in the U.S., which means over $4,000,000 a day is generated by the states from sales of driving records.

A state's fee structure can also vary by the type of access method. For example, 17 states charge more per record for electronic access than for manual, and 6 states charge more for manual processing than electronic. A number of states charge set-up fees and/or annual fees to online subscribers, generally under $100 per year. Some states require extensive deposits or even performance bonds to be placed as collateral.

Key Data Found On Motor Vehicle Records

Nationally, the information found on each state's record is somewhat standardized, but there are notable differences among states.

License Status

As mentioned, status information indicates the license class, if any restrictions or endorsements, and if the license is valid or under a suspension, etc.

Traffic Violations and Accidents

The heart of the driving record is a list of traffic tickets resulting in a conviction. The only time you will see a pending conviction is if the incident involves a situation that triggers an immediate suspension – such as with alcohol related matters – or if an alleged violator fails to appear in court.

Typical information on a driving record includes date of violation, date of conviction, location of incident, points assessed, and description or descriptive code of the violation. Other possible pieces of information include the state statute related to the violation, the type of court, and court location. Accident involvement is also reported, but reporting who is at fault is spotty at best. If there is no conviction appearing with the date of the accident, this usually indicates involvement with no fault, but not always depending on the state.

Withdrawals and Administrative Actions

DMV officials often use the term *withdrawal actions*. The most common actions are suspensions, revocations, and disqualifications. Sometimes a withdrawal may be triggered by a specific violation or series of violations. At other times the withdrawal may be administered by a judge or a DMV official.

Personal Information about the Driver

Personal information found on an MVR may include the licensee's address, height, weight, date of birth. As a rule, Social Security Numbers and medical information is always redacted and never released to record requesters. As mentioned, the release of personal information on motor vehicle records is governed by the DPPA, based on if for a permissible use or if the consent of the subject is given.

However, the level of compliance with the Act is inconsistent from state-to-state; some states have stricter policies than the Act. Some states never release personal information and there are states that make available records either with or without personal information. The State Summary pages at the end of this chapter indicate when states offer *sanitized* (no personal information) records to the public.

Record Reporting and Data Retention

How far back records go and what is reported are aspects of MVRS that vary from state to state. The standard reporting period for most states is at least three years for moving violations and from five to ten years for administrative actions. However, a number of states provide for a longer time period on a standard record, and many states offer options for more in-depth records. For example, besides a three-year record, Georgia also provides a seven-year record, Vermont an eight-year record, and Pennsylvania a complete lifetime record. Extra fees may be involved to purchase these. How long the states keep record data varies also. Federally mandated data retention and reporting standards for commercial (CDL) drivers require the retention period to be fifty-five years.

What data appears on reports also varies by state. Some states do not report certain low level moving violations, especially to insurance companies. Accident reporting is not consistent, neither is the length of time shown for previous suspensions or major convictions such as alcohol-related incidents.

The state summaries pages indicate some of these variances.

Vehicle and Vessel Records

Vehicle records available include ownership and titles, registrations, vehicle identification numbers (VINs), license plates, and liens placed on vehicles. Ownership and title records of vehicles can generally be ordered as either a current record or as a historical record showing all previous owners. Title data can indicate if a vehicle was at one time a junk vehicle or if the vehicle was once a subject of title washing (previously branded as a salvage or flood-damaged vehicle), or perhaps a government vehicle previously.

Usually the same state agency that administers driving records also administers vehicle records. In some states vehicle records are controlled by an entirely different state government department or division. Also, in some states the liens on vehicles are recorded at the county or at the Secretary of State's Office where UCCs are filed.

Decoding a VIN

VIN stands for "vehicle identification number." This number is internationally recognized as the way to identify an individual vehicle. When buying a used vehicle, many people and dealers check the history of a VIN with a private vendor to help make an informed decision about the quality and value of the vehicle. Vehicles have a metal plate stamped with unique VIN located somewhere on the dashboard or door, but the VIN may also be found attached to other locations on the vehicle.

A VIN consists of 17 characters (vehicles manufactured before 1981 may have fewer characters) in a highly coded but strict format structure. A simple overview of how is decode a VIN by the character position is shown below.

Position	Explanation
1	The country where vehicle manufactured

2	The vehicle manufacturer
3	The make
4-8	Unique characteristics, such as the body style or engine
9	A check digit to help identify VIN fraud
10	The model year
11	The location where assembled
12-16	The assembly line sequence number

A code table that shows all the possible meanings for each position is a very extensive document, and it changes frequently. Web resources to decode a VIN include:

- www.autocheck.com
- www.cardetective.com
- www.carfax.com
- www.decodethis.com

About Vessels

Vessels and watercraft that weigh more than five tons are registered with the U.S. Coast Guard, www.st.nmfs.noaa.gov/st1/CoastGuard/. Another handy location to search for larger vessels, or to search by lien or title, is the Coast Guard's National Vessel Documentation Center found at www.uscg.mil/hq/g-m/vdoc/poc.htm.

Smaller vessels, usually those for pleasure or sport, are registered through a state motor vehicle department or a state environmental agency such as a Fish & Game Department.

The types of vessel records available from state agencies are very similar, with different terms used sometimes for the registration or plate type data. Not all states title watercraft, and those that do generally only require titles if over a certain length or motorized. Similar requirements may be imposed when registration is mandatory.

Vehicle and Vessel Record Access

There are many similarities between accessing driving records and vehicle records, especially if records are administered by the same agency that handles driver records. Regardless of which agency oversees vehicle recordkeeping, record access is affected by DPPA as described for driving records. The access methods for vehicle records are similar to the methods used for driving records; however, not every state offers online access. A few states offer status checks, see the state profiles section later in this chapter.

The same description above holds true for vessel records *if* the vessels are administered by the same motor vehicle agency. When watercraft and watercraft records are governed by a different government agency, the access policies are usually not governed by DPPA. In these states certain records may be more open to access, but generally access is governed by administrative rules or even by statute.

Vehicle record data that includes personal identifiers is never sold for marketing purposes, as per DPPA.

The state searching tips pages indicate when the state government agency administering vehicle records or vessel records is separate from the agency that oversees driving records.

Accident or Crash Reports

First, be aware that many states use the term "crash reports" and will bristle if you use the term "accident reports." Also, there are usually two types of accident records for each incident – the reports filed by the citizens involved and the reports prepared by the investigating officers. Copies of a *citizen's* accident report are not usually available to the public and are not reviewed herein. For the purposes of this publication, we will use the term accident reports and designate those records as reports prepared by the investigating officer.

Generally, accidents investigated by local police officials or minor accidents where the damage does not exceed a reporting limit (such as $1,000), are not available from state agencies.

Usually an entity known as the *State Police* or *Department of Public Safety* maintains the database of accident reports. Some of these agencies make records open, but most do not. Generally, record access is only given to a person involved in the accident or to an entity representing one of the parties involved, or when a party involved gives written consent. Sometimes accident records are open after a designated time period passes. Accidents reports involving a fatality are often held for a longer time period before the record is open to the public.

When records are maintained by the same agency that holds driving records, the DPPA guidelines are followed with regards to honoring record requests.

Typical information found on a state accident report includes drivers' addresses and license numbers as well as a description of the incident. Accident reports are normally not available online.

There is no overall national database of historical accident information maintained by either a government agency or by private enterprise. A good rule of thumb is accident records must be obtained from the investigation agency.

For detailed information about each state's procedures regarding when accident reports must be filed and how to obtain record copies, see *The MVR Book* by BRB Publications. [17]

Motor Vehicle Record Searching Tips by State

This section contains state specific record searching tips, including:

- When coding is used on the make-up of a driver's license number
- When sanitized records are available to the public
- Free web look-ups for license or vehicle status checks
- When the agency administering vehicle records and/or vessel records is not that same agency administering driving records
- Where vehicle and vessel lien records may be accessed
- Additional searching tips of note

Alabama

Driving Records – Maintained by Department of Public Safety. Personal information is only available if a record is accessed online. Mail or walk-in requesters do not receive records with personal information.

Vehicle Records – Maintained by Department of Revenue. County of registration is coded by the first number on a license plate as follows: 1 is Jefferson, 2 is Mobile, 3 is Montgomery; numbers 4 through 67 correspond to an alphabetical listing of the remaining counties, thus 4 is Autauga and 67 is Winston.

Vessel Records – Maintained by Department of Conservation and Natural Resources. Liens are found at the central state location for UCC filings, call 334-242-5231.

Alaska

Driving Records – Sanitized records are not available. Fax requests accepted for pre-approved accounts. Liability insurance is not required in areas where registration is not required, with the exception of a driver who has received a ticket for a violation of 6 points or more within the last 5 years and is ordered to have liability insurance. A list of these locations is shown at www.alaska.gov/dmv/faq/manins.htm.

Vehicle Records – Sanitized records are not available.

Vessel Records – Boats are registered with the DMV. Liens are filed with the Department of Natural Resources, Recorder's Office, 907-762-2104. The DMV does not record lienholders for boats.

---

[17] Published annually by BRB Publications, www.brbpub.com

Arizona

Driving Records – Sanitized records are not available. MVD allows customers to electronically view and print their own 39-month uncertified driving record at www.servicearizona.com. The $3.00 fee requires use of a credit card.

Vehicle Records – Sanitized records are not available. A title history will show liens.

Vessel Records – Records maintained by the Game & Fish Department. Lien records are not maintained here and must be researched at the county recorder offices.

Arkansas

Driving Records – Sanitized MVRs not available. Driver Services offers a monitoring and notification system for employers to track incidents of drivers. Commercial Driver Watch permits employers to receive notification on the change in the driver license status for registered employees. Visit www.arkansas.gov/driverwatch/index.html.

Vehicle Records – The Office of Motor Vehicles maintains title, registration, and lien records for vehicles and mobile homes. Social Security Numbers are not released.

Vessel Records – Also, this agency registers vessels; however, lien records on boats are found at the county level or at Secretary of State.

California

Driving Records – The DMV offers the public an Occupational License Status for these categories: ATV School, Dismantler, Distributor, Driving School, Lessor-Retailer, Manufacturer, Mature Driver, Program, Registration Services, Remanufacturer, Traffic Violator School, Transporter, Vehicle Dealer (including Autobroker), and Vessel Agent at https://mv.dmv.ca.gov/olinq2/welcome.do.

The Department offers a Pull Notice Program to provide employers and regulatory agencies with an ongoing method to monitor driver records. The employer enrolls specified drivers in the program and is notified when the record has activity. For more information visit the website at www.dmv.ca.gov/vehindustry/epn/epnformlist.htm or write the DMV care of the Employer Pull Notice Unit - H265 or call 916-657-6346.

Vehicle Records – A casual requester must state the purpose and/or use of the information. Records will be withheld for ten days, pending notification to the subject who can then, if he/she wishes, object to the release of information (CVC 1810(b)).

Vessel Records – Vessel records may be obtained from the Department of Motor Vehicles. Liens are filed here. Name searches for vessels are permitted, but you must use the state form. The vessel owner is notified and has 10 days to respond if the owner does not want information released.

Colorado

Driving Records – Sanitized MVRs not available from the MVD. Convictions on the record indicate an accident occurred or not by a (Y/N.(Thus, accidents are not reported on the driving record if the driver was not convicted of a violation.

Vehicle Records – Sanitized records not available from the MVD. A search will provide the vehicle description, the name and address of the owner, and lien information if there is a lien on the vehicle. To obtain vehicle lien records, the VIN and (if possible) title number and Form DR 2539 are required. Handicap and Disabled Vet plate information is not released.

Vessel Records – The Colorado State Parks maintains records for boats, snowmobiles, and off-highway vehicles. Lien information is not recorded here and must be searched at the Department of Revenue.

Connecticut

Driving Records – The first two digits of the nine-digit DL indicate, by odd or even year, the driver's month of birth, and the seven additional numbers are the next available sequential numbers. Vendors may not transmit records via the Internet unless acceptable safeguards are imposed. Driver history records do not contain address information. Sanitized records are not available.

Vehicle Records – The standard fee is $20.00 for a title search which includes lien data.

Vessel Records –The DMV maintains the registration file for boats. All motorized boats and all boats over 19 1/2 ft must be registered. Boats are not titled.

Delaware

Driving Records – The DL is one to seven numbers and is computer generated; there is no coding. Zeros are not placed in front if number is less than seven digits. Accidents are only reported when a conviction is rendered. Sanitized records are only released on a case-by-case determination.

Vehicle Records – Sanitized records are only released on a case-by-case determination. The DMV has records of liens.

Vessel Records – The Department of Natural Resources and Environmental Control registers all personal watercraft. Registration information is considered confidential and this agency follows DPPA guidelines. However, the agency will verify information over the phone with a yes or no response only. Liens are filed at the Secretary of State and are not found at this location.

District of Columbia

Driving Records – DMV records do not contain personal information. Some SSNs are still used as DLs. It will take until at least 2010 for all the SSNs to be replaced.

Vehicle Records – Permission of driver/owner required for record; no personal data released. Liens records held here at DMV.

Vessel Records – Lien, title and registration records maintained by the Metropolitan Police Department, Boat Registration Unit, 202-727-4582 http://mpdc.dc.gov/mpdc/site/default.asp.

Florida

Driving Records – The DL is one letter followed by twelve numbers. The letter corresponds to the first letter of the last name. No sanitized records are available. A free status check is found at https://www6.hsmv.state.fl.us/dlcheck/dlcheckinq (note: the last letter is Q not G) for any FL driver license number. Only the license number is used to access an MVR. No personal information is released.

Another status site gives an insurance update and allows parents to view the driving record of their children under 18. Go to https://www6.hsmv.state.fl.us/DLCheck/main.jsp. Check the status of a HAZMAT endorsement at https://www2.hsmv.state.fl.us/.

Vehicle Records – To research by name, for current vehicle information, the DOB and city are required. The fee for non-certified computer printouts of VIN, registration, lien, and tag (plate) checks is $ .50 per request. Enter title # or VIN to check vehicle status at https://www6.hsmv.state.fl.us/rrdmvcheck/mvcheckinq.

Vessel Records – Same agency manages vessel records. A written request is required for all searches. Florida works with the local county tax collectors' offices in recording titles and registrations; this permits real-time connection.

Georgia

Driving Records – No sanitized records available. Drivers may view or download a non-certified copy of their driving record at https://online.dds.ga.gov/onlineservices/MVRInfo.aspx. Fees involved. Records maintained by Department of Driver Services.

Vehicle Records – MVD at the Department of Revenue controls records, lien data is available here also. A vehicle insurance status check is free on the web at https://mvd.dor.ga.gov/vincheck/VinCheck.aspx. Also, there is a web inquiry program for GA dealers only. In addition, email requests may be sent to motorvehicleinquiry@rev.dor.ga.gov.

Vessel Records – Georgia Department of Natural Resources, Boat Registration Office, 800-366-2661. Liens are filed at the county level and do not show on records found at this agency.

Hawaii

Driving Records – Hawaii does not have a separate state department or division that manages and regulates all motor vehicle and driver functions. The Hawaii Department of Transportation, Motor Vehicle Safety Office is responsible for program co-ordination of five separate county-responsible agencies. The Traffic Violations Bureau, Abstract Section, 808-538-5530, processes MVR requests. No personal information is released.

Vehicle Records – Hawaii does not have a statewide Department of Motor Vehicles. Vehicle Registration is managed by each county government.

Vessel Records – Records held by Land and Natural Resources, Div. of Boating & Recreation, www.hawaii.gov/dlnr/dbor/dbor.html, 808-587-1963. Requests must be in writing and describe reason for the search. Liens are filed at the Bureau of Conveyances, but information is made available from the aforementioned agency.

Iowa

Driving Records – Records are released to casual requesters without consent, but no personal information is released. For MVRs and vehicle records, if ordered by a private investigator, the request form mandates that a copy of the Iowa state PI license be attached. This applies to a licensed security company as well.

Vehicle Records – Without Consent Vehicle histories, title research, registration research, and owner name research are available on vehicles, mobile homes, motorcycles, and trailers. See above about PIs.

Vessel Records – Boats, snowmobiles, and all-terrain vehicles are registered and titled at the county recorders' offices. Boats with liens must be titled.

Idaho

Driving Records – DL is 2 alpha, 6 numeric, 1 alpha. If no consent, records without personal information are released. When requesting driver records, if you do not provide the individual's SSN/DLN or if it differs from the information you provide, the driver's license number will not be disclosed. The SSN is never disclosed. The state refers to the driving record as a DLR (Driver License Record). Accidents are not reported on the driving record.

Vehicle Records – The prefix to the passenger plates designates the county of issuance. The code is the numeric sequence of the first initial of the county with that initial (i.e. Butte is the 10th county starting with B, so the prefix is 10B). If no consent, records without personal information are released, same agency as with MVRs. Liens here.

Vessel Records – Idaho Parks & Recreation, 208-514-2480, ext 306. Registration records are open to the public. Record information can be verified or provided; however state statutes forbid the release of commercial lists. Lien record information must be searched at the UCC Division at state, call 208-334-3191.

Illinois

Driving Records – DL is one letter and eleven numbers, coding is not released. A non-exempt requester must provide the purpose of the request and receives data without addresses and personal information. Before information is released, there is a ten-day waiting period while the Driver Services Dept notifies the subject.

Vehicle Records – Personal information is not released for non-business purposes, from Vehicle Services Dept.

Vessel Records – Department of Natural Resources, Records and Legal Services, 217-557-0180, http://dnr.state.il.us. All watercraft must be registered and titled unless only used non-motorized on a private lake. Liens are recorded with this agency.

Indiana

Driving Records – The DL is 10 numbers, the first 3 digits denote the License Branch where issued. Casual requesters can obtain records but without personal information.

Accident Reports – Records have been privatized. Copies of accident reports may be obtained from an agency working within the offices of the State Police Department. Address requests to Holt, Sheets & Associations, Vehicle Crash Records Sections, 100 N Senate, Room N301, Indiana Government Center, Indianapolis 46204, 317-233-5133

Vehicle Records – The name of the county of issuance appears on the top of the plate along with a corresponding number from 1 to 98 per an alphabetical list of the 92 counties. Thus 1 is Adams, 2 is Allen, etc. Two counties have additional assigned numbers; Marion County has 93, 95, 97, 98, and 99 while Lake County has 94 and 96 assigned. The title history will show liens. Casual requesters receive sanitized records.

Vessel Records – Indiana is a title and registration state: all motorboats and jet skis valued over $3,000 when new must be titled and registered by same agency maintaining driver and vehicle records.

Kansas

Driving Records – Effective July 1, 2004 all licenses are issued an assigned number consisting of the letter "K" plus eight numbers. Until that date, the SSN was also used as a license number. The SSN could still show as a valid number until July 2010. Generally, motor vehicle records cannot be released without consent.

Vehicle Records – The Dept of Revenue maintains registration and lien information on vehicles and unattached mobile homes.

Vessel Records – Department of Wildlife and Parks, Boat Registration, Pratt KS, 67124-8174 620-672-5911, www.kdwp.state.ks.us. Boats are not titled in Kansas. Liens are recorded at the county level with the Register of Deeds. Registration requests must be in writing with an explanation of why the information is needed.

Kentucky

Driving Records – The DL or ID consists of a combination of a single alpha and eight numerals. The alpha corresponds to the first initial of last name, but if name changes license number does not. A three-year driving record without personal information or accidents may be obtained http://dhr.ky.gov/DHRWeb, fees involved.

Vehicle Records – The agency will not do a name search. Passenger plates have county of issue printed on bottom; commercial plates do not.

Vessel Records – Records can be obtained from the Division handling vehicle records. Only motorized boats must be titled and registered. Title and registration information is available from 1992 to present. Prior records are kept by county clerks. Direct questions to 502-564-2737.

Louisiana

Driving Records – DL is even digits preceded by two zeros (e.g. 001234567). No sanitized records released by DPS.

Vehicle Records – No sanitized records released. The state closed the walk-in counter. Lien records are here with DPS.

Vessel Records – Department of Wildlife & Fisheries, 225-765-2898 www.wlf.state.la.us. Release of registration records is subject to very strict criteria. No titles issued; liens are filed at parish courts.

Maine

Driving Records – Drivers convicted of an offense for OUI under drugs or alcohol will have an asterisk displayed on their license for 10 years. Casual requesters without consent can obtain records, including online, but personal information is shielded, except for the personal information submitted with the request. The BMV offers a Auto Fax Back program enabling the requester to order a driving record over an automated telephone system. Driver CrossCheck allows employers to automatically receive notification about changes to the driving records of employees.

Vehicle Records – Without consent, the vehicle records released by the BMV contain no personal information.

Vessel Records – ATV and snowmobile records as well as boat records are maintained by the Department of Inland Fisheries and Wildlife. Mobile homes are only required to be registered if they are being moved.

All mobile homes records (including lien records) are maintained by the municipality in which the mobile home is located. All motorized boats must be registered; boats are not required to be titled. Liens are not shown and must be searched with the Secretary of State, 207-624-7760.

Maryland

Driving Records – The DL is 1 letter and 12 numbers. The letter represents the first letter of driver's last name. The twelve numbers are coded in groups of three, creating a unique total number: the first three digits are coded to the last name; the second three to the first name; third group to the middle name; and the last group is coded to the month and day of birth. Using Form DR-057 requesters may obtain a non-certified record without personal information; consent is not needed. The MVA implemented the **License Monitor System (LMS)** for employers and insurance companies who need to monitor their employees' or their insured drivers' driving records for violations and suspension.

Accident Reports – Copies of accident reports investigated by the State Police, except if occurred in the city of Baltimore, can be requested from: Maryland State Police, 410-298-3390. Records are open after 60 days.

Vehicle Records – Title service agents offer services related to MVA certificates of title, registrations, drivers' licenses, certified copies of records, and other related documents. Fees vary. A listing of agents is found at www.marylandmva.com/VehicleServ/REG/titleagents.htm. Using Form DR-057 requesters may obtain a non-certified record from the MVA without personal information; consent is not needed.

Vessel Records – Department of Natural Resources, Licensing & Watercraft Division, 410-260-3220, www.dnr.state.md.us. All motorized boats must be titled and registered. Lien records are blocked and not released. However, when asked the Department will indicate with a yes or no if a lien exists.

Massachusetts

Driving Records – In Massachusetts there are two agencies that provide driving records. The Registry of Motor Vehicles (RMV) provides records to employers and for personal use. The Merit Rating Board's MVRs are used for private passenger automobile insurance purposes. Casual requesters without consent can obtain records without personal information.

Vehicle Records – Lien information is automatically provided by the Registry as part of registration and title information. Casual requesters without consent can obtain records without personal information.

Vessel Records – Massachusetts Environmental Police, 617-626-1610 www.mass.gov/dfwele/dle/elereg.htm. State law requires all boats 14 ft or over to be titled. Records from 2000 forward are available by telephone. SSNs, DOBs, and subject phone numbers are not released. This agency maintains lien record information and will release lien holder names and addresses.

Michigan

Driving Records – The format of the DL is one letter followed by twelve numbers coded as follows: three numbers for the last name, three numbers for the first name, three numbers for the middle name, and three numbers for the birth month and day. Because a small number of drivers' names and birth dates have the same number, MI began using the first initial of the last name with the code 726 or 727 to assign drivers a unique driver license number. BUT Michigan will be changing their numbering system with the implementation of the forthcoming Business Application Modernization (BAM) project.

Casual requesters without consent can obtain records without personal information. Fax and phone requesting is available for pre-approved, established accounts or for those obtaining their own records. Results are returned by mail. Major credit cards are accepted. This agency also provides accident reports in the same manner.

Vehicle Records – Casual requesters can obtain records, personal information redacted. Lien records available here. A Repeat Offender Registration Status Inquiry to check the eligibility of a vehicle purchaser is at http://services.sos.state.mi.us/repeatoffender/inquiry.aspx.

Vessel Records – The Department of State, Record Lookup Unit that handles driver and vehicle records also has vessel records and liens.

Minnesota

Driving Records – The driver license number is one letter followed by twelve numbers. Until 12/2004, the letter represents the first letter of the last name; the numbers represent a coding of the last name, the first name, the middle name and date of birth. Casual requesters can obtain records, personal information redacted.

A Status Report of the driver license is available at www.mndriveinfo.org using the DL# as input. There is no fee; no personal information is released.

Vehicle Records – If no notarized consent, casual requesters can only obtain records without personal information. For a free status report, (no personal information released) enter a MN plate or registered VIN at https://dutchelm.dps.state.mn.us/dvsinfo/mainframepublic.asp.
Counties are coded on plates in alphabetical order respectively from 01 to 87. The coding is as follows: 01 is Aitkin, 02 is Anoka...and 87 is Yellow Medicine. Code 88 is used for Foreign.

Vessel Records – Department of Natural Resources, Information Education and Licensing Bureau, 651-296-2316 (Registration); 296-7007 (Titling). Lien information found here.

Mississippi

Driving Records – The license number is a randomly nine-digit number in the same format as a Social Security Number, with the first three digits being 800 (i.e. 800-11-1111). No sanitized records released.

Vehicle Records – Please note there are two bureaus – Title Bureau and Motor Vehicle Bureau (MVLB) – within the Tax Commission which furnish information. They are both located at 1577 Springridge Rd, Raymond, 39154. Be sure to address mail requests accordingly. Without consent, records are not available.

Vessel Records – Wildlife, Fisheries and Parks Department, 601-432-2186, www.mdwfp.com. The department will do a record search with a boat number or name at no fee; however, they will screen calls to insure that the purpose of the request complies with DPPA. Liens are shown.

Missouri

Driving Records – The DL is the SSN (issued prior to 12/17/05) or an assigned number consisted of one alpha and five to nine numbers or nine numbers only. Sanitized records released to casual requesters. Phone, fax and email requesting available for approved account holders.

Vehicle Records – Without consent, records are released, but personal information is blocked. Lien information shows on title records.

Vessel Records – Motor vehicle Bureau also handles watercraft records. Lien information shows on title records.

Montana

Driving Records – Since October 1, 2005, Montana driver licenses and IDs are issued with a system generated 13 digit number. Previous number could be the SSN or the first initial of the last name followed by 8 randomly generated numbers. Sanitized records are available if no consent. A Public User web service is offered for record access; no personal data released.

Vehicle Records – Title and Registration Bureau handles vehicle records including liens. Sanitized records are available if no consent. Public User service also available for vehicle records, fees involved.

Vessel Records – All boats must be titled and registered. Records, including liens, are maintained at the agency above.

The Temporary Registration Permit site at https://app.mt.gov/trp/client allows registered users to create, reissue and void Temporary Registration Permits for recently purchased vehicles. Searching for a vehicle by Vehicle Identification Number is also available.

Online access is available (see above), otherwise the $6.00 search fee must be included with requests. All requests in writing must be on the state form. Turnaround time is normally 10 to 12 days. Lien information shows on the title. Records are available from 1988 to present.

Nebraska

Driving Records – One letter (A, B, C, E, G, H, or V) and 3 to 8 digits make up the license number. Without consent, no records are released.

Vehicle Records – First number(s) of the plate designate county of issuance, except in Douglas, Lancaster and Sarpy counties. The list of the 93 numbers and counties can be obtained from the DMV. Current title and registration information on vessels can be obtained from this agency, but lien records, including liens on vessels, are maintained by the County Treasurer in the county where the owner resides.

Vessel Records – See above.

Nevada

Driving Records – Without Consent, records are released, but all personal information is blocked. Nevada offers a retrieval phone-in system at 775-684-4590. Callers must have an assigned five-digit account number for access. Pre-approved callers can request up to 5 MVRs at a time.

Vehicle Records – The Department of Motor Vehicles also blocks personal information of vehicle records if consent not given. Same telephone system for driving records offered for vehicle records

Vessel Records – Department of Wildlife, Attn: Boat Registration, 775-688-1511 www.ndow.org. All motorized boats must be registered and titled. The boat registration, hull number, or name of owner is needed to search. SSN is blocked. Current lien-holder name and address released.

New Hampshire

Driving Records – DL is two numbers, three letters, then five numbers; coded as follows: birth month (two digits); the first letter of the last name; the last letter of the last name; the first letter of the first name; the year of birth (two digits); day of birth month (two digits); and a computer "twin" number (usually one, never a zero). Casual requesters may not obtain records.

Vehicle Records – Bureau of Titles and the Registration Section are at different locations at the Dept. of Safety. Each oversees the appropriate records. The Bureau of Title oversees requests for lien information. Casual requesters may not obtain records.

Vessel Records – The Department of Safety also maintains the database of boat registrations. The same privacy provisions apply as those to vehicle records. Liens on boats are recorded with the Secretary of State, call 603-271-3242.

New Jersey

Driving Records – First letter of last name and fourteen numbers. For example, DL Number "S5778-40771-01024" of John Smith is interpreted as follows: S is first initial of last name of the driver, 5778

coded as next four letters of last name (i.e., <u>mith</u>), 407 coded as first name (John), 71 coded ass middle initial (J.), 01 coded as birth month for males (January) (if Female then 51), 02 is year of birth (1902), 4 coded as eye color (blue). Vendor's representing end user clients with a permissible use must first submit a client list complete with name, address, phone number, and client's intended use. The CAIR provides driver status information to entities such as school transportation providers, vehicle rental companies, and other approved businesses for a fee of $2.00 per inquiry

Vehicle Records – For vehicle and vessel registration, use Motor Vehicle Services, Attn: Certified Information, PO Box 146, Trenton, NJ 08666, 609-292-6500 or in-state at 888-486-3339. For vehicle and vessel ownership, use Motor Vehicle Commission, Special Titles, PO Box 017, Trenton, NJ 08666-0017. Motor Vehicle Services maintains registration, title, and lien information on all vehicles including mobile homes and boats. Also, the MVC issues motorboat and Jet Ski licenses for use on fresh, non-tidal waters or lakes, creeks or rivers not affected by tidal conditions. SSNs and medical information are not released.

Vessel Records – See above.

New Mexico

Driving Records – Records without personal information are released to businesses, consent not needed. SAMBA's (see above) FleetWatch Service provides automated driver monitoring for risk management and loss control. Monthly reports identify invalid drivers, note new citations, and highlight past and current license renewal dates. For more information go to www.samba.biz or call 505-797-2622, option 3.

Vehicle Records – There is no fee for VIN, plates, registration or lien information, certified copies or histories from microfilm from the Vehicle Services Bureau. The Motor Vehicle Division also maintains the record database for boat registrations; however, lien information on boats under 10 feet in length is filed with UCCs at the Secretary of State's office.

Vessel Records – See above.

New York

Driving Records – New York assigns randomly selected nine-digit numeric Client Identification Numbers to all driver licenses and non-driver ID cards. By mail or in person, the DMV will provide sanitized, printed "Abstract of Operating Record" showing license status and type, traffic convictions, suspensions, revocations and accidents, but not motorist(s address. The License Event Notification Service (LENS) enables an organization to file with DMV a roster of employees or volunteers who drive on the organization's behalf. The LENS program will notify the organization if a new event posts to a registered driver's record.

Vehicle Records – Lien/Title Status Check displays the date the title was issued by the DMV, number of liens (if any), and the lien holder. No personal information is displayed. Enter the VIN, vehicle model year, and vehicle make at www.nysdmv.com/titlestat/default.html. Otherwise, a requester without permissible use or consent may not access another's vehicle record.

Vessel Records – The DMV issues titles for model year 1987 and newer boats at least 14 feet long and are registered in NYS. This includes homemade boats manufactured on or after 8/1986 if a model year is not designated. Lien data is included on some registrations.

North Carolina

Driving Records – DL is one to twelve numbers; the DMV indicates most new numbers start with four zeros, such as "00008..." If no consent, casual requesters cannot obtain records. A record service at https://edmv-dr.dot.state.nc.us/DrivingRecords/DrivingRecords allows NC citizens to purchase a NC driving record online. Requesters must first apply for a PIN which is disclosed by email.

Vehicle Records – Casual requesters that do not qualify as a permissible users under DPPA can only obtain records without personal information.

Vessel Records – Wildlife & Resource Commission, Transaction Management, 800- 628-3773, http://216.27.49.98. All motorized boats and all sail boats over 14 ft must be registered. Effective 01/07, titles are mandatory; previously this was optional. Now all liens are filed here and are shown on Title Certificates.

North Dakota

Driving Records – The DL is an alpha numeric combination comprised of nine characters beginning with the first three letters of the last name (if last name is only two letters, an "X" is added). At https://secure.apps.state.nd.us/dot/dlts/dlos/welcome.htm one may view and print a limited record. The fee is $3.00 per record and a use of a credit card is required. A limited record does not include convictions more than three years old, convictions assigned less than three points, suspensions/revocations/cancellations that have been satisfied and are more than three years old, or any crash information. A free status check is at https://secure.apps.state.nd.us/dot/dlts/dlos/requeststatus.htm.

Vehicle Records – If no consent, records are released without personal information. Liens are automatically shown on an ownership search. A written request on "Form SFN-51269" is required.

Vessel Records – North Dakota Game & Fish Department, 701-328-6335. All motorized boats and all sailboats must be registered. No titles are issued here. This agency does not follow DPPA; records are considered open to the public. Liens are filed with UCC filing locations at either the county or state.

Ohio

Driving Records – DL is two letters followed by six numbers. Records without personal information are not sold but driver can view record at https://www.dps.state.oh.us/netsys/netdb/ENGLISH/MMENU.asp. There is no fee.

Vehicle Records – The Ohio BMV website at https://www.dps.state.oh.us/atps offers a free search by either title number or identification number, but the results do not include personal information. The site also includes information on watercraft. The title information available from the web page is obtained from Ohio county title offices. Title information may not exist in the system and on this web page for titles issued prior to March 1993 because all Ohio county offices were not automated until then.

Vessel Records – Natural Resources Department, Division of Watercraft, 614-265-6480, www.dnr.state.oh.us. Only Watercraft Agents issue registrations (at the county level). Only Country Clerks of Court write titles. But this agency has access to all records. Lien information will be provided, but you must first request it in writing.

Oklahoma

Driving Records – Records Management Division, Attn: MVR DESK Records are released without consent but they do not contain personal information.

Vehicle Records – Oklahoma Tax Commission, Motor Vehicle Division Oklahoma has an elaborate coding system for plates. The MVD has a 252- page book that describes all codes for all vehicles for all types of plates. No vehicle records are released without consent; information is only released to statutorily qualified requestors. The Tax Commission holds lien records for both vehicles and boats.

Vessel Records – See above.

Oregon

Driving Records – All newly issued numbers are seven digits; the older format is one to nine numbers. A sanitized record (no personal information) is available. IVR is an automated record inquiry system by telephone available only to record inquiry account holders. The ARS Program allows users who have a Record Inquiry Account to submit a name list and DMV will automatically produce a printed driving record whenever a conviction, accident or suspension is posted to the record.

Vehicle Records – IVR also provides for vehicle records. To set-up an account or more information, please call 503-945-5312. Sanitized records are available.

Vessel Records – Oregon State Marine Board, 503-378-8587 www.boatoregon.com. Titles and registrations are issued on all motorized boats and on sailboats over 12 ft. Lien information is shown on the title record.

Pennsylvania

Driving Records – No record information is released without consent. All signed agreements forbid the requester from using the Internet as a means to transmit data to end-user clients without express written permission from PennDOT. While the state does not offer a monitoring system or notification program to employers or insurance companies to track incidents of drivers, account holders who employ commercial drivers or school bus drivers can apply for unlimited electronic access to driver records.

Vehicle Records – Encumbrance/lien information is not considered public information and is only available per DPPA guidelines.

Vessel Records – Fish and Boat Commission, 717-705-7940, www.fish.state.pa.us. The agency follows the FCRA regarding the release of boat registration and ownership information. Liens are filed here.

Rhode Island

Driving Records – The DL is seven numbers. The first two numbers represent the year of issuance, the third digit represents the location where was license issued, and the last four digits are sequential numbers. A (V(and six numbers indicates a disabled veteran. If no consent, no record is released to mail or walk-in requesters. There is a record available online that does not report personal information and can be ordered by a casual requester with the consent of the subject not needed.

Vehicle Records – No consent, no vehicle record. Lien records here at Registry of Motor Vehicles.

Vessel Records – Department of Environmental Management, Office of Boat Registration, 401-222-6647. All boats over 14 ft must be titled and registered. Lien information will show on a title record. For casual requesters, this agency will not release the name and address of a lien holder, but will indicate whether a lien does exist.

South Carolina

Driving Records – Without consent, casual requesters cannot obtain a driving record but may obtain an online summary including points history and current status at www.scdmvonline.com/dmvpublic.

Vehicle Records – To causal requesters, the DMV will not release name and address information, but will confirm validity of name and address if provided by requester. Lien records here.

Vessel Records – Department of Natural Resources, Registration & Titles, 803-734-3857. All motorized boats must be titled and registered. All boat motors must be titled. There is a distinction between a boat title and a motor title. Sailboats 14 ft and over must be titled and registered. A title search request will show any liens.

South Dakota

Driving Records – No records are released, even without personal information, if consent is not given. Pre-approved accounts may order records by phone. In state requesters must pay a 4% tax on all record requests.

Vehicle Records – The first 1 or 2 numeric characters on a plate designate the county of issuance. There are 66 (1-65 + 67) codes, but they are not in alphabetical order. We suggest calling the state for this information, if needed. The DMV has lien data.

Vessel Records – The DMV took over the registration process for boats in 1992. Liens and registration records are available for boats 12 foot or longer and motorized boats. Liens on smaller boats are filed with UCCs at the Secretary of State.

Tennessee

Driving Records – Records are released by the Dept of Public Safety without personal information to casual requesters.

Vehicle Records – On July 1, 2006 by Executive Order from the Governor, the Title and Registration Division of the Tennessee Department of Safety was moved to the **Tennessee Department of Revenue**. This Division is now known as **Taxpayer & Vehicle Services**. Without consent, records are strictly limited and requests are reviewed on a case-by-case basis. If released, personal information is blocked. Trailers used for the transportation of boats are exempt from both title and registration.

Vessel Records – Wildlife Resources Agency, Boating Division, 615-781-6585 www.state.tn.us/twra. All motorized boats and all sailboats must be registered; there are no titles. All lien information is found at the Secretary of State. One may request records via email to darren.rider@state.tn.us.

Texas

Driving Records – DL is eight numbers, beginning with 0, 1, or 2. No sanitized records are released. Texas offers employers a free annual driving check of school bus drivers.

Vehicle Records – No sanitized records are released from the Vehicle Titles and Registration Division. No name checks performed.

Vessel Records – Parks and Wildlife Department (TPWD), 512-389-4828. Record checks can be processed by any TPWD Law Enforcement Field Office. History requests may be submitted to any of these offices, but results are returned by Headquarters. Lien information will show on title reports with the microfilm report showing complete lien history. The name and/or registration number is required. All requests must be in writing and contain the following phrase in the request: *"The information obtained will be used for a lawful purpose."*

Utah

Driving Records – DL can be four to ten numbers, but currently only nine digit numbers are being issued. In the future ten digit numbers will be utilized. If consent is not presented, records are not released to casual requesters.

Vehicle Records – State Tax Commission provides access for ownership and lien records for vehicles, boats, and mobile homes. Utah also has a program for dealerships and financial institutions requesting lien-holder information. The state will not do a (name check(nor release medical records, SSNs, or insurance information.

Vessel Records – See above. All boats manufactured in 1985 or newer must be titled. All boats except canoes must be registered.

Vermont

Driving Records – If no consent, records without personal information are released

Vehicle Records – The DMV maintains records on vehicles, motor homes, trailers, and boats. Lien record information is provided to all of these conveyances. Potential lien-holders are provided a (yes or no(answer when asking about liens on a vehicle.

Vessel Records – See above. All boats that operate with an attached motor must be registered.

Virginia

Driving Records – Social Security Numbers are being phased out as the driver license number. All licenses issued since July 1, 2003 display a computer generated random number consisting of an alpha character followed by eight numbers. Consent from the driver is required for release unless the record is being provided to law enforcement, a government entity, the DMV or if an employer is requesting records on a CDL driver. No sanitized records are released.

Vehicle Records – Prospective Purchaser Inquiry (PPI) produces a summary about a vehicle. Requester must provide the vehicle's make, model and VIN. This fee service does not contain personal information about the vehicle's previous owners. Visit https://www.dmv.virginia.gov/dmvnet/ppi/intro.asp.

Vessel Records – Game & Inland Fisheries Department, 804-367-6135 www.dgif.virginia.gov. All motorized boats must be registered and titled. Non-motorized boats sailboats over 18 ft are titled. Liens are included on the record. The records are open to the public to the extent that information is released with either a title or hull #. Submit either the title or hull #. Name searches are not performed.

Washington

Driving Records – DL is first five letters of last name, first initial, middle initial, three numbers, and two letters or numbers (i.e., WASHI G E 222 O3). Coding of the last five characters is not released due to security reasons; however, this code is widely known among commercial MVR vendors and insurance industry personnel.

Either the driver's license number or full name (with middle initial) and date of birth are needed when ordering an MVR. If all three identifiers submitted, the state will search using only the license number. Many ongoing requesters prefer to not use the license number and submit only the name and date of birth. This is because the license number can be confusing as it may contain "Os," "0s," and asterisks (*).

A Driver Status Display is free at https://fortress.wa.gov/dol/ddl/dsd. User can verify validity of license and ID cards. All responses are in a yes or no format. No personal information is provided.

The Department operates a monitoring system for insurance companies to review the driving records of existing policyholders for changes to the driving record.

Vehicle Records – No sanitized records are released. Telephone service is available to authorized users. A commercial Internet search known as IVIPS (Internet Vehicle/Vessel Information Processing System) is available for pre-approved accounts to obtain line holder data. The Department maintains the database for registrations, titles, and liens for vehicles, mobile homes, and boats.

Vessel Records – See above.

West Virginia

Driving Records – A seven digit alpha/numeric series, with no correlation to type of license issued, is used as follows(A000001 - A999999; E000001 - E999999; S000001 - S999999; B000001 - B999999; 1X00001 - 1X99999; F000001 - F999999; C000001 - C999999; XX00001 - XX99999; D000001 - D999999; and 0000001 – 0999999.

If no consent presented, no records are released; however, the state permits the requester to use the "Message Forwarding Service" that enables the state to forward a request to the license holder to approve the record request. There is a $5.00 service fee plus the cost of the MVR.

Vehicle Records – The DMV maintains records including liens for vehicles, boats, and unattached mobile homes. Same Message Forwarding Service is available as above.

Vessel Records – See above. All boats with a motor or a sail must be titled and registered.

Wisconsin

Driving Records – DL is one letter followed by thirteen numbers. The coding of driver license numbers is as follows for A5364683945805: A- first letter of last name; 536- coded from last name; 468- coded from first name and middle initial; 39- birth year; 458- coded month and day of birth, sex; 05 code for tie-breaker/check-digit.

Sanitized MVR records not available, but check the status of a driver license free at www.dot.wisconsin.gov/drivers/online.htm. The status can be requested using the DL, SSN and DOB, or by using the full name and DOB. Employers of commercial motor vehicle drivers may enroll in the Employer Notification Program. For more information or to register, call 608-266-0928 or email dotiinq@dot.state.wi.us.

Vehicle Records – The DOT maintains the database for vehicle titles, registrations, and liens. Sanitized records are not provided but at https://trust.dot.state.wi.us/pinq/PinqServlet?whoami=pinqp1 is a free license plate check. Wisconsin also offers a free title inquiry at https://trust.dot.state.wi.us/totl/totlservlet?whoami=totpl

Vessel Records – Boat and ATV information is with the Department of Natural Resources. 608-266-2107. All motorized or sail boats 16 ft and over must be titled and registered. All motorized or sail boats under 16 ft must be registered. Lien information appears on the title record. Record information can be requested by the owner name or boat registration number. There is no fee if under 10 records. 10 records or more is considered a bulk records request and fees follow the Electronic Records Instructions, which can place fees as high as $200.

Wyoming

Driving Records – The driver's license is nine numbers (six numbers, hyphen, three numbers; i.e., 101565-142). Numbers are computer-generated with a (check digit.(An ID card is composed of two numbers, hyphen, then seven numbers. Casual requesters cannot obtain records without consent.

Vehicle Records – On a license plate, the numbers 1 to 23 preceding the Bucking Horse image designate the county of issuance. Note that Apportioned Plates have no county designated and no alpha characters. The county codes for these 23 numbers are as follows: 1-Natrona; 2-Laramie; 3-Sheridan; 4-Sweetwater; 5-Albany; 6-Carbon; 7-Goshen;

8-Platte; 9-Big Horn; 10-Fremont; 11-Park; 12-Lincoln; 13-Converse; 14-Niobrara; 15-Hot Springs; 16-Johnson; 17-Campbell; 18-Crook; 19-Uinta; 20-Washakie; 21-Weston; 22-Teton; and 23-Sublette.

Wyoming vehicle titles and lien filings are processed by the local county clerks' offices in the county seat of the county of residence. The DOT maintains the record database.

Vessel Records – Wyoming Game and Fish Department, Watercraft Section, 307-777-4575. Wyoming does not title boats. All motorized boats must be registered. Simple name search requests are honored. There is no fee to do a registration record search by fax or phone. Liens are not recorded here, but at the county level.

Working With Public Record Vendors

As mentioned in Chapter 1, if you type the words *public records* into any search engine, the resulting list will be filled with people-searching sites and URLs that offer many links to free record searching.

This chapter is not concerned with these types of services and vendors. They serve a purpose and some are very useful, but many are designed to help consumers and not record search professionals.

This chapter takes a look at working with vendors who provide direct professional public record search services within these six distinct categories—

1. Distributors with Proprietary Databases
2. Gateways
3. Search Firms
4. Local Document Retrievers
5. Verification and Screening Firms
6. Private Investigation Firms

Knowledge of how each of these vendor types operates and how they fit within the **Information Food Chain**[18] is valuable when searching for the vendor most suitable for your needs.

Distributors with Proprietary Databases

Distributors, generally, are automated public record dealers who combine public sources of bulk data and/or online access to develop their own in-house database. Also known as or database providers or data aggregators, they collect or buy public record information from government repositories and reformat the information in useful ways for clients. They may also purchase or license record data from different sources or other information vendors, like telephone listing companies.

Vertical or Horizontal

By nature, many of these entities are either vertical (multiple types of info collected on a local or regional basis) or horizontal (dedicated single purpose type of info collected on regional or national basis). An example

---

[18] A term coined by Mr. Leroy Cook, founder of ION (www.pihome.com).

of a **vertical distributor** is Court PC of Connecticut This vendor maintains a database of "Connecticut Superior Court civil and domestic case records, and discloseable criminal/motor vehicle felony and misdemeanor convictions" back to 1985 and earlier. For a closer look, visit www.courtpcofct.com.

An example of a **horizontal distributor** is Aristotle (www.aristotle.com). Aristotle purchases voter registration records nationwide and sells customized lists to political candidates and political parties.

Some distributors are **both vertical and horizontal**. An example is ChoicePoint (www.choicepoint.com), a company with multiple divisions offering access to many and varied nationwide databases for a wide variety of clients.

When a database vendor sells data, the vendor is bound by the same disclosure laws attached to the original government repository. Access restrictions can range from zero for recorded documents, level three sexual predators, etc., to "severe restrictions" for voter registration, motor vehicle records, etc.

Gateways

Gateways are similar to distributors except gateways do not warehouse records – they merely provide a sophisticated pipeline to access existing databases. Gateways provide clients with an automated electronic access to 1) multiple proprietary database vendors and/or 2) government agencies online systems. Gateways provide "one-stop shopping" for multiple geographic areas and/or categories of information. Gateways are very evident on the Internet; we see them advertising access to records for many different purposes.

Gateways may also be designated vendors for certain government agencies. As mentioned in Chapter 1, the state affiliates of the National Information Consortium (NIC) manage and market eGovernment services on behalf of 21 states and a number of local governments without spending taxpayer dollars. NIC services range from the general information look-ups at states' web pages to managing record access subscription accounts for MVRs, UCC filings, and court records. Visit the NIC web page at www.nicus.com for a list of all affiliates and services.

Companies can be **both Primary Distributors and Gateways**. For example, a number of online database companies are both primary distributors of corporate information and also gateways to real estate information from other primary distributors.

Search Firms

Search firms furnish individual clients with public record search and document retrieval services. Search firms use online services and/or through a network of specialists including their own employees or correspondents (see Retrievers below). Search firms may rely on other vendors such as distributors, gateways and/or networks of retrievers, or they may go direct to the government agency. Combining online proficiency with document retrieval expertise, search firms may focus either on one geographic region – like New England – or on one specific type of public record information – like criminal records. There are literally hundreds of search firms in the U.S. Examples include GA Public Records from Texas and Motznik Information Services from Alaska.

Record Retrievers

Somewhat similar to a search firm is a Local Document Retriever or simply, a Record Retriever. Retrievers are hands-on researchers for hire who visit government agencies in-person. Using a record retriever is an excellent way to quickly access records in jurisdictions where clerks do not perform record searching.

Retrievers' clients typically request name searches or document retrieval services for the purpose of legal compliance (e.g., incorporations), employment screening, lending, real estate (e.g., abstracting) or for litigation purposes. Retrievers do not necessarily review or interpret the results or issue reports in the sense that investigators do, but rather return the results of searches along with document copies. Since retrievers or their personnel go directly to the agency to look up information, they may be relied upon for strong knowledge on record searching at the courthouses or recording offices they cover. Retrievers tend to be localized and are used by search firms who offer a national network of retrievers.

Record retrieving is not necessarily a profession. Many vocations offer record retrieval services including private investigators, process servers, genealogists, and paralegals. There are at least 3,000 active local public record document retrievers in the U.S.

Members of the Public Record Retriever Network (PRRN) are listed by state and counties they serve at www.brbpub.com/PRRN. This organization has set industry standards for the retrieval of public record documents. Members operate under a Code of Professional Conduct. An article from PRRN that gives advice on how to order a search from a record retriever is found later in this chapter.

Verification and Screening Firms

Verification firms provide services to employers and businesses when a subject has given consent for the verification. In this category are pre-employment screening firms and tenant screening firms (both governed by the Fair Credit Reporting Act - FCRA), motor vehicle record vendors (governed by the Drivers Privacy Protection Act – DPPA), and firms that provide prior employment and academic verification checks. Since verification and screening firms usually only perform their services for clients who have specifically received consent from the subjects, they do not warehouse data for resell purposes.

The service provided by a pre-employment screening company is often called a background screen or background report. Their service should not be confused with an investigation as provided by private investigators (see below) or with search firms with an Internet presence. Tot find a screening company visit the web page of the National Association of Professional Background Screeners (NAPBS) at www.napbs.com. Examples of a verification service are ReferencePro found at www.referencepro.com and the National Student Clearing House at www.studentclearinghouse.org.

Private Investigation Firms

Private investigators use public records as tools rather than as ends in themselves. Depending on the purpose, investigators use public records in order to create an overall, comprehensive "picture" of an individual or company. The investigator interprets the information gathered in order to identify further investigation tracks. They summarize their results in a report compiled from all the sources used. In many instances, a private investigator doing an investigation does not have the consent of the subject.

An investigator may perform the types of services traditionally thought of as detective work, such as surveillance. Many investigators also act as search firms or record retrievers and provide search results to other investigators. As mentioned, some investigators also offer pre-employment screening.

Other Vendors of Note

There are two other types of vendors worthy of mention that often provide public records as part of their services. The Association of Independent Information Professionals (AIIP), at www.aiip.org, has over 700 experienced professional information specialist members from 21 countries. Information Professionals are extremely knowledgeable in online research of full text databases. Information Professionals typically gather information intended to help their clients make informed business decisions, with each project being unique. Often they specialize in a particular subject such as patents or competitive intelligence.

A similar organization is the Society of Competitive Intelligence Professionals (SCIP), see www.scip.org. Per their web "...SCIP provides education and networking opportunities for business professionals working in the rapidly growing field of competitive intelligence (the legal and ethical collection and analysis of information regarding the capabilities, vulnerabilities, and intentions of business competitors)."

Which Type of Vendor is Right for You?

The next question is "Which type of vendor is the right one to use for the public record information I need?" To guide you to the proper vendor type, ask yourself the following questions—

What is the Frequency of Usage?

Setting up an account with a primary distributor may give you an inexpensive per search fee, but some may charge a monthly minimum requirement that will be prohibitive to a casual requester. Ask if there is an ala carte per-search option. If your requests are few, you sometimes are better off using a vendor who accesses from a distributor.

What is the Complexity of the Search?

The importance of hiring a vendor who understands and can interpret the information in the final format increases with the complexity of the search. Pulling a corporation record in Maryland is not difficult, but doing a true criminal record search in Maryland, when only a portion of the felony records are online, is not so easy.

Thus, part of the answer to determining which vendor or type of vendor to use is to become conversant with what is and is not available from government agencies. Without knowing what is available and what restrictions apply, you cannot guide the search process effectively.

What are the Geographic Boundaries of the Search?

A search of local records close to you may require little assistance, but a search of records nationally or in a state 2,000 miles away will require the use of a vendor who effectively covers that area. Many national primary distributors and gateways combine various local and state databases into one large comprehensive system available for searching. However, if your record searching is narrowed by a region or locality, then a source that specializes in a specific geographic region may be a better alternative.

Of course, you may want to use the government agency online system, if available, for the kind of information you need.

What Privacy Protections are in Place?

The national news is full of stories about identity theft problems experienced by companies that hold personal information in vast customer files. These companies thought they had adequate protection in place, but evidently they did not. These same concerns are or should be applicable when choosing a public record vendor who receives record requests containing the personal identifiers of search subjects.

It is quite fair to ask a vendor for their policy statement on the management of personal identifiers, security measures and protections are in place.

For example, ask how they process and store paperwork or computer files with DOBs, and SSNs. Do they use encryption when sending content over the web? Do they use a shredder? Are their computers password protected? How long is the data retained? Vendors operating from home are perhaps even more susceptible to privacy theft concerns. Do they put the trash out at the curb weekly, trash that contains faxes, orders, even record search results? Are friends of family members able to access the business computer when they are not home?

The following is an example of key points that can or should be included in a privacy protection policy:

> *XXX agrees that all information provided by the Customer shall be maintained by the XXX in strict confidence and disclosed only to individuals whose duties reasonably relate to the legitimate business purposes for which the information is submitted.*

> *XXX agrees to take reasonable care to protect the confidential personal or consumer identification information provided by the Customer, including physical and network security systems. XXX agrees to use proper and timely destruction procedures for all materials and computer files that contain personal identification information provided by the Customer. XXX will not sell or otherwise distribute to third parties any information received, except as otherwise required by law or agreed upon in writing between XXX and the Customer.*

Where to Find a Public Record Vendor

Another common question is how to locate the right vendor for a particular type of public record or record searching need.

There are several proven approaches. Perhaps the easiest way to find a vendor is by *word of mouth*. Asking colleagues who they use or recommend works well.

A second suggestion is to look for a trusted trade or professional association that is somehow connected to the particular need or reason for the record search. This works in two ways, by direct connection or by association. If you are looking for an employment screening firm, then go to the web page for the National Association of Professional Background Screeners and search for members. Because employment screeners use driving record vendors and criminal record vendors, this is also good place to find vendors who provide services to screening companies and have joined as associate or affiliate members.

In the *Searching A thru Z* chapter you will find a list of over 80 professional trade associations that are connected to public records.

Another option is to look for vendor lists on the web. BRB Publications has a lookup of over 800 public record vendors by record category and states covered at www.brbpub.com/pubrecsites_ven.asp. This list also shows who are distributors and gateways by record type.

Tips on Analyzing Vendor Databases

Once you find a vendor or possible vendor to use, it is important to ask questions about the public record data you will be receiving. The article below, written by Mr. Lawrence Lopez, is very helpful to this end. It provides key questions to ask a database vendor, but also for examining the effectiveness of a government database.

Mr. Lopez, a licensed private investigator and investigative reporter, has conducted numerous seminars for professional organizations and associations. Mr. Lopez is owner of Strategic Research, www.srresearch.com, and can be reached at larrylopez@srresearch.com. We sincerely thank him for contributing this article.

Tips on Searching Record Databases

By Lawrence Lopez

A database is only as good as what is inside – and how you can get at it. Here are some questions to ask vendors:

What jurisdictions does the database cover? Is it all 50 states? All the counties within each state or just some of them? All the cities within each county?

How far back does the data go in each jurisdiction? Is that 'all data,' or just 'some data?' For example, when court clerks start a database, they typically include all cases filed AFTER that date and all the cases that were filed BEFORE but still active. Usually they will not enter closed cases before the database was created. So, while a database that began in 2000 may have a few cases from 1985, a vendor should not claim the database goes back to 1985.

Is old data ever purged? Connecticut's official court sites drop thousands of old cases every year, while a private database, Court PC of Connecticut, keeps them. On the other hand, the official state site has housing and small claims cases, which Court PC of CT does not. Which leads to the next question.

What kinds of data does the database include? Are all files at the recorder's office included or just the land deeds? Just recorded land deeds or registered land as well? Is it all civil cases or just those where a business is one of the parties? All types of litigation, or just cases where money is involved? All money cases, or just those above a certain amount? Does the data include mental health cases, or divorces, or wills?

Does the database list all parties to each transaction? Some real estate databases, for example, may list only the first name on each side: If Joe Smith, Mary Smith and the Smith Family Trust buy a house from Jane Doe, John Doe and the 123 Main Street Trust, you may not find the record by searching for Smith Family Trust or John Doe.

How frequently is the data refreshed? Nightly? Monthly? Quarterly? If you are looking for someone who recently moved – or died – you need to know how old the data in the database is.

How was the data assembled? All other things being equal, the fewer times the data is entered, the fewer the errors there are likely to be. A vendor who downloads a computer tape directly from the government agency that compiled it is likely to have fewer errors than a vendor who sends abstractors into the agency to go through the records by hand and type up a list. In addition, abstractors often enter less data, so their creations are likelier to list just the first parties' names, or to include just money-related filings.

How is the data entered by the source? If all you are searching is fields (i.e. Last Name, Address, etc.) there is more potential for mischief than if you are searching the full text. For example, court clerks in Massachusetts often enter the LastName in the FirstName field or both the first and last names in the same LastName field. If the database you use allows you to search only by fields, you will miss many cases. If the database is full text, then you'll find the last name no matter what (assuming it is spelled correctly, of course).

How is the search parsed? Does the database allow you to use wildcards when you search? Will a search for John Doe find someone who is Dr. John Doe or John Doe, Jr. (or "John Doe as trustee and executor for Mary

Roe"?) Does it allow Boolean searching? How does it handle equivalents: for example, if you are searching for First National Bank will your search also turn up any record that is written in the database as 1st National? If you search for Theodore Roosevelt will that also get you the entries for Teddy Roosevelt?

When you search the database, are you searching everything or just an index to it? For example, most locator databases draw on a lot of datasets but use one or more of the three main credit-headers – Experian, Equifax and TransUnion – as their backbone. But even if the vendor draws from all three headers in the detailed search, does your initial search – the one that leads to the details screen – draw on all three or just on one? And, importantly, how old is the index?

There are, of course, a lot of other questions you may want to ask, depending on what type of data you are seeking.

Tips When Hiring a Record Retriever

On-site record retrievers represent a key link in the information food chain. If you hire a retriever and are not clear at the outset what you expect a record retriever to do for you, you may be asking for trouble. Major misunderstandings can be avoided if the expectations between the retriever and the client are clearly understood.

The article below is provided by the Public Record Retriever Network (PRRN).

A Checklist to Use Before You Place An Order With A Record Retriever ...

Here are ten aspects of a search we think are essential to review before you hire a retriever.

1. Determine Exactly What Type of Records You Want Searched

You must always be crystal clear about what information you need. Do not give the retriever vague instructions. For example regarding **Criminal Searches**

An order to do a "criminal record search" is not an adequate description. Is it for felonies only, for felonies and misdemeanors, or for both? If misdemeanors are desired, should the search include DWI's? Is a federal court search also required?

2. Determine Where Do You Want to Search

Frequently this question is associated with the previous question. Simply make sure to ask if there is more than one location where the information requested might be obtained. Court locations provide a complex example in a number of states and counties. A county may have two courts with the same jurisdictions, but without a combined index to search. Or, municipal courts in a county may have overlapping jurisdiction with the state court in the county with respect to misdemeanors. You must determine if you wish the retriever to search all or only part of the county court structure.

Another consideration is which county to search. There are over 8,000 ZIP Codes that cross county lines. Your may wish to independently check which county is correct for the given address or ZIP Code of the subject. The retriever can perform a more thorough job by searching in highly populous contiguous counties where additional records might be located.

3. Decide the Time Period to Search

When hiring a retriever, you need to give specific instructions on how far back to make the search. Better yet, ask what is the retriever's norm or standard search period for that particular county. Many local jurisdictions have computerized an index to records, but the index may only go back a limited number of years. If the date range of the index does not meet your needs, the retriever will need to perform a separate, manual search of the older records.

4. Know the Subject's Name

You should develop standards to determine if the subject name you give a retriever is adequate for searching.

Individual names such as "George H. Ruth" may be adequate for your purposes, or you may want to ask whether the middle initial is known, especially if the name is common. "G. Herman Ruth" may create real search problems for a retriever if you don't know what the "G" stands for.

You will need to state clearly in your request the names you wish to be searched and any constraints or limitations on search procedures due to the form of the name. A retriever may be expected to find common variations of the subject name, but cannot, nor is responsible to, determine all the weird variations that a keypuncher might inflict on a name.

5. Let the Retriever Know if You Anticipate Records or Hits

Public record searching is not a test. It always helps the retriever to know if you are aware of any records that now exist on the subject. You may say,

"That's none of his or her business, the retriever is hired to do the search." That's OK, but you realize that public records can be mis-indexed by the filing officers or court personnel. Most retrievers will extend their search procedures beyond their usual thorough methods if they did not get a hit when one was anticipated.

Another consideration is when a government office charges a lot for copies, and automatically makes copies for all searches. If you know the subject has multiple cases, you may ask the retriever to advise a more cost-efficient way to search the records without incurring substantial copy charges.

6. Prepare to Ask How the Search Will be Conducted

Has anyone ever asked this question? Everyone should ask.

Public record searches are performed at the actual court, or recorder records office, by human beings. Keep in mind the methods of storage and retrieval of public records can vary from one government agency to another. Who performs that actual search? Some agencies require that the names to be searched for be handed over to the clerk who performs the actual search. Some agencies have computer terminals that a researcher can view in person. The researcher may have to type in each name, or the researcher may review a list of names to see if the applicant's name appears. Some agencies index names in other searchable formats such as ledgers, microfiche, or microfilm. Some of these ways may be an official search, and some are unofficial but provided by the agency.

Therefore, it is incumbent upon you to ask the retriever about the possible search methods and clarify how you wish the search to be performed. If for legal reasons you require an "official search" (one done by the government office itself and certified) make that requirement clear at the outset.

In those jurisdictions where a retriever has the option of searching on a private, third party database rather than on the official database of the agency, the retriever should never conduct a search on the private database without your expressed permission.

7. Know What Documents You Want to Obtain or What Results You Want Reported

Obtaining documents can be quite costly. Perhaps you think you are asking for a list or index of public records on a subject and the retriever hands you copies of 500 UCC filings. Make sure you find out first if you have no choice but to obtain documents as part of a search. The retriever should inform you of the possibility of excessive copy costs in advance of performing the search.

What if the retriever finds an exact name match, but another identifier (like a DOB) does not match? What if the first and last name match as well as the DOB, but the middle initial does not? Do you want to have this information reported to you? A good idea is to ask the retriever what his/her standard procedure is when near matches occur. Keep in mind that there have been lawsuits filed by employers when a close match is not reported that was a positive "hit" on a criminal record.

8. Know Your Deadline

Let the retriever know when you need the results and ask if you have a reasonable time expectation. In those jurisdictions where government personnel must perform the search you need to know if the normal turnaround time does not fit your needs. In those situations, ask if the government agency offers an expedited service for an additional fee. You may need to adjust your expectations.

9. Determine How You Want the Results Given to You

Be clear on how you expect the form of delivery of the search results. Do you want results and documents by fax, by telephone, email, overnight courier, or by regular mail? Ask if there are different fees for different delivery methods.

10. Keep a Written Log of the Request

The nine items summarized above should indicate your complete instructions. If you have an ongoing relationship with a retriever, that retriever should maintain a standard set of client instructions for your orders. If you are working with a new or relatively new retriever, you will lose nothing by being comprehensive with your instructions. Keep a log with the date and time the order was placed, the time and method of expected delivery, and to whom you spoke if you placed the order by telephone. Using standard, written procedures will minimize the chances of making a mistake and help insure your instructions are legible and complete.

Chapter 9

Archives (National)

The National Archives and Records Administration (NARA) is America's record keeper and it serves as the archival arm of the federal government. NARA not only preserves documents and materials related to the U.S., but also ensures people can access the information. NARA maintains regional archives of historical documents that tell the stories of America's history - records on immigration, genealogy, census, military, presidential libraries, to name a few .

There are over 30 locations nationwide with specific locations holding designated records. Also, there are *affiliated archives* with records that by formal, written agreement with NARA are accessioned holdings of the National Archives.

Examples of locations include the records of U.S. Congress held by the Center for Legislative Archives in the National Archives Building in Washington, DC. The Rotunda in that building displays the U.S. Constitution, the Bill of Rights, and the Declaration of Independence. Federal population census records from 1790-1930 are available for research at the National Archives Building in Washington, DC, and in Regional Archives throughout the country.

NARA's immigration records holdings are found in the genealogy section's Immigration Records or Naturalization Records. There are some passenger arrival records from ships.

Federal Record Centers (FRCs) are also part of NARA. These centers hold closed case files from Federal U.S. District Courts civil and criminal and Bankruptcy Courts. See the *Searching Federal Court Records* chapter for information on how to obtain cases files.

The NARA web page at www.archives.gov has detailed information regarding documents, images, and how to research.

Below are a few selected locations, including the FRCs. To find all the NARA locations, visit www.archives.gov/locations.

NARA Headquarters

U.S. National Archives and Records Administration 8601 Adelphi Rd, College Park, Maryland 20740-6001; 1-86-NARA-NARA or 1-866-272-6272; local 301-837-2950; local fax 301-837-1617; frc@nara.gov

National Personnel Records Center (NPRC) (St. Louis)

The U.S. central repositories of personnel-related records for both military and civil service.

Civilian Division - 111 Winnebago St. St. Louis, MO 63118-4126; 314-801-9250; fax: 314-801-9269; cpr.center@nara.gov

Military Division - Military Personnel Records, 9700 Page Ave, St. Louis, MO 63132-5100. 314-801-0800; fax: 314 801-9195; MPR.center@nara.gov

Note: For detailed information on how to research military records, go to the *Military* section later in this chapter.

Federal Record Centers with U.S. District and Bankruptcy Court Records

Central Plains Region FRC/Archives (Kansas City, MO)

For Iowa, Kansas, Missouri, and Nebraska. 2312 East Bannister Rd, Kansas City, MO 64131; 816-268-8000; kansascity.archives@nara.gov

Great Lakes Region FRC/Archives (Chicago)

For Illinois, Indiana, Michigan, Minnesota, Ohio, and Wisconsin. Located at 7358 South Pulaski Rd, Chicago, IL 60629-5898 Archives-773-948-9050; Bankruptcy-773-948-9030; fax-773-948-9051; Court Records less than 30 years old - 773-948-9030; Court Records more than 30 years old - 773-948-9001; chicagoreference@nara.gov

Great Lakes Region FRC/Archives (Dayton)

Holds bankruptcy records for the Northern & Southern District Courts of Ohio. 3150 Springboro Rd, Dayton, OH 45439-1883, 937-425-0600; fax: 937-425-0640; Bankruptcy: 937-425-0629; fax: 937-425-0649

Mid-Atlantic Region FRC/Archives (Philadelphia)

For Delaware, Maryland, Pennsylvania, Virginia, and West Virginia.

Archives: 900 Market St, Philadelphia, PA 19107-4292 215-606-0100, fax: 215-606-0116; Records: 14700 Townsend Rd, Philadelphia, PA 19154-1025, 215-305-2000; fax: 215-305-2038

Northeast Region FRC/Archives (Boston)

For Connecticut, Maine, Massachusetts, New Hampshire, Rhode Island, and Vermont. Frederick C. Murphy Federal Ctr, 380 Trapelo Rd, Waltham, MA 02452-6399, 781-663-0130; fax: 781-663-0154; waltham.archives@nara.gov

Northeast Region FRC/Archives (New York City)

For New York, New Jersey, Puerto Rico, and the U.S. Virgin Islands. (For Bankruptcy records, see Lee's Summit, MO.) 201 Varick St, 12th Fl, New York, NY 10014; 866-840-1752; fax: 212-401-1638, newyork.archives@nara.gov

Northeast Region Archives (Pittsfield, MA)

For Connecticut, Maine, Massachusetts, New Hampshire, Rhode Island, and Vermont. 10 Conte Dr, Pittsfield, MA 01201-8230, 413-236-3600; fax: 413-236-3609; pittsfield.archives@nara.gov

Lee's Summit, MO FRC –

The Lee's Summit facility stores and services records from Federal bankruptcy courts in New Jersey, New York, Puerto Rico, the U.S. Virgin Islands as well as from most U.S. Department of Veterans Affairs offices nationwide. 200 Space Center Dr, Lee's Summit, MO 64064-1182; Bankruptcy Div: 816-268-8100; fax: 816-268-8159

Rocky Mt Region FRC/Archives (Denver)

For Colorado, Montana, New Mexico, North Dakota, South Dakota, Utah, and Wyoming. North and South Dakota records created before 1972 are held in Kansas City. Denver Federal Center, Bldg 48, PO Box 25307, Denver, CO 80225; 303-407-5700; fax: 303-407-5707

Pacific Region FRC (Anchorage, AK)

654 W Third Ave, Anchorage, Alaska 99501-2145; 907-261-7820; fax: 907-261-7813; alaska.archives@nara.gov

Pacific Alaska Region FRC (Seattle)

For Idaho, Oregon, and Washington. Located at 6125 Sand Point Way NE, Seattle, WA 98115; 206-336-5115; fax: 206-336-5112; Seattle.archives@nara.gov

Pacific Region FRC/Archives (Riverside, CA)

For Arizona, and Clark County NV; also Los Angeles, San Bernardino, San Diego, Santa Ana, and Santa Barbara, CA. Records Mailing: NARA, Caller Service 8305, Perris, CA 92572; Records Physical: NARA, 23123 Cajalco Rd, Perris, CA 92570; 951-956-2000 to schedule an appointment. Archives: 24000 Avila Rd, 1st Fl, East Entrance, Laguna Niguel, CA 92677-3497; 949-360-2641

Pacific Region FRC (San Francisco)

For northern and central California, Nevada (except Clark County), Hawaii, American Samoa, and the Trust Territory of the Pacific Islands.

1000 Commodore Dr, San Bruno, CA 94066-2350; 650-238-3501; fax: 650-238-3510; sanbruno.archives@nara.gov

Southeast Region FRC (Atlanta)

For Alabama, Florida, Georgia, Kentucky, Mississippi, North Carolina, South Carolina, and Tennessee. Records: 4712 Southpark Blvd, Ellenwood, GA 30294; 404-736-2820; fax: 404-736-2931. Archives: 5780 Jonesboro Rd. Morrow, GA 30260; 770-968-2100; fax: 770-968-2547; atlanta.archives@nara.gov

Southwest Region FRC (Fort Worth, TX)

For Arkansas, Louisiana, Oklahoma, and Texas.

Records: 1400 John Burgess Dr, Fort Worth, TX 76140 817-551-2000; fax: 817-551-2037. Archives: 501 W Felix St, Bldg 1, Ft Worth, TX 76115-3405

Washington, DC Area FRC

Washington National Records Center (WNRC) in Suitland, Maryland 4205 Suitland Rd, Suitland, MD 20746-8001. Court record research: 301-778-1520; agency records: 301-778-1510; delander.reid@nara.gov

Aviation Records

Accidents

The Federal National Transportation Safety Board (NTSB) maintains an aviation accident database with information from 1962 forward about civil aviation accidents and selected incidents within the U.S., its territories and possessions, and in international waters. Six different queries are available. Preliminary reports are posted within days; final reports may take months before posted. Some information prior to 1993 is sketchy. www.ntsb.gov

Aircraft, Airlines, Pilots

The main government information center regarding certification for pilots, airmen, airlines, aircraft and for aircraft registration/ownership, and airports is the Federal Aviation Administration (FAA). The website is www.faa.gov, the toll-free phone number is 866-835-5322.

One of the leading private information resource centers for searching flights, pilot certifications, and regulatory overviews is Albuquerque-based Landings.com, 702-920-8298. Visit www.landings.com for many excellent searching links and background information.

Another extremely in-depth source of aviation information of every kind is Jane's Information Group. Jane's reference, news and analysis information covers the areas of security, defense, aerospace, transport, public safety and law enforcement for not only aviation, but also for vessels and railroads. The North America office is located in Alexandria, VA. They can be reached at 800-824-0768 or visit www.janes.com to access many free searches. Offices are found throughout the world.

Another industry leader in aviation information collection, analysis and distribution is Cincinnati-based Aviation Research Group; phone 800-361-2216 or visit www.aviationresearch.com. They offer a free aircraft registration search on the web. Search Canadian aircraft information at www.tc.gc.ca/aviation/activepages/ccarcs/index.htm.

Airports

One of the best private sites to find detailed information for free about an airport, including ownership and management, is www.airnav.com. You can search by state or by U.S. Territory.

Another excellent resource is GCR & Associates. Visit www.gcr1.com and click on the Airport IQ link for airport master records and reports.

Air Associations

With well over 400,000 members, the Aircraft Owners and Pilots Association (AOPA) calls itself the largest, most-influential aviation association in the world. AOPA, 421 Aviation Way, Frederick, MD 21701, 301-695-2000, www.aopo.org.

The International Air Transportation Association (IATA) represents 250 airlines. Four U.S. offices and one Canadian office are found at their web page www.iata.org. While there is not a lot of public record related information, this association is a good venue to learn about airport planning and safety.

Registration Numbers

The International Civil Aviation Organization (www.icao.int) maintains aircraft registration standards for participating countries. Each aircraft (over a certain weight) must be registered with a national aviation registration mark and number. This registration is shown on the plane. Different countries have different registration schemes. For example, the U.S. uses an "N" followed by 1 to 5 additional characters as the aircraft registration number as follows:

- N1 to N99 (reserved for only FAA internal use)
- N100 to N99999
- N1A to N9Z
- N1AA to N9ZZ
- N10A to N99Z
- N10AA to N99ZZ
- N100A to N999Z
- N100AA to N999ZZ
- N1000A to N9999Z

Each registration must start with a number other than zero, can not end in more than two letters, may not contain the letters I or O.

Private aircraft usually use their registration as their radio call-sign, but most commercial aircraft use the ICAO airline designator or a company call-sign.

Pre-1950s aircraft sometimes have a second letter in its identifier, but is not really part of the identification identifying the category of aircraft. For example, NC12345 is the same registration as N12345.

These categories may still appear on antique aircraft:

- C = standard
- L = limited
- R = restricted
- X = experimental

As mentioned, each country has its own unique registration mark scheme. For example, Canadian registrations start with C, Panama is HP, and Cyprus is 5B. For a list of country registration codes, go to www.icao.int/icao/en/anb/fls/alpha_State.pdf

Banks & Financial Institutions

Where to find public information about an individual bank or lending institution can be confusing because there are five federal regulator agencies for five different types of entities. Each regulator maintains a database when formal enforcement actions must be taken against the entities they regulate. The information below details these regulators. Enforcement actions against institutions or their affiliated parties can be found at the website of the institution's regulator.

Also, the Office of the Comptroller of the Currency (OCC) maintains a variety of public information about the national banking system. See the Treasury Department section in later in this chapter under the *Federal Agency Sanctions and Watch Lists* section.

Federal Deposit Insurance Corporation (FDIC)

The FDIC supervises the following entities and has the statutory authority to take enforcement actions against them—

- FDIC-insured state chartered banks that are not members of the Federal Reserve System
- FDIC-insured branches of foreign banks
- Officers, directors, employees, controlling shareholders, agents, and certain other categories of individuals (institution-affiliated parties) associated with such institutions

Their Institution Directory is found at www2.fdic.gov/idasp/index.asp. At www.fdic.gov/bank/individual/enforcement/index.html you may view **enforcement actions**. Order printed copies of the enforcement orders from the Public Information Center at 3501 North Fairfax Drive, Room E-1002, Arlington, VA 22226, 703-562-2200. Send questions to regs@fdic.gov.

Federal Reserve Board

Banking Search Pages, Institution Characteristics, Reports

The Federal Reserve supervises the following entities and has the statutory authority to take formal enforcement actions against them—

- State member banks
- Bank holding companies
- Non-bank subsidiaries of bank holding companies
- Edge and agreement corporations
- Branches and agencies of foreign banking organizations operating in the United States and their parent banks
- Officers, directors, employees, and certain other categories of individuals associated with the above banks, companies, and organizations (referred to as "institution-affiliated parties")

The National Information Center Institution Search at www.ffiec.gov/nicpubweb/nicweb/SearchForm.aspx allows you to search the Federal Reserve's database for an institution's current and non-current information by name and location. Also, you may search www.ffiec.gov/nicpubweb/nicweb/SearchForm.aspx?pS=2 for U.S. Branches and Agencies of Foreign Banking Organizations (FBOs). At both sites, an institution's profile will be displayed in the results. Each institution's name is a hyperlink to its characteristic information, including institution type, location, and primary federal regulator. Links to structure will only be displayed when available.

Links to the following reports will be displayed only if that information is available for the selected institution—

- The **Organization Hierarchy Report** is information regarding ownership if the subject institution is part of a multi-level, "tiered" organization.
- The **Institutions Acquired** page displays acquisitions made by the subject institution.
- The **Institution History** page displays a chronological list of changes to the institution's characteristic and structure information.
- The **Branch Locator** locates and lists the branches a domestic bank operates.

Financial Reports are also accessible from the Institutions' Profile page, only if data exists for reports provided at this site.

Enforcement Actions

Generally, the Federal Reserve takes formal enforcement actions against the entities listed above for violations of laws, rules, or regulations, unsafe or unsound practices, breaches of fiduciary duty, and violations of final orders. Since August 1989, the Federal Reserve has made all final enforcement orders public.

Search at www.federalreserve.gov/boarddocs/enforcement/search.cfm.

National Information Center

The National Information Center (NIC) is a central repository of overall data about banks and other institutions for which the Federal Reserve has a supervisory, regulatory, or research interest. The website provides access to detailed information about banking organizations. www.ffiec.gov/nicpubweb/nicweb/nichome.aspx

Office of the Comptroller of the Currency

The Office of the Comptroller of the Currency (OCC), a bureau of the U.S. Department of the Treasury, charters, regulates, and supervises all national banks and federally chartered branches and agencies of foreign banks that are not members of the Federal Reserve System. The OCC has the statutory authority to take action against Institution-Affiliated Parties (IAPs) including:

- Officers, directors, and employees,
- A bank's controlling stockholders, agents, and certain other individuals.

Information may be requested on formal enforcement actions against the above entities for violations of laws, rules or regulations, unsafe or unsound practices, violations of final orders, violations of conditions imposed in writing, and for IAP's breaches of fiduciary duty.

Search Enforcement actions at www.occ.treas.gov/enforcementactions/. To obtain a paper copy of an order, agreement, or directive, fax the request to the OCC's Public Disclosure Room at 202-874-4448. A FOIA request should be addressed to Comptroller of the Currency, Disclosure Officer, Mail Stop 3-2, Washington, DC 20219.

National Credit Union Administration

The National Credit Union Administration (NCUA) is the independent federal agency that charters and supervises federal credit unions. The web page www.ncua.gov offers plenty of research and data access; one can pull a PDF file listing of all credit unions in the United States. Administrative orders back to 1991 are posted at www.ncua.gov/administrative_orders/Admin/administrative.html. The agency is located at 1775 Duke St, Alexandria, VA 22314-3428, 703-518-6300.

Office of Thrift Supervision

The Office of Thrift Supervision regulates thrift associations. To find enforcement actions and orders, go to www.ots.treas.gov, click on *Enforcement* found at the lower left bottom of the page under Public Info. The mailing address and phone is Office of Thrift Supervision, 1700 G. Street, NW, Washington, DC 20552, 202-906-6000.

Canada

The intent of this section is to present a quick but useful guide to many Canadian resources related to public record and information searching. The section is organized by topic; a number of web pages are presented.

Business Related Information

Industry Canada – (Covers Many Record Types)

One of the most useful web pages belongs to is Industry Canada (www.ic.gc.ca/epic/site/icl.nsf/en/home). For example, this web resource leads to records of **bankruptcies, business names, copyrights, corporations, mergers, patents, trademarks, and even unclaimed funds**. For a complete index listing of everything found at this site, go to www.ic.gc.ca/epic/site/icl.nsf/en/h_00013e.html.

Public Security Findings

The System for Electronic Document Analysis and Retrieval (SEDAR) is a filing system developed for the Canadian Securities Administrators. This is the **Canadian version of EDGAR**. www.sedar.com Email questions to sedarwebmaster@cds.ca.

Criminal Records

Royal Canadian Mounted Police (RCMP)

The Information and Identification Services of the RCMP is a point of contact to the central repository of criminal record data in Canada, similar to the FBI in the U.S. The RCMP operates an automated central police database known as the Canadian Police Information Centre (CPIC) is the. Municipal and provincial police services in Canada also have their own systems, as do the court systems (see below.)

Criminal record searches are performed by the Civil Fingerprint Screening Services (CFSS) of the RCMP. Search requirement include a signed release and set of fingerprints. The RCMP does not provide name checks. You must contact the local police service or provincial court system for name searches. RCMP, National Police Services Building, Loading Dock #1, Information and Identification Services, Civil Fingerprint Screening Services, 1200 Vanier Parkway, Ottawa, Ontario K1A 0R2, Telephone - 613-998-6362.

Correctional Service of Canada

The Correctional Service of Canada (CSC) is the Canadian government agency responsible for administering sentences with a prison term of two years or more imposed by the court system. CSC is responsible for managing institutions of various security levels and supervising offenders under conditional release in the community. Records are not public. See www.csc-scc.gc.ca

National Parole Board of Canada

For questions relating to the status of pardon applications, call 800-874-2652. Request must include subject's signature. Mailing address for is Pardon Section, Clemency and Investigations Division, National Parole Board, 410 Laurier Avenue West, Ottawa, Ontario K1A 0R1. www.npb-cnlc.gc.ca

Court System and Court Records

Canadian court records are public information. The court system in Canada is similar to the U.S. system in that there is a federal court system with a supreme court and there are provincial systems with upper and lower courts.

An informative resource about the Canadian Court System, including how organized, is the Department of Justice. Go to www.justice.gc.ca/en/dept/pub/trib.

Below are links to the judicial systems of each province. The links will lead to extensive information about each province's system including some online accessible databases.

Alberta – www.albertacourts.ab.ca

British Columbia – www.courts.gov.bc.ca

Manitoba – www.gov.mb.ca/justice

New Brunswick – www.gnb.ca/cour/index-e.asp

Newfoundland – www.justice.gov.nl.ca/just

Northwest Territories – www.nwtcourts.ca

Nova Scotia – www.gov.ns.ca/just

Ontario – www.attorneygeneral.jus.gov.on.ca/english

Prince Edward Island – www.gov.pe.ca/courts

Quebec – www.justice.gouv.qc.ca/english/accueil.asp

Saskatchewan – www.sasklawcourts.ca

Yukon – www.justice.gov.yk.ca/prog/cs/courts.html

Bankruptcy Records

As mentioned above, visit the Industry Canada site at www.ic.gc.ca/epic/site/ic1.nsf/en/h_00000e.html.

Supreme Court Decisions

The Canada Supreme Court Reports (decisions) are published in English and French. For information about the Supreme Court Library, contact library@scc-csc.gc.ca or phone 613- 996-8120 or visit www.scc-csc.gc.ca. The Court directs online searches of decisions to a web page managed by the University of Montreal. Visit:

http://scc.lexum.umontreal.ca/en/index.html

Tax Court Judgments

http://decision.tcc-cci.gc.ca/en/index.html

Court Martial Appeals Court

www.cmac-cacm.ca/index_e.html

Government & Legislation

Canadian Government on the Internet

This government site is a **master site** with links to federal, provincial, and municipal sites. http://canada.gc.ca

Parliament

www.parl.gc.ca/common/index.asp?Language=E

Consolidated Acts, Regulations, and Legislation

http://laws.justice.gc.ca/en/

Legislation

Canadian Laws and regulations at
http://laws.justice.gc.ca/en/index.html

Transportation and Motor Vehicle

Aircraft

www.tc.gc.ca/aviation/activepages/ccarcs/index.htm

Motor Vehicle Records

In general, a signed release is required to obtain a driving record or vehicle-related record, especially if the record contains personal information. Many provinces license or authorize third parties to provide record access. For example, these authorized agencies are called

Registries in Alberta; in Ontario sanitized driving and vehicle records may be obtained from kiosks and mall kiosks.

Addresses and web links to each province are provided below. The links are very useful to learn how motor vehicle records are managed by the provinces.

Alberta

Motor Vehicle Division, Alberta Registries, 780-427-7013
www.servicealberta.gov.ab.ca/mv/operator.cfm

British Columbia

ICBC, Driver Testing & Vehicle Information, 250-978-8300
www.icbc.com/licensing/

Manitoba

Manitoba Public Insurance, Driver and Vehicle Licensing
Driver Records and Suspensions
Driver 204-985-0980, Vehicle 204-945-7366   www.mpi.mb.ca/

Lien information, call the Personal Property Registry at 204-945-3123.

New Brunswick

Department of Public Safety, Licensing & Records Branch
Driver (or Vehicle) Records, 506-453-3992
www.gnb.ca/0276/vehicle/index-e.asp

Lien information is released only to parties involved, call 506-453-2817 or visit www.snb.ca

Newfoundland

Motor Vehicle Registration, Driver Records Division, 709-729-2519
www.gs.gov.nl.ca/gs/mr

Lien searches have been privatized; search private company list at www.gs.gov.nl.ca/cca/cr/

Northwest Territories

Dept. of Transportation, Motor Vehicle Div, Yellow Knife Registries, 867-873-7487, 867- 873-7406 www.dot.gov.nt.ca/

Lien info available at a different office, 876-873-7493.

Nova Scotia

Services of Nova Scotia, Driver Records Section
902-424-5851; 800-898-7668 outside Halifax metro area
www.gov.ns.ca/snsmr/rmv

Ontario

Driving records: Ministry of Transportation
Licensing Administration Office, Data Access Unit, 416-235-2999

Order records online (results mail return) at
www.dlcheck.rus.mto.gov.on.ca/Scripts/OrderForm.asp

Vehicle records: Ministry of Transportation, Licensing Admin. Office, Special Inquiry Unit, 416-235-2999
www.mto.gov.on.ca/english/dandv/

Lien information is shown only when a Used Vehicle Information Package (UVIP) is purchased. Purchase a vehicle history, VIN, plate search, or UVIP at www.omvic.on.ca/services/ also a Used Vehicle Information Package (UVIP).

Prince Edward Island

Highway Safety Division, Driving Records Section, 902-368-5210
Registrar of Vehicles 902-368-5200, 902-368-6847

Lien information is released only at courthouses.

Quebec

Driving Records Division, SAAQ, 418-643-7620; 800-361-7620
www.saaq.gouv.qc.ca/en/index.php

Before buying a vehicle or obtaining a lease you can obtain a vehicle record including previous owners from the SAAQ.

Saskatchewan

Driver Abstracts, Saskatchewan Government Insurance
306-775-6198, 306-751-1249 www.sgi.sk.ca

Yukon

Department of Motor Vehicles. Yukon Territory, 867-667-5315
www.community.gov.yk.ca/motorvehicles/newmvindex.html

Lien information available from Corporate Affairs, 867- 667-5442.

Ship Registrations

http://daryl.chin.gc.ca:8000/basisbwdocs/sid/title1e.html

Transportation Liens

With registration, a Commonwealth-wide vehicle Lien Check Service to identify liens on personal property that is a motor vehicle, trailer, mobile home, airplane, boat or outboard motor is online at https://pprs.acol.ca/lc/index.do

Search Engines and Phone Books

AltaVista Canada

This is the Canadian version of AltaVista, with access to millions of Canadian-specific web pages. http://ca.altavista.com

Google Canada

This is the Canadian version of Google with most of the same features as the U.S. version. www.google.ca/

InfoSpace

In the North America section, click on Canada to find Yellow Pages and White Pages. www.infospace.com/home/white-pages/world

Other Phone books

White Pages - www.canada411.ca/eng/person.html

Yellow Pages - www.yellowpages.ca/index.html

Copyrights

In the U.S., the Copyright Act of 1976 and its major revisions enacted in 1978 and 1998, (www.loc.gov/copyright/title17/) govern the use of copyrighted works, including literary works; musical works including words; dramatic works including music; pantomimes and choreographic works; pictorial, graphic, and sculptural works; motion pictures and other audiovisual works; sound recordings; architectural work, but **not** titles, names, short phrases, and slogans; familiar symbols or designs; variations of typographic ornamentation, lettering, or coloring; mere listings of ingredients or contents; ideas; procedures; methods; systems; processes; concepts; principles; discoveries; devices; works of common property, nor containing no original authorship like calendars, rulers, and public lists or tables

Since 1978, copyright protection subsists from the time the work is created in fixed form and ordinarily given a term enduring for the author's life plus 70 years after. For works made for hire, and for anonymous and pseudonymous the duration of copyright is 95 years from publication or 120 years from creation, whichever is shorter. The copyright in the work of authorship immediately becomes the property of the author who created the work. Only the author or those deriving their rights through the author can rightfully claim copyright. In the case of works made for hire, the employer and not the employee is considered the author.

For further info see www.copyright.gov or contact the U.S. Copyright Office at:

Library of Congress
Copyright Office
101 Independence Avenue, SE
Washington, DC 20559-6000
202-707-3000

Foreign Copyrights

In 1989 the U.S. joined the Berne Convention which is an entity that guarantees copyright protection for authors in all member nations. The

Convention does not require registration, a copyright symbol, or notification of any kind on authors' publications; so one should assume that *all worldwide* Internet works are copyrighted and protected by the Berne Convention. Circular 38a, *International Copyright Relations of the United States*, lists the nations that honor U.S. copyrights. Other countries' copyright laws are more restrictive than U.S. laws. U.K. and Canada do protect their government publications.

www.wipo.int/treaties/en/ip/berne/

Website Copyrights

Placing content or pages from others' websites into your own webpage is called "framing" (or inlaying) and can be infringement or copyright.

To determine what can be legally downloaded, copied, and printed from the web, users should look for terms and conditions and links detailing the permissions given by the site owner. Usually, commercial sites permit reproduction for personal use or for non-profit or educational purposes but not for commercial purposes or making of multiple copies to be distributed. U.S. federal websites are not protected by copyright and can be copied; their content is in the public domain. But content of state government websites is likely to be protected by law. Content from U.S. patent documents and federal legal documents can also be copied, but proprietary information from private parties attached to federal documents is protected by law. Non-profit groups, such as associations, may copyright their material. Never delete copyright notices from search results.

Copyright Information Online

A free search the Library of Congress database is found at www.copyright.gov/rb.html

Search Canadian copyrights free at:

http://strategis.ic.gc.ca/app/cipo/copyrights/displaySearch.do?language=eng

A copyright availability search is one of many national and international IP, trademark and copyright services for a fee from Thomson Compumark at http://compumark.thomson.com/do/cache/off/pid/13.

Corrections Records

(*See Incarceration Records*)

Credit Reporting Bureaus

Of course, credit reports are not public record. Credit reports are derived from the financial transactions of people or businesses. **Private companies maintain this information; government only regulates access.** Certain credit information about **individuals** is restricted by federal law, such as the Fair Credit Reporting Act, and state laws. Credit information about **businesses** is not restricted by law and is fully open to anyone who requests (pays for) it.

Major Credit Bureaus – Individual

A credit report on an individual essentially has two parts — the credit header and the credit history. A credit header is essentially the upper portion of a credit report containing the Social Security Number, age, phone number, last several addresses, and any AKAs. A credit header can be purchased separately, but recently the access to credit header information (see below) was closed to many business entities.

These are the major U.S. providers of credit information on individuals:

Equifax

Equifax Credit Information Services, Inc
P.O. Box 740241, Atlanta, GA 30374
Fraud Alert - 888-766-0008
Purchase Report: www.equifax.com/credit-report-history/
or call 800-685-1111

Experian

Experian lists two primary locations in the U.S.:

475 Anton Blvd, Costa Mesa, CA 92626, 714-830-7000
955 American Lane, Schaumburg, IL 60173, 847-517-5600

Order by phone or Fraud Alert: 888-397-3742
Disputes: 888-397-3742

TransUnion

Although headquartered in Chicago, TransUnion accepts mail at two addresses:

P.O. Box 6790, Fullerton, CA 92834
P.O. Box 1000, Chester, PA 19022

Fraud Assistance: 800-680-7289 or email to fvad@transunion.com
Disputes: 800-916-8800
Free credit reports - call 877-322-8228 or online at
https://www.annualcreditreport.com/cra/index.jsp

Major Credit Bureaus – Business

As mentioned, credit information of a business is not restricted by law and is fully open to anyone who requests and pays for it. Listed below in alphabetical order are the names and web pages of the major players maintaining proprietary databases of business credit information.

BusinessCreditUSA – www.businesscreditusa.com

ClientChecker – www.clientchecker.com/business_credit_reports.htm

Dun & Bradstreet – www.dnb.com

Equifax Business – www.equifax.com/commercial/en_us

Experian Business – www.experian.com/business/bcr.html

Kroll Factual Data – www.krollfactualdata.com

The Credit Header Ban and Gramm-Leach-Bliley

The Gramm-Leach-Bliley Act (GLBA), also known as the Financial SVCS Modernization Act of 1999, provided limited privacy protections against the sale of private financial information. The Act did not deny access to public record sources or databases that may contain age, SSN, phone, prior addresses, and AKAs. The Act only forbade financial institutions from disclosing this data.

This Act took affect on July 1st, 2001, an important date for skiptracers, fraud investigators, and other businesses that rely on "credit headers." Previously, credit headers had always been available without the consent of the individual subject. Per the Act and a federal court ruling, beginning July 1st 2001, access to credit header information was treated in the same manner as access to credit reports – there must be permission granted by the individual. Therefore, those businesses shut-off from using credit headers had to investigate alternative sources of public records.

Impact of Changes

The impact was far ranging. Credit bureaus were restricted from selling the above-mentioned data to information vendors who compiled their own proprietary databases. But there is one alternative for entities that rely on using credit header information. The data is grandfathered. Provider companies that purchased files from the credit bureaus can continue to sell the data to their customers. Although data will never be updated from the credit bureaus, the existing data can still be used without the restrictions imposed by the ruling.

Education Records

Per the Family Educational Rights and Privacy Act (FERPA), the education records of students are not public record unless used as general directory information. There must be consent to release records containing personal information.

However, what is very much public record is the accreditation of schools. This section looks at how to find the location of a school, determine if it is accredited, and how to recognize *diploma mills*. This section also looks at the steps involved for verification of attendance or degree of a student. Information about the FERPA is found in the Appendix.

Accreditation of Colleges and Universities

Searching accreditation resources is perhaps the best way to find a post-secondary institution. A school's accreditation must be issued by an organization – accreditor body – that has been **recognized** by the U.S. Department of Education (USDE) and/or the Council for Higher Education Accreditation (CHEA). To be "recognized" means that an accrediting body must meet the quality standards of at least one of these two respective organizations. Schools may operate without accreditation, as long as a state grants the authority to operate. The schools that operate without accreditation *and* without authority are generally known as "diploma mills."

Both CHEA and the USDE provide online search capabilities to find accrediting bodies and accredited schools.

The USDE publishes a database of Postsecondary Educational Institutions and Programs Accredited by Accrediting Agencies, and State Approval Agencies Recognized by the U.S. Secretary of Education, available at www.ope.ed.gov/accreditation. The database lists approximately 6,900 postsecondary institutions and programs, each accredited by an accrediting organization recognized by the USDE.

U.S. Department of Education
400 Maryland Avenue, SW, Washington, DC 20202
1-800-872-5327; Fax- 202-401-0689

The CHEA searchable database includes accrediting bodies, nearly 7,000 schools and also 17,000 accredited programs. The search function is based on the school name and includes geographical filters. See www.chea.org/search/default.asp.

Council for Higher Education Accreditation
One Dupont Circle NW, #510, Washington, DC 20036
202-955-6126; Fax-202-955-6129
chea@chea.org

Each accrediting organization's list of institutions or programs is prefaced by a brief description of the accredited status of the institutions or programs, and the year for which the list is accurate.[1]

Some accrediting organizations and their institutions and programs appear in both the CHEA database and the USDE database. Others may appear in one but not both. Whether in CHEA or USDE, accrediting organizations identified in the database have been "recognized."

An alternative to finding a school or university, although not a complete list, is searching www.google.com/intl/en_extra/universities.html.

The Accrediting Bodies

Generally, accrediting entities are of two types:

   1. Regional associations   2. Specialized accrediters

Specialized accreditors focus on **topics** – religion (ABET, for example), teaching (NCATE, for example), or health, social work, music, etc.

Regional associations focus on a school's **overall programs**.

For most U.S. institutions with liberal arts programs, one of the six following regional associations of colleges and schools takes primary accrediting responsibility for the entire school. The list below includes the name of the accrediting association, web address, the phone number, and the list of the states or territories covered by the association. These are excellent resources should you have questions about an institution in a particular state. All provide web look-ups of the institutions they accredit.

Regional Accrediting Associations

MSACHE (or simply **MSA**) Middle States Association of Colleges and Schools, 215-662-5606, www.msche.org. DE, DC, MD, NJ, NY, PA, Puerto Rico, Virgin Islands

NEACHE (or **NEASC CIHE**) New England Association of Schools and Colleges, 781-271-0022, www.neasc.org. CT, ME, MA, NH, RI, VT. The New England Association of Schools and Colleges Commission on Technical and Career Institutions is a separate entity within NEACHE.

NCACHE (or simply **NCAC** or **NCA**) North Central Association of Colleges and Schools, 800-621-7440. www.ncahigherlearningcommission.org. AZ, AR, CO, IL, IN, IA, KS, MI, MN, MO, NE, NM, ND, OH, OK, SD, WV, WI, WY

NWCCU (or simply **NASC**) Northwest Commission on Colleges and Universities, 425-558-4224, www.nwccu.org. AK, ID, MT, NV, OR, UT, WA

---

[1] The information in the CHEA database is supplied by the accrediting organizations. It is reformatted but otherwise not edited by CHEA.

SACSCC (or simply **SACS**) Southern Association of Colleges and Schools, 800-248-7701, 404-679-4500, www.sacs.org. AL, FL, GA, KY, LA, MS, NC, SC, TN, TX, VA

WASC (erroneously known as WACS) Western Association of Schools and Colleges: Senior College Commission, 510-748-9001, www.wascweb.org. CA, HI, territories of Guam, American Samoa, Federated States of Micronesia, Republic of Palau, Commonwealth of the Northern Marianas Islands, the Pacific Basin, and East Asia, and areas of the Pacific and East Asia where American/International schools or colleges may apply to it for service. WASC-JR is separate entity within WASC for accrediting junior colleges.

Specialized Accrediters

Colleges and universities wish to emphasize their accreditations. Many provide a convenient hot link to their *Accreditations Page*. Usually one of the six regional accreditors appears first (if applicable), followed by a list of specific-topic accrediters. The list of specialized accrediters clues you in on the types of programs the school offers. For instance, NCATE indicates an accredited program for teachers. AVMA indicates veterinary medicine. A list of accreditation acronyms is found at www.aspa-usa.org/resources/acronyms.html.

Education Records– What to Check

Business owners, managers, and others have an interest in verifying or knowing that anyone hired does actually possess the educational credentials claimed on a resume, application, or during a job interview. Employment screeners, licensing boards, HR staffs, and security personnel verify educational credentials as a main line of defense against the most-often lied about claim on these documents – one's education history and qualifications.

There are four primary pieces of information to verify–

1) The school attended does exist.

2) The school is accredited by an approved accrediting body.

3) The subject attended the school during the time period claimed.

4) A degree was actually granted to the subject as claimed.

If the position involves proof of course-taking, then–

5) The student's completed the courses of study for any degree are granted are shown on an official copy of their school transcripts.

Inquires about items 1 and 2 can be made from CHEA, USDE, one of the accreditors, or from vendor's compiled database of this information. Items 3, 4, and 5 can be made through the school's Registrar's office.

Diploma Mills, Degree Mills, Accreditation Mills, Fake Paper

Have you received a spam email with a subject line saying "Get a degree now" or "Get credit for what you deserve"? Imagine how many job-hungry applicants might respond and take a shot at passing themselves off as more educationally qualified than they are.

Webster's Dictionary describes a Diploma mill as:

> *An institution of higher education operating without supervision of a state or professional agency and granting diplomas which are either fraudulent or because of the lack of proper standards worthless.*

A diploma mill issues a paper 'diploma' that the student has paid for, and the student performs little or no actual study. Some diploma mills go so far as to provide a phone number or email address for verification-seeking screeners to use for verification. The phone or an email address is directed to a fake registrar's office, including a very convincing, live fake registrar who will confirm the schools existence and even gets uppity if you suggest there is a fraud.

Identifying Diploma Mills

CHEA has an instruction page on identifying Degree Mills at www.chea.org/degreemills/default.htm

A good overall diploma mill identifier is the College and University section in BRB Publication's PRRS-Web or on the CD product.

Several of the best places to view lists of known diploma mills and unaccredited colleges are at Oregon's Diploma Mills site at www.osac.state.or.us/oda/unaccredited.aspx and at Michigan's 'Not Accredited by CHEA' list at www.michigan.gov/documents/Non-accreditedSchools_78090_7.pdf.

The Bear's Guide to Earning a Degree Non-traditionally and *Bears' Guide to Earning Degrees by Distance Learning* provide good background on off-beat learning and distance education issues and answers.

Tips on Verifying Student Records

Verifying Attendance or Degree via the School

Traditionally, a verification request is sent by mail or fax to the school's Registrar office, but increasingly Registrar offices accept phone and email requests. Many now provide online, interactive request forms. Some schools require a signed release from the student. Verifications are usually free, but not always. Confirmations *may* be faxed back although you may ask to school to confirm their results via phone. Requests should include a DOB, SSN, and the name used during attendance. Gender and approximate or exact years of attendance should be mentioned, and always be concise about where verification results should be returned – your address, phone, company name, etc. If you mail a request, be sure to include a SASE.

Verifying Through NSLC or degreechk.com

Nearly 25% of schools have outsourced verification duties to a third-party vendor. There are two primary vendors that are under contract with higher education schools to provide verification services on behalf of schools. This outsourcing ostensibly takes the tasks out of the hands of cost-conscious registrar offices. Fees are involved and requesters must generally provide the subject's signed release. By far the largest vendor is the National Student Loan Clearinghouse (NSLC), 703-742-4200, fax- 703-318-4058, in Herndon, VA, www.nslc.org. Another verification provider with a shorter list of participating schools is Credentials Inc. of Northfield, IL 60093, 847-716-3000, www.degreechk.com.

Both vendors also provide a transcript copy service, though their transcript participating school lists are substantially smaller then their bread-and-butter service – verifications.

Acquiring Transcript Copies

Most schools make verifications without cost to the requester, but not so for transcripts copies. Fees for each transcript copy vary from $1.00 to $20.00 each, but usually around $5.00. Items to include in a written transcript request are the same as with a verification, with an emphasis on a providing the student's signed release. Often transcription request forms are found online at the schools web page. Credit card payment *may* be allowed.[2] A number of schools offer *Unofficial Transcripts* as a cost-saving measure, the benefit being that an unofficial copy can be returned by fax or email. Official copies are usually mailed back.

A school may outsource its transcript fulfillment duties to a 3rd party vendor, but this is rare.

Finding a Closed School and its Records

The applicant's resume reads "Attended Aakers' Business College in Fargo, ND." But when one seeks to verify the applicant's attendance there, the school is found to be closed. Perhaps the applicant is claiming they attended there but didn't, knowing that verifications there might be hard to come by!

Closed schools within a state are registered through an education-related state agency. The records may be maintained by the agency or the agency may know who does and have some mechanism in place to

---

[2] A good source of information about Registrar's request procedures and fees is found in BRB Publication's *PRRS* or *The National Directory to College & University Student RecordsCD.*

help you either 1) identify the current location of the closed schools student records, or 2) the agency may perform the record check for you. This is also true for transcript requests, but, depending on the state, transcripts and student attendance/degree information may not always be found at the same place.

Closed private institutions such as military or seminary schools are a different story. Their records may have been transferred to another school, a nearby same-denomination school, or simply held by a surviving alumnus.

Knowing of the difficulty and urgency of your search request, the state agency can usually handle phone requests or is quick to instruct you how to correctly submit your request. Search online at http://wdcrobcolp01.ed.gov/CFAPPS/FSA/closedschool/searchpage.cfm

Links to Other Educational Organization Sites

Below are some additional resources of value.

- Association of Governing Boards (AGB), www.agb.org
- American Assoc. of University Women (AAUW), www.aauw.org
- American Assoc. of Univ. Professors (AAUP), www.aaup.org/aaup
- American Federation of Teachers (AFT), www.aft.org
- Association of Community College Trustees (ACCT), www.acct.org
- The Carnegie Foundation for the Advancement of Teaching, www.carnegiefoundation.org
- The College Board, www.collegeboard.com
- Council for Advancement & Support of Edu,cation, (CASE) www.case.org
- National Education Association (NEA), www.nea.org/index.html

General Education Diplomas (GED)

Not everyone graduates from high school. But later a person may pass a high school equivalency test and receive a General Education Diploma (GED). A database of GED recipients is maintained at the state level by the agency that oversees adult education. A GED record search will verify if someone truly received a GED certificate for high school education equivalency. Many of these state agencies will verify over the phone the existence of a GED certificate or give a "yes-no" answer by fax. Copies of transcripts or diplomas usually require a fee and a sigend release. Search requirements include the name of the student at the time of the test and a general idea of the year and test location. GED records are not useful when trying to locate an individual.

BRB's *Public Record Research System* provides detailed information on each state's GED office with record searching requirements.

High School Records

Searching for high school records can be a difficult task. Over the years, schools can close, merge, or be renamed. A high school name can be misspelled or not quite remembered.

There are several excellent websites that provide comprehensive lists and data pertaining to high schools as well as junior highs and elementary schools.

The site maintained by Standard and Poors at www.schoolmatters.com provides detailed information on each school including the school's address, telephone number, total students and also very detailed comparisons on performance matters. Click on the *Site Map* to begin an alpha search on a state basis.

Check out the subscription site at www.schoolinformation.com. Designed for entities marketing products to schools, this resource is valuable if extensive searching or due diligence is required.

Also, a Google search will reveal a number of state lists.

Of course, an on-site visit of a school is a good way to view a yearbook to find pictures and activity information about individual students.

Elections

(See Voter Registration Records)

Employment Screening

A critical function of employment screening is the searching and use of public records. Employment screening is not an investigation; it is *a verification.* Also known as a pre-employment background check, employment screening verifies the information on a job application or resume. Common sense dictates that employers wish to minimize the liability for negligent hiring if the actions of an employee could harm the public in a job-related situation. Also, there are many federal and state laws requiring background checks be conducted for certain jobs, such as positions working with children or the elderly.

A background check usually involves obtaining a criminal record search, verification of previous employment, verification of education or similar credentials, and sometimes obtaining a driving record report. Also, a background check often will verify that the Social Security Number of the applicant is not that of a deceased person or belongs to someone else.

The Gold Standard – The FCRA

When background checks are conducted for an employer by a third party – a pre-employment screening firm – compliance with the federal Fair Credit Reporting Act (FCRA) is required. Although the law uses the word "credit" the FCRA goes well beyond the scope of credit reports. The background check is called a "consumer report." And the pre-employment screening firm is known as a "consumer reporting agency" (CRA).

The purpose of the FCRA is to protect the confidentiality of the applicant and promote the accuracy of a report. The FCRA requires employers to obtain a job applicant's consent before performing record checks. The FCRA dictates that the most recent record database available must be used for record checking. Strict compliance rules go into affect if "adverse information" not previously disclosed is uncovered on an applicant, or on a current employee, which could affect the employment.

In general, the FCRA compliance rules do not apply if employers conduct background checks themselves, such as when reference checks are by their conducted human resource departments.

A number of states have their own version of the FCRA, California being notable. There are also many states with laws that dictate the types of criminal records that can be used when hiring decisions are made. For example, some states do not allow the use of misdemeanor records and others disallow the use of arrest records without convictions.

With a myriad of laws and compliance issues, employment screening is not an easy business to operate and it is very competitive. Some individuals think it is an easy business to start with a chance to make easy money. This is not true, especially so in states that require a employment screening company to have a private investigator's license.

PI or CRA?

There is another issue that is a red flag. Some private investigators offer pre-employment screening to their clientele, but do not realize they are consumer reporting agencies and bound by the mandates of the FCRA. Here is a quick story which illustrates the confusion. Several years ago I gave a short presentation on criminal record databases to a group of private investigators. At the beginning of the talk I asked for a show of hands of how many people in the room did pre-employment screening for employers. About 85% of the attendees indicated they did. Several questions later I asked how many people in the room were Consumer Reporting Agencies and only 15% of the attendees indicated they were.

> If someone providing employment screening to employers does not know that they are a consumer reporting agency, the door is wide open to many bad things, including negligent hiring lawsuits. Most of the private investigators that I know are quite knowledgeable about FCRA compliance. But if you are an investigator who is not knowledgeable about the FCRA and you offer employment screening services, I strongly recommend that you speak to your attorney and find ways to become better educated on FCRA compliance issues.

The Appendix has additional information about the FCRA, including a link to the Act. A great resource of information is the trade association for employment and tenants screeners – the National Association of Professional Background Screeners (NAPBS). Visit www.napbs.com. For detailed information about background screening, we recommend *The Safe Hiring Manual* by Lester S. Rosen (Facts on Demand Press, 2007).

Environment

Many of the environmental public records held by the government rest at two locations: the Environmental Protection Agency and the National Library of Medicine. The content to follow looks at each agency and public records associated with health hazards. At the end of this section, be sure to check out the write-up on **Scorecard**, a pollution information site.

Environmental Protection Agency (EPA)

The EPA's Environmental Facts Warehouse is a good starting place to search for environmental information. Go to www.epa.gov/enviro. Below are descriptions of some of the more useful search features.

EnviroMapper combines interactive maps and aerial photography to display various types of environmental information, including air releases, drinking water, toxic releases, hazardous wastes, water discharge permits, and Superfund sites. The site creates maps at the national, state, and county levels that can be linked to environmental text reports. Go to www.epa.gov/enviro/emef/.

The EPA's Office of Enforcement and Compliance Assurance (OECA) works with EPA regional offices, state governments, tribal governments and other federal agencies on compliance with the nation's environmental laws. See www.epa.gov/compliance/index.html.

OECA offers online access to its database called Enforcement & Compliance History Online (ECHO). Search the database for inspection, violation, enforcement action, and penalty information about compliance and enforcement information on approximately 800,000 regulated facilities. ECHO can be found at www.epa-echo.gov/echo.

For a web search of cases and settlements go to http://cfpub.epa.gov/compliance/cases, additional information can be found at www.epa.gov/compliance/civil/index.html.

Federal law requires facilities in certain industries, which manufacture, process, or use significant amounts of toxic chemicals, to report annually on their releases of these chemicals to the EPA Toxics Release Inventory Program. Superfund sites are those throughout the United States and its territories which contain substances that are either designated as hazardous under the Comprehensive Environmental Response, Compensation and Liability Act (CERCLA), or identified as such under other laws. For information about the Superfund sites on the National Priorities List, email superfund.docket@epa.gov. Superfund sites are at http://cfpub.epa.gov/supercpad/cursites/srchsites.cfm. Search EPA Records of Decisions (ROD) at www.epa.gov/superfund/sites/rods.

National Atlas (Department of the Interior)

The Department of the Interior maintains some dynamic web pages with usable data and map making abilities. At www.nationalatlas.org, click on either the Environment or Geology tabs. Maps can be created based on EPA criteria.

National Library of Medicine (NLM)

Household Products Database

This resource indicates the chemical ingredients found in household products and who manufactures specific brands. The database contains information on over 7,000 products. Email tehip@teh.nlm.nih.gov or visit http://householdproducts.nlm.nih.gov.

TOXMAP

TOXMAP (http://toxmap.nlm.nih.gov) is a Geographic Information System (GIS) from the National Library of Medicine (NLM) that uses maps of the United States to help users visually explore data from the EPA's Toxics Release Inventory (TRI) (www.epa.gov/tri/) and Superfund Programs.

TOXMAP helps users create nationwide or local area maps showing where TRI chemicals are released on-site into the air, water, and ground. It also identifies the releasing facilities, color-codes release amounts for a single year, and provides multi-year chemical release trends, starting with 1987. Maps can also show locations of Superfund sites on the National Priority List (NPL) at www.epa.gov/superfund/sites/npl, listing all chemical contaminants present at these sites. Users can search the system by chemical name, chemical name fragment, and/or location (such as city, state, or ZIP code). TOXMAP also overlays map data such as U.S. Census population information, income figures from the Bureau of Economic Analysis, and health data from the National Cancer Institute (www.cancer.gov) and the National Center for Health Statistics (www.cdc.gov/nchs).

Specifically, the data shown in TOXMAP comes from these resources:

- EPA's Toxics Release Inventory (TRI)
- EPA's Superfund Program
- Hazardous Substances Data Bank
- TOXLINE (Toxicology Bibliographic Information) - www.nlm.nih.gov/pubs/factsheets/toxlinfs.html
- Agency for Toxic Substances and Disease Registry (ATSDR)- www.atsdr.cdc.gov/
- National Atlas of the United States of America (USGS) - www.nationalatlas.gov/

For detailed information about HSDB or TOXNET, contact:

National Library of Medicine
Specialized Information Services
Two Democracy Plaza, Suite 510
6707 Democracy Boulevard, MSC 5467
Bethesda, MD 20892-5467
Telephone 301-496-1131, fax: 301-480-3537

TOXNET

TOXNET, the Toxicology Data Network, provides multiple databases on toxicology, hazardous chemicals, environmental health, and toxic releases. TOXNET is managed by the Toxicology and Environmental Health Information Program within the National Library of Medicine (NLM). TOXNET provides free access at http://toxnet.nlm.nih.gov for easy searching of the following databases—

- HSDB® (Hazardous Substances Data Bank) is a factual database focusing on the toxicology of over 5,000 potentially hazardous chemicals. www.nlm.nih.gov/pubs/factsheets/hsdbfs.html
- IRIS (Integrated Risk Information System) is a database from the U.S. Environmental Protection Agency (EPA) containing carcinogenic and non-carcinogenic health risk information on over 500 chemicals.
- The ITER (International Toxicity Estimates for Risk) database contains data in support of human health risk assessments on over 600 chemical records.

- CCRIS (Chemical Carcinogenesis Research Information System), developed and maintained by the National Cancer Institute (NCI), contains over 9,000 chemical records with carcinogenicity, mutagenicity, tumor promotion, and tumor inhibition test results.
- GENE-TOX (Genetic Toxicology) is a toxicology database created by the U.S. Environmental Protection Agency (EPA) containing genetic toxicology test results on over 3,200 chemicals.
- Tox Town (see above)
- Household Products Database (see above)

Haz-Map® links jobs and hazardous tasks with occupational diseases and their symptoms. The approximately 1,000 chemicals and biological agents in the database are related to industrial processes and other activities such as hobbies. The linkage indicates the potential for exposure to the agents. The 180 occupational diseases and their symptoms are associated with hazardous job tasks. This association indicates an increased risk for significant exposure and subsequent disease.

To reach TOXNET by telephone, call 301-496-1131.

Tox Town

Also provided by the National Library of Medicine, this interactive web page is a great source of non-technical descriptions of chemicals, assorted links to selected, authoritative chemical information, and lists everyday locations where one might find toxic chemicals. http://toxtown.nlm.nih.gov/

Scorecard

Scorecard is a very popular web resource for information about pollution problems and toxic chemicals. Per their web page, "Find out about the pollution problems in your community and learn who is responsible. See which geographic areas and companies have the worst pollution records. Identify which racial/ethnic and income groups bear more than their share of environmental burdens. Then take action as an informed citizen - you can fax a polluting company, contact your elected representatives, or get involved in your community." Visit www.scorecard.org.

Federal Agency Sanctions & Watch Lists

This section examines public record databases of individuals and companies that have sanctions, violations, enforcement actions, or warnings initiated against them by one of these federal government departments—

- Commerce Department
- Food & Drug Administration
- GSA – Government Services
- Human Health Care Services Department
- Justice Department
- Labor Department
- Occupational Safety & Health Administration
- State Department
- Treasury Department

Note: To find enforcement actions taken by the Federal Reserve, see the Banks & Financial Institutions Section. To find enforcement action involving stocks and securities see the Securities and Securities Dealers Section.

Commerce Department

The Bureau of Industry and Security (BIS), part of the U.S. Department of Commerce, provides the three lists described below that are relevant to import/export transactions. www.bis.doc.gov

Denied Persons List

The purpose of the Denied Persons List is to prevent the illegal export of dual-use items before they occur and to investigate and assist in the prosecution of violators of the Export Administration Regulations. www.bis.doc.gov/dpl/default.shtm

Unverified List

This is a list of parties whom BIS has been unable to verify in some manner in prior transactions. The Unverified List includes names and countries of foreign persons who in the past were parties to a transaction with respect to which BIS could not conduct a pre-license check ("PLC") or a post-shipment verification ("PSV") for reasons outside of the U.S. Government's control. If you would like to be informed when

changes occur to the Unverified List, consider subscribing to the BIS Email Notification Service.
www.bis.doc.gov/enforcement/unverifiedlist/unverified_parties.html

Entity List

The Entity List, available in PDF or ASCII text format, is a list of parties whose presence in a transaction can trigger a license requirement under the Export Administration Regulations. The original pupose of this list was to inform the public of entities whose activities imposed a risk of diverting exported and reexported items into programs related to weapons of mass destruction. Now the list includes those with any license requirements imposed on the transaction by other provisions of the Export Administration Regulations. The list specifies the license requirements that apply to each listed party.
www.bis.doc.gov/entities/default.htm

FDA – Food & Drug Administration

FDA regulates scientific studies that are designed to develop evidence to support the safety and effectiveness of **investigational drugs (human and animal), biological products, and medical devices**. Physicians and other qualified experts ("clinical investigators") who conduct these studies are required to comply with applicable statutes and regulations intended to ensure the integrity of clinical data on which product approvals are based and, for investigations involving human subjects, to help protect the rights, safety, and welfare of these subjects.

For further information about the lists below, contact the Food and Drug Administration, Office of Enforcement, 5600 Fishers Lane, HFC-230, Rockville, MD 20857; 240-632-6853, fax: 240-632-6861.

FDA Enforcement Report Index – Recalls, Market Withdrawals, and Safety Alerts

The FDA Enforcement Report, published weekly, contains information on actions taken in connection with agency regulatory activities. Activities include Recall and Field Correction, Injunctions, Seizures, Indictments, Prosecutions, and Dispositions. A record of all recalls (Class I, II, and III), including pre-1995, can be found at www.fda.gov/opacom/Enforce.html.

Visit www.fda.gov/opacom/7alerts.html for the most significant product actions of the last 60 days, based on the extent of distribution and the degree of health risk. These recalls on the list are mainly Class I, the most serious category.

Information regarding individuals sanctioned by the FDA may be accessed through the FDA bulletin boards. For more information, contact the PHS Alert System Manager, Office of Research Integrity, 1101 Wootton Parkway, Rm 750, Rockville, MD 20852, 301-443-5330.

Debarrment List

The FDA maintains a list of individuals and entities that are prohibited from introducing any type of food, drug, cosmetics or associated devices into interstate commerce. The list is found at www.fda.gov/ora/compliance_ref/debar/

Disqualified or Totally Restricted Clinical Investigator List

FDA may disqualify a clinical investigator if the clinical investigator has repeatedly or deliberately failed to comply with applicable regulatory requirements or the clinical investigator has repeatedly or deliberately submitted false information to the sponsor or, if applicable, to FDA. A disqualified or totally restricted clinical investigator is not eligible to receive investigational drugs, biologics, or devices. www.fda.gov/ora/compliance_ref/bimo/disqlist.htm

Partially Restricted Clinical Investigator List

All clinical investigators who have agreed to certain restrictions with respect to their conduct of clinical investigations are listed at www.fda.gov/ora/compliance_ref/bimo/restlist.htm

Search for all clinical investigators who previously agreed to certain restrictions, which have now been removed, at www.fda.gov/ora/compliance_ref/bimo/rest_removed.htm

Adequate Assurances List

All clinical investigators who, under regulations in effect until 1987, have provided FDA with adequate assurances of their future compliance with requirements applicable to the use of investigational drugs and biologics. www.fda.gov/ora/compliance_ref/bimo/asurlist.htm

GSA – Government Services

Excluded Party List

The Excluded Parties List System (EPLS) contains information on individuals and firms excluded by various Federal government agencies from receiving federal contracts or federally approved subcontracts and from certain types of federal financial and non-financial assistance and benefits. Note that individual agencies are responsible for the timely reporting, maintenance, and accuracy of their data this single comprehensive list of. Information shown may include names, addresses, DUNS numbers, Social Security Numbers, Employer Identification Numbers or other Taxpayer Identification Numbers, if available and deemed appropriate and permissible to publish by the agency taking the action. www.epls.gov

Human Health Services, Department of

Excluded Individuals/Entities (LEIE)

The LEIE maintained by the Office of Inspector General (OIG) for the Department of Human Health Services is a list of currently excluded parties for convictions for program-related fraud and patient abuse, licensing board actions, and default on Health Education Assistance Loans. The purpose is to prevent certain individuals and businesses from participating in Federally-funded health care programs. The database may be searched online or the database may be downloaded from the web page. The searchable database is found at http://exclusions.oig.hhs.gov/. The downloadable database is at http://oig.hhs.gov/fraud/exclusions/database.html.

Health Education Assistance Loan (HEAL)

Between 1978 and 1998, the Health Education Assistance Loan (HEAL) program provided federal insurance for educational loans made by private lenders to more than 156,000 graduate health profession students. Students included were in schools of medicine, osteopathy, dentistry, veterinary medicine, optometry, podiatry, pharmacy, chiropractic, health administration or clinical psychology. New HEAL loans were discontinued September 30, 1998.

By law, HEAL borrowers in default on their loans are published quarterly. They can be searched by name, discipline, state, amount due and school. For details, visit http://defaulteddocs.dhhs.gov/search.asp

Justice Department

There are a number of Divisions within the Justice Department that maintain news articles, stories, records lists, and most wanted lists that can be very useful for research and investigation purposes.

Bureau of Alcohol, Tobacco, Firearms and Explosives

Below are four resources:

- Federal Firearms License Validator - https://www.atfonline.gov/fflezcheck
- Most Wanted List - www.atf.gov/wanted/index.htm
- Out of Business Records - 800-788-7133, ext. 1590
- Federal Firearms Licensees list local or nationwide - 202-927-8866

Bureau of Investigation (FBI)

The FBI's Most Wanted Site at www.fbi.gov/wanted.htm contains numerous lists to search, including kidnappings, missing persons, unknown bank robbers, and others. Department FOIA instructions are found at http://foia.fbi.gov/foia_instruc.htm. You can request online.

Drug Enforcement Administration (DEA)

Search DEA fugitives at www.usdoj.gov/dea/fugitives/fuglist.htm by Field Division, from a map showing by the states within each division. Major international fugitives and captured fugitives also found here.

Labor Department

Labor and Labor Unions

The Office of Labor-Management Standards (OLMS) in the U.S. Department of Labor is the Federal agency responsible for administering and enforcing most provisions of the Labor-Management Reporting and Disclosure Act of 1959, as amended (LMRDA). The LMRDA is meant to ensure basic standards of democracy and fiscal responsibility in labor organizations representing employees in private industry, unions representing U.S. Postal Service employees and other Federal employee organizations. OLMS does not have jurisdiction over unions representing solely state, county, or municipal employees. OLMS responsibilities include:

- **Public Disclosure of Reports** – Labor unions, their officers and employees, employers, labor relations consultants, and surety companies must file reports which are public information and available for disclosure at OLMS offices.

- **Compliance Audits** - OLMS has responsibility under the LMRDA to audit local unions for records review and to verify LMRDA compliance.

- **Investigations** - OLMS staff conduct investigations to determine if violations of the LMRDA provisions have occurred and to protect and safeguard union funds and assets. OLMS must refer information it uncovers regarding possible embezzlement violations by union officers or employees to the U.S. Attorney who decides if criminal prosecution is warranted.

- **Education and Compliance Assistance** - Among the services OLMS provides are education and compliance assistance programs to promote voluntary compliance and conducting seminars and workshops about the law in general or about specific areas per regulations by the LMRDA.

The OLMS Internet Public Disclosure Room web page enables users to (1) view and print reports filed by unions, union officers and employees, employers, and labor relations consultants for the year 2000 and after and reports filed by unions for trusts in which they have an interest, (2) order reports for the year 1999 and prior, and (3) search the union annual financial reports for the year 2000 and after and the trust reports for key data items. Also, searchers can generate a number of reports comparing data saved from multiple searches.

Visit   www.dol.gov/esa/regs/compliance/olms/rrlo/lmrda.htm   or contact the U.S. Department of Labor, Statutory Programs, Washington, D.C. 20210, or phone 202-693-0126.

Occupational Safety & Health Administration (OSHA)

The purpose of the Occupational Safety & Health Administration (OSHA) is to insure employee safety and health in the U.S. by setting and enforcing standards in the workplace. OSHA partners with the states for inspections and enforcements, along with education programs, technical assistance and consultation programs.

There are a number of searchable databases at OSHA (www.osha.gov). For example you can search by establishment name for information on over 3 million inspections conducted since 1972. Click on *Establishment Search.* The default option searches inspections for closed cases; however, a separate search may be made of open cases. Searches must be performed in using no longer than a five-year date range. You can also search by the North American Industry Classification Code (NAIC) or the Standard Industrial Classification Code (SIC).

Another useful search is of the Accident Investigation database. This database contains abstracts dating back to 1984 and injury data dating back to 1972. Another available search is the OSHADocket. This is a rulemaking master file that includes the materials that are collected and reviewed in reaching decisions concerning the change or creation of an OSHA regulation.

The OSHA web page offers overall access to a wealth of education and training information. For more information, reach the Occupational Safety & Health Administration at 200 Constitution Avenue, NW, Washington, DC 20210.

State Department

ITAR Debarred List

A list compiled by the State Department of parties who are barred the International Traffic in Arms Regulations (ITAR) (22 CFR §127.7) from participating directly or indirectly in the export of defense articles, including technical data or in the furnishing of defense services for which a license or approval is required, is found at www.pmddtc.state.gov/debar059.htm

Nonproliferation Sanctions Lists

The State Department maintains lists of parties that have been sanctioned under various statutes and legal authority. **Seven separate lists** are found at the web page including Sanctions for the Transfer of

Lethal Military Equipment and under Missile Sanctions laws. www.state.gov/t/isn/c15231.htm

Treasury Department

Specifically Designated Nationals (SDN) List

The U.S. Department of the Treasury, Office of Foreign Assets Control (OFAC) publishes a list of individuals and companies owned or controlled by, or acting for or on behalf of, targeted foreign countries, terrorists, international narcotics traffickers, and those engaged in activities related to the proliferation of weapons of mass destruction. The site also shows indicates individuals and entities that are not country-specific. Collectively, these individuals and companies are called "Specially Designated Nationals" or "SDN." Their assets are blocked and U.S. persons generally prohibited from dealing with them.

In addition, the Export Administration Regulations require a license for exports or re-exports to any party in any entry on this list that contains any of the suffixes "SDGT", "SDT", "FTO" or "IRAQ2". OFAC's "Hotline" is 1-800-540-6322. www.treas.gov/offices/enforcement/ofac/sdn/

Federal Contractor & Vendor Eligibility

An avenue of public record data sometimes overlooked is the licensing of individual and businesses to do business for the U.S. government.

Business Partner Network

The Business Partner Network is designed to be the single source for vendor data for the Federal Government. The web page at www.bpn.gov gives access to the CRR and OCRA (see below), as well as the Excluded Parties Listing System. (See the GSA entry under *Federal Agency Sanctions and Watch Lists* above.)

Central Contractor Registration (CCR)

The Central Contractor Registration (CCR) registers all companies and individuals that sell services and products to, or apply for assistance from, the federal government. The CCR validates the registrant information and electronically shares the secure and encrypted data with the federal agencies' finance offices to facilitate payments. There are several exceptions to registration, generally related to military or emergency operations. Also, registration data is not publicly available if the reason for registration involves national security.

The 450,000+ registrants at CRR are searchable online using a DUNS number, company name, or other criteria at https://www.bpn.gov/CCRSearch/Search.aspx. The CCR Assistance Center can be reached at 888-227-2423.

Online Representations and Certifications Application (ORCA)

The ORCA system allows contractors to enter company data regarding certification needed on federal contracts. This is a publicly accessible database, but it does require the subject's DUNS number. Go to https://orca.bpn.gov.

Small Business Administration (SBA)

The SBA maintains a database of Dynamic Small Business (DSBS) that, while primarily self-certified, does indicate certifications relating to 8(a) Business Development, HUBZone or Small Disadvantaged Business status. Visit http://dsbs.sba.gov/dsbs/search/dsp_dsbs.cfm

To find woman-owned, veteran-owned and service disabled veteran-owned specific profiles in this same SBA database, go to the Quick Market Search screen at http://dsbs.sba.gov/dsbs/search/dsp_quicksearch.cfm

For more information about SBA and government contracting, visit www.sba.gov/aboutsba/sbaprograms/gc/index.html

FBI Records

The Criminal Justice Information Services (CJIS) complex in West Virginia is the largest division in the FBI and is the central repository for criminal justice information. Programs under the CJIS Division include the National Crime Information Center (NCIC), Uniform Crime Reporting (UCR), the Integrated Automated Fingerprint Identification System (IAFIS), the NCIC 2000, the Interstate Identification Index (III), and the National Incident-Based Reporting System (NIBRS).

The FBI exchanges criminal history record information with officials of state and local governments for employment and licensing, which includes volunteers, and other similar non-criminal justice purposes, if authorized by a state statute (providing the statute is approved by the U.S. Attorney General).

The records of the FBI are not open to the public, except to the subject. Below is information about some of the significant CJIS databases.

National Crime Information Center (NCIC) 2000

The National Crime Information Center (NCIC) 2000 is an automated database of criminal justice and justice-related records maintained by the FBI that serves more than 90,000 criminal justice and law enforcement agencies nationwide. The record database includes records of wanted and missing persons, stolen vehicles, identifiable stolen property including firearms, subjects of protection and restraining orders, violent gang and terrorist members, and immigration violators. The sources of information include counties, states, and federal agencies.

Interstate Identification Index (III) System

Interstate Identification Index (III) System is not a database, but an index with a "pointer system" of persons arrested for felonies or serious misdemeanors under state or federal law. It serves for the interstate exchange of criminal history records and includes identification information such as name, date of birth, race, and sex, FBI Numbers and State Identification Numbers (SID). 48 States are participating members (ME, VT, DC, and U.S. Territories are not).

The National Instant Criminal Background Check System (NICS)

The National Instant Criminal Background Check System (NICS) is used by gun dealers to screen persons applying for firearms. NICS index contains records of over 4 million people prohibited from possessing a firearm. The NICS records are provided by federal and state agencies on individuals who have been (a) dishonorably discharged from the Armed Forces; (b) are unlawful users of or addicted to a controlled substance; (c) have been adjudicated as a mental defective or been committed to a mental institution; (d) are illegal or unlawful aliens; or (e) have renounced their U.S. citizenship. In addition, the NICS automatically checks criminal history records to identify convicted felons and those convicted of misdemeanor crimes of domestic violence and also checks NCIC files for active wanted persons, protection orders, and deported felons. Part of the search includes using personal identifiers to match records in the NCIC and the III.

The Integrated Automated Fingerprint Identification System (IAFIS)

The IAFIS, the largest biometric database in the world, contains the fingerprints and corresponding criminal history information for more than 47 million subjects in the Criminal Master File. The fingerprints and corresponding criminal history information are submitted voluntarily by state, local, and federal law enforcement agencies. In general, agencies receive electronic responses to criminal ten-print fingerprint submissions within two hours and within 24 hours for civil fingerprint submissions.

Public Request for a Copy of Record

Only the subject of the identification record can request a copy of his/her own FBI Identification Record. The request must be accompanied by satisfactory proof of identity (consisting of name, date and place of birth, and a set of roll-inked fingerprint impressions) and a certified check or money order for the $18 processing fee. The FBI will not provide copies of arrest records to individuals other than the subject of the record. Mail the request to:

> FBI CJIS Division – Record Request
> 1000 Custer Hollow Road
> Clarksburg, West Virginia 26306

Foreign Country Resources

Seven topic headings are presented below. Canada has its own section in this chapter, presented previously.

Business Entities

Foreign Business Entity Designations

In the U.S., the name of a corporation is usually followed by Inc. Or if a Limited Liability Corporation then LLC, etc. Foreign companies have different endings, extensions, or security identifiers. Knowing these foreign company terms may be quite useful in an investigation. For example, AG means the entity is a "stock corporation" in Austria, Germany or Switzerland.

CorporateInformation.com, provided by Wright Investors' Service, is an excellent source to find these foreign company extensions. Visit the web page at www.corporateinformation.com/Company-Extensions-Security-Identifiers.aspx. This page fully explains what these terms mean and where they are used. If you don't know where a company is based, this list of identifiers may very well help narrow your search.

Foreign Stock Exchanges

A valuable resource to learn specifics about foreign business entities that have publicly traded shares is the stock exchange agency within that particular country. Generally, each of these exchanges will have its own monitoring and oversight group. Below are three recommended resources to find these foreign exchanges—

- www.wall-street.com/foreign.html

- www.tdd.lt/slnews/Stock_Exchanges/Stock.Exchanges.htm
- http://en.wikipedia.org/wiki/List_of_stock_exchanges

Foreign Country Company Database Vendors

There are some good vendor resources that offer a wealth of information for searching news, market research, products, trade names, industries ownership, mergers and acquisitions data. Of course, you will have to pay to get the "good stuff" but most of the vendors listed below offer some data for free or on a trial basis.

- Kompass - www.kompass.com
- SkyMinder - www.skyminder.com
- Bureau van Dijk - www.bvdep.com

Currency

An excellent website is the Universal Currency Converter at www.xe.com/ucc/. An easy-to-use table allows one to determine a true rate of exchange. Plug in an amount of money from one country to determine its value in another. The site also lists countries' currency symbols and codes.

Diplomats

The Office of the Chief of Protocol publishes the Diplomatic List, which consists of accredited diplomatic officers of foreign embassies within the United States, and publishes Foreign Consular Offices, a complete listing of the foreign consular offices in the United States. The links to the most recent lists are found at www.state.gov/s/cpr/rls/.

Embassies Located in U.S.

There is a plethora of information available on the web pages maintained by foreign county embassies in the U.S., including addresses, detailed data about the country, and links to their government agencies. Of course, the sites use the English language.

If a country does not have a web link, a good place to find information is http://projectvisa.com.

Country	Embassy Web Page
Afghanistan	www.embassyofafghanistan.org/
Algeria	www.algeria-us.org/
Angola	www.angola.org/
Armenia	www.armeniaemb.org/

Country	Embassy Web Page
Australia	www.usa.embassy.gov.au/
Austria	www.austria.org
Azerbaijan	www.azembassy.us/
Bangladesh	www.bangladoot.org/
Bahrain	www.bahrainembassy.org/
Belarus	www.belarusembassy.org/
Belgium	www.diplobel.us/
Belize	www.embassyofbelize.org/
Benin	www.beninembassy.us/
Bolivia	www.bolivia-usa.org/
Bosnia-Herzegovina	www.bhembassy.org/
Botswana	www.botswanaembassy.org/
Brazil	www.brasilemb.org/
Brunei	www.bruneiembassy.org/
Bulgaria	www.bulgaria-embassy.org/
Burkina	www.burkinaembassy-usa.org/
Burundi	www.burundiembassy-usa.org/
Cambodia	www.embassyofcambodia.org/
Cameroon	www.ambacam-usa.org/
Canada	http://geo.international.gc.ca/can-am/washington/menu-en.asp
Chile	www.chile-usa.org/
China	www.china-embassy.org/eng/
Colombia	www.colombiaemb.org/
Costa Rica	www.costarica-embassy.org/
Croatia	www.croatiaemb.org
Cyprus	www.cyprusembassy.net/home/
Czech Republic	www.mzv.cz/wwwo/?zu=washington
Denmark	www.ambwashington.um.dk/en
Dominican Rep	www.domrep.org/
Egypt	www.egyptembassy.net/
El Salvador	www.elsalvador.org/
Estonia	www.estemb.org/
Ethiopia	www.ethiopianembassy.org/index.shtml
Fiji	www.fijiembassydc.com/
Finland	www.finland.org/en/
France	www.ambafrance-us.org/
Gambia	www.gambiaembassy.us/
Georgia	http://embassy.mfa.gov.ge
Germany	www.germany.info/relaunch/index.html

Country	Embassy Web Page
Ghana	www.ghana-embassy.org/
Great Britain	www.britainusa.com/
Greece	www.greekembassy.org/Embassy/content/en/Root.aspx
Grenada	www.grenadaembassyusa.org/
Guatemala	www.guatemala-embassy.org/main.php
Guinea	http://guineaembassy.com/
Guyana	www.guyana.org/govt/foreign_missions.html
Haiti	www.haiti.org/
Holy See	www.holyseemission.org/
Honduras	www.hondurasemb.org/
Hungary	www.huembwas.org/
Iceland	www.iceland.org/us
India	www.indianembassy.org/newsite/default.asp
Indonesia	www.embassyofindonesia.org/
Iran	www.daftar.org
Iraq	www.iraqiembassy.org/
Ireland	www.embassyofireland.org
Israel	www.israelemb.org/
Italy	www.ambwashingtondc.esteri.it/ambasciata_washington
Jamaica	www.jamaicanconsulatechicago.org/
Japan	www.us.emb-japan.go.jp/english/html/index.htm
Jordan	www.jordanembassyus.org/new/index.shtml
Kazakhstan	www.kazakhembus.com/
Kenya	www.kenyaembassy.com/
Korea	www.koreaembassyusa.org/
Kyrgyz Republic	www.kyrgyzembassy.org/
Laos	www.laoembassy.com/
Latvia	www.latvia-usa.org/
Lebanon	www.lebanonembassyus.org/
Lesotho	www.lesothoemb-usa.gov.ls/
Liberia	www.embassyofliberia.org/
Liechtenstein	www.liechtenstein.li
Lithuania	www.ltembassyus.org/
Luxembourg	www.luxembourg-usa.org/
Macedonia	www.macedonianembassy.org/
Mali	www.maliembassy.us/
Marshall Ils	www.rmiembassyus.org/
Mexico	http://portal.sre.gob.mx/usa/
Micronesia	www.fsmembassydc.org/
Moldova	www.embassyrm.org/

Country	Embassy Web Page
Mongolia	www.mongolianembassy.us/default.php
Mozambique	www.embamoc-usa.org/
Myanmar	www.mewashingtondc.com/
Namibia	www.namibianembassyusa.org/
Nepal	www.nepalembassyusa.org/
Netherlands	www.netherlands-embassy.org/homepage.asp
New Zealand	www.nzembassy.com/home.cfm?c=31
Niger	www.nigerembassyusa.org/
Nigeria	www.nigeriaembassyusa.org/
Norway	www.norway.org/Embassy/embassy.htm
Palau	www.palauembassy.com/
Panama	www.embassyofpanama.org/
Papua, N Guinea	www.pngembassy.org/
Peru	www.peruvianembassy.us/
Philippines	www.philippineembassy-usa.org/
Poland	www.polandembassy.org/
Portugal	www.portugal.org/index.shtml
Qatar	www.qatarembassy.net/
Romania	www.roembus.org/
Russia	www.russianembassy.org/
St. Vincent - Grenadines	www.embsvg.com/
Saudi Arabia	www.saudiembassy.net/
Sierra Leone	www.embassyofsierraleone.org/
Serbia and Montenegro	www.serbiaembusa.org/
Singapore	www.mfa.gov.sg/washington/
Slovak	www.slovakembassy-us.org/
South Africa	www.saembassy.org
Spain	www.maec.es/subwebs/embajadas/Washington/en/Home/paginas/home.aspx
Sri Lanka	www.slembassyusa.org/
Sudan	http://sudanembassy.com
Suriname	www.surinameembassy.org/
Sweden	www.swedenabroad.se/Start____6989.aspx
Tajikistan	www.tjus.org/
Tanzania	www.tanzaniaembassy-us.org/
Thailand	www.thaiembdc.org/index.htm
Tunisia	http://tunisiaembassy.org/
Turkey	www.turkishembassy.org/
Turkmenistan	www.turkmenistanembassy.org/

Country	Embassy Web Page
Uganda	www.ugandaembassy.com/
United Arab Emirates	http://uae-embassy.org/
Ukraine	www.mfa.gov.ua/usa/en/news/top.htm
Uruguay	www.uruwashi.org/
Uzbekistan	www.uzbekistan.org/
Venezuela	www.embavenez-us.org/
Vietnam	www.vietnamembassy-usa.org/
Yemen	www.yemenembassy.org/
Zambia	www.zambiaembassy.org/
European Union	www.eurunion.org

International Driving Permit

Established by the United Nations, the International Driving Permit (IDP) is a document that enables a foreign country to recognize that a visitor has valid driver's license issued from a home country. The IDP establishes the right for a person to drive in another country when the IDP is accompanied by an original driver's license.

According to the Federal Trade Commission, the U.S. Department of State has authorized only two organizations in the U.S. to issue IDPs to U.S. Citizens – The American Automobile Association (AAA) and the American Automobile Touring Alliance (National Auto Club). Below are the web pages for these two organizations.

- www.aaa.com/vacation/idpf.html
- www.nationalautoclub.com/

Per the FTC, there are several myths circulating about IDLs. Per the FTC the following statements are NOT TRUE about IDLs:

- IDLs authorize consumers to drive legally in the U.S. even if they don't have state-issued licenses or if their state-issued licenses have been suspended or revoked;
- IDLs can be used to avoid points or fines affecting state-issued drivers' licenses; and
- IDLs can be used as photo ID in the U.S.

For more information, visit the FTC at www.ftc.gov/bcp/conline/pubs/alerts/driveralrt.shtm

Patents

See World Intellectual Property Organization (WIPO) in the Patents section.

Trademarks

An astounding list of international trademark resources is found at www.ggmark.com/#International_Trademark_Law

Genealogy Resources

(Also see Vital Records)

Perhaps the most well-known resource of genealogical information is the Church of Jesus Christ of Latter-day Saints (Mormon Church). The Church has been actively gathering and preserving genealogical records worldwide for over 100 years. One may access genealogy records on-site at churches across the nation and on foreign soil. The genealogy site is www.familysearch.org.

There are several other, huge genealogical sites that have collected public record information along with historical documents from various sources. Below are a few recommended sites and starting points for genealogy record searching, presented in alphabetical order.

- Ancestry Hunt provides an extensive list of genealogy search engines. Go to www.ancestryhunt.com.

- Cyndi's List – www.cyndislist.com – Since 1996 this site has grown to 250,000 links in 180 categories.

- Generations Network – www.ancestry.com, www.genealogy.com and www.myfamily.com. With more than 5 billion names and 23,000 searchable databases, Ancestry.com is a signficant online resource for family history information with perhaps the largest collection of historical records.

- The National Genealogical Society in Arlington, VA is a membership organization dedicated to dissemination of genealogical sciences and literature. Founded in 1903, The Society offers research services, conferences, a learning center, home courses, competitions, links lists, and person-to-person services. See www.ngsgenealogy.org or 800-473-0060.

- Rootsweb – www.roostweb.com – is an easy-to-use search engine with many accessible databases. A good place to start is http://searches.rootsweb.com.

GIS and Mapping

GIS is the acronym used for Geographic Information System. Commonly associated with maps, GIS data can be displayed in a variety of product types with many associated uses. GIS can link and layer data attributes to specific criteria, such as addresses to people or parcels to building.

GIS property details are then used by the assessing offices at the county or municipality level for taxation and real estate associated matters. Although they may appear intimidating, GIS mapping websites maintained by these government offices usually have a search mechanism for finding parcels, addresses, and sometimes, but not always, property owner names. A GIS website's search feature is not always displayed prominently, but many assessor sites have them.

For more information about GIS visit www.gis.com.

To find GIS searching sites, visit one of the many free public record link sites. One site that does an excellent job of maintaining links is www.netronline.com.

For more information about searching real estate records, see the *Searching Liens and Recorded Documents* chapter.

Incarceration Records

Incarceration records are criminal-related records of inmates housed or formerly housed at jails and prisons. Since jails are usually found at the local level and hold a variety of inmates, *jail records* are often a mix of persons with misdemeanor sentences and persons being held until transport to a state of federal facility. Jails records are probably the least useful to professional record searchers. *Prisons records* refer to inmates held in state prisons and federal prisons. The details found in prison records vary widely by location and content.

Use of Incarceration Records

Although incarceration records are often used to populate many of the so-called national criminal record databases maintained by vendors, they are not true criminal records; they are criminal–related records. This terminology is a big distinction if you are doing research that requires a high level of due diligence, such as hiring or doing a background check per the Fair Credit Reporting Act. Incarceration records are useful, but they should not be relied upon as a primary data source. However, the **federal prison records** (see below) can be a **very useful resource** when attempting to verify the identity of persons who are subjects of criminal records data obtained from the federal courts.

A website devoted to information about prisons and corrections facilities is the Corrections Connection (www.corrections.com). One of the most recognized sites in community of correction entities, the Corrections

Connections has very informative data, along with a number useful links and inmate locator searching sites.

Federal Prison Records

The Federal Bureau of Prisons offers an Inmate Locator and a Facility Locator at www.bop.gov. The Inmate Locator contains records on inmates incarcerated or released from 1982 to present.

Record Searching Tips

When searching, use the middle initial if possible. Inmates shown as being in a Regional Office are serving a concurrent state sentence in a state prison. Inmates shown as being in a Community Corrections Management (CCM) center are in a contract "halfway house" (not in the CCM). "IN TRANSIT" means the inmate has been moved from a BOP facility, and may or may not be returned. It is possible that a record may exist for an individual who was in BOP custody but never served a sentence of incarceration (e.g., a person was detained pre-trial but criminal charges were dismissed, held as a material witness, held for civil contempt).

For record data prior to 1982 Requests related to post-1982 releases must be sent to:

Federal Bureau of Prisons
Attn: Inmate Locator
320 First St., N.W.
Washington, DC 20534

Include the inmate name with middle name or initial, DOB or approximate age at time of incarceration, race, and approximate dates when in prison.

State Prison Systems

Each state has a government agency that manages the corrections departments and prisons. State systems may and do vary. For example, in Delaware there is one unified system; there are no county or municipal correction or jail systems and no separate probation system. Some states have facilities run by vendors, such as New Mexico with six adult facilities run by private enterprise.

Record Searching Tips

To a varying degree, these state agencies consider the inmate records to be public and will process information requests. Many states offer web pages with inmate locators or look-ups. The level of information available varies widely from state to state. Some have extensive, detailed information often going back many years, some sites even include pictures.

The web pages of several private companies are great resources to find links and searchable inmate locators to state prison systems. Check www.theinmatelocator.com and www.inmatesplus.com. Also most of the free public record links lists sites (such as www.searchsystems.net and www.brbpub.com) offer searching links.

VINElink is the online version of VINE (Victim Information and Notification Everyday), the National Victim Notification Network. This service allows crime victims to obtain timely and reliable information about criminal cases and the custody status of offenders 24 hours a day. Victims and other concerned citizens can also register to be notified by phone, email or TTY device when an offender's custody status changes. VINE provides a number of inmate locator links throughout the U.S. at https://www.vinelink.com/vinelink/initMap.do.

IRS Records

There are only a handful of records that may be accessed from the IRS, not all are public.

Income Verification

The Income Verification Express Service (IVES) program is used by mortgage lenders and others within the financial community to confirm the income of a borrower during the processing of a loan application. One may obtain a full return or just the income informational info (the W-2). The written consent of the taxpayer is required. The IRS provides the requested information generally within 2 business days to a third party.

Visit www.irs.gov/individuals/article/0,,id=161649,00.html.

A private company provides a similar service for employers. See TALX's W-2 Express at www.w2express.com.

Seized Property

Check what the IRS is auctioning at www.ustreas.gov/auctions/irs/.

Charitable Organizations

A Cumulative List of Organizations is a list of organizations eligible to receive tax-deductible charitable contributions. The IRS offers an online search at www.irs.gov/charities/article/0,,id=96136,00.html. The web page also has separate searching for revocations, deletions, and suspensions from the Cumulative List.

Lobbyists

The IRS monitors what can be deducted as donations to a PAC. To search these donations, See the *Politics – Donations & Lobbyists* section later in this chapter.

Media

The media is an often overlooked resource for finding clues to public records and public record trails. Researching 24-hour news outlets, press releases, company announcements, trade journals and magazines is a good way to find many leads. Although many resources are online, a good starting point is often the local library. Below are some research sources and tips that should prove helpful.

News Journalism

One of the best in print collection of news resources is *Find It Online* by Facts on Demand Press. The chapter titled News Resources Online in the latest edition is filled with excellent material handy for an investigator or journalist.

Links to thousands of newspapers, radio and TV stations, magazines, and foreign outlets are found at two excellent web pages: www.editorandpublisher.com and www.newslink.org.

A couple of web pages specializing in magazine stories are http.findarticles.com and www.highbeam.com.

Investigative Reporters & Editors, Inc. is without a doubt the leading trade association for journalists. They promote high standards while providing educational services to reporters, editors and others interested in investigative journalism. Visit ther web page at www.ire.org.

CNN provides a web page to obtain transcripts of broadcasts. Visit http://transcripts.cnn.com/TRANSCRIPTS/.

Back Issues in Print

The United States Book Exchange is a non-profit organization which supplies back issues of scholarly periodicals, trade journals, popular magazines and other serials to libraries worldwide. Visit them at www.usbe.com.

A good resource for a list of stores selling back issues of a magazine is presented at www.trussel.com/books/magdeal.htm.

For resources on newspapers, call the Historic Newspaper Archives at 800-221-3221. A unique regional service for the past six months of New York newspapers is Dependable Delivery at 212-586-5552.

Web Resources

The web offers resources that are free, but as with most extensive reference resourcess, you have to pay for the good stuff.

Fee-Based Resources

One of the advantages of the fee-based resources is the length of time stories are kept available. Depending on the service, some vendors maintain comprehensive data dating back 40 years or more. The following entities are highly recommended by Cynthia Hetherington:

- Factiva (www.factiva.com)
- LexisNexis (www.nexis.com/research)
- EBSCO (www.ebsco.com)
- InfoTrac (www.infotrac.com)
- ProQuest (www.proquest.com)

Free Resources

The following article is taken from the text of the *Business Background Investigations* book by Cynthia Hetherington. We thank Ms. Hetherington for allowing us to reprint her copyrighted material.

Tips from a Professional

Websites that offer free access to news stories usually allow searching by either topic or by location. Here are five sites that I feel are excellent for investigations.

The two sites below are organized **by topic**.

- **News Directory** (www.newsdirectory.com) Drill down by topic; use this site to get free newspaper sources online.

- **Google News** (www.news.google.com) Offers current news (within 30 days) and is an excellent source for local news with approximately 4,500 news sources worldwide.

The three sites below are organized **by location**.

- **NewsLibrary.com** (www.newslibrary.com) Search by location and by available news on a specific topic.

- **Newspapers.com** (www.newspapers.com) Includes international locations.

- **Thepaperboy** (www.thepaperboy.com) Includes national *and* international locations.

Journalists and the Media

The Reporters Committee for Freedom of the Press is a nonprofit organization dedicated to providing free legal assistance to journalists and media lawyers. They can be reached at 1101 Wilson Blvd, Suite 1100, Arlington, VA 22209, 800-336-4243. The web page is an excellent resource of articles and facts. www.rcfp.org

Military Records

National Personnel Records Center (NPRC)

Military service records are kept by the National Personnel Records Center (NPRC) which is under the jurisdiction of the National Archives and Records Administration. The address is the National Personnel Records Center, Military Personnel Records, 9700 Page Avenue, St. Louis, Missouri 63132, 314-801-0800 fax: 314-801-9195, www.archives.gov/veterans/military-service-records/

The type of information released to the general public is dependent upon the veteran's authorization. Also, the **key to searching military records** is form SF-180 (or a signed release). The **key military record** is the DD-214. Federal law [5 USC 552a(b)] requires that all requests for records and information be submitted in writing. Each request must be signed and dated. The NPRC categorizes two types of requesters:

With the Veteran's Authorization

The veteran (or next-of-kin if the veteran is deceased) must authorize release of information. The authorization must 1) be in writing; 2) specify what additional information or copies are requested that NPRC may release; and 3) include the signature of the veteran or next-of-kin.

Without the Veteran's Authorization

A request for information by the general public (someone who is not next of kin) is treated as a FOIA request. A "limited amount of information" is released. See below.

Using Form SF-180

The SF-180 is a form specifically used to request military records. If you wish to search the records of an individual and the subject does not provide you with the DD-214, then you must use the SF-180 to request a copy of the DD-214. The SF-180 can be requested in writing from the NPRC or can be downloaded as a pdf file. The form and instructions are found at www.archives.gov/st-louis/military-personnel/standard-form-180.html. The SF-180 can also be obtained from the Department of Defense, Federal Information Centers, local Veterans Administration offices, and from veterans' service organizations.

A veteran or the veteran's next of kin may use the eVetRecs system at www.archives.gov/veterans/evetrecs/ to create their request for a copy of the DD-214, or may mail or fax the SF-180.

Use of the SF-180 is not mandatory. The request must be in writing and signed by the requester. Include as much as the following as possible - the veteran's complete name used while in service, the service number or SSN, branch of service, and dates of services if known. The DOB is helpful. If the records were part of the 1973 fire, then including the place of entry, discharge, and last unit of assignment is quite helpful.

The turnaround time for most requests takes about 10 days plus mail time. However, records involve in a 1973 fire or older records which require extensive search efforts may take 6 months or more to complete. Reconstruction requests are taking on average 4.5 weeks to complete.

About the DD-214

DD-214 is the name of the document that military personnel receive when discharged from the U.S. Navy, Army, Air Force, Marine Corp, or Coast Guard. There are actually a number of different copies of the DD-214 with different sets of information. A discharged service person receives Copy 1, which has the least information. Copy 4 gives the nature of the discharge – General, Honorable, Dishonorable, Undesirable – and details of service. There are codes that characterize the service record including SPD (Separation Program Designator), SPN (Separation Program Number) and RE (Re-Entry). For a discharged service person to get Copy 4, the subject must actually ask for it.

Using Miliatry Records for Employment Screening Purposes

Per Les Rosen, author of the *Safe Hiring Manual*..."In order to avoid potential EEOC claims, an employer should treat a dishonorable discharge in the same fashion as a criminal conviction ... A general discharge or undesirable discharge may or may not have any bearing on employment and generally should not be the basis of an employment decision.

"The best advice may be to use the basic DD-214 to confirm a person was in fact in the military, then ask for the names of references from their military service to obtain job-related information that would be relevant to an employment decision."

Military Branches - Internet Sources

The Official Sites include—

www.army.mil	U.S. Army
www.af.mil	U.S. Air Force
www.navy.mil	U.S. Navy
www.usmc.mil	U.S. Marine Corps
www.arng.army.mil	Army National Guard
www.ang.af.mil	Air National Guard
www.uscg.mil/default.asp	U.S. Coast Guard

National Gravesite Locator

The Nationwide Gravesite Locator maintained by the U.S. Department of Veterans Affairs includes burial records from many sources. Go to http://gravelocator.cem.va.gov/j2ee/servlet/NGL_v1.

If you cannot locate the person you are searching for online, provide the following in writing on each individual: full name, including any alternate spellings; date and place of birth; date and place of death; date from which the individual entered active duty; and military service branch. Most requests take approximately four weeks for a reply. Write to U.S. Department of Veterans Affairs, National Cemetery Administration (41C1). Burial Location Request, 810 Vermont Ave., NW, Washington, DC 20420.

Missing Persons

A links list of missing persons compiled by state agencies is free at www.ancestorhunt.com/missing-persons.htm. View the FBI Kidnapping and Missing Persons Investigations web page free at www.fbi.gov/wanted/kidnap/kidmiss.htm. The privately operated Doe Network lists international missing persons and unidentified victims at www.doenetwork.org. Search the National Center for Missing Adults database at www.theyaremissed.org/ncma/index.php. Another private site – America's Most Wanted – features missing persons and missing children profiles at www.amw.com.

Where found, County Sheriff websites often provide County Missing Persons web pages; these same sheriff websites may include most wanted lists, sexual predators, warrants, arrests, DUIs or other types of local pages as a public service.

Most Wanted Lists

Many federal agencies (and some international agencies) have a web page of a Most Wanted List with name searching capabilities. A web page with links to lists maintained by the FBI, U.S. Marshall, the Bureau of Alcohol, Tobacco, and Firearms (ATF), The Drug Enforcement Administration (DEA), and even the U.S. Postal Service is found at www.usa.gov/Citizen/Topics/MostWanted.shtml.

A quick way to find each state's Most Wanted Lists is at www.ancestorhunt.com/most-wanted-criminals-and-fugitives.htm.

Where found, County Sheriff websites often provide data on County Most Wanted individuals. These same sheriff websites may include missing persons, sexual predators, warrants, arrests, DUIs and other types of local pages as a public service. For those interested in these sites, www.searchsystems.net does a good job of collecting these URLs.

Native Americans

Court Records

National Tribal Justice Resource Center

Per their web page, The National Tribal Justice Resource Center is "...the largest and most comprehensive site dedicated to tribal justice systems, personnel and tribal law. The Resource Center is the central national clearinghouse of information for Native American and Alaska Native tribal courts." The Resources tab on the web page gives access to Tribal Court Codes & Constitutions, Tribal Court Opinions from over 18 tribes, and a Tribal Court Directory to locate contact information for tribes and locate tribal courts, on the web.

The Center is located at 4410 Arapahoe Ave, #135, Boulder, CO 80303, 303-245-0786. www.tribalresourcecenter.org/

Tribal Court Clearinghouse

Sponsored by the Tribal Institute, the Tribal Court Clearinghouse is a comprehensive website established in June 1997 to serve as a resource for American Indian and Alaska Native Nations, American Indian and Alaska Native people, tribal justice systems, victim services providers, tribal service providers, and others involved in the improvement of justice in Indian country. *The General Guide to Criminal Jurisdiction in Indian Country* is an excellent and in-depth source; they have offices in Anchorage AK, West Hollywood CA, and St. Paul MN. www.tribal-institute.org/index.htm

Native Organizations and Federal Agencies

The Tribal Institute's Links Page

There is no reason to list and describe the many Federal government agencies and native organizations involved with Native Americans when the Tribal Institute does such a great job of providing this information. Go to http://tribal-institute.org/lists/fed_agen.htm.

OSHA

(See Occupational Safety & Health Administration in the Federal Sanctions and Watch Lists section)

Passport Records

Passport Records for Issuances 1925 – Present

Passport Services maintains United States passport records for passports issued from 1925 to the present. These records normally consist of applications for United States passports and supporting evidence of U.S. citizenship, and are protected by the Privacy Act of 1974, (5 USC 552(a)). Passport records do not include evidence of travel such as entrance/exit stamps, visas, residence permits, etc., since this information is entered into the passport book after it is issued.

The Privacy Act allows persons to obtain copies of their own records and the records of their minor children. The requester's notarized signature and a copy of requestor's valid photo identification are required along with any information that would help locate the records. A search for one's passport record is free with the notarized request.

Third Party Requests

Third party requesters may obtain a record with a $60 fee per name as long as one of the following is also included in the request:

- Notarized consent from the owner of the passport record,
- Proof of guardianship,
- Death certificate, or
- Court order signed by a judge of competent jurisdiction requesting the U.S. Department of State to release passport records.

The only exception to this requirement is when the owner of the passport records was born 100 years or more ago. The third party request does not have to be notarized.

All requests for passport records issued from 1925 to present should be mailed to:

Department of State, Passport Services
Research and Liaison Section, Rm 500
1111 19th St N.W.
Washington, DC 20524-1705
or call 202-955-0447

Passport Records for Issuances Prior to 1925

The National Archives and Records Administration maintains records for passport issuances prior to 1925. Write to:

National Archives and Records Administration
Archives 1, Reference Branch
8th & Pennsylvania Ave. NW
Washington, DC.

Patents

United States Patent and Trademark Office

Search the United States Patent and Trademark office (USPTO) databases for full-text patent information on U.S. patents granted since 1976 and full-page images since 1790 at www.uspto.gov/go/pats/. Patents issued from 1790 through 1975 are searchable only by patent number, issue date, and current US classifications. The USPTO's text-searchable patent database begins with patents granted since 1976.

Note that neither assignment changes nor address changes recorded at the USPTO are reflected in the patent full-text or the patent full-page images.

A search may also be conducted at any of the Patent and Trademark Depository Libraries throughout the U.S. These libraries have copies of patents in multiple formats arranged in numerical order, classification search tools, automated search aids, and photocopy facilities. All states have at least one library location; there are six library locations in California. To find a library location, go to www.uspto.gov/go/ptdl.

The Patent Application Information Retrieval (PAIR) system permits third parties to obtain information on published applications on issued patents, status of maintenance fee payments, and if a reissue application or reexamination request has been filed. PAIR can be accessed at http://portal.uspto.gov/external/portal/pair.

For further help or to find the number assigned to a patent, call the Official Search Unit at 703-308-2733.

How Long do Patents Remain in Affect?

Per the USPTO web page "For applications filed on or after June 8, 1995, utility and plant patents are granted for a term which begins with the date of the grant and usually ends 20 years from the date you first applied for the patent subject, to the payment of appropriate maintenance fees. Design patents last 14 years from the date you are granted the patent. Note: Patents in force on June 8 and patents issued thereafter on applications filed prior to June 8, 1995 automatically have a term that is the greater of the twenty year term discussed above or seventeen years from the patent grant."

Other Patent Record Resources

The World Intellectual Property Organization (WIPO)

The World Intellectual Property Organization (WIPO) is a specialized agency of the United Nations. It is dedicated to promoting the effective use and protection of intellectual property worldwide. WIPO offers an international patent search at www.wipo.int/pctdb/en/

Other Vendors of Note

There are a few reliable vendors who offer patent searching as alternatives to the USPTO, including in alphabetical order:

- www.freepatentsonline.com
- www.google.com/patents
- www.patentgenius.com
- http://scientific.thomson.com/products/dwpi (Derwent patent index)
- www.surfip.gov.sg/

Politics – Donations & Lobbyists

A description of all the possible resources dealing with political parties, politicians, and elections would no doubt fill several books. The intent of this section is to present resources and information regarding political donations and lobbying, both of which are matters of public record.

Political Action Committee – PAC

The purpose of a Political Action Committee (PAC) is to raise money in the support of political candidates. PACs usually represent businesses large or small, or special interest groups such as unions or the NRA, etc.

PACs must register at the state or federal level, depending on the purpose of the PAC, and follow pre-set guidelines. For example, at the federal level, a PAC can give no more than $5,000 per candidate per election and no more than $15,000 annually to a national political party. PACs may receive no more than $5,000 per individual, per another PAC, or per a party committee per year.

Since PACs are a matter of public record, the registration information and donations are searchable by the public. Search locations follow.

Lobbyist

Lobbyists are individuals paid to communicate with public office holders in order to influence government decisions. As with PACs, lobbyists must be registered at the government level where they are trying to influence votes. The registration of lobbyists is a matter of public record.

Federal lobbying firms are required to file a separate registration for each client. A lobbying firm is exempt from registration for a particular client if its total income from that client for lobbying activities does not exceed and is not expected to exceed $6,000 during a semiannual period.

A lobbyist is not the registrant unless he/she is self-employed. In that case, a self-employed lobbyist is treated as a lobbying firm.

Organizations employing in-house lobbyists file a single registration. An organization is exempt from registration if its total expenses for lobbying activities do not exceed and are not expected to exceed $24,500 during a semi-annual period.

Federal Agency Resources

Federal Election Commission (FEC)

The Federal Election Commission (FEC) administers and enforces the Federal Election Campaign Act (FECA), which is the statute that governs the financing of federal elections. The FEC is entrusted with disclosing campaign finance information, enforcing laws that limit or prohibit contributions, and overseeing the public funding of Presidential elections.

To locate information about the political donations go to the Federal Election Commission's website at www.fec.gov. There are some excellent search tools under the Campaign Finance Reports and Data tab. Also, try the Search the Disclosure Database and Using FEC Public Records tabs. The FEC is located at 999 E Street, NW, Washington, DC 20463 and can be reached at 800-424-9530.

Internal Revenue Service

The IRS monitors what can be deducted as donations to a PAC or by a PAC. At the Political Organization Filing and Disclosure web page http://forms.irs.gov/politicalOrgsSearch/search/basicSearch.jsp one can search for all electronic and paper submissions of Form 8871 Political Organization Notice of Section 527 Status, and Form 8872 Political Organization Report of Contributions and Expenditures. Also searchable from this site are the paper submissions of Form 990 Return of Organizations Exempt from Income Tax, which is the form filed by many public charities and other exempt organizations.

U.S. Senate Office of Public Records

Lobbyists must register with the Senate to disclose who hired them, how much they are paid, what issues or bills they are lobbying on, and the federal agencies they are contacting. Five criteria can be searched at once at http://sopr.senate.gov.

The Office of the Clerk for the U.S. House of Representatives maintains a web page at http://lobbyingdisclosure.house.gov that offers information about lobbying at the House, but the organization does not offer a searchable online database.

Agent for a Foreign Principal for Political Reasons

The Foreign Agents Registration Act (FARA) requires indviduals acting as agents of foreign principals in a political or quasi-political capacity to make periodic public disclosure of their relationship with the foreign principal, as well as activities, receipts and disbursements in support of those activities. The FARA Registration Unit of the Counterespionage Section (CES) in the National Security Division (NSD) is responsible for the administration and enforcement of the Act.

Search at www.usdoj.gov/criminal/fara/links/search.html. Public information relating to the Foreign Agents Registration Act (FARA) may be obtained in person at the FARA Registration Unit Public Office located at the Department of Justice, Registration Unit, 1400 New York Avenue, N.W. 1st Floor - Public Office #100, Washington, D.C. 20005.

State Agency Resources

The following table gives the web page resource for finding public record data for PAC contributors and registered lobbyists within the particular state. Interestingly, there is no overall pattern to where these agency sites can be found. Some are at the "elections" site, some at the various secretary of states, some sites are maintained by the state legislatures, and other sites are part of a government agency dealing with ethics.

State Political Donations and Lobbyist Registration Chart

AL	PAC resources are found at www.sos.alabama.gov/vb/election/pacsrch1.aspx. Download the current list as a PDF. The current list of lobbyists is at www.ethics.alalinc.net/news/lobbyist_list.pdf
AK	Campaign and financial disclosures at https://webapp.state.ak.us/apoc/ Search for lobbyists at www.state.ak.us/apoc/lobcov.htm
AZ	Search lobbyists at www.azsos.gov/election/lobbyist. Search PACs at www.azsos.gov/cfs/CampaignFinanceSearch.htm
AR	A PAC and lobbyist search is at www.sos.arkansas.gov/elections/ce/index.php
CA	Find lobbyists at http://cal-access.ss.ca.gov/Lobbying/ Find PACs at http://cal-access.ss.ca.gov/Campaign/Committees/
CO	Click on Lobbyists at www.elections.colorado.gov/DDefault.aspx. Click on Campaign Finance Online Database at www.elections.colorado.gov/DDefault.aspx?tid=
CT	Search lobbyists at https://www.ctose.net/reportRequest/index.asp. Search PACs at www.ct.gov/seec/cwp/view.asp?a=2650&Q=329402&seecNav=|
DC	Search PAC and lobbyists at http://ocf.dc.gov/WebsiteReports/filertype.asp
DE	Search lobbyists at www.delawaregov.us/pic/index.cfm?ref=74391. For PACs, click on View Reports online at http://elections.delaware.gov/information/campaignfinance/campaignfinance.shtml
FL	Find lobbyists at www.leg.state.fl.us/lobbyist/. Find PACs at http://election.dos.state.fl.us/campfin/cfindb.shtml
GA	Data on lobbyists and campaign finance data is found at www.ethics.ga.gov/EthicsWeb/main.aspx
HI	Lobbyists data at www.state.hi.us/ethics/noindex/pubrec.htm. PACs at Campaign Spending Commission at http.hawaii.gov/campaign/NC/nc.htm
ID	Lobbyist data at www.idsos.state.id.us/elect/lobbyist/lobinfo.htm. PAC data at www.idsos.state.id.us/eid/index.htm
IL	Lobbyists data is at www.cyberdriveillinois.com/departments/index/lobbyist/home.html. PAC data is at www.elections.state.il.us/. Click on Campaign Disclosure
IN	Lobbyist data is at https://secure.in.gov/apps/ilrc/registration/browse. PAC data is at www.indianacampaignfinance.com/INPublic/inSearch.aspx
IA	Lobbyist data is at www.legis.state.ia.us/Lobbyist.html. For PAC go to www.state.ia.us/government/iecdb/index.htm and click on campaigns.
KS	Lobbyist and PAC data at www.kansas.gov/ethics/

KY	Lobbyists data at http://klec.ky.gov/reports/employersagents.htm. Search PACs at http://kref.ky.gov/
LA	Lobbyists and PACs at www.ethics.state.la.us/
ME	Lobbyists and PACs at www.mainecampaignfinance.com/public/home.asp
MD	Lobbyist at http://ethics.gov.state.md.us/listing.htm. Search PACs at www.elections.state.md.us/campaign_finance/index.html.
MA	Lobbyist data at www.sec.state.ma.us/lobbyist/LobbyistSearch/PublicSearch.asp?action=P PACs at www.mass.gov/ocpf/
MI	Lobbyists at http://miboecfr.nicusa.com/cgi-bin/cfr/lobby_srch.cgi. PACs at www.michigan.gov/sos/0,1607,7-127-1633_8723---,00.html
MN	Lobbyists and PACs at www.cfboard.state.mn.us/
MS	Lobbyists at www.sos.state.ms.us/elections/Lobbying/Lobbyist_Dir.asp. PACs at www.sos.state.ms.us/elections/CampFinc/
MO	Lobbyists at www.mec.mo.gov/Ethics/Lobbying/LobElecReports.aspx. Search PACs at www.mec.mo.gov/Ethics/CampaignFinance/CF_PublicSearch.aspx
MT	Lobbyists and PACs at http://politicalpractices.mt.gov/
NE	Lobbyists at www.unicam.state.ne.us/web/public/lobby. PACs at http://nadc.nol.org/
NV	Lobbyists at www.leg.state.nv.us/lobbyistdb/index.cfm. PACs from http://sos.state.nv.us/
NH	PACs and Lobbyists are found at www.sos.nh.gov/elections.htm
NJ	PACs and Lobbyists at www.elec.state.nj.us/PublicInformation/GAA_Annual.htm
NM	PACs and Lobbyists at www.sos.state.nm.us/Main/Ethics/EthicsHome.htm
NY	Lobbyists found at https://www.nytscol.org/lobby_tracker/search.pl. For PACs go to www.elections.state.ny.us and click on Campaign Finance tab.
NC	Lobbyists at www.secretary.state.nc.us/Lobbyists/LSearch.aspx. PACs at www.sboe.state.nc.us/
ND	Lobbyists at www.nd.gov/sos/lobbylegislate/lobbying/reg-mnu.html. PACs at www.nd.gov/sos/campfinance/dis-report.html
OH	Lobbyist at www.jlec-olig.state.oh.us/AgentandEmployerLists.htm. PACs at www.sos.state.oh.us/, click on Campaign Finance
OK	Lobbyists at www.state.ok.us/~ethics/lobbyist.html. For PACs, contact the Ethics Commission at 405-521-3451. Data not online.

OR	Lobbyists at www.oregon.gov/OGEC/public_records.shtml. PACs at www.sos.state.or.us/elections/c&e/
PA	Lobbyists at www.palobbyingservices.state.pa.us/Act134/Public/RegistrationSearch.aspx. PACs at www.dos.state.pa.us/campaignfinance/site/default.asp?bcelNav=|
RI	Lobbyists at www.sec.state.ri.us/resources_for/lobbyist.html. PACs at www.elections.ri.gov/CampFinance/cfmain.htm
SC	For Lobbyists and PACs, visit www.ethics.sc.gov/
SD	www.state.sd.us/applications/ST12ODRS/LobbyistViewlist.asp?cmd=resetall for Lobbyists. PACs at www.sdsos.gov/electionsvoteregistration/campaignfinance.shtm
TN	Lobbyists and PACs at www.state.tn.us/tref/
TX	Lobbyists and PACs at www.ethics.state.tx.us/
UT	Lobbyists and PACs at http://elections.utah.gov/
VT	Lobbyists and PACs at http://vermont-elections.org/soshome.htm
VA	Lobbyists at http://secure01.virginiainteractive.org/lobbyist/cgi-bin/search_lobbyist.cgi. Search PACs at www.sbe.virginia.gov/cms/Campaign_Finance_Disclosure/Index.html
WA	Lobbyists and PACs at http://web.pdc.wa.gov/
WV	Lobbyists at www.wv.gov/Offsite.aspx?u=http://www.wvethicscommission.org. PACs at www.wvsos.com/elections/cfreports/
WI	Lobbyists at http://ethics.state.wi.us/Scripts/2003Session/OELMenu.asp. PACs at http://elections.state.wi.us/section.asp?linkid=325&locid=47
WY	Lobbyists at http://soswy.state.wy.us/election/lob-list.htm. PACs at http://soswy.state.wy.us/election/pac.htm

Private Agencies of Note

Follow the Money

Per their web page www.followthemoney.org, the National Institute on Money in State Politics is "a nonpartisan 501(c)3 tax-exempt charitable organization dedicated to accurate, comprehensive and unbiased documentation and research on campaign finance at the state level. The Institute develops searchable databases, makes them available to the public online, and analyzes the information to determine the role campaign money plays in public policy debates in the states."

Money Line

The Congressional Quarterly and *St. Petersburg Times* operate CQ MoneyLine, found at http://moneyline.cq.com/pml/home.do. There are a number of free searches offered to find political campaign donors and lobbyists. There is even a search to find donors from one state who contribute to candidates in other states. PAC contributors are also searchable. This excellent web page also has many, many other database searches available on a subscription basis only.

Open Secrets – The Center for Responsive Politics

The Center for Responsive Politics is a non-partisan, non-profit research group based in Washington, D.C. that tracks money in politics and its effect on elections and public policy. The Center conducts computer-based research on campaign finance issues for the news media, academics, activists, and the public at large. The web page at www.opensecrets.org is extremely comprehensive and offers searching of the Center's database that tracks contributions. The Center is located at 1101 14th St NW, #1030, Washington, DC 20005 and can be reached at 202-857-0044.

Public Agenda

Found at www.publicagenda.org, Public Agenda's nonpartisan Issue Guides distill facts and analysis from major news and public opinion sources. The non-partisan group's site provides public opinion polls and analyses of different campaign finance policy options.

Vote Smart

The Vote Smart site at www.vote-smart.org/index.htm tracks campaign contributions for more than 13,000 candidates and elected officials nationwide and includes voting records and evaluations by special interest groups.

Privacy

Privacy Laws - See the Appendix

The **Appendix** profiles eight important federal laws that impact privacy and the distribution of information.

Do Not Call – Opt Out Sites of Note

The means that direct marketing companies obtain information to create direct marketing lists is NOT through public records, but through devices like the following:

- Grocery Store "Discount" Cards
- Sweepstakes
- Product Warranties and Registrations

There are organizations, including the Federal Government's Do Not Call Registry, that assist the public to remove their names and addresses from marketing list organizations are—

- Center for Democracy and Technology
  http://opt-out.cdt.org/moreinfo/
- Do Not Call.com - www.donotcall.com
- National Do Not Call Registry - https://www.donotcall.gov
- Optout Prescreen.com - https://www.optoutprescreen.com/?rf=t
- Direct Marketing Association Opt Out
  https://www.dmachoice.org/MPS/

Identity Theft Vulnerability

www.identitysweep.com is a private company website that sells identity theft prevention products online but it offers ID theft news and a free vulnerability test that may be helpful in determining your weaknesses.

Privacy Rights Advocates

There are a number of organizations who represent the privacy interests of the consumer. Some of these groups are extremely one-sided in their approach to many issues. Other groups, while certainly advocating privacy rights, also demonstrate an understanding of the legitimacy of certain information requests from legitimate businesses with permissible use per statute vs. the purposes associated with data aggregators who cause harm by violating the privacy rights of unsuspecting individuals.

The entities listed below are thought of very highly for their excellent programs to help individuals who have privacy concerns.

Privacy Rights Clearinghouse

We purposely placed this organization at the top of this list. Their web page supplies plenty of good information acknowledging the importance of balancing privacy with legitimate protection needs for the public good. The section called *Privacy Today* is excellent. www.privacyrights.org

World Privacy Forum

This is another top organization with plenty of informative data on the web page. They do a lot of work towards protecting medical information. www.worldprivacyforum.org

PrivacyExchange

This web page, a product of The Center for Social & Legal Research, is an excellent global information resource. www.privacyexchange.org

Occupations & Licensing Boards

Professional occupational licensing, certifications, and registrations are generally a matter of public record, intended to protect the public from fraud and the unqualified. The Council on Licensure, Enforcement, and Regulation (CLEAR) is an organizational resource for entities or individuals involved in the licensing, non-voluntary certification or registration of hundreds of regulated occupations and professions. The set of definitions for occupational regulation that CLEAR provides is well said:

> **Registration** The least restrictive form of occupational regulation, usually taking the form of requiring individuals to file their names, addresses, and qualifications with a government agency before practicing the occupation. This may include posting a bond or filing a fee.

> **Certification** The state grants title protection to persons with certifications. Uncertified individuals may practice the same or similar job duties, but specialized titles are reserved only for individuals who have the related certification.

> **Licensure** The most restrictive form of professional and occupational regulation. Under licensure laws, it is illegal for a person to practice a profession without first meeting state standards."

Source: www.clearhq.org/

Types of Agencies Involved

With the above definition in mind, there are several, general types of agencies involved with the registration, licensing, or certification of credentials.

Private Entities

For many professions, the certification body is a private association that has set the licensing or certification standards. An example is the American Institute of Certified Public Accountants, which sets the standards for becoming a Certified Public Accountant (CPA).

Many other professional licenses are based on completion of the requirements of professional associations. In addition, there are many professional designations from such associations that are not recognized as official licenses by government. These designations are basic certifications in fields that are so specialized that they are not of interest to the states, but rather only to the professionals within an industry.

For example, the initials "CFE" indicate an individual is a Certified Fraud Examiner and has met the minimum requirements for that title from the Association of Certified Fraud Examiners.

See the Trade Associations section later in this chapter for resources that may oversee credentialing.

State Entities

A state agency can administer the registration, certification, and occupational licensing of an individual intending to offer specified products or services in the designated area. If registration alone is required, there may not be a certification status showing that the person has met minimum requirements. Using the CPA example above, the New York State Education Department, Office of the Professions, oversees the preparation, licensure, and practice of its CPAs.

Businesses may also fall under the administration of state entity, per statute. For example, a state may require business registration for an entity to do business or offer specified products or services in a designated area, such as registering a liquor license. Some business license agencies require testing or a background check. Others merely charge a fee after a cursory review of the application.

Often the state agencies are referred to as **licensing boards**. Sometimes many, many boards are under the direction of one specific branch of regulatory government. An example is health care related vocations. The BRB Publication's database of occupational licensing boards lists over 8,750 individual job titles or businesses that are administered for licensing, registration or certification by 1,976 different state entities. Some level of online searching of names and even enforcement actions for over 5,000 of job titles or businesses.

Local Entities

Local government agencies at both the county and municipal levels require a myriad of business registrations and permits in order to do business (construction, signage, sell hot dogs on a street corner, etc.) within their borders. If you decide to check on local registrations and permits, call the offices at both the county — try the county recording office — and municipal level — try city hall — to find out what type of registrations may be required for the person or business you are checking out. Several of the free links lists sites will connect you to online searching sites if available.

Searching Tips

When you verify credentials, be aware of what distinguishes each type, which in turn could alter the questions you ask. While some agencies consider their information private and confidential, most agencies freely release at least some basic data over the phone or by mail.

Research indicates that many agencies appear to make their own judgments regarding what specifically is private and confidential in their files. For example, approximately 45% of the agencies indicate that they will disclose adverse information about a registrant, and many others will only disclose selected portions of the information or merely verify a credential.

In any event, the basic rule to follow when you contact a licensing agency is to ask what specific kinds of information are available.

What Information May Be Available

An agency may be willing to release part or all of the following—

- Field of Certification
- Status of License/Certificate
- Date License/Certificate Issued
- Date License/Certificate Expires
- Current or Most Recent Employer
- Social Security Number
- Address of Subject
- Complaints, Violations or Disciplinary Actions

Fees

There is no charge to verify if a particular person is licensed; this can usually be done by phone. You should expect that receiving basic information will only involve a phone call – or an Internet search – and that you will not be charged for obtaining a status summary.

Anything more extensive will generally incur costs. The fee for copies or faxes ranges from $.25 to $2.00. A fee of $5 to $20 usually applies to written requests. This is due to the fact that written certifications give more information than verbal inquiries, i.e. disciplinary action, exam scores, specific dates. A fee of $25 or more is typical for a list of licensed professionals. For example, a hospital might need a roster of registered nurses in a certain geographic area.

Searching State Resources

As mentioned above, sometimes professional associations will provide a membership list.

A links list to perform online name searching of over 5,000 entities is provided free at www.brbpub.com/default.asp.

CareerOneStop, a unique web resource for job seekers, provides information about finding certifications by occupation or industry, and licenses by occupation or agency. Agencies details are provided, but the site indicates that content is only updated every two years. Visit www.careeronestop.org

A number of private vendors also compile lists from these agencies and make them available online or on CD-ROM. We do not necessarily suggest these databases be used for credential searching because they may not be complete, may not be up-to-date, and may not contain all the information you can obtain directly from the licensing agency. However, these databases are extremely valuable as supplemental sources of background information on an individual or company that you may wish to do business with.

Recalls

There are several excellent resources that cover product recalls.

Six federal agencies with vastly different jurisdictions joined together to create www.recalls.gov. Searching is arranged by these topics: boats, consumer products, cosmetics, environment, food, medicine, and motor vehicle. Various search capabilities are offered. You can do a "name search" or use the tabs to find lists of recalls by product type.

Two of the more popular search sites found above are the vehicle recall site at www-odi.nhtsa.dot.gov/cars/problems/recalls/recallsearch.cfm and the FDA site of their recalls (Class I, II, and III), including pre-1995, at www.fda.gov/opacom/Enforce.html. Enforcrment actions and alerts are found at www.fda.gov/opacom/7alerts.html.

The U.S. Consumer Product Safety Commission is another great recall resource, go to www.cpsc.gov.

Another resource avenue to check are private companies or industries that monitor recalls on products associated with their businesses, for example Home Depot and *Consumer Reports* magazine. You can Google for these and others.

Securities and Securities Dealers

There are a number of primary agencies who oversee the regulatory and compliance issues that deal with publicly traded securities or with security dealers. These agencies have the authority to investigate issues related to compliance or improprieties. Hence, these agencies are excellent resources to search for enforcement actions.

Perhaps the most well-know and informational federal agency, the Securities and Exchange Commission (SEC), is presented first. The other federal agencies are presented in alphabetical order, followed by a look at the state agencies.

SEC – Securities & Exchange Commission

The SEC oversees the participants in the securities world, including securities exchanges, securities brokers and dealers, investment advisors, and mutual funds.

EDGAR

EDGAR – the **E**lectronic **D**ata **G**athering **A**nalysis and **R**etrieval system – was established by the SEC as the means for companies to make required filings to the SEC by direct transmission. EDGAR provides an extensive online repository of U.S. corporation information available online. The record searching site at EDGAR is www.sec.gov/edgar/searchedgar/webusers.htm. EDGAR also offers a guide on how to search publicly traded companies, go to www.sec.gov/investor/pubs/edgarguide.htm.

A number of private vendors offer access to EDGAR records along with some added features and searching flexibilities. Recommended sites include www.edgar-online.com, www.secinfo.com, www.edgarlive.com, and www.lexisnexis.com.

For more information about content in EDGAR and other SEC information related to corporations, see the *Searching Business Entities Records* chapter.

Enforcement Actions

SEC-related enforcement actions are viewable online at www.sec.gov/divisions/enforce/enforceactions.shtml and include civil lawsuits brought by the Commission in Federal court, administrative proceedings as instituted and/or settled, opinions issued by Administrative Law Judges in contested administrative proceedings, and opinions on appeals issued by the Commission on appeal of Initial Decisions or disciplinary decisions issued by self-regulatory organizations (e.g., NYSE or NASD).

Litigation Actions

This web page, www.sec.gov/litigation.shtml, contains links to information on SEC enforcement actions, opinions issued by the Commission, briefs filed by SEC staff, trading suspensions, and notices concerning the creation of investors' claims funds in specific cases. Three links are mentioned below.

At www.sec.gov/litigation/litreleases.shtml there are informative press releases concerning **civil lawsuits** brought by the Commission in federal court. The list is in date order and not searchable by name.

At www.sec.gov/litigation/suspensions.shtml there are SEC **trading suspensions** with historical data to 1995, in date order.

At www.sec.gov/divisions/enforce/claims.htm are lists of **investors' claims funds**. The SEC enforcement cases are shown in which a Receiver, Disbursement Agent, or Claims Administrator has been appointed. Funds that are recovered and available for investors will be distributed according to an approved plan.

In addition to seeing whether a claims fund has been established, you may want to find out whether a private class action lawsuit has been filed against a company. See *Securities Class Action Clearinghouse* to follow later in this chapter.

Financial Industry Regulatory Authority (FINRA)

Formerly the National Association of Securities Dealers (NASD), the Financial Industry Regulatory Authority (FINRA) is a resource to investigate brokers and brokerage firms. FINRA oversees over 5,000 brokerage firms, 172,000 branch offices, and more than 665,000 registered securities representatives. FINRA is probably the largest non-governmental regulator for all securities firms doing business in the U.S.

The website at www.finra.org allows name searching of an individual or a brokerage firm registered in FINRA. The user can download an eight-page Adobe Acrobat PDF file that outlines the subject's history, including employment. Brokerage firms also are searchable for any disciplinary actions taken against a company, or brokers who are involved with arbitration awards, disciplinary, and regulatory events. You can reach FINRA at 301-590-6500.

North American Securities Administrators Association (NASAA)

The North American Securities Administrators Association (NASAA) is devoted to investor protection. NASAA members license firms and their agents, investigate violations of state and provincial law, file enforcement actions when appropriate, and educate the public about investment fraud. NASAA members also participate in multi-state enforcement actions and information sharing.

The NASAA web page (www.nasaa.org/home/index.cfm) contains links to individual state, provincial, and territorial jurisdictions for securities laws, rules and regulations. Headquartered in Washington DC, NASAA can be reached at 202-737-0900.

Central Registration Depository (CRD)

The Central Registration Depository (CRD) is a collaborative effort of NASAA, FINRA, and the SEC. The CRD, a centralized filing system of licensed broker-dealers, was developed by state securities regulators, NASAA, FINRA, and the SEC. CRD reports are available through state regulatory authorities. A list is located at the NASAA web page.

National Futures Association (NFA)

The National Futures Association (NFA) is a self-regulatory organization to safeguard the U.S. futures.industry. NFA's web page permits name searching of individuals or firms. Results indicate any arbitration or regulatory action filed against any NFA listed individual or firm. Visit www.nfa.futures.org or call the Chicago headquarters at 312-781-1300.

Securities Class Action Clearinghouse

Class Action Suits

The Securities Class Action Clearinghouse provides detailed information relating to the prosecution, defense, and settlement of federal class action securities fraud litigation. The Clearinghouse maintains an index of filings since passage of the Private Securities Litigation Reform Act of 1995. The Clearinghouse contains copies of more than 21,500 complaints, briefs, filings, and other litigation-related materials filed in these cases. This content is maintained by the Stanford Law School and Cornerstone Research. Visit http://securities.stanford.edu.

State Security Agencies

As mentioned in the *Searching Business Entities Records* chapter, every state has its own securities laws – often referred to as **"Blue Sky Laws"** – that are designed to protect investors against fraud. The records of the filings by companies registering under the Blue Sky Laws, as well as any records of legal actions, are held by designated state regulatory securities agencies. The state agencies that oversee these records also, usually, license and hold records of brokerage firms, their brokers, and investment adviser representatives doing business there.

These records are open to the public although they are not generally found online. Rather than list each state's address and web page, we suggest the reader visit the North American Securities Administrators Association (see above) or the links found at www.seclinks.com/id16.html.

Sexual Predator Records

Sexual offenses include aggravated sexual assault, sexual assault, aggravated criminal sexual contact, endangering the welfare of a child by engaging in sexual conduct, kidnapping, and false imprisonment. Under Megan's Law, sex offenders are classified in one of three levels or "tiers" based on the severity of their crime as follows: Tier 3 (high); Tier 2 (moderate); and Tier 1 (low).

Sex offenders must notify authorities of their whereabouts. Also, there is a notification process when a registered sex offender moves into a community. Neighbors are notified of Tier 3 offenders. Registered community organizations involved with children such as schools and day care centers are notified of Tier 3 and Tier 2 offenders. Local law enforcement agencies are notified of the presence of all Tiers of sex offenders.

The information provided by local law enforcement includes the offender's name, description of offense, personal description, photograph, address, place of employment or school, and a description of the offender's vehicle and license plate number.

Sexual offenses include aggravated sexual assault, sexual assault, aggravated criminal sexual contact, endangering the welfare of a child by engaging in sexual conduct, kidnapping, and false imprisonment.

Usually, the state agency that oversees the criminal record repository also administrates a Sexual Offender Registry (SOR).

Record Resources

The National Sexual Offender Registry at www.nsopr.gov, coordinated by the Department of Justice, is a cooperative effort between the state agencies hosting public sexual offender registries and the federal government. The website has a national query to obtain information about sex offenders through a number of search options including name, Zip Code, county, and city or town. The site also has an excellent, detailed overview of each state's SOR policies and procedures.

Nearly every state offers a free search of registered sexual offenders who are living within the particular state. A quick search on the web will reveal many of the typical links list sites that offer these links to state SOR URLs.

Skiptracing

Skiptracing is finding the location of missing persons such as heirs, debtors, spouses, absconders, or witnesses. Often the purpose is so service of process can be performed.

Mr. Michael Dores, founder of Merlin Information Services, is one of the nation's leading authorities on skiptracing. His company provides databases to investigative professionals who skiptrace, look for assets, run background checks or perform investigative work. Mr. Dores has been kind enough to provide an overview about skiptracing for this book and we sincerely thank him. To reach Merlin Information visit www.merlindata.com.

Tips From a Professional

"Skiptrace" is an investigative term meaning "locate people and businesses." It does not always imply that people have "skipped town," although sometimes this is the case. A skiptrace may include a search for people who witnessed an accident, are recipients of unclaimed funds, or want to reunite family members. In general, "skiptracing" covers any legitimate reason to find someone.

Using an Electronic Cross-Directory

An electronic cross-directory is an essential tool for any successful skiptracer. A cross-directory is a computerized national database of residences and businesses designed to be searched by name, address or telephone number. The primary function of a cross-directory is to provide information to assist the skiptracer in locating a subject. Utilized correctly, a cross-directory will lead to the location of at least 50% of all subjects before any money is spent searching other databases. A cross-directory may not always lead you directly to your subject; however, it will lead you to someone who may know of your subject's whereabouts—a key source in solving a skiptrace.

Begin every skiptrace with a cross-directory search of the subject's last known address to determine the name and phone number of the current resident. A call to this person may determine that the subject still lives at the last known address, or may lead to a friend or relative who lives at that address and knows the whereabouts of your subject. If a last known phone number is provided, check the cross-directory to see who is listed at that phone number. You may find a good address for the subject or spouse's name that will help in locating your subject. Searching by last known address could also help you determine the correct spelling of the subject's last name. For instance, a search using the subject's last known address could determine that Robert Smith is actually Rupert Schmidt.

Use the cross-directory to search for neighbors at the subject's previous addresses. These people may provide location information on your subject.

A search for individuals with the same last name as the subject in the last known city or ZIP Code may yield possible relatives who know the subject's current address. To find the relative who lives closest to your subject, start with the subject's last name and enter the five-digit ZIP Code.

To broaden your search, search by last name and state, or last name and county. Sometimes even a last name search encompassing the entire country will lead to a relative who can provide subject location information. Start and end each assignment with the cross-directory for skiptracing success.

Public Records and Public Information

Another primary resource that skiptracers use is public records. Below is a list of the most useful public record types.

- Motor Vehicle Title Documents (Access to some data is restricted by the Driver's Privacy Protection Act as well as several state laws.)
- Real Property Deed Transfers
- Real Property Assessors' Records
- UCC Filings
- Corporate Filings, LLCs and LLPs
- City Business Licenses
- Fictitious Business Names / Assumed Name Filings
- Sales Tax Permits
- Court Indexes—Civil, Criminal, Small Claims, Traffic, Bankruptcy
- Professional Licenses

Another valuable resource is the information found in proprietary databases maintained by private companies. But access to this data may be regulated by state or federal law. For example, Merlin Information Services offers this type of information for authorized purposes only.

Importance of Historical Data

A key skiptracing component is the ability to access historical data. This is essential when solving tough cases and locating people when the only clue is very old information. This information is the starting point for tracing the subject forward to his or her current location. Merlin is committed to maintaining historical information as well as current information. Because public records are obtained from government agencies who systematically purge old data from their files each year, sometimes the only place to find historical data is from a vendor that makes a commitment to maintaining historical information.

Telephone and Communications

Area Codes - North American Numbering Plan (NANPA)

NANPA is an integrated telephone numbering plan serving the United States, its territories, and 18 other North American countries; Canada, Bermuda, Anguilla, Antigua & Barbuda, the Bahamas, Barbados, the British Virgin Islands, Cayman Islands, Dominica, Dominican Republic, Grenada, Jamaica, Montserrat, St. Kitts and Nevis, St. Lucia, St. Vincent and the Grenadines, Trinidad and Tobago, and Turks & Caicos.

NANPA holds overall responsibility for the administration of NANPA numbering resources, subject to directives from regulatory authorities in the countries that share participate in the NANP. www.nanpa.com/guide/guide.html

Key online searches include:

- Area code maps - Select a state and see area code boundaries.
- Central office code assignments - Find out what codes are assigned or available for assignment in each geographic area code
- Area code search - Get information about individual area codes, including dialing plans and pointers to planning letters with split/overlay information.
- Electronic mailing lists - Sign up to obtain the latest information on area code assignments and other areas of numbering interest.

Yellow and White Pages

www.yellowpages.com or www.superpages.com or www.addresses.com

Phone/People Finders

InfoSpace http://ypng.infospace.com/ lets you search by place and business type or name; results give address, phone, fax, and like results. www.411X411.com has a commercial appearance and will connect you to other finder services if you let it.

Phone List Services

Telephone number services such as www.infousa.com and Dun & Bradstreet's www.zapdata.com offer mailing-list services. Through various public records, news accounts, and telephone interviews, D&B has amassed a large amount of very specific contact information that can be purchased by the batch or in small doses. The lists are targeted for marketing purposes but investigators can use purchased lists to locate a target or subject by occupation, geography, or hobby.

Free Directory Service for Cells

Cell phone companies are charging us $1.00 to $1.75 or more for 411 information calls when they don't have to. Most of us do not carry a telephone directory in our vehicle, which makes this situation even more of a problem. When you need to use the 411 information option, simply dial 800 FREE 411 or 800-373-3411 without incurring any charge at all. Program this into your cell phone.

Location & Service Provider Finders

There are several search service tools that provide the location and service provider for a telephone number. A good one is given here.

FoneFinder   Search by 7 digits of the telephone number or by city or ZIP Code at www.fonefinder.net/

Media Links

A great resource to find news media links is www.gebbieinc.com. Search for TV stations, radio stations, daily and weekly newspapers, magazines. You can search by magazine topic. Results give websites.

Tenant Screening

Tenant screening is an essential service to landlords and property managers that help them make informed decisions about prospects applying to rent or lease a property. Tenant screening components typically involve a credit report and public records of criminal actions and evictions. Evictions, frequently called forcible detainers, are civil actions where a judgment has been rendered against a renter or leaser entity for non-payment. The court record will indicate plaintiff, defendant, disposition and amount of judgment. These court records are generally held in the assigned division at either a general or limited jurisdiction court, depending on the state.

Tenant screening, when performed by a third party, falls under the scope of the Fair Credit Reporting Act, thus tenant screeners are Consumer Reporting Agencies. The affect of the FCRA is covered in other places in this book. See the Appendix and also the *Employment Screening* section in the *Searching A thru Z* chapter.

Trade Associations

Trade Associations and their websites provide a wealth of information. They are useful for not only industry knowledge, but also for finding members and entities with strong ties as vendors. Here is a short list of associations with strong ties to public records or public record searching. The list is presented in order of the acronym.

AALL	American Assoc. of Law Librarians	www.aallnet.org/index.asp
AAMVA	Amererican Assocociation. of Motor Vehicle Administrators	www.aamva.org
AAPL	American Assoc. of Professional Landmen	www.landman.org
ABA	American Bar Association	www.abanet.org/home.html
ABA(2)	American Banking Association	www.aba.com/default.htm
ABFE	American Board of Forensic Examiners	www.acfei.com
ABI	American Bankruptcy Institute	www.abiworld.org
ABW	American Business Women	www.abwahq.org
ACA	Association of Collectors & Professionals	www.acainternational.org
ACFE	Association of Certified Fraud Examiners	www.acfe.com
AFIO	Association of Former Intelligence Officers	www.afio.com
AICPA	Assoc. of Certified Public Accountants	www.aicpa.org/index.htm
AIIP	Assoc. of Independent Information Professionals	www.aiip.org
AIPLA	Amer. Intellectual Property Law Association	www.aipla.org
ALA	American Library Association	www.ala.org
ALTA	American Land Title Association	www.alta.org
AMA	American Management Association	www.amanet.org/index.htm
APA(2)	American Psychological Association	www.apa.org
APG	Association of Professional Genealogists	www.apgen.org
ASIS	American Society for Industrial Security	www.asisonline.org
ASLET	American Soc. of Law Enforcement Trainers	www.aslet.org
ASSE	American Society of Safety Engineers	www.asse.org
ATA	American Truckers Association	www.trucking.org
ATLA	Association of Trial Lawyers of America	www.atlanet.org
CDIA	Consumer Data Industry Association	www.cdiaonline.org
CII	Council of Intl Investigators	www.cii2.org
DMA	Direct Marketing Association	www.the-dma.org
EAE	Environmental Assessment Association	www.iami.org
EMA	Employment Management Association	www.shrm.org/EMA
EPIC	Evidence Photographers Intl Council	www.epic-photo.org
FBINAA	FBI National Academy Association	www.fbinaa.org
IAAI	Intl Association of Arson Investigators	www.fire-investigators.org
IAHSS	Intl Assoc. of Healthcare Security & Safety	www.iahss.org
IALEIA	Intl Assoc. of Law Enforcement Intel. Analysts	www.ialeia.org
IASIR	Intl Assoc. of Security & Investigation Regulators	www.iasir.org
IIAA	Independent Insurance Agents of America	www.iiaba.net
INA	Intl Nanny Association	www.nanny.org
INOA	Intl Narcotics Officers Association	www.ineoa.org
INTA	Intl Trademark Association	www.inta.org
ION	Investigative Open Network	www.ioninc.com
IREM	Institute of Real Estate Management	www.irem.org

LES	Licensing Executive Society	www.usa-canada.les.org
MBAA	Mortgage Bankers Association of America	www.mbaa.org
NAC	National Association of Counselors	http://nac.lincoln-grad.org
NACM	National Association of Credit Managers	www.nacm.org
NAFE	National Association of Female Executives	www.nafe.com
NAFI	National Association of Fire Investigators	www.nafi.org
NAHB	National Association of Home Builders	www.nahb.org
NAHRO	National Assoc. of Housing & Redevelopment Officials	www.nahro.org
NAIS	National Assoc. of Investigative Specialists	www.pimall.com/nais/
NALA	National Association of Legal Assistants	www.nala.org
NALFM	National Association of Law Firm Marketers	www.legalmarketing.org
NALI	National Association of Legal Investigators	www.nalionline.org
NALS	NALS… Association of Legal Professionals	www.nals.org
NALSC	National Assoc. of Legal Search Consultants	www.nalsc.org
NAMSS	National Association of Medical Staff Svcs	www.namss.org
NAPBS	Nat. Assoc. of Prof. Background Screeners	www.napbs.com
NAPIA	National Assoc. of Public Insurance Adjustors	www.napia.com
NAPPS	Nat. Assoc. of Professional Process Servers	www.napps.org
NAR	National Association of Realtors	www.realtor.com
NAREIT	Nat. Assoc. of Real Estate Investment Trusts	www.nareit.com/library/index.cfm
NARPM	Nat. Assoc. of Residential Property Mgrs	www.narpm.org
NASA	National Association of Screening Agencies	www.n-a-s-a.com
NAWBO	National Assoc. of Women Business Owners	www.nawbo.org
NBFAA	National Burglar & Fire Alarm Association	www.alarm.org/
NCISS	National Council of Investigation & Security Svcs	www.nciss.org
NCRA	National Court Reporters Association	www.verbatimreporters.com
NCRA	National Credit Reporting Association	www.ncrainc.org
NDIA	National Defender Investigator Association	www.ndia.net
NFIB	Nat. Federation of Independent Businesses	www.nfib.org
NFIP	National Flood Insurance Program	www.fema.gov/business/nfip/
NFPA	National Federation of Paralegal Association	www.paralegals.org
NGS	National Genealogical Society	www.ngsgenealogy.org
NHRA	National Human Resources Association	www.humanresources.org
NICB	National Insurance Crime Bureau	www.nicb.org
NLG	National Lawyers Guild	www.nlg.org
NPPRA	National Public Record Research Association	www.nprra.org
NSA	National Sheriffs' Association	www.sheriffs.org
PBUS	Professional Bail Agents of the United States	www.pbus.com
PIHRA	Profs in Human Resources Association	www.pihra.org
PRRN	Public Record Retriever Network	www.brbpub.com/prrn
REIPA	Real Estate Information Providers Assoc.	www.reipa.org
SCIP	Society of Competitive Intelligence Professionals	www.scip.org
SFSA	Society of Former Special Agents of the FBI	www.socxfbi.org
SHRM	Society of Human Resources Management	www.shrm.org

SIIA	Software & Information Industry Association	www.siia.net
SILA	Society of Insurance License Administrators	www.sila.org
SLA	Special Libraries Association	www.sla.org
USFN	America's Mortgage Banking Attorneys	http://imis.usfn.org
W.A.D	World Association of Detectives	www.wad.net

Trademarks & Service Marks

United States Patent and Trademark Office

The U.S. Patent and Trademark Office (USPTO) reviews trademark applications for federal registration to determine if an applicant meets the requirements for federal registration. The USPTO does not decide who has the right to *use* a mark. Even without a registration, someone may still *use* any mark adopted to identify the source of your goods and/or services. Once a registration is issued, it is up to the owner of a mark to enforce their rights in the mark based on ownership of a federal registration.

Per the United States Patent and Trademark office (USPTO):

- A trademark is a word, phrase, symbol or design, or a combination of words, phrases, symbols or designs, that identifies and distinguishes the source of the goods of one party from those of others.

- A service mark is the same as a trademark, except that it identifies and distinguishes the source of a service rather than a product.

USPTO employees cannot conduct trademark searches for the public. However, the Electronic Business Center offers searching at www.uspto.gov/ebc/index_tm.html. There is no fee to search, but there are charges for certified copies.

Trademarks Key Resource

An astounding list of international trademark resources is found at www.ggmark.com/#International_Trademark_Law

The Canadian version of Google, with most of the same features as the U.S. version, has trademark information. www.google.ca/

Unclaimed Funds

Unclaimed funds refers to money, stocks, bonds, dividends, utility deposits, vendor payments, gift certificates and insurance proceeds held by state or federal agencies who are looking for rightful owners. The Unclaimed Property Division is responsible for returning money, stocks, bonds, dividends, utility deposits, vendor payments, gift certificates and insurance proceeds of any type to the rightful owners.

Nearly every state provides a link to find unclaimed monies, and national links list are easily found on the web.

A great resource is the National Association of Unclaimed Property Administrators (NAUPA), a non-profit organization affiliated with the National Association of State Treasurers. At www.unclaimed.org, one may do national searches or find a profile of the state agency responsible for holding unclaimed funds, including a link to the state's free web search page. Another important feature that NAUPA offers is its list of various U.S. government agencies who hold unclaimed assets.

A recommended vendor is Missing Money at www.missingmoney.com. Their site provides searchable state web pages and also state instructions for obtaining states' unclaimed property claim forms with instructions.

Unions

U.S. Department of Labor

Union Management and Reporting

The Office of Labor-Management Standards (OLMS) in the U.S. Department of Labor is the Federal agency responsible for administering and enforcing most provisions of the Labor-Management Reporting and Disclosure Act of 1959, as amended (LMRDA). The LMRDA is meant to ensure basic standards of democracy and fiscal responsibility in labor organizations representing employees in private industry, unions representing U.S. Postal Service employees and other Federal employee organizations. OLMS does not have jurisdiction over unions representing solely state, county, or municipal employees.

OLMS responsibilities include:

- **Public Disclosure of Reports** - Labor unions, their officers and employees, employers, labor relations consultants, and surety companies. Must file reports which are public information and available for disclosure at OLMS offices.

- **Compliance Audits** - OLMS has responsibility under the LMRDA to audit local unions for records review and to verify LMRDA compliance.

- **Investigations** - OLMS staff conduct investigations to determine if violations of the LMRDA provisions have occurred and to protect and safeguard union funds and assets. OLMS must refer information it uncovers regarding possible embezzlement violations by union officers or employees to the U.S. Attorney who decides if criminal prosecution is warranted.

- **Education and Compliance Assistance** - Among the services OLMS provides are education and compliance assistance programs to promote voluntary compliance. OLMS conducts seminars and workshops about the labor laws in general or about specific areas per regulations by the LMRDA.

Contact the U.S. Department of Labor, Statutory Programs, Washington, D.C. 20210, phone 202-693-0126.

Search Union Reports and Constitutions and Bylaws

The OLMS Internet Public Disclosure Room web page enables one to search extensive public record information about unions. Users may 1) view and print reports filed by unions, union officers and employees, employers, and labor relations consultants for the year 2000 and after and reports filed by unions for trusts in which they have an interest, (2) order reports for the year 1999 and prior, and (3) search the union annual financial reports for the year 2000 and after and the trust reports for key data items. Also, searchers can generate a number of reports comparing data saved from multiple searches. Go to www.dol.gov/esa/regs/compliance/olms/rrlo/lmrda.htm

- Search for basic information on specific labor organizations by searching Union Annual Financial Report Forms LM-2, LM-3, or LM-4. Information includes the union's net assets, investments, charitable contributions, salaries, etc.

- The Payer/Payee Search gives information about payers and payees of unions.

- The Officer/Employee Search gives information about union officers and employees.

- One may download archive files that contain raw data of union and financial information as reported for public disclosure under provisions of the LMRDA.

- One may order copies of LM-2, LM-3, and LM-4 Union Annual Financial Reports; LM-1 Labor Organization Information Reports; and Union Constitutions and Bylaws

- Access employer and labor relations consultant reports (LM-30)

U.S. Railroad Retirement Board

This federal agency provides good information about former railroad workers and workers collecting benefits. It follows Privacy Act and FOIA rule. U.S. Railroad Retirement Board, 844 N. Rush St, Chicago, IL, 60611, 312-751-7139. www.rrb.gov/

Private Resources on Unions

Big Labor.com

Big Labor is sponsored by Union Communication Services Inc. Per their website "Every U.S.-based union with a website – national and local – can be found on the Big Labor list in one of three ways: by the union's full name, by its acronym, (examples: UAW, IBT) or by its common short-hand name (examples: Auto Workers, Teamsters)." www.biglabor.com

Unions.org

Unions.org manages a searchable database of union organizations across the U.S. Search by state to find a specific union or find a links list of existing unions in that state. www.unions.org

Job Tracker

Working America, an AFL-CIO affiliate, offers a unique search for companies who are "endangering their workers" or involved in cases with violations under the National Labor Relations Act. The database contains information on more than 60,000 companies nationwide. Search by ZIP Code, state or company name, or search by specific industry to see the detailed information. The Job Tracker database is at www.workingamerica.org/jobtracker.

Vehicle Records

(See Motor Vehicle Records chapter)

(For vehicle recalls,see Recalls earlier in this chapter)

Vessels and Watercraft

(See Motor Vehicle Records Chapter)

Vital Records

(Also see Genealogy Resources earlier in this chapter)

This section looks at searching vital records that are somewhat current and where they can be searched before hitting archive locations. For information about searching historical vital records, see the *Genealogy Resources* section in this chapter.

Usually birth, death, marriage and divorce records can be searched at the local (county) level and/or at the state vital records office, which is usually part of a state health agency. If a certificate is needed, birth, death and marriage certificates are usually issued by the state; divorce certificates from the county or local entity.

Vital records are not necessarily public records. Some states place limitations ranging from 50 to 100 years before records are open. In general, birth records are the most restrictive, death records the least restrictive, and marriage and divorce records somewhere in between. But the degree of restrictiveness may also depend on if a certified record is needed or if merely a computer printout will suffice.

Requesting Records from a State or County Agency

Always provide as complete as possible information on a subject and the event. Include all possible names, nicknames and even alternative spellings. Try to include the date of the event or at least a range of years. Some agencies charge for each year or number of years searched. Other request criteria depend on the record type. For example, when requesting a birth record, include full names of parents, including mother's maiden name, race, the location or county, name of hospital if known, and obviously the date of birth. The wife's maiden name is helpful when requesting a marriage record.

If requested by mail, be sure to always provide an SASE, complete information about yourself (including a copy of your driver's license), if and how you are related to the subject, and the reason for the request. The latter two are especially important if the agency restricts access to only those related to the subject.

County offices have limited personnel to perform vital record searches, and are often overwhelmed with genealogical queries. State agencies may take as long as 6 weeks to process a request unless an expedite fee is paid upfront.

Working with Vital Record Vendors

There are several national vendors who specialize in providing vital records to clients, with a special emphasis on doing so on an expedited basis. Perhaps the most well-known one-stop shop is VitalChek Express Certificate Service at www.vitalchek.com. VitalChek has developed relationships with many of the state vital record agencies and is often promoted as the way to obtain records if you need to order by fax or online. Another vendor with similar services and direct ties to Ancestry (a vendor specialized in genealogy records) is Vitalrec.com found at http://vitalrec.com. This web page provides some excellent links and good basic searching information about each state.

If you use a search engine, you will find many other reputable vendors who offer various modes of access to many vital record searching sites. Many of them obtain records from other sources, create a proprietary database or gateway, then offer a "people search" approach to finding records on individuals. Some are quite useful and are mentioned below.

Birth Records

A birth record will contain the mother's full maiden name, the father's full name, the name of the child, the date of the birth, and the county or place name where the birth took place. Sometimes addresses of parents, the race, and even the parents' occupations are shown.

Check out www.birthdatabase.net. Type in a name and approximate age and it will give a list of individuals with same name or a variant spelling, the DOBs, and the state of record location.

Death Records & the Death Index of U.S. Social Security Admin

The Social Security Death Index (SSDI) contains the records of deceased persons who were assigned a SSN. Data is generated from the master death file of the U.S. Social Security Administration (SSA). The data is not searchable from a SSA site but a number of vendors purchase the data and make it available to the public. To obtain record information from the SSA, it is advised to send an FOIA request with the $7.00 fee.

Vendors offer a search of the SSDI. The search is often coupled with a SSN verification that verifies a particular SSN has been issued and from what state and date range of the possible year issued.

A good free search source of the SSDI is at a site maintained by Ancestry.com at http://ssdi.genealogy.rootsweb.com/cgi-bin/ssdi.cgi.

Free search of 80,690,794+ retired-due-to-death Social Security Numbers or search by name at http://ssdi.rootsweb.com or search at www.ancestry.com/search/db.aspx?dbid=3693.

Obituaries

The database search by Obituary Central at www.obitcentral.com has not only obituaries, but also cemetery searches. The data gets stronger as you go further back in time. The site shows many resources and other links of interest. Also, search obituaries at www.ancestry.com/search/obit/.

The Nationwide Gravesite Locator

The Nationwide Gravesite Locator maintained by the U.S. Department of Veterans Affairs includes burial records from many sources. Go to http://gravelocator.cem.va.gov/j2ee/servlet/NGL_v1.

Marriage Records

On a marriage record, you can at least find the full name of the bride and groom, the date of the marriage, and county where the marriage took place. Many marriage records include other information such as the names and birthplaces of the bride's and groom's parents, the addresses of the bride and groom, information about previous marriages, and the names of witnesses to the marriage.

The web abounds with marriage record sources, most of which are genealogy based. Besides the sites mentioned above, try www.genealinks.com/register.htm.

Divorce Records

Divorces are administered by the local courts, so obtaining records of divorces will vary by county. Divorce records are sometimes source records of information on property, living children, the ages of the husband and wife, and may lead to other data such as marriage records or even birth dates of children.

Here are some facts about searching divorce records.

- In AR, DE, ID, IL, KS, MD, MI, MN, MS, OH, UT, and VA the state agency will only verify a divorce; records are at the county level.
- GA, MA, NV, ND – state agency will indicate county where divorce occurred only; records at the county level.
- In AZ, CT, IA, LA, MO, MT, NM, OK, PA, RI, and WV records are only available at the county level.
- IN – divorce index at State Library; records at county level.
- NY – records at county level prior to 1963.
- VT – records at Dept of Health if divorce occurred within past 5 years.

Voter Registration

Voting registration records are public record sources of addresses, voting history, and sometimes telephone numbers. Every state has a central election agency or commission, and all have a central repository of voter information collected from the local level agencies per federal mandate HAVA (Help America Vote Act of 2002, Public Law 107-252).[3]

The degree or level of accessibility to these records varies widely from state to state. Seventeen states and DC permit unrestricted access to voter registration rolls. These states generally permit the purchase of voter registration data on CD. Fees range from $2.50 (AR) to $500 (CO) for a statewide list.

Thirty-three states place restrictions for record access at the state level. Generally, these states restrict access for only political or research purposes. Political purposes include purchase by political parties or candidates to solicit votes. However, all of these restrictive states permit the look-up of voter registration lists at the local level. The local level can be the county, the parish (LA), or at a municipal level.

Record data released generally includes name, address and telephone numbers, unless specifically blocked by the registrant. We believe all states and local agencies block the release of Social Security Numbers.

The chart to follow shows which states are restrictive and which are open, when local registration is at the municipal level, and if online access to status of one's registration is available.

Authorized Use of State Voter Registration Chart

State	Record Restriction Policy
AK	Unrestricted. There are six regional elections offices besides the headquarters in Juneau. Each has access to the election records database.
AL	Political purposes only
AR	Unrestricted
AZ	Political purposes only, and only at the county level
CA	Political or pre-approved purposes
CO	Unrestricted. Verify Voter Registration at www.elections.colorado.gov/DDefault.aspx?
CT	Unrestricted. Local access is at the city or town level.
DC	Unrestricted. Check status at www.dcboee.org/voterreg/vic_step1.asp
DE	Unrestricted
FL	Unrestricted
GA	Political or research purposes only. Name and DOB needed to search unofficial registration information at http://sos.georgia.gov/cgi-bin/Locator.asp. The results will provide address and district-precinct information. No SSNs released.
HI	Political purposes only. List requests are referred to county clerks.
IA	Political purposes only.
ID	Political or research purposes only.
IL	Political purposes only.
IN	Political purposes only.
KS	Political or research purposes only.
KY	Political or research purposes only. With first and last name and DOB, search voter status search at https://cdcbp.ky.gov/VICWeb/index.jsp.
LA	Unrestricted

---

[3] South Dakota is exempt from HAVA.

State	Record Restriction Policy
MA	Political purposes only. Local access is at the city or town level.
MD	Political purposes only.
ME	Unrestricted. Local access is at the city or town level.
MI	Unrestricted
MN	Political purposes only
MO	Political or research purposes only
MS	Unrestricted
MT	Political or research purposes only. Access records at http://app.mt.gov/voterfile/select_criteria.html
NC	Unrestricted. Online access free (A DOB is needed for best results.) at www.sboe.state.nc.us/votersearch/seimsvot.htm.
ND	Exempt from HAVA, no centralized DB offered. Local level only
NE	Political purposes only. A voter registration status link is found at https://www.votercheck.necvr.ne.gov/
NH	The statewide system DB is only open to political candidates. All records kept by Town Clerks are open to view or for purchase with no restrictions at local level.
NJ	Political or research purposes only
NM	Political purposes only
NV	Unrestricted
NY	Political purposes only
OH	Unrestricted
OK	Unrestricted
OR	Political or research purposes only
PA	Political purposes only
RI	Political purposes only. Local access is at the city or town level. Search at www.sec.state.ri.us/vic/
SC	Political or research purposes only. Free check of registration status is offered at www.scvotes.org/check_your_voter_registration
SD	Political purposes only
TN	Political purposes only
TX	Political or research purposes only
UT	Unrestricted
VA	Political purposes only. Verify registration status at www.sbe.virginia.gov/cms/Online_Services/Index.html
VT	Unrestricted. Best access is at the city or town level.
WA	Political purposes only. Voter information is also kept at the local level by the County Auditor (except King County where records are kept by the Dept of Records and Elections).
WI	Unrestricted
WV	Political purposes only. Search to see if someone is registered at www.wvvotes.com/voters/am-i-registered.php
WY	Political purposes only

Weather

Historical facts on weather topics are sometimes critical in court cases. Below are several informative sites and resources that present weather information and a variety of calculators to assist planning.

- **AccuWeather** - www.accuweather.com
- **CompuWeather** - www.compuweather.com
- **Forensic Meteorology Associates** - www.forensic-weather.com
- **Heat Index Chart** - www.crh.noaa.gov/pub/heat.php

For official records of temperature go to—

- www.ncdc.noaa.gov
- www.compuweather.com
- www.weatherworksinc.com

Workers' Compensation

Every state has an agency that administrates workers' compensation cases and records; there is no national database. Workers' compensation benefits are paid to people who have suffered an injury during the performance of their jobs. Workers' compensation records will contain the date of the incident, employer, insurance company, type of injury, body part injured, time lost, and if there is a job-related disability. Obviously, these records are useful in background investigations and fraud cases. However, most records are considered to be confidential or at least certain portions of each case file are. They're usually only released to parties involved in a case or by subpoena. Generally what is considered public record by some states is limited to determining if a subject has filed a claim, and decisions, awards or orders in disputed cases.

States that release at least a portion of workers' compensation files to the public are California, Florida, Illinois, Ohio, Oklahoma, and Wisconsin. In most other states, a signed release is necessary

Several state offer online access to some information. In Florida, access to the claims history database is provided online at www.fldfs.com/wc/databases.html, all personal information has been redacted. Case status for Illinois cases at shown at www.iwcc.il.gov. In Nebraska, workers' comp record requests may be made at www.nebraska.gov/WC/records.phtml. Unless specifically requested, responses will be limited to first and subsequent reports filed within the last five (5) years.

Access and the ADA

One reason records are confidential is that they may contain medical information, but the primary reason is the Americans with Disabilities Act (ADA). This act prohibited state workers' compensation boards from disclosing information as part of the pre-employment screening process. Per the ADA, *a review of workers' compensation histories may only be conducted after a conditional job offer has been made* and when medical information is reviewed. However, the ability to conduct this type of review is still subject to individual state statutes, which vary widely and can be stricter than the ADA. For example, Nevada disallows a record search for post-hire purposes. More information about the ADA and a web link to the Act is found in the Appendix.

World Wide Web

Web Pages' "Public Records"

There is plenty of public information that can be found about a web page. A number of useful resources report who owns a URL and how to contact them, the webmaster, the software, and even if an address has been blacklisted.

Search for a URL at http://whois.domaintools.com to find physical details about a website including meta description, registry creation and expiration dates, server details, webmaster contact info, and its all-important basic WhoIs record of the registrant. At the URL above, click on 'wiki article about ~' and the www.aboutus.com site displays what the public sees as your main page opens and other public details about your site.

InterNIC (www.internic.net) provides public information and other useful information on popular web topics – viruses, IP address, website content, registries. InterNIC provides a simple WhoIs lookup. Another good IP search site is ARIN at www.arin.net/whois/index.html.

VeriSign provides a list of North American website registrars. Go to www.verisign.com/information-services/index.html and click on Find a Registrar.

See www.norid.no/domenenavnbaser/domreg.en.html for foreign registries.

Other Web Page Resources and Tools

- The Internet Corporation for Assigned Names and Numbers (ICANN) is a network of inter-related sites who manage the naming system for the millions of internet sites. From www.icann.net you may link to www.icann.org (operations), www.internic.net (instructions for names and registrations), www.iana.org (numbering), www.alac.icann.org (advisory), and www.gac.icann.org (government advising). There is also an ICANN chat forum.

- The WhoIs page at www.networksolutions.com/whois can conveniently tell you if a name is available or not and under what suffix, also lets you search for expired domain names.

- An excellent tool for analyzing a website is the NetSolutions' WhoIs search at www.networksolutions.com/whois/index.jsp. Results include who owns or registered a site, the IP address, a screen capture of the home page, traffic ranking, more.

- To find out if anyone is imitating your site to steal your customers use the Domain Search feature at http://domain-search.domaintools.com. This can also be used as an alerting tool that lets you know when someone uses registry terms too similar to your own.

- Use the Xenu web check tool for reports on URLs and broken links. Go to http://home.snafu.de/tilman/xenulink.html and download the free Xenu's Link Sleuth. You can check the status of a list of URLs by posted a list on the site and Xenu will generate a report.

- To find the IP address (e.g 200.100.100.80) you are using on your computer go to www.palserv.com/ipdisp.html or www.whatismyipaddress.com.

- To find information about an email address, check www.theultimates.com/email/.

- A "reverse" email address finder is at InfoSpace at www.infospace.com/home/white-pages/reverse-email.

- Historical web pages can be found at the WayBack Machine at www.archive.org/index.php. Another resource is GigaBlast at www.gigablast.com and Search Engine Showdown at www.searchengineshowdown.com

Privacy and Public Record Laws

Public records are meant to be used for the benefit of society.

As a member of the public, you or someone in authority is entitled to review the public records held by government agencies. Whether you are a business owner, a reporter, an investigator, someone looking for a lost relative, collecting on a debt, or even a father trying to check on your daughter's first date, you can access public records to meet your needs.

The legal framework surrounding the right to access rests on three major tenets—

1. The Public has a broad right of access to government information.

2. The Government may not discriminate when disseminating public information.

3. Copyright-like restrictions on the use of public information are antithetical to the goal of widely disseminated government information.

The government is bound to facilitate the public's access to government held information. There is no requirement that an individual show "a need" for the information requested as a precursor to receiving access unless such access is precluded by legislated restrictions.

Of particular interest to the public record requesters and vendors is the legal precedent that information, like money, has a time value. Information delayed can be information denied or due diligence ignored. The significance here is that governmental agencies are required to make information available in a timely manner. Not doing so is to discriminate between requestors. The basis of court decisions concerning information access is that "equal" means nonexclusive and nondiscriminatory; "timely" means without undue delay.

Public or Not Public?

Often public records are confused with public information and restricted information. Further, all three of these records information types may very well contain personal information. As a result many people confuse the three categories, lump them into one and wonder how "big brother" accumulated so much information. The reality is that much of this information is given willingly.

Public Record

A public record is generally a record of an incident or action filed or recorded with a government agency for the purpose of notifying others – the "public" – about the matter. The deed to your house recorded at the local recorder's office is a public record – it is a legal requirement that you record with the local recorder. Anyone requiring details about your property may review or copy the documents.

According to BRB Publication's *The Sourcebook of Public Record Information* the definition of public records is—

> "Those records maintained by government agencies
>
> that are open without restriction to public inspection,
>
> either by statute or by tradition."

Public Information

Government is not the only "big brother" that gathers information. Non-government entities collect public information that is freely furnished in order to facilitate communications. An example of public information is your telephone number listing in the phone book. Your address is public information for mail or delivery needs.

Sometimes individuals and business entities freely furnish information when asked in the course of purchasing products. Warranties on products and magazine subscriptions are perfect examples.

Restricted Information

Some information is not available unless the requester has prior approval or the requestor qualifies based on the intended use of the record content. Typical access restrictions on government-held data placed by law are based on either the use of the data or on who the requester is, or both. A public purpose is served by keeping the information out of non-qualified hands. Typical examples are accident reports (in some states), birth certificates (in many states), and the medical portion of a worker's compensation record (in all states).

Personal Information

Personal information is any information about a person or business that the person or business might consider private and confidential in nature. Personal information may be found in public records, public information, and restricted information. A Social Security Number (SSN), an address, a date of birth (DOB), a person's weight or height are all examples of personal information. Such information will remain private to a limited extent unless it is disclosed to some outside entity that could make it public.

Another term that is widely used by public record vendors and end-users of records is ***personal identifiers***. In order to determine if a record truly belongs to an individual who is subject of a search, there must be some matching personal information. Unless there are enough identifiers available to match, a searcher runs the risk of having a *false positive* match.

The increased number of identity theft incidents has precipitated well-deserved scrutiny on the manner in which personal information is maintained by and is accessible from government agencies and private sector information vendors. The identity theft problem is driving legislation toward more and more restrictions on the dissemination of personal information. These legislative acts and administrative rules are not only providing identity theft protection to the public, but also adding to the red tape procedure for those with a permissible and ongoing use of the data. This in turns creates added expenses for many consumer transactions like when obtaining a loan or buying insurance or checking out a possible new employee.

So How Does Personal Information Enter the Information Highway?

Personal information enters the information highway in two ways – voluntarily and statutorily.

In a **voluntary** transaction, you share personal information of your own free will. In a **statutory** transaction, you disclose personal information because the law requires you to do so.

Examples of Statutory Disclosure

- Your weight, height, eye color, and date of birth on a driver's license application
- Your Social Security Number, income and children's names and ages on your tax return
- Your address on a deed

Examples of Voluntary Disclosure

- Your telephone number listed in a telephone directory
- Your address and date of birth on a product warranty card
- Your estimated annual income on a magazine subscription form

Disclosure

Let us take this one step further. Disclosure of personal information by government agencies is controlled by either statute or usage or traditional practice. Disclosure of information by private parties is either unregulated (uncontrolled) or regulated by statute.

Statute (Government)

There are several prime examples of where disclosure is controlled by statute.

- The Freedom of Information Act and The Privacy Act dictate the rules for dissemination of information by Federal agencies.

- The Drivers Privacy Protection Act directs the states to impose restrictions on access to personal information found in driver and vehicle records.

- Most states have statutes limiting access to certain types of court records such as juvenile and adoption cases.

Usage (Government)

Most court records (civil, criminal, probate) are open to public inspection by historical tradition.

Regulated (Business)

The Fair Credit Reporting Act (FCRA) limits access to an individual's credit history for only permissible purposes.

Unregulated (Business)

Many businesses collect customer demographics which they consider highly confidential. Some businesses sell their customer lists for solicitation by other businesses.

Some groups try to self-regulate

Therefore, depending on the statutes, regulations, usage, and company policies, personal information may be fully open to access by the public, restricted in some way, or kept closed and entirely confidential.

Government Records can be Open, Restricted, or Closed

Quite simply, records held by government agencies fall into three categories – open, restricted, or closed. The only truly public record information is that which is entirely open without restriction to anyone who wants to find it.

Typically, restrictions are placed by law and by tradition on information where there is public purpose that is served by cloaking or blocking the information from non-qualified interests. Further, there are two typical types of restrictions – **prior approval** and **use**.

Prior Approval Restriction

Access to many types of records requires the prior approval of the subject. For example, many state criminal record repositories will not release a copy of a criminal history record without the notarized permission or fingerprints of the subject or both.

Use Restriction

Use restrictions require the requester to demonstrate that the purpose of the request meets a legal or regulatory requirement and the requester will be subject to penalties for breaking the rules. For example, the Driver's Privacy Protection Act (DPPA) directs states to follow as a minimum a list fourteen permissible uses for which records with personal information can be released for certain uses. Beyond those uses, the requester must produce a signed release form the subject before obtaining the record with personal information.

Records closed to the public may not necessarily be entirely inaccessible. For example, the FBI's National Criminal Information Database is considered closed and not accessible to the general public, but is legally accessible by law enforcement officials for specific investigative uses. Another example is that some county juvenile court case records can only be released to someone through an order of the court. You will find that often closed records can only be obtained with a subpoena.

Private Enterprise: Unregulated or Regulated

This is the vocabulary describing the accessibility to information held by private organizations, businesses, associations, etc. Unregulated information held by an organization about its customers, members, and others may be kept confidential or be disclosed at their discretion. Regulated information consists of information held by a private organization when access to which is controlled by law of government regulation, such as access to a person's credit information is regulated by the Fair Credit Reporting Act (FCRA).

Frequently, information in the hands of private organizations is in fact the same information as in the hands of a government agency. It is important to note that public records compiled by private companies for resale purposes must follow the same access and restriction regulations as the related government jurisdiction. With the vast online information systems containing literally billions of pieces of information about people and businesses, the users of these private systems often do not even think about the source. More information about public record vendors in found in Chapter 8

Federal Legislation Impacting Information Exchange

Seven federal acts are profiled below.

Fair Credit Reporting Act (FCRA) – 15 USCA Section 1681 et seq (1970)

www.ftc.gov/os/statutes/031224fcra.pdf

The Fair Credit Reporting Act (FCRA) was the first major Federal Law enacted to protect privacy. The Act deals with consumer credit and states how a financial report on a consumer may be used. Even though the term "Credit" appears in the name of the law, the FCRA goes well beyond the regulation of credit reports.

FCRA also prohibits the inclusion of obsolete data, describes information which must be released to the Government, outlines how a consumer can learn what is on file, and permits the challenge of incomplete or inaccurate data.

An important point to keep in mind is that the law primarily regulates what third parties do. The FCRA establishes specific requirements and rules for a pre-employment background report, called a Consumer Report, which is usually much broader in scope than just a credit report. A Consumer Report can include a wide variety of obtained information concerning job applicants, such as criminal and civil records, driving records, civil lawsuits, reference checks, and any other information obtained by a Consumer Reporting Agency (CRA). Therefore, the FCRA fundamentally controls the information on applicants that is assembled, evaluated, or disseminated by certain third parties and used for employment purposes.

When first passed in 1970, the FCRA was primarily meant to promote confidentiality, privacy, accuracy, and relevancy regarding information gathered about consumers. The law was extensively amended in 1996 with changes effective September 30, 1997. That amendment substantially overhauled the use of consumer reports for employment purposes by providing greater protection to consumers. Other important amendments were made in 1998 and additional amendments were passed in 2003. Recent revisions of the FCRA add text on employment screening (refer to that chapter). As the figurative gold standard for employment screening, the FCRA imposes extensive legal liabilities on companies which furnish information to credit reporting agencies. The revision requires companies which "regularly furnish information about any consumer to a credit reporting agency" to notify the consumer in advance and to adopt procedures for assuring accuracy and resolving disputes.

Privacy Act – 5 USCA Section 552A (1974)

www.usdoj.gov/oip/privstat.htm

The Privacy Act was enacted because—

- The collection and use of personal information by the U.S. Government infringes on personal privacy.

- The increased use of computers and sophisticated technology enhances the possibility of harm to individual privacy.

- The misuse of information can threaten one's employment, insurance, and credit opportunities.

- The right to privacy is a fundamental personal right of all citizens even though it is not stated expressly in the U.S. Constitution.

The Act protects the individual who decides what records kept by the Government are important to him/her. The Act permits the individual to insist that those records be used only for their intended purpose. The Privacy Act pertains only to personal records in the custody of the Executive Branch of the U.S. Government, and the requested record must pertain to the requestor, or the requestor must be the legal guardian of the individual of record. Each agency is required to publish a descriptive list of the record systems from which information can be retrieved using a personal identifier. The Federal Register has material concerning how information is stored and maintained, and how it can be retrieved.

The Privacy Act is a companion act to the Freedom of Information Act. An individual can preclude release under the FOIA by citing the Privacy Act. See the chart at end of this chapter for state privacy and FOIA websites.

The Right to Financial Privacy Act (RFPA)) 12 USCA Section 3401 et seq (1978)

www4.law.cornell.edu/uscode/12/ch35.html

The RFPA protects the right of customers in financial institutions. The Intent of this Act is to keep financial records private and free from unjustified governmental investigation. While this act appears to have no direct impact of information requests from private individuals, it is important to be aware of the existence of this Act.

The Americans with Disabilities Act (ADA) – 42 USCA 12291 Section 501 (1990) & 29, 47 USCA

www.usdoj.gov/crt/ada/cguide.htm (Guide to Disability Rights Laws)

The ADA prohibits employment discrimination that may occur in testing, by undue standards, or job segregation. Employers cannot make pre-employment inquiries concerning whether the applicant has a

312 ✳ *The Public Record Research Tips Book* ~

disability and, if so, how severe the disability unless it concerns the ability to perform job-related functions. An employer may require a post-offer physical or obtain information if everyone has the same requirements and results are maintained in a confidential record. A Workers' Compensation history is legal for use in the hiring process as part of the post-offer contingency or medical review.

Under the ADA, there are only three valid reasons to rescind a job offer – the applicant lied; the applicant is a threat to self and/or others, and/or the applicant is unable to perform essential job functions. However, nothing in the ADA prohibits nor restricts "an insurer, hospital – or any other agent or entity that administers benefit plans or similar organizations from underwriting risks, classifying risks, or administering such risks that are based on or not inconsistent with state law."

Driver's Privacy Protection Act (DPPA)
18 U.S.C. § 2721 et. Seq

www4.law.cornell.edu/uscode/18/2721.html

The Driver's Privacy Protection Act Title XXXI - Protection of Privacy of Information in State Motor Vehicle Records - was attached as an amendment to the Violent Crime Control Act of 1994 and was signed by President Clinton late in the Summer. The intent of the DPPA is to protect the personal privacy of persons licensed to drive by prohibiting certain disclosures of information maintained by the states. States were given three years to comply.

The Act prohibits disclosure of personal information from the driver history, vehicle registration, title files held by state DMVs, except for 14 defined "permissible uses" unless consent is given by the subject o fthe record search. An amendment to the Act also defines Personal Information and Highly Restricted Personal Information.

In general, the permissible uses permit ongoing, legitimate businesses and individuals to obtain full record data, but with added compliance procedures.

Sarbanes-Oxley Act Section 404

www.govtrack.us/congress/bill.xpd?bill=h107-3763

The Sarbanes-Oxley Act of 2002 (Pub. L. No. 107-204, 116 Stat. 745), also known as the Public Company Accounting Reform and Investor Protection Act of 2002 and commonly called SOX or Sarbox is a U.S. federal law signed into law on July 30, 2002.

This far-reaching law radically changed the landscape of corporate governance, controls, audits and financial disclosures, and even employment checks. SOX established new or enhanced standards for all U.S. public company boards, management, and public accounting firms. SOX does not apply to privately held companies. Sarbanes-Oxley contains 11 titles with specific mandates and requirements for financial reporting.

Freedom of Information Act (FOIA) – USCA Section 552 (1966)

www.usdoj.gov/oip/

Fundamentally, the federal FOIA provides for public disclosure of information held by administrative agencies of the U.S. Government. Thus, the FOIA allows access to all records in custody of the Executive Branch unless specifically exempted. Such disclosure may be withheld when disclosure would cause harm to a governmental function; e.g., invasion of privacy, trade secret disclosure, etc. Specifically, the most commonly recognized exceptions are: personal information which clearly invades personal privacy; commercial trade information belonging to a private entity which the government has because of a contract of for regulatory purposes; and information withheld for security reasons; e.g., government investigatory files.

FOIA is considered a general access statute and is the broadest of all such statutes. The requestor need not have any personal interest in the information requested nor does there need to be a reason for the request. Most Federal agencies have issued instructions which covers what constitutes "readily available" information and how to get it, how to get "other" information, and the "right of review" process in cases when access is denied.

FOIA George Washington University provides a helpful guide to FOIA at www.gwu.edu/~nsarchiv/nsa/foia_how_use.html including tutorials, also addresses to FOIA-related offices.

The Federal Register and the Code of Federal Regulation (CFR) have material concerning how information is stored in Federal administrative agencies, how it is maintained, and how it can be retrieved. See www.gpoaccess.gov/nara/index.html

Family Educational Rights and Privacy Act (FERPA) (20 U.S.C. § 1232g; 34 CFR Part 99)

www.ed.gov/policy/gen/guid/fpco/ferpa/index.html

This Federal law protects the privacy of student education records. The law is applicable to all schools who receive funds from the U.S. Dept. of Education.

Generally, schools must have written permission from the parent or eligible student to release any information from the student's education record. However, FERPA allows schools to disclose those records, without consent, to school officials, other schools to which a student is transferring, officials for audit or evaluation purposes, those in connection with financial aid to a student, accrediting organizations, to officials in health and safety emergencies, justice authorities.

Schools may disclose, without consent, "directory information" such as a student's name, address, phone, date and place of birth, honors and awards, and dates of attendance. Schools must tell parents and eligible students about directory information and allow parents and eligible students a reasonable amount of time to request that the school not disclose directory information about them.

For additional information call 202-260-3887 or write:

Family Policy Compliance Office, U.S. Department of Education 400 Maryland Avenue SW, Washington, D.C. 20202-5920

State Privacy Laws

The federal FOIA law applies only to federally maintained records; each state has its own FIOA rules. States are free to enact their own privacy laws and these are usually stricter and more specific than the federal laws they supersede. The same is true of state FOIA laws.

The Reporters Committee for Freedom of the Press has a superb website full of incredible information and search tools about state privacy laws. Look for *The Open Government Guide* (formerly called Tapping Officials' Secrets) at www.rcfp.org.

Another excellent web page with links and explanations is the Freedom of Information Center, managed by The National Freedom of Information Coalition. The Freedom of Information Center web page shows links to each state's FOIA-related laws. Visit http://foi.missouri.edu/index.html. The Coalition is hosted by the Missouri School of Journalism, which is also the headquarters for IRE – Investigative Reporters and Editors. The Freedom of Information Center is located at the University of Missouri-Columbia, 133 Neff Annex, Columbia, MO 65211, 573-882-9157.

These sites above are not limited to material about state laws. Both have plenty of information about privacy and federal laws including FOIA.

Public Record Searching Glossary

Abatement   1) Equal reduction of recovered debts by all creditors when there are not enough funds/assets to pay in full; 2) Removal of a problem that is against private or public policy, or endangers others, including nuisances; 3) Equal reduction of benefits to heirs when an estate is too small to fully pay beneficiaries.

Abeyance   If its owner cannot be determined, then property and shipped goods are 'in abeyance.'

Abscond   1) Leave a jurisdiction to avoid being arrested or served legal papers; 2) Unanticipated leaving with stolen goods or funds.

Abstract   Summary of a record or document such as abstract of title to real property, or an abstract of judgment.

Abstraction   Taking away with intent to harm or deceive.

Accusation   1) Charging someone with a crime by legal indictment via a Grand Jury or filing of charges by a District Attorney; 2) statement that a named person committed a crime or wrong.

Acknowledgement   Copy of a filed document indicating it has been accepted and filed in the jurisdiction indicated.

Acquittal   A not-guilty verdict absolving an accused party of guilt, that is, not proven guilty beyond a reasonable doubt. Release or absolution.

Addendum   Pages attached as second or additional pages, often on UCC financing statements. An 'Amendment Addendum' is a 2nd page to a UCC-3 amendment.

Adjudication   Legal process by which a case or claim is settled. May also be the final pronouncement of judgment in a case or claim.

Adjudication Withheld   The court will withhold a decision until a future date. Usually some sort of probation is added and if the defendant complies with the conditions for a specified period of time, case dismissed!

Affidavit   A voluntarily, written statement of fact, confirmed by oath.

a.k.a   'also known as' - when someone uses different initials, a nickname, a maiden, or married name. See also Alias.

Alias   False name used in substitution of a legal name on official documents and for official purposes. Nicknames are not considered aliases. May be noted as 'a.k.a' - also known as - on criminal records.

Allegation   Statement of 'claimed fact' contained in a criminal charge, complaint, or an affirmative defense.

Amendment   1) In UCCs, a broad term applied to all filings affecting a initial financing statement; this may also be a termination, continuation, assignment or release. 2) addition to or alteration of a motion, bill, constitution, etc.

Amnesty   Government's blanket abolition of an offense, with the legal result those convicted/charged are unbound and freed from the charge and/or sentence.

Answer   Defendant's written response to the plaintiff's complaint.

Antitrust Acts or Laws   Laws to protect trade and commerce from unlawful practice.

Apostille   1) Added note in a document's margin; 2) quick version of authentication of a document, usually foreign ones.

Appeal   A complaint to a superior court to review the decision of a lower court.

Appellate Court   A court having jurisdiction of appeal and review. Not a trial court.

Appraise   Professionally evaluate the value of property, or in certain cases the loss of value or cost of replacement due to damage.

Archived Filings   Lapsed, old, or unnecessary filing entries in a folder separate from active documents.

Arraignment   Calling the accused to come before the court to hear charges and/or enter a plea.

Articles of Incorporation   A document filed with the Secretary of State outlining a newly-created business, equivalent to announcing a corporation.

Assess   Set a value on property usually for the purpose of calculating real property taxes. Usually conducted by county assessor though the official name may vary.

Assignment   When a secured party gives all or part of the rights to another party, i.e., a bank sells a loan to a 2nd bank.

Bankruptcy Petition   Formal document or request by a debtor to a bankruptcy court to obtain relief from creditors.

Bearer Share   Unregistered security payable to the holder; shares can be privately bought, exchanged, sold.

Bench Warrant   A process delivered by the court directing a law enforcement agency to bring a specified individual before the court.

Beneficial Owner   A person not listed as a company owner but can buy and sell its shares.

Bind Over   1) Put under bond to appear in court; 2) when a case is shifted from a lower court to a higher court.

Board of Directors   Governing body of a corporation elected by the shareholders.

Bond   A certificate of obligation, either unsecured or secured with collateral, to pay a specified amount of money within a specified period of time. In a criminal matter, meeting the bond requirements is in exchange for release from custody.

Bond Forfeiture   Bond forfeiture occurs when a case has been disposed and a fine is to be paid or has been. If it is a first offense, it is listed on the record but not classified as a conviction; any other time it is classified as a conviction.

Breach   To break. Common breaches are 1) breach of contract - breaking its terms; 2) breach of duty or breach of trust; 3) breach of peace by causing a disturbance by acts that break public tranquility, such as violence; 4) breach of warranty by not telling the truth knowingly or innocently about title to property.

Brief   Written document submitted to the court that contains case facts and cites relevant laws in support of one's position.

Bylaws   In a corporation, bylaws are the regulations and basic rules the company operates under.

Calendar   List of cases to be called for trial before a particular court.

Capias   Latin, meaning 'That You Take.' This is the name for several types of writs that require a law enforcement official take a named defendant into custody.

Cause of Action   One or more related charges combined and made against a defendant for wrongs committed

Certificate of Existence/or/Status   State-issued document that indicates an entity is incorporated of qualified.

Certification   An agency's proof, often a stamped impression on a cover page, that a document is authentically from their records. Usually a fee is involved

Chattel   Item of personal property which is movable, unlike real estate.

Citation   Order issued by a law enforcement officer requiring appearance in court to answer a charge. Bail is not accepted in lieu of appearance.

Civil Disorder   Violent public disturbance by three or more people which causes danger, damage or injury to property or persons.

Class Action   Lawsuit filed by one or more people on behalf of themselves and a larger group of people who are similarly situated.

Coercion   Use of physical force or threats to compel someone to commit an act against their will.

Collateral   Security pledged for the payment of a loan, for instance an item of property or agriculture of the debtor.

Collusion   When two persons - or a business via their officers or employees - enter into a deceitful agreement, usually secret, to defraud or gain an unfair negotiating advantage over a 3rd party, competitor, or consumers.

Comity   When one court defers to the jurisdiction of another court where both would have the right to handle the case.

Commutation; Commute a Sentence   When an individual presently incarcerated and serving an active sentence has their sentence 'commuted' or reduced 1) by any length of time, 2) to make parole eligible, 3) to time served which would immediately release the individual.

Complainant   Person or entity who begins a lawsuit by filing a complaint; is 'plaintiff' or petitioner.

Compounding Crime   The receipt by an individual of consideration in exchange for an agreement not to prosecute or inform on someone who they know has committed a crime.

Concurring Opinion   Agrees with the opinion reached, but does not agree with the reasoning.

Conditional Discharge   A conviction. Court issues the discharge from the jail and requires defendant to comply with some conditions. Regardless whether defendant complies with rules or not, he/she is still convicted (GUILTY) and case can never be expunged.

Conditional Release   Release from a correctional facility before full sentence has been served which is conditioned on specific behavior. If conditions are not met, the individual may be returned to the facility.

Consent Degree & Order   Agreement by both parties to the terms of a settlement made under the sanction of the court.

Conservator   Guardian and protector appointed by a judge to protect and manage the financial affairs of another's daily life due to old age or physical or mental limitations.

Continuation   1) in court, a postponement judicially granted; 2) in UCCs, an amendment the extends a financing statement's effectiveness for 5 years, if filed within 6 months of the filing's lapse date.

Contract   Agreement with specific terms between 2 or more persons or entities; one agrees to do something in return for a consideration, payment.

Conversion   Document filed with Sec. of State or equivalent that changes an entity to another type of entity.

Contempt of Court   An act committed which serves to obstruct the court in its administration or authority.

Contiguous   Connected or 'next to' - usually referring to adjoining counties or real estate.

Conversion   Unauthorized taking of another's property.

Corporate Kit   Collection that includes compliance tools – corporate seal, stock certs, bylaws, board resolutions, bookkeeping.

Correction Statement   1) in publication, an after-the-fact explanation or modification usually concerning a legal liability; 2. A UCC record indicating a financing statement is inaccurate or wrongfully filed.

Count/Charge   An offense named in a cause of action. A cause of action may contain multiple counts or charges, each relating to the others but identifying a separate offense.

Court Costs   Fees for expenses that a court passes on to attorneys, who then pass them on to their clients or to the losing party. The prevailing party in a lawsuit is usually awarded court costs.

Court of Record   Court where the permanent record of all proceedings is held.

Creditor   Person or entity to whom a debt is owed.

Criminal Nonsupport   Failure to pay child support

Cross Complaint   Defendant in a civil suit assets a cause of action against the plaintiff or cross-complainant.

Culpability   Blame, or degree of responsibility for a crime. Degrees - purposeful, knowingly, recklessly, or by negligence.

Cumulative Sentence   A sentence that takes effect after a prior sentence is completed for crimes tried under the same cause of action.

Custody   When an individual is held by authorities. Custody assignments can include- close, medium, minimum 1, minimum 2, minimum 3, etc.

Customs Court   Federal court established 1926 to hear appeals from decisions of customs officials.

De Novo   Usually used as 'Trial De Novo.' New trial or one that is held for a second time, as if there had been no previous trial or decision.

Dead Docket   Case never went to trial. The case can be re-opened if new evidence is submitted.

Debenture   Long term debt security issued mainly to evidence unsecured corporate debt.

Deed   Written document which transfers title/ownership or an interest in real property to another person.

Defamation   Making untrue statements about another which damages their reputation. If the defamatory statement is printed or broadcast, then it is libel. If oral, it is slander.

Defendant   A person against whom a cause of action is taken.

Deferred Adjudication of Guilt   The final judgment is delayed for a period of time. Can be likened to probation before a final verdict. If 'probation' is completed without incident, the charges are usually dropped and the case is dismissed. During the 'probationary period' the disposition is not necessarily considered a conviction

Deferred Discharge   Dismissed and considered a non-conviction.

Deferred Probation   The judge doesn't make a finding of guilt; he assigns probation. If probation is completed without incident, the charges are usually dropped.

Deferred Sentence   Postponement of the pronouncement of the sentence.

Defraud   Knowingly misrepresenting facts to cheat or trick.

Degree (First, Second, or Third, A, B or C)   Classification assigned to a crime, depending on circumstances, for purposes of determining punishment. First degree is considered most serious than third; A is more serious than C. Degrees may be assigned to the actual crime (i.e.: murder in the first degree or second degree) or the class of crimes (i.e.: felony or misdemeanor).

Deposition   Taking and recording testimony of a witness under oath before a court reporter while away from the courtroom before trial. A deposition is part of permitted pre-trial discovery investigation

Deuce   Slang for a drunk driving charge.

Directed Verdict   A determination by a jury, made at the direction of the judge. A directed verdict happens in cases where there has been a lack of evidence, an overwhelming amount of evidence, or where the law is in favor of one of the parties.

Discharge   Bankruptcy court action releasing a debtor from some or all of their debts.

Disclosure Statement   Any added review of financial matters relating to a debtor's bankruptcy.

Discovery   Pre-Trial procedure used by the parties to gain facts and information about the case.

Dismissal Without Leave After Deferred Prosecution   Charges dismissed after specified time (90 days to 1 year) provided certain conditions have been met such as participating in specified program of anger control or drug counseling or providing community service, etc.

Disposition/Disposed   The final settlement in the matter. Examples of disposed cases are those with a finding of guilt (conviction), innocence, or acquittal.

Dissenting Opinion   Summary statement that disagrees with the court's majority opinion.

Dissolution   1) A Divorce; 2) document filed with Sec of State or equivalent that ends a domestic entity.

Diversion Program   To set aside. A court direction which calls a defendant, found guilty, to attend a work or educational program as part of probation. May include some type of anger management, drug rehab, etc. If the condition of program is met, charge may be considered non-conviction.

Diversity of Citizenship   Crime or claim which extends between citizens of different states. This is one of the grounds that can be used to invoke the jurisdiction of the U.S. Federal District Court.

Docket Number   unique number that identifies an offender or case.

Docket Record; Docket Sheet   A court's official record of proceedings and calendar of upcoming cases

Double Jeopardy   Placing someone on trial a second time for an offense for which they have been acquitted previously. This is specifically prohibited by the U.S. Constitution, even if new incriminating evidence is unearthed.

Due Diligence   1) A reasonable and expected measure of attention taken for a particular action. Not measurable by an absolute standard, but dependant on the situation. 2) Employer's responsibility to protect the public/clients by adequately checking employee's/hiree's background.

Due Process of Law   Procedures followed by law enforcement and courts to insure the protection of an individual's rights as assigned by the Constitution.

DUI, DWI   Driving Under the Influence.

E-Filing; Electronic Filing   A transmission, usually in real time and automatically, of a filing directly into a government database.

Ejectment   Lawsuit brought to remove a party who is occupying real property. Do not confuse this with unlawful detainer, an eviction suit against a tenant. Ejectment is against someone who has tried to claim title to a property.

Eminent Domain   Power of a federal, state, county or city government, school district, hospital district or other gov't agency to take private real estate for public use, with or without the permission of the owner, who is entitled to just compensation.

Encumbrance   Claim or lien on a parcel of real property. These include: mortgages, deeds of trust, recorded abstracts of judgment, unpaid real property taxes, tax liens, easements, mechanic's liens, and water or timber rights.

Exhibit   During a court proceeding an item or document submitted to the court as evidence.

Ex parte   Means 'on one side only.' When an act is 'for one party only.' For example, in an Ex parte proceeding, only one party to the case is heard.

Expunge/Expungment   When a record of an offense is expunged it will not appear on a released criminal history. The record may be destroyed or sealed after a certain period of time. Records may be expunged in juvenile cases or upon satisfactory completion of a court-ordered probation, diversion, and/or class(s).

Extradition   Surrender of an individual accused or convicted of a crime by one state to another.

Family Offenses, Nonviolent   Unlawful, nonviolent acts by a family member or legal guardian that threaten the physical, mental, or economic well-being or morals of another member. These are not classifiable as other offenses like Assault, Incest, Statutory Rape, etc. Examples- Abandonment, Desertion, Neglect, nonsupport.

FCRA   Fair Credit Reporting Act.

Felony/ Fraudulent Conversion   Similar to embezzlement or theft. An example of felony conversion is if someone sold goods for a company, and kept the money instead of turning it in to the company.

Fictitious Business Name   Public name other than the official name, usually created for branding and advertising purposes, and filed with the Sec of State or equivalent office.

Finding of Fact   Determination made by the court or jury based on evidence presented.

Fixture   Equipment attached to real estate as to be part of the premises. Its removal would do harm to the building or land value.

Foreclosure System whereby a party who has loaned money secured by a mortgage or deed of trust on real property, or has an unpaid judgment, requires sale of the real property to recover the money due, unpaid interest, plus the costs of foreclosure.

Franchise Tax Status A state tax department certificate showing that an entity is incorporate and qualified in that jurisdiction.

Impersonation - Falsely representing one's identity or position and acting in the character or position assumed in order to deceive others and thereby gain a profit or advantage, enjoy some right or privilege, or subject another person or entity to an expense, charge, or liability.

Full Disclosure The need to tell the whole truth about any matter that the other party should know in deciding to buy or contract.

Garnish Obtain a court order directing a party holding funds or about to pay wages to an alleged debtor to set that money aside until the court determines how much the debtor owes the creditor.

General Jurisdiction Court that hears a wide range of topics, both criminal and civil.

Good Standing Certificate See Certificate of Existence/or/Status.

Grantor/Grantee Index Set of books or computerized lists found in the County Recorder or Recorder of Deeds office which shows recorded transfers of title by deed (as well as liens, mortgages, deeds of trust and other documents affecting title). Each yearly index is usually alphabetized by the last names of grantors - the party transferring title - and grantee, the recipients.

Gross Misdemeanor Serious misdemeanor.

Guardian Person appointed by a judge to care for a minor child or incompetent adult personally and manage that person's affairs.

Habeas Corpus A writ requesting a trial or the release of a prisoner.

Habitual Violator To have committed the same offence three times. Can also be charged as a habitual offender.

HAVA See Help America Vote Act, the.

Hearsay Second-hand verbal evidence - a witness is not telling what they know personally, but what others have said.

Help America Vote Act, The or HAVA. Establishes a program to provide funds to States to replace punch card voting systems, to establish the Election Assistance Commission, and to otherwise provide assistance with administration of certain Federal election laws and programs, minimum election standards for Federal elections.

Hostile Possession Occupancy of real property coupled with a claim of ownership regardless of the recorded title holder.

Illegal Immigrant An alien/non-citizen who entered the US without government permission or stayed beyond the termination date of a visa.

Impeach 1) to discredit the testimony of a witness by proving they has not told the truth or been inconsistent, introduced contrary evidence. 2) charge a public official with a public crime - punishment is removal from office.

Incompetency Lacking the ability to handle one's affairs due to mental or physical incapacity. Before incompetency is officially declared by a court, a hearing must be held with the person.

Incontrovertible Evidence Evidence proving a fact so conclusively that by no stretch of the imagination can it be untrue. Examples: dna tests, fingerprint matches.

Incorrigible One who is incapable of reform.

Indictment A formal, written accusation made by the grand jury.

Infraction Violation of local ordinance or state statute usually resulting in a fine or limited period of incarceration. This term usually in traffic offenses.

Injunction Court order prohibiting a person from doing a specified act for a specified period of time.

Insider Trading Using confidential information about transactions or a business gained through employment there or through a stock brokerage to buy or sell stocks/bonds based on private knowledge the value will go up or down.

Insolvency   Having more debts/liabilities than assets available to pay them.

Instrument   1) as evidence, an object used to perform some action, often in an assault. 2) a written legal document - a contract, lease, deed, will, bond.

Intangible; Intangible Property   Items such as company stock or 'goodwill' that represent value but are not necessarily tangible, accountable objects.

Interrogatories   A discovery procedure where a party under oath must answer questions in writing about the case to the opposing party.

Intervention   1) where a 3rd party such as an authority enters into a dispute. 2) Procedure agreed upon by a judge where a 3rd party may join an ongoing lawsuit. A petition to intervene and a hearing occur first. and not just before trial commences.

Intestacy   Having died without a valid will. If the dead person has property it is distributed via probate according to statutes - by the law of descent and distribution - and laws dealing with marital and community property.

Involuntary Dismissal   Dismissed due to lack of prosecution or lack of evidence.

Jeopardy   Danger of being charged with or convicted of a particular crime.

Joinder   Joining together of several lawsuits or parties all in one lawsuit provided the issues and facts are the same for all.

Judgment Lien   An encumbrance arising when a judgment is filed.

Judicial Discretion; Judicial Notice   Judge's power to make decisions on certain matters without being bound by precedent or rules established by statutes. Judicial Notice is authority of a judge to accept as facts certain matters of common knowledge such as the sun will rise again.

Jurisdiction   A court's power to question facts, apply law, make decisions and judgments.

Jurisdiction of Organization   State where an entity is incorporated or where its chart documents are filed.

Jurisprudence   Study of Law and legal questions; law subjects entirely.

"K"   Shorthand symbol for 'contract' in legal professional circles.

Lapsed Date   How long a record will continue to be visible after its term as expired. For UCCs a record remains for 1 year. A UCC is active 5 years after its file date.

Legacy   Gift of personal property or money to a will's beneficiary. Synonymous with 'bequest.' Legacy usually refers to any gift from the deceased's estate; technically, legacy does not include a device such as real property.

Legal Malice   An act, committed without just cause or excuse, intended to inflict harm or cause death

Legalese   Sometimes arcane, specialized, and convoluted jargon of legal scholars and lawyers.

Legatee   Person or organization receiving a gift or money under the terms of the deceased's will.

Lesser-included Offense   Crime that is proved by same facts as a more serious crime.

Levy   1) act of a legislative body to create a tax. 2) seize property upon a writ issued by the court to pay a money judgment granted in a lawsuit. The levy may be made by a sheriff or other official at the request of the judgment holder, and the property is sold at a sheriff's sale to provide money to satisfy the judgment. 3) earthen embankment for flood control.

License   Permission to perform a particular act or conduct business.

Lien   Official claim or charge against property or funds for an amount owed for services rendered or payment of a debt.

Limited Jurisdiction   Type of court with a set range of case types, either by topics heard or dollar limits.

Liquidate   Sell assets of a business, then paying bills and dividing the remainder among shareholders, partners, investors.

Lis Pendens   1) written notice that a lawsuit has been filed which concerns the title to real property or some interest in that real property. 2) Control the court acquires over property in a pending litigation until a final decision reached.

Listing Certificate   or Good Standing Long Form. This document shows all charter documents filed for an entity at that agency.

Litigant   A party to a lawsuit.

Litigation; Litigious   Lawsuit or other resort to the courts to determine a legal matter or question. Someone litigious constantly brings or prolongs legal actions, particularly when the legal maneuvers are unnecessary or unfounded.

Living Trust   Generic name for any trust agreement that comes into existence during the lifetime of the person(s) creating the trust. Commonly it is a trust where the trustors/settlors receive benefit from the trust's profits during their lifetimes. Include also- irrevocable trusts, insurance trust, charitable remainder trust, and certain specialized trusts to manage assets.

Living Will   Document where a person appoints someone as his/her proxy or representative to make decisions on maintaining extraordinary life-support if they becomes too ill or are certain to die. Also known as a durable power of attorney.

Long-arm Statute   Law giving local court jurisdiction over an out-of-state company or individual whose actions caused damage locally or to a resident. Legal test - whether the out-of-state defendant has contacts sufficiently substantial within the state.

Malfeasance; Misfeasance   Intentionally doing something either legally or morally wrong, with no right to do so; involves dishonesty, illegality or knowingly exceeding authority for improper reasons. Misfeasance is committing a wrong or error by mistake, negligence or inadvertence, but not by intentional wrongdoing.

Malice   Intentional wrongdoing of a civil wrong like libel or a criminal act like assault or murder, with the intention of doing harm to the victim.

Malice Aforethought   Planning to commit an unlawful act without just cause or excuse.

Mandate   1) mandatory order or requirement under statute, regulation, or by a public agency; 2) orders a public official or public body to comply with the law; 3) order of an appeals court to a lower court to comply with an appeals

Material Witness   Person who has information pertinent to a lawsuit or criminal prosecution significant enough to affect the case outcome.

Mediation   Attempt to settle a legal dispute through participation of a 3rd party mediator, all working to find points of agreement among those in conflict and arrive at a fair result.

Medical Sanction   Identifies an individual or employers who have had sanctions brought against them for crimes that committed in associations with certain state or government funded agencies. Parties with sanctions against them are excluded from billing Medicare, Medicaid, child care and social services, and may also be excluded from Federal health care programs.

Memorandum of Law   Written argument stating the legal authority, statutes and case decisions on points of law.

Misdemeanor   Crime punishable by a fine and/or county jail time for up to one year; not a felony.

Moral Turpitude   Business or inter-related group of businesses who control so much of the production or sale of a kind of a product to control the market, including prices and distribution.

Moratorium   Suspension of activity, particularly voluntary suspension, perhaps as a cooling off period.

Motion   Formal request made to a judge for an order or judgment.

National Death Locator   Database that matches a social security number with a decedent's name, birth date, and death date. Additional information may include the state and year of Social Security issuance, the city and state of last residence, and zip code of beneficiary receiving a death benefit.

National Wants and Warrants   Fairly complete nationwide list of outstanding warrants for extraditable offenses.

Negligence   Flagrant and reckless disregard of the safety of others. Willful indifference.

Negotiated Plea   See Plea Bargain.

No Bill or No True Bill   The decision by a grand jury that it will not bring indictment against the accused on the basis of the allegations and evidence presented by the prosecutor.

No Contest   A plea in which the defendant does not contest the charge. This has the same effect as a guilty plea except the conviction cannot be used against the defendant in a civil suit.

No Papered   Charges were not pursued. (This is a legal term in Washington, DC)

No Probable Cause   There was not sufficient reason to bring case to trial.

Nolle Pros or Nolle Prosequi   Latin phrase used by the district attorney or plaintiff when they do not wish to prosecute or proceed with the action.

Nolo Contendre   Latin phrase used by a defendant to say "I do not wish to contest." This plea in a criminal case has the legal effect of pleading guilty. See No Contest.

Non-Feasance   Failure of an agent or employee to perform a task agreed upon.

Nuisance   Unwarranted, unreasonable, and/or unlawful use of property that causes inconvenience or damage to others.

Obstruction of Justice   Attempt to interfere with law enforcement officers or the judicial system, including threatening witnesses, improper talk with jurors, hiding evidence, interfering with an arrest.

Obtain Property under False Pretense   The misrepresentation of the value of something. Passing bad check.

OCC Filing/or/Retrieval   Documents filed with the Office of the Comptroller of the Currency.

Offense Qualifier   Indicates what role the offender played in the commission of a crime. 11 possibilities are- principal, attempted, conspiracy to attempt, conspiracy, accessory before the fact, accessory to attempt, Aid and Abet, accessory after fact, solicit, solicit to attempt, unknown.

Officers, Corporate   Individuals appointed by the Board of Directors to carry out policies and make day to day decisions.

Official Misconduct   Illegal or improper acts under the guise of official authority by a public official that violates their duty to follow the law and act on behalf of the public good.

Official Search   Search performed at the record location and certified to be true and correct, with a attesting seal or official's signature.

Omission   Failure to perform an act agreed to where there is a duty to an individual or the public to act, or where it is legally required. 2) inadvertently leaving out a word, phrase, or language from a contract or other document.

Opinion   Explanation of a court's judgment that may set a precedent or may be needed in an appeal. Legal reasoning on which a judgment is based.

Order   Mandate or direction given by the court deciding a point or providing direction for the next course of action.

Pander   To provide products or services which cater to sexual gratification of others. To entice another into prostitution.

Parcel   Defined piece of real estate, often resulting from the division of a large land area.

Parole Violation   An act that does not conform to the terms of parole.

Partial Verdict   Trial result where the jury finds the defendant guilty of one or more charges but not guilty of all.

Patent Infringement   Permissionless Manufacture or use of an invention or improvement owned by gov't patent by someone else.

Peace Bond   Bond required of a person as part of a court order to guarantee they will stay away from another they have threatened or bothered.

Peer Review   Examination/evaluation of a professional's or technician's performance by a board or committee of people in the same occupation.

Penalty   1) amount agreed in advance to be paid if payment or performance is not made on time. 2) after conviction for a crime, money fine or forfeiture of property ordered by the judge.

Pending Charge or Case   Charge for an offense not yet been disposed of by the court.

Peremptory   Final, absolute and not entitled to reconsideration or delay.

Perfected   Having completed all legal steps necessary.

Petitioner   One involved in the initiation of a legal action.

Physician-patient Privilege   Obligation and right of a physician to refuse to testify in a legal proceeding about any statement made to them by a patient on the basis their is confidential.

Pilferage   Theft of little things usually from shipments or baggage.

Piracy   Crime of robbery of ships or boats, now applied also to theft of intellectual property.

Plaintiff   Party who initiates a lawsuit demanding damages, performance, or court determination of rights.

Plea   The defendant's formal answer to a charge.

Plea Bargain   A plea of guilt to a lesser offense in return for a lighter sentence.

Pleadings   In a civil case, written statements by the parties that defines the premise for their claims.

Police Powers   A state's enforcement rights and powers 'not delegated to the United States include protection of the welfare, safety, health, morals of their public. Police powers include licensing, inspection, zoning, safety regulations, quarantines, working conditions, law enforcement.

Post Mortem   Examination of a dead body to determine cause of death, generally called an autopsy.

Power of Attorney   Written document signed by a person giving another the power to conduct the signer's business.

Practice   1) a legal law business or conduct law as a business; 2) habit or custom as shown by repeated action; 3) repeat an activity to improve skills.

Precedent   1) situation that must exist before the next step; 2) prior reported opinion of an appeals court establishing the legal rule or authority in the future on the same question.

Pre-Clearance   Review of corporate documents prior to their being officially filed.

Preliminary Hearing   Meeting before the judge to determine if a person charged with a felony should be tried for that crime, based on some substantial evidence that they committed the crime. Preliminary hearing are held in the lowest local court but only if the prosecutor has filed the charge without asking the Grand Jury for an indictment.

Preliminary Injunction   Court order made in the early stages of a lawsuit or petition that prohibits parties from doing an act which is in dispute, thereby maintaining the status quo during procedures.

Premeditation   Plotting, planning, deliberating before doing something. Is an important consideration in murder.

Preponderance of the Evidence   Based on the more convincing evidence and its probable truth or accuracy, and not on the amount of evidence as commonly believed.

Presumption of Innocence   Fundamental protection for a person accused of a crime that requires the prosecution prove its case beyond a reasonable doubt.

Pre-Sentence Diagnostic   When an offender has been convicted of a crime but not sentenced, a diagnostic report is prepared at the request of the court to help determine the appropriate sentence.

Pre-Trial Intervention   An extensive background check to help determine if charges will be pressed.

Privilege Against Self Incrimination   Right to refuse to testify against oneself in any legal proceeding where testimony may be used against them.

Pro Bono   Legal work performed by lawyers without pay to help people with legal problems and limited funds, or provide legal assistance to organizations involved in social causes.

Pro Se   Party to a lawsuit who represents himself.

Probation   Relief of all or part of a sentence on the promise of proper conduct.

Proceeding   A legal filing, hearing, trial, or judgment in a lawsuit or criminal prosecution. Collectively called legal proceedings.

Promissory Note   Written promise by a person to pay a specific amount of money/principal to another.

Proprietary Rights   Rights that go with ownership of real property or a business.

Public Access Terminal   Computer terminal connected to that agency's database that the public may use to look up names or case numbers. Almost always free, this may be as simple as an index or as complex as case record images. There may be a copy charge to print documents found.

Public Domain   1) in copyright law, the right of anyone to use previously copyrighted materials after the copyright period expired. Usually the last possible date for copyright protection would be 50 years after the author's death. 2) lands and waters owned by government.

Public Use   Only purpose for which private property can be taken/condemned by the government's power of eminent domain. Public use includes: schools, streets, highways, hospitals, gov't buildings, parks, reservoirs, flood control, slum clearance/redevelopment, public housing, public theaters/stadiums, safety facilities, harbors, bridges, railroads, airports, terminals, prisons, jails, public utilities and other purposes deemed beneficial to the public.

Punitive Damages   Award in a lawsuit for malicious, evil, or fraudulent acts as a punishment and to set an example to others.

Quash/Quashed   Declined to prosecute but with the option to reopen the case.

Qualification   In order to do business, registration required of a business within a state or jurisdiction other than where it was originally or officially registered.

Quasi-judicial   Actions of an agency, board, or other gov't entity where they perform hearings, orders, judgments, or other activities similar to those of courts.

Question of Law; of Fact   Issue in a case that relates to determination of what the law is, how it is applied to the facts, and other purely legal points in contention. Questions of fact are decided by the jury or only by the judge if there is no jury.

Quitclaim Deed   Real property deed which transfers/conveys only that interest in the property that the grantor has title to.

Quorum   Number of participants required to be present before a meeting can conduct business.

Ratification   Confirmation of an action that was not pre-approved or may not have been authorized.

Receivership   A court's appointment of a responsible party to take custody of the property, business, rents and profits of a party to a lawsuit pending a final decision. Agreement where a receiver controls the financial receipts of one who is deeply in debt/insolvent for the benefit of creditors.

Reckless Endangerment   An act which does or could cause injury to another, not necessarily with intent.

Referendum   Process where the repeal or approval of an existing statute or constitutional provision is voted upon.

Remand   To return an individual to custody pending further trial, or to return a case from an appellate to a lower court for further proceedings.

Remedy   Any means to achieve justice in matters where legal rights are involved.

Rescission   When the parties cancel a contract by mutual agreement.

Replevin   An action or writ to recover personal property said or claimed to be unlawfully.

Respondent   The party required to answer a petition, a court order, or writ. Usually respondent required to take some action, halt an activity, or obey a court's directive.

Restitution   Return to the proper owner their property or the monetary value of their loss.

Restraining Order   An order prohibiting a specified action until such time that a hearing on an application for an injunction can be held.

Retired (as Disposition)   The case can be brought up within the next year if the individual is arrested for anything. It is the judge's decision and only he can take action. If the individual remains "clean," then the case can be dismissed.

Record Retriever   Individual or firm who performs public record searches or retrieves public record documents.

Revised Article 9   July 1, 2001 revision of the UCC Code accepted by all states, amending the section on secured transactions.

Revivor   A request to return an entity in bad standing to good standing.

Revocation   Cancellation.

Rights   1) Collection of entitlements such as justice, due process, privacy, to own - a person may have that are protected by the gov't, or courts, or under a contract agreement. 2) Slang for the information which must be given by law enforcement officers to a suspect.

Row Offices   Refers to county agencies with a county courthouse. In addition to courts, row offices may include assessor, auditor, register of deeds (land records), GIS-mapping, tax collector, voter registration/elections, and sometimes sheriff.

Sanction   1) Financial penalty imposed by a judge on a party or attorney for a violation. 2) Impose a fine or penalty as part of a judge's duty to maintain both order and fairness in court. 3) Impose constraints on trade against a country. 4) allow, approve.

Schedules   Bankruptcy petitioner's list of debtor's debts and assets.

Sealed Records   Court records or decisions a judge orders kept from public view.

Secreting Lien Property   Hiding property that has a lien filed against it.

Secured Party   In a security agreement, in whose favor a security interest has been created, and perhaps also their duties and liabilities.

Secured Transaction   Where a lien is filed against collateral being held for repayment of a loan.

Serious Misdemeanor   Having a more severe penalty than other misdemeanors.

Service of Process   Official delivery of legal document copies or delivery by mail or in person of documents to opposing attorneys or parties.

Sharp Practice   Lawyer using misleading statements, threats, improper use of process, tricky, or dishonorable means barely within the law.

Sheriff Sale   Auction sale of property held by the sheriff pursuant to a court order to seize and sell the property to satisfy/pay a judgment.

Simple Assault   Unlawful physical attack on another person where neither the offender displays a weapon, nor the victim suffers obvious severe or aggravated bodily injury or loss of consciousness.

Slander   Defamation verbal communication. Making false and malicious statements about another.

Solicitation   Asking, urging or enticing.

Solvency   Having more assets than liabilities/debts.

Status: Closed   No further action will occur on this case; cannot be reopened at later date.

Statute of Limitations   Law that sets the maximum period one can wait before filing a lawsuit. There are statutes of limitations on bringing criminal charges, too (homicide generally has no time limitation.)

Stipulation   Essential condition to an agreement between two parties in a court proceeding.

Stricken   To eliminate or expunge.

Subpoena; Subpena   Court order for a witness to appear for deposition or trial.

Successive Sentences   Imposition of the penalty one after the other for each of several crimes, as compared to concurrent sentences which happen at the same time.

Summary Judgment   Judge's final determination that there are no genuine issues of fact or law.

Suspended Sentence   Deferment of punishment usually over a period of probation.

Summons   Court document issued as a lawsuit is filed, stating name of both plaintiff and defendant, case title and file number, court and its address, name and address of plaintiff's attorney, and instructions as to the need to file a response.

Surrender   1) In business, a statement filed with the Sec of State that an entity no longer intends to do business in their jurisdiction. 2) Turn oneself in to authorities; 3} to give up that which is requested or ordered.

Surrogate's Court   Similar to Probate Court.

Suspended Sentence   Penalty applied by a judge to a defendant convicted of a crime which the judge suspends so long as the defendant performs certain services, makes restitutions, stays out of trouble or meets other conditions.

Swear   1) declare under oath that one will tell the truth; failure to tell the truth and do so knowingly is the crime of perjury. 2) install into office by administering an oath.

Tainted Evidence   Or 'fruit of the poisonous tree.' Information obtained by illegal means or acquired by illegal search/seizure.

Tangible Property   Assets that are physical articles; things; not "incorporeal" assets such as rights, patents, copyrights and franchises. Tangible property is also known as personality.

Tax Clearance   Certificate issued by a tax department that shows that an entity has complied with its official tax obligations.

Tax Court   Federal agency with courts in major cities to hear taxpayers' appeals from decisions of the IRS.

Tax ID Number   Unique number assigned to a business by the IRS and used to identify it to federal regulatory agencies.

Tax Lien   Lien filed on an individual/company by a governing agency for unpaid taxes.

Tax Sale   Auction of a taxpayer's property conducted by the federal government or a local authority to collect unpaid taxes.

Tenant   One who occupies real property owned by another based upon an agreement between the two.

Testator or Testatrix   Person who has written a will that is in effect at their death.

Testify   Give oral evidence under oath in answer to questions posed at trial or at a deposition. Opposing attorneys may cross-examine.

Theft of Services   Obtaining services without consent through deception, theft, tampering, etc.

Theft/unauthorized   Means the person used someone else's information, credit card, check, or something similar.

Time Served   Period a criminal defendant has been in jail, often while awaiting bail or awaiting trial. Often a judge will give a defendant credit for time served.

Title Abstract   History of the chain of title.

Tort   French for "wrong" - civil wrong or wrongful act, whether intentional or accidental, causing injury to another.

Trade Name or Trademark   Also known as a fictitious Business Name; name of a business or one of its products which, by use of the name and public reputation, identifies the product as that of the business. Trademark is a distinctive design, picture, emblem, logo or wording affixed to goods for sale to help identify the source.

Trial Court   Court that holds the original trial, not appeals.

Trial de Novo   When an appeals court holds a trial as if no prior trial had been held. Trial de novo is common on appeals from small claims court judgments.

Tribunal   Originally meaning '3 judges,' any court, judicial body or board who has quasi-judicial functions. Examples- a planning, zoning, or utility commission.

Truncated Files   Destroyed or partially destroyed. Unable to obtain more information.

Trust or Trust Fund   Entity created to hold assets for the benefit of certain persons or entities.

UCC   See Uniform Commercial Code.

UCC-1, UCC-3, UCC-11   UCC-1 Form is a financing agreement for using personal property such as equipment to secure a loan under the provisions of the Uniform Commercial Code. UCC-3 is usually an amendment to a UCC-1 filing. UCC-11 is the form used to request a search.

Ultimate Fact   Conclusion of fact logically deduced from other evidentiary facts.

Unconscionable   Referring to a contract or bargain so unfair - or signed under duress or misunderstanding - to a party that no reasonable or informed person would agree to it. Similar to an adhesion contract where one party has taken advantage of a person dealing from weakness.

Underwrite   1) agree to pay an obligation that may arise from an insurance policy. 2) guarantee by investment in a business or project.

Undo Influence   Pressure used to force someone to give up an asset or thing of value. Key is the influence was so great on a party to a contract or will had that they lost the ability to exercise their judgment and gave into pressure.

Uniform Commercial Code   Statutes governing the conduct of business, sales, warranties, loans, agreements secured by personal property, negotiable instruments, and other commercial matters.

Unlawful Detainer   Keep possession of real property without a right. Examples- lease expired, after being served with a notice to vacate, or being a squatter.

Unlawful Entry   Entry without force and without permission by means of fraud or other wrongful act.

Usury   Charging more interest than is permitted by law for a loan.

Vacate (Judgment)   To make void; to cancel.

Variance   Exception to a zoning ordinance, authorized by the appropriate governmental body such as a town council.

Venire   List from which jurors may be selected.

Venue   Geographic area where the case or claim occurred, within which a court with jurisdiction can hear and determine a case. A Change of Venue - the moving of a case from one court to another - may be granted when the court does not think the defendant can get a fair trial in that area or for the convenience of the parties in a civil case.

Verification   1) declaration under oath or upon penalty of perjury that a statement or pleading is true, located at the end of a document. 2) act of a college/university registrar to affirm a student's attendance or degree.

Vested   Having an absolute right or title, when previously the holder had only an expectation.

Voluntary Dismissal   The court or district attorney dismisses legal charges.

Vexatious Litigation or Action   Filing a lawsuit in the knowledge that it has no legal basis, with its purpose to bother, embarrass, annoy, or cause legal expenses to the defendant.

Vicarious Liability   Also imputed liability. Attachment of responsibility to a person or entity such as an employer for harm or damages caused by another such as an employee.

Vigilante Justice   Punishing another person without any legal authority.

Voice Case Information System   or VCIS. A dialup system that allows access to federal court information, usually bankruptcies. Fees for records found.

Waiver by Magistrate   Charges are waived after the defendant agrees to pay a fine. The defendant is not prosecuted on this charge.

Waiver of Jury   The right to a jury trial is waived and the judge makes the decision of guilt or innocence.

Warrant   Court order authorizing a law enforcement official to arrest or perform search and seizure.

Warranty; Express or Implied   Statement of good quality of merchandise, or clear title to real estate, or that a fact stated in a contract is true. Express warranty is a definite written statement; implied warranty is based on circumstances of the sale or contract.

White Collar Crime   General term for crimes involving insider trading, commercial fraud, swindles, cheating consumers, embezzlement and other dishonest business schemes.

Widow's Election   The choice a widow must ponder: to accept what her husband left her in his will OR accept what she would receive by the Laws of Succession.

Will Contest   Lawsuit challenging the validity of a will and/or its terms. Some bases for contesting a will include validity, competency of the testator at signing, undue influence, a 2nd will.

Willful   Act intentional, consciously and directed toward achieving a purpose. Some willful conduct with wrongful or unfortunate results may be deemed stubborn, malicious, hardheaded.

Wobblers   Offenses that can be tried as either a felony or a misdemeanor.

World Court   Voluntary court founded by the United Nations in 1945 to hear international disputes.

Writ   A written court order, or a judicial process.

Wrongful Entrustment   Allowing an unlicensed driver to operate a motor vehicle.

Youthful Offender   Classification of youths and young adults, generally older then juveniles. In the 18 to 25 year age group, these individuals are sometimes given special sentencing consideration for the purpose of rehabilitation, sometimes through education and counseling.

Youthful Training Act   Usually a non-conviction. Used for juvenile first-time offenders. It may be reported on a criminal record. If the juvenile complies with the sentence, case will be dropped from the record when the offender reaches adulthood.

Zoning   Official system of developing a city or county plan where various geographic areas – zones - are restricted to certain uses/development, such as industrial, light industrial, commercial, light-commercial, agricultural, single-family residential, multi-unit residential, parks, schools and other purposes.

Index